MARTIN SHARP

HIS LIFE AND TIMES

JOYCE MORGAN

ALLEN&UNWIN
SYDNEY • MELBOURNE • AUCKLAND • LONDON

First published in 2017

Allen & Unwin
83 Alexander Street
Crows Nest NSW 2065
Australia
Phone: (61 2) 8425 0100
Email: info@allenandunwin.com
Web: www.allenandunwin.com

Cataloguing-in-Publication details are available
from the National Library of Australia
www.trove.nla.gov.au
ISBN 978 1 76011 175 5

Set in 12/16.7pt Minion Pro by Midland Typesetters, Australia

Printed and bound in Australia by Griffin Press

10 9 8 7 6 5 4 3 2 1

MIX
Paper from responsible sources
FSC www.fsc.org FSC® C009448

The paper in this book is FSC certified.
FSC promotes environmentally responsible,
socially beneficial and economically viable
management of the world's forests.

CONTENTS

1	Beginnings	1
2	The little prince	20
3	Art versus Alfs	36
4	The trials of Martin Sharp	52
5	'Filthy and disgusting'	68
6	The white-ant of Bellevue Hill	81
7	Swinging London	96
8	The Pheasantry	111
9	'I need to be possessed by something bigger than me'	127
10	Back and forth	143
11	The Yellow House	159
12	Ginger Meggs School of Arts	176
13	The embassy of enchantment	191
14	Wirian	203
15	The king in yellow	216
16	'While often extreme and eccentric …'	230
17	Loss and reconciliation	249
18	Eternity	264

Acknowledgements	284
Select bibliography	287
Notes	291
List of artworks	321
Index	325

CHAPTER 1

BEGINNINGS

Beyond the rambling house with its upright wooden panels, red turret roof and sweeping verandah, the lawn sloped down to the rock-lined shore. On long summer days, a seven-year-old boy combed the ledges and water's edge, searching for treasures washed up by the tide.

He entered rock shelters with ceilings blackened by ancient fires. He found traces of shells from middens left by Aboriginal people before whitefellas arrived on their land. The ghostly outlines of hands, in ochre and clay, were stencilled on sandstone walls. They hinted at sacred ceremonies and dreaming stories passed down the generations. The Dharawal people once hunted wallaby and bandicoot in the bushland, and the river still yielded mussels, oysters and pipis.

In the blue-green water, the boy dropped pieces of bread to see what fish he could attract. Bream flashed silver and black in the waters kept crystal clear by nearby mangroves. And occasionally in the river's depths he caught a glimpse of luminescent blue gliding in and out of the weeds and labyrinth of rocks: a majestic blue groper. He was the king of this enchanted underwater realm. The rare sight of the solitary fish, as long as a grown-up's outstretched arms, filled the boy with awe. Long after the boy became a man, the mysterious creature glided across his dreams.

The childhood days spent at Telford, his maternal grandparents' riverfront holiday house, were among the happiest of Martin Sharp's life. There his imagination could run as wild as the deer he stalked in the native bushland that encircled the house. Rainbow lorikeets with red beaks, orange breasts and green wings and sulphur-crested cockatoos darted through the stands of eucalypts. At Telford, his eyes first opened to the beauty of the natural world.

The 32-acre property was less than fifty kilometres, but a world away, from his childhood home in Sydney's dress-circle suburb of Bellevue Hill, where he grew up as the only son and sole grandson of one of the city's wealthiest families.

In the 1940s Telford was reached either by a boat across the Port Hacking River or a bumpy track through the Royal National Park south of Sydney. During the school holidays when Martin went there, the constraints of the city were left behind. There was no school bell to wake him each day at 6.30am, and no uniform inspections or tedious maths lessons. The shyness that at times overcame him was irrelevant along the riverbank.

He was often in the company of women—his mother and maternal grandmother, or his nanny. His industrialist grandfather Stuart Douglas Ritchie had business in Newcastle most weeks. His doctor father, Henry Sharp, had his practice in the city, but sailed down from Sydney in his boat on weekends.

Although Martin had no siblings, he did not lack for playmates at Telford. The caretaker's cottage was shouting distance from the main house, and here lived Alfred Skinner, his wife, Ida, and their children, Jan and Ian. Together the three children collected frogs, putting them in a white enamel bowl covered by a mosquito net; the luminous pink markings on their brown heads fascinated Martin.

Martin shared games and cups of tea and the occasional cigarette with his two playmates, who were about his own age. He was drawn to the warmth inside the little cottage, more modest than his grander house up the hill. There were scones with fresh cream from the property's cow. Class barriers that might have kept him apart from a caretaker's children in the city didn't apply at Telford.

Besides, the lives of the Ritchie and Skinner families had long been intertwined. The Sydney factory of the Ritchie Bros, which made railway carriages, trams and agricultural implements, had employed both Alfred Skinner and his father over the years. Martin was six when his grandfather asked Alfred to become Telford's caretaker. Alfred's tasks included hand-milking the cow and fetching supplies by boat across the river at the hamlet of Lilli Pilli, half a kilometre away, dodging the sandbar that appeared at low tide.

At times Martin was joined at Telford by friends from Sydney. They sailed together in Martin's clinker wood dingy. And they fished with him. Martin spent hours fishing; he knew the movements of the fish, their feeding patterns and the time of day when they would appear. He was a silent, obsessive angler who understood and anticipated the behaviour of the different kinds of fish.

Martin watched people sailing in wooden skiffs hired from a boatshed at Lilli Pilli. At art school years later he would paint an image of people fishing from three little boats on this sparkling river, oblivious to the lone boy watching from the shady shore. Martin saw how men baited their hooks with weed so as to catch shy blackfish and learned how best to catch them himself. He enjoyed the dramatic fight that ensued when a fisherman reeled in a large fish and attempted to land his struggling catch.

He put such observations to use beyond fishing, for Martin wasn't averse to playing tricks. When he spotted one of his parents' more stilted friends, an aide-de-camp to the New South Wales governor, arriving at the wharf one day, Martin appeared to be struggling to land a giant fish. The boy wrestled with his line and sought help from the visitor. Martin handed over his line and the aide-de-camp reeled in a kerosene tin. Even as a boy, Martin could orchestrate a laugh at another's expense.

Visitors arriving by boat rather than by road walked uphill past a vast bunya pine and crossed a lawn where croquet had been played early last century. In front of the house was a weathered seat, its grey stone covered in lichen, positioned to take in the lawn and river view. The front door opened onto a lounge with a huge fireplace on the left. The room's dark wood panelling, which also covered the pitched ceiling, created a sombre interior. The room contained a piano on which his father played, a gramophone and his mother's stack of 78 rpm records. But at times he felt an uneasy silence and sadness in the big house that he did not understand.

As an adult Martin often described himself as an only child of an only child. It implied a solitary responsibility, a burden even, to guard the memories, knowledge and artefacts of his lineage. For without siblings, cousins, aunties and uncles, there was no one to protect or impart the family stories. And these mattered to Martin. They mattered a great deal.

On his mother's side, he was the third in a dynasty of only children, for his grandfather also had no siblings. Indeed, Martin was an only child of an only child of an only child. In him were invested all their hopes and dreams for the future.

His paternal side was more populous. Martin's father had four siblings, who each had several children. Martin had more than a dozen first cousins. But Martin identified closely with his mother's line. Hers was a world of immense wealth and privilege, a world of nannies, servants and chauffeur-driven cars. By the time Martin was born, his maternal grandfather, Stuart Ritchie, was one of Australia's richest men. But the Ritchies—like America's Vanderbilts or Carnegies, with whom they invite comparisons—didn't start out that way.

The first Ritchie to set foot in Australia grew up in the Scottish town of Paisley. Just outside Glasgow, the town was the centre of the textile industry in the mid-nineteenth century when its most famous product, paisley shawls, became the height of fashion. Although wages were lower in Paisley than in the Scottish capital Edinburgh, spinners, dyers and weavers were drawn from elsewhere to the town's plentiful work. But a depression in the early 1840s saw many mills close, which may have been why one of the town's dyers embarked on a long and risky journey.

John Ritchie set sail for Australia and arrived in Sydney in 1848 with his family, which included his twelve-year-old Paisley-born son Robert Adam. Robert's older brother—a shipwright also called John—had already emigrated to Sydney, and that may have prompted the decision to seek a better life in the distant colonial town.

The Ritchies brought more hope than money, for few with wealth ever willingly embarked on the perilous journey to the other side of the world. They arrived as free settlers just as New South Wales was poised to abolish convict transportation in the infant colony of fewer than 200,000 inhabitants.

Young Robert worked in a woollen mill at Parramatta before the discovery of gold in New South Wales in 1851. Gold fever was in the air. Robert sniffed the wind, quit his job and headed over the Blue Mountains to the Turon goldfields about 250 kilometres north-west of Sydney. There he joined hundreds of impoverished men hoping to dig and pan their way to riches, but within eighteen months Robert Ritchie was back in Parramatta. It was a less precious metal than gold that would make his fortune.

He became apprenticed to a local blacksmith before setting up his own business making agricultural tools. Construction of Australia's first railway began in Sydney in 1850 and Robert Ritchie once again scented opportunity, this time with more success as he began making rails, railway carriages and wagons. The business thrived and he began expanding. By 1879 he had acquired a site at Auburn and opened a branch in the Newcastle suburb of Wickham.

Robert Ritchie added political influence to his industrial might. He became a Parramatta alderman, a member of the New South Wales

Legislative Assembly and a free-trade advocate. He was opinionated, persuasive and hot-tempered, and so combative in council debates he was dubbed the 'lecturer-general'. A lean man with a long nose, prominent ears and a look of steely determination, his resemblance in later life to his great-great-grandson is apparent.

Robert Ritchie's company merged with Hudson Bros in 1884 and he managed their Clyde works. Two of his sons, John and James, formed Ritchie Bros and oversaw the Wickham and Auburn factories. In the same year, James married Ada Bewick, daughter of a railway engineer, in Newcastle's Christ Church Cathedral.

Robert Ritchie remained active in business and politics, despite bouts of ill health and 'sluggish action of the bowels', his rather too detailed obituary noted. He was in his mid-fifties when, in August 1891, he inspected the Ritchie Bros Auburn iron factory and soon after suffered stomach pains. The next day his condition was critical and his family was summoned. The industrious Scotsman died of peritonitis at his Auburn Road home the same night.

He was 'a man of ceaseless mental activities' but whose political contribution was as 'more the captious and destructive critic than the constructive man of action'. This self-made man of ideas, enterprise and ambition laid the foundations of the wealth that would flow to Martin.

A lengthy dispute ensued between the Ritchies and Hudsons over aspects of the 1884 merger soon after Robert Ritchie's death. The case dragged on for years before being settled in the Ritchies' favour in 1896, when they received a substantial settlement. This payout may have allowed James Ritchie, Martin's great-grandfather, to purchase in 1914 Telford, the Port Hacking property that played such a vital role in the artist's life.

Ritchie Bros prospered and by the end of World War I employed more than 800 men at its Auburn works. James Ritchie was an advocate for business and industry, a man of iron literally and metaphorically who opposed any government encroachment that might threaten his fortune, especially moves by them to manufacture railway rolling stock. The government should stick to owning the tracks and carriages, not making them, he argued.

James Ritchie became president of the industry body, the Iron Trades Association, at a time of growing industrial unrest. He took an unwavering line against workers' ability to strike: they should be brought before the courts and fined, he told a Royal Commission into the Industrial Arbitration Act. He became chairman of Newcastle's Commonwealth Steel, a company Ritchie Bros had helped found during World War I.

When he died in December 1925, James Ritchie was hailed as a pioneer of the iron industry. The wealth and influence he had amassed were reflected in the scale of his funeral, which began with a service at the family home in Woodside Avenue, Strathfield. More than a hundred men—family members, captains of industry, aldermen and employees—attended his burial in Rookwood Cemetery.

Among the chief mourners was his forty-year-old son and heir, Stuart Douglas Ritchie, who, on his father's death, inherited Telford and the family business. By then Stuart Ritchie was married, having wed Vega Kopsen in 1911 in a match that united two Sydney families who had prospered in a new land.

Vega was the daughter of manufacturer and ship chandler William Kopsen of Strathfield. He, too, was a self-made man. Born in Stockholm and orphaned at fifteen, Kopsen arrived in Sydney in 1868 and worked as a cook and a shepherd and later established a timber business. His interests were wide, including anthropology, geology and botany. He was a Congregationalist, a leading member of Sydney's Swedish community and was instrumental in the erection of a monument at Sydney's Kurnell to Daniel Solander, the Swedish botanist who landed in Australia with Captain Cook.

Stuart and Vega Ritchie's daughter and only child, Joan Sheila, was born in 1915. She grew up at the family's substantial home on

The Boulevarde, Strathfield, and attended Meriden College, an Anglican girls' school. A career was not an option for a wealthy young woman in the 1930s. Instead, she led the privileged but proscribed life of a young socialite centred around parties, horseracing and tennis. With her school days over, at nineteen she accompanied her parents on an overseas business trip, sailing to London and New York and staying at the finest hotels, including the Hyde Park Hotel in Knightsbridge and The Plaza in New York.

Joan and her parents moved from Strathfield after her father bought a mansion in Sydney's Bellevue Hill in the mid-1930s. With its harbour views, the elegant two-storey residence was in the Arts and Crafts style, with a carriage porch and upper-storey bow window. It was built in 1923 to a design by prominent Sydney architects Halligan and Wilton, who had previously created Kingsclere in Macleay Street, Potts Point, one of Sydney's first residential high-rise buildings. Wirian, at 3 Victoria Road, Bellevue Hill, was an impressive home for a captain of industry. Stuart Ritchie became a director of Commonwealth Steel, sitting alongside the most prominent Australian industrialist of his day, Essington Lewis.

The first Sharp to arrive in Australia charted a different course to the Ritchie family. William Henry Sharp would become a leading trade unionist and a founding father of the Australian Labor Party.

He was born the son of a clergyman in Dickens-era London in 1844, where *A Christmas Carol*—the tale of the city's poverty, social injustice and the crippled Tiny Tim—had been published just a few months earlier. He grew up on the banks of the Thames, near Millbank Prison, which housed hapless convicts awaiting transport to Australia.

William Sharp became an apprentice to the Queen's printer Eyre and Spottiswoode. He married eighteen-year-old Eliza Alice Ramsay in 1869 and after their first child, Alfred Ramsay Sharp, was born, the family sailed to America where William Sharp continued his trade in Boston and Chicago. But their stay in America was short-lived and a year later the family returned to London where their second son, Walter Alexander Ramsay Sharp, was born in 1875. Their joy at their new son's arrival was tempered by the death of infant Alfred around the same time.

A desire for a healthier climate prompted William Sharp to sail from England for a second time. Although he would never live there again, he retained a lifelong interest in England's folklore and London's history. This time his destination was Australia. He arrived in Sydney with his family in 1887 and they settled in Raglan Street, Mosman, on Sydney's lower North Shore. When two more sons followed, they were also given Ramsay as a middle name. Even the family home was named Yasmar, an inversion of his wife's maiden name.

His new life afforded few luxuries. He raised his family in an atmosphere that was spartan and valued 'stern effort'. William Sharp worked in Sydney for the Government Printer and joined the newly formed trade union, the New South Wales Typographical Association. He became a delegate to the Trades and Labor Council, the peak trade union body, and its president in 1891. His election came as union membership and muscle was growing. By then, nearly a quarter of the colony's working men were union members, among the most unionised workforces in the world.

The 1890s was a period of industrial turmoil in Australia. The decade began with the national maritime strike, whose aftermath had a profound effect on the labour movement. The strike began over pay and conditions to seamen, but spread until 28,500 workers, including coalminers, were on strike around the country. The strike was unsuccessful—maritime wages were cut—and this fuelled a recognition that industrial action alone was not enough to effect social change. A political voice was needed.

In New South Wales, the Trades and Labour Council moved to create a political party to contest elections in 1891. Meetings were called to form branches of this party, the Labour Electoral League of New South Wales. The first meeting—a landmark in Australian labour history—was held in Sydney's Balmain in April. A few nights later, 500 people gathered inside the Protestant Hall on Castlereagh Street near Hyde Park to form the first East Sydney branch. William Sharp chaired the meeting, the crowd applauding as he told them that workers would never secure their just rights until they had proper political representation. There was much cheering and hear-hearing as various speakers advocated state socialism, championed the rights of the working class and condemned the 'squattocracy'.

William Sharp was elected to the New South Wales Legislative Assembly for the seat of Redfern in 1891. He favoured electoral reform and advocated 'one man, one vote' (until 1904, only men had the right to vote). He opposed the system that existed, which favoured the wealthy by giving multiple votes to those who held property in more than one electorate. This was abolished in 1893.

But his life in Australia was not without tragedy. Two years before he died, the steamship *Tahiti* was leaving Sydney for New Zealand on a clear afternoon when it collided with a Sydney Harbour ferry, the *Greycliffe*, in November 1927. The steamer was three times the size of the ferry it cut in half. The little ferry sank with the loss of forty lives, many of them children returning home from school. It remains Sydney's worst maritime disaster. Among the victims was William Sharp's grand-daughter, fifteen-year-old Hazel. It would be another tragedy involving the deaths of children on Sydney Harbour that would dominate the life of William Sharp's great-grandson.

William Sharp's oldest surviving son, Walter Alexander Ramsay Sharp, chose to study medicine, a decision that surprised his parents. He graduated from Sydney University in 1902 and undertook further medical studies in Scotland, Ireland and Germany before returning to Australia in 1906. He became a country doctor with a practice in Candelo in the Bega Valley of southern New South Wales where he was a well-known figure—not least because he was the first doctor in the district to do his rounds by motor car instead of on horseback.

He married a Bega woman from a family of graziers, Elizabeth Ritchie, known as Bessie; despite her surname, she was unrelated to the Ritchies on Martin's maternal side. The wedding at St John's Anglican Church, Bega, in June 1907, was a large affair with 160 guests who showered the couple with gifts of silverware and even a piano.

Their first child, Henry—Martin Sharp's father—was born the following year. Twins, Alan and Katharine, were followed by Frank and Elizabeth, the youngest. The family moved to Sydney in 1913, eventually settling in Vaucluse Road, Vaucluse. In Sydney, Bessie Sharp would host an annual Christmas gathering of the extended Sharp family. She was a strong-willed woman, one of the first in New South Wales to get a driving licence, and an accomplished pianist. She was conscious of social standing and keen to see her children well educated and well married.

Walter Sharp became one of Sydney's best-known medical practitioners. He had a Macquarie Street practice and a long association with Sydney Hospital, including as an honorary surgeon and tutor in surgery. He had a strong sense of public service, gave lectures on public health and received an OBE in 1936 for services to social welfare. His will provided for the establishment of a prize in surgery in memory of his parents. The William Henry and Eliza Alice Sharp Prize is still awarded by Sydney University.

A Congregationalist, Walter was religious and well read. Politically, he was the polar opposite of his trade unionist father. Walter once presided over a meeting of the conservative Liberal and Reform Association in Candelo, at which the town was derided as a 'hotbed of Labor sympathisers'. He later supported the United Australia Party, the forerunner of the Liberal Party. He was a Vaucluse Municipal Council alderman for about a decade, during which time he took part in a heated debate over the proposed erection of flats in his dress-circle suburb, a move he opposed arguing they attracted a 'degenerate' element.

Henry Sharp was raised in a more prosperous household than the spartan atmosphere of his father's early years, and grew up playing the piano and singing. He was among the first intake of boys enrolled in Cranbrook School, which his father helped found, when it opened in 1918. The school had been a residence for the Tooth brewing family and later the New South Wales governor before it was bought by a group of businessmen and churchmen who wanted to establish an Anglican boys' school in Sydney's Eastern Suburbs.

When his school days were completed, Henry followed his father's footsteps and studied medicine at Sydney University. He lived on campus at St Paul's, the male Anglican college. He had a musical and theatrical streak, and became involved in Sydney University's Dramatic Society, performing in and penning plays. He retained an interest in music, playing the piano at family events throughout his life.

Henry graduated in 1935 and became a resident medical officer at Sydney Hospital. Two years later he set sail for England, earning his passage as ship's doctor. Among the passengers, a young Sydney woman caught his eye.

The heady scent of roses, sweet peas and stocks filled the ballroom in Sydney's elegant Australia Hotel. The dance floor was surrounded by tables at which sat some of the city's most fashionable young women, in dresses of tulle, georgette and satin.

The centre of attention was a petite young woman with golden hair and blue eyes wearing a turquoise taffeta gown. Her tight bodice and full skirt emphasised her tiny waist. A spray of white lilies-of-the-valley and mauve orchids enhanced the blue-green of her dress.

Joan Ritchie was attractive, wealthy and vivacious. And the dinner dance, amid the marble and mahogany of the Victorian-era hotel, was to celebrate her twenty-first birthday. Her parents spared no expense to see their only daughter cross the threshold into womanhood and become one of the city's most eligible women.

Joan—or Jo, as she was known—set sail with her parents for England soon after the grand party. The journey was timed to coincide with the coronation of King George VI in May 1937. Aboard the ship, she was drawn to the ship's young doctor. Romance blossomed between Jo and Henry, who at twenty-eight was seven years older than the young socialite.

There was no doubt much talk aboard ship about another romance and the controversial events that had led to the forthcoming coronation. The previous king, Edward VIII, had abdicated in December 1936 after less than a year on the throne so he could marry the divorced American socialite Mrs Wallis Simpson. The romance between Edward and the twice-married Mrs Simpson scandalised Britain. She was seen as immoral and a gold-digger, an unsuitable royal consort. Opposition to their marriage was widespread, including from the Church of England, of which the king was the nominal head, which did not allow divorcees to remarry while their spouses remained alive. Divorce was rare and frowned on. Women divorcees especially carried with them a whiff of disgrace.

By the time the ship docked in the United Kingdom, Jo and Henry were in love. But Henry was about to begin a three-year appointment at London's Lewisham Hospital. Knowing they must separate would have added piquancy to what began as a shipboard romance. Theirs would be a long-distance courtship.

A few months after Henry took up his London appointment, his father died in Australia, aged only sixty-two. Walter Sharp left an estate of £19,000, a sizeable sum at a time when the average male wage for factory workers was less than £250 a year. Newly widowed, Bessie Sharp was well provided for and well connected when she left Australia in mid-1938 to visit Henry in London during a seventeen-month overseas trip. By then her two other sons, Alan and Frank, had begun medical studies in Australia and daughter Katharine had married; this left only her youngest child, Elizabeth, to accompany her. In England, Bessie launched Elizabeth into high society. The young woman was presented at court by Lady Game, wife of the former New South Wales Governor Sir Philip Game, and went hunting in Oxfordshire.

Political storm clouds gathered over Europe and by September 1939, England was at war with Germany. The outbreak of war meant Bessie and Elizabeth's return to Australia was delayed. The women used the time to pass their Red Cross and first-aid tests. The delay no doubt afforded Bessie time to discuss with Henry his future and especially his intentions towards the young heiress Jo Ritchie, by now back in Sydney.

With Henry's three-year appointment in London at an end, he returned to Australia. He sailed the Atlantic, took a troop train across the United States and boarded the SS *Monterey* to cross the Pacific to Australia. He arrived just a few days before his engagement to Jo was announced in August 1940. Jo's parents held an afternoon tea party at Wirian to celebrate the betrothal.

The couple married at St Mark's Church, Darling Point, on 7 December 1940. Henry was thirty-two and Jo was twenty-five. The Gothic Revival church was a fashionable choice for society weddings long before it was the scene of Elton John's first marriage and the fictional nuptials in the movie *Muriel's Wedding*. A marquee was erected in the grounds of Wirian for the reception; here family, friends and even Hippy the family dog mingled.

The newlyweds made their home at 25 Cranbrook Lane, Bellevue Hill, in a Provencal-style villa with banked lawns down to Cranbrook Road and views over Rose Bay across the harbour to Manly. Jo's parents lived at Wirian, about a ten-minute walk away, while Henry's widowed mother lived at the Astor, an elegant 1920s apartment building in Macquarie Street in the city.

With the war continuing, Jo and Henry had little time together to adjust to their new roles as husband and wife. Henry joined the

Royal Australian Air Force as a medical officer soon after his return from England. Within a couple of months of marriage, he was on the move again. He worked initially aboard a recruiting train that travelled to country districts interviewing young men unable to make the journey to the city to join up. Within six months of their marriage, Jo was pregnant.

Separation from her young husband, impending motherhood and apprehension for the future took a toll on Jo, who became tearful at times. She even wished she wasn't expecting a child, telling Henry in a letter 'then I could be with you'. It would not be the only time she expressed unease about motherhood. Henry was away for their first wedding anniversary. Heavily pregnant, Jo wrote to him expressing her love and fears. 'I get the feeling that you don't love me and that you aren't happy. Darling if you could get a bit sentimental and romantic at times, it would be such a help.' Even before Martin's birth, cracks in the marriage were becoming apparent.

The war had just reached Australia's shores when Martin Ritchie Sharp was born on 21 January 1942. Darwin, the country's most northern city, lay smouldering from the Japanese bombing two days earlier, in which more than two hundred people had died. More than four thousand kilometres south in Sydney, Martin entered the world at St Luke's Hospital, Elizabeth Bay. The maternity wing was within a converted Victorian mansion, Lulworth, the childhood home of Nobel prize-winning author Patrick White.

The birth announcement in *The Sydney Morning Herald* was succinct: 'to the wife of Flight-Lieutenant Henry Sharp—a son'. Martin's mother was unnamed, an omission unusual even by the standards of the time. But Jo Sharp would exert a defining influence on the life and work of her only child.

Henry had little time with his baby son. Within six months of Martin's birth he was shipped off to England. There he was attached to the RAAF's 453 Spitfire squadron as its medical officer and later squadron leader. He was based for a time at Drem in Scotland where, in a lighter wartime moment, the BBC captured the squadron's Christmas party. In a photograph of the event, Henry is a tall, confident figure as he stands in uniform near the microphone with a cigarette in hand. The keen singer joined his fellow servicemen in a chorus of 'Along the Road to Gundagai' in a morale-boosting broadcast to Australia.

His squadron's work was fraught with danger. It undertook air patrols over Britain, escorted bombers over enemy-controlled Europe and conducted strikes. As a medical officer, Henry held the fate of his men in his hands and that burden weighed on him. 'He said the worst thing was having to declare someone fit, because you often never saw them [again],' Martin later recalled.

Back in Australia, Jo was among a generation of young war wives adjusting to motherhood without their husbands. Although, unlike the vast majority of them, she had the assistance of a series of nannies to help her. Jo took delight in her infant son and was amused at his early awareness of anatomy. She relayed how 22-month-old Martin, in bed with her one morning, observed her underarm hair: 'Mum's broom' was his comment. He was a child with a temper, prone to sticking out his bottom lip and yelling.

Henry was away when Martin was christened in Cranbrook School chapel a few weeks after his third birthday. Jo had an afternoon tea party for him afterwards and then went out for the evening. She was maintaining a hectic social life: there were cocktail parties at Government House, drinks and luncheons with friends, trips to the races, casual buffets and grand dinners.

Roma Leonard was ushered into the elegant drawing room at Wirian. The seventeen-year-old was a country girl from Goulburn, and unfamiliar with luxurious surroundings. Her family was poor and, when she applied for the position of Martin's nanny, her father was away at the war. She had no previous experience. But Mrs Ritchie, who conducted the interview, liked the young woman and she was hired.

Jo does not appear to have met Nurse Roma, or Nursie as she was known, until December 1944, when she arrived at Cranbrook Lane, where she lived for about five years. 'She is lovely looking,' Jo noted in her diary. Indeed she was, with a mane of thick, dark wavy hair. Jo, too, liked the young woman. They became almost like sisters, Roma recalled years later. Jo would ask Roma's opinion on what clothes she should wear and how to do her hair; she took an interest in the nanny's boyfriends. And when Roma entered the Miss Australia quest a couple of years later, Jo loaned her a circular silver pendant of her own to wear.

Martin adored Nursie. Of all his nannies, she was his favourite. With Jo often out at social events, she was arguably the most constant female presence in his early formative years and the pair formed a close bond. The bond is apparent in a photograph taken at the Royal Easter Show. As Martin stands between Jo and Roma, he leans against his nanny. When she gave him a copy of Dr Seuss's *Horton Hatches the Egg* for Christmas when he was almost four, she addressed it to 'the sweetest little boy in the world'. Martin still treasured the book as an adult.

Jo was ambivalent about motherhood, despairing of her son's behaviour and her lack of maternal feelings. She told Henry their toddler son was 'quite one of the naughtiest—rudest—bad-mannered kids I've ever met—but he's so good looking. That is all that saves me "doing away" with him at times … I've had Martin at the moment—had him completely. I do wish I could get less nervy . . . and more placid. I think it is an awful sense of duty that makes me "feel" anything, nothing maternal.'

Jo feared an exhausted Nursie was poised to quit, because Martin was so demanding she rarely got an unbroken night's sleep. Jo, too, was worn out, and only slept through the night if she took a sleeping pill. While Henry was still in England, Jo refers to Martin but not by name, telling Henry 'the child has just been to see me'. It is a curiously arm's-length way to refer to their two-year-old son.

Uneasy with her role as a mother, Jo's relationship with her mother-in-law was also at times a source of friction. Bessie Sharp and Jo were both strong women, but with different temperaments. Bessie's outlook was Victorian and restrained. She disapproved of gambling. Jo loved horseracing, proudly telling Henry how her mother's horse Petruchio had won at Rosehill.

The two women were too different to ever really get on together, Jo told Henry. Jo was irritated by Bessie's approach to children and marriage: 'I am still being told what a constant joy babies are and that people ought to go on having baby after baby to keep marriages together. All I can say if that's all that they kept their husbands with I feel sorry for them.' She asked Henry if he would have married her if she could not have had children. While she feared she might disappoint him as a mother, she promised to be a good wife: 'a hell of a good one'.

She invariably addressed her letters to 'My darling Henry' and she looked for the silver lining in their continued separation: 'The more we are parted the more we'll adore each other when we do "get together" again.' Yet she hinted again at the disparity of their feelings and sought reassurance: ' . . . you love me a little bit—don't you? I worship you.'

Exhausted after a week of sleepless nights when Martin, recovering from an illness, stood in his cot for hours and yelled, Jo wondered if she had the patience to be a good mother. But with Martin recovered, her pride in her son was restored when she took him to a tea party. In a new linen suit and white shoes, he was turning heads. 'I heard quite a few people asking who he was ... he was as tall as all the three-year-olds, he's going to be a giant.'

Jo appeared far happier on her second wedding anniversary than her first. Reassured by a 'gloriously sloppy' cable from Henry and fortified by a celebratory glass of Pimm's, she was amused by Martin's bedtime comment as he said his prayers. She wrote: 'he got through God bless Mummie and Daddy, and God bless Marka (what he calls himself) and make him a girl—(instead of a good boy) what do you think he meant? Does he want to be a girl or does he want a girl?'

Henry returned from the war in 1945. But once again he had little time to spend with his growing son. Committed to a year's service after the war ended, Henry went initially to the RAAF's section of Concord Hospital before moving to South Australia as principal medical officer.

Martin was four by the time his father returned for any length of time to the Cranbrook Lane family home. The boy wondered who the stranger was who was demanding the attention of the woman whose undivided focus he had had for most of his short life.

CHAPTER 2

THE LITTLE PRINCE

The Cranbrook Lane villa was filled with elegantly dressed friends. There were parties on the lawn, where the chink of glasses, laughter and the reassuring sounds of Bing Crosby and Rudy Vallée carried on the summer breeze. Martin recalled the early years after his father returned from the war as happy, sociable times when his parents appeared content.

Martin's father, like many of his generation, rarely discussed the war. 'It was quite jolly for a while there,' Martin said. 'I knew nothing about the war really, it wasn't mentioned. You wouldn't have known they'd been through such a heavy time … It must have had an enormous impact, but they seemed to keep the world together with cocktail parties.'

Henry went into general practice and began studying dermatology. Jo bought him a print for his Macquarie Street surgery, a copy of van Gogh's *The Artist on the Road to Tarascon*, an image that made an enduring impression on Martin.

Jo purchased the print from Carl Plate's Notanda Gallery in Rowe Street. With its coffee shops, bars, teahouses and galleries, many run by recent European migrants, this stylish laneway between Castlereagh and Pitt Streets was the closest Sydney got to bohemia. Sydney's arty crowd sipped their first espressos there, while wealthy visitors and guests of the Australia Hotel, which ran alongside it, browsed its bespoke tailors and imported Parisian millinery in its tiny boutiques.

Rowe Street, which fell to the wrecker's ball in the 1970s along with the Australia Hotel, appealed to the fashionable Jo. She helped out in the city's first charity shop, which raised money for Martin's kindergarten and which was located there.

———

Jo encouraged Martin's early creativity. He called her his first art teacher. His first 'drawing' was in a letter Jo wrote to Henry. The two-year-old had scribbled on the paper. When Jo asked Martin what it was, he insisted it was an animal. Jo made collages from figures cut from fashion magazines, and encouraged Martin to cut out his favourite images to paste in books. A Campbell's soup can—long before Warhol turned the image into an icon—is among those he cut out and pasted into an early collage. One of his first images is of a sailing ship. He painted it on a cotton sheet when he was sick in bed aged about six. His mother kept the image and framed it. But to fit it in the frame, she cut off some eagles he had included—much to his annoyance.

He was surrounded by cartoons. His maternal grandfather, who sketched as a boy, loved cartoons, especially those by *The Bulletin* magazine's popular Livingston 'Hop' Hopkins and Phil May. His grandmother cut cartoon strips from the newspapers, including the hapless *Boofhead*, and made little books of them for her grandson. Martin learned to read with the aid of cartoons. The illustrations for *A Christmas Carol* were his entree to Dickens, even though he found its image of the Grim Reaper pointing a long skeletal finger disturbing. He first saw a statue of Mickey Mouse in his mother's cabinet and was captivated by it.

Jo took him to see films. As a treat before returning to school one holiday, they went to see Danny Kaye in *Hans Christian Andersen*. But Martin was disappointed because the movie was more about Andersen's life than the fairytale characters he created. Walt Disney's *Fantasia* made a bigger impression, but its closing *Night on Bald Mountain* section, with its god of evil, demons and harpies, terrified him.

Martin was surrounded by books: *Biggles* albums, *Winnie-the-Pooh*—he loved the drawings by E.H. Shepard, who also illustrated *The Wind in the Willows*. His favourite book was Antoine de Saint-Exupéry's illustrated tale *The Little Prince*. It tells of a prince from a tiny planet who encounters narrow-minded grown-ups, and a fox who tells him that the important things in life are visible only to the heart.

Martin's father was a great reader, although he preferred poetry and classics to comics. From his father he got a love of literature and poetry, from his mother a love of art. 'Jo's family were a lot looser about what you read. My uncles and aunts thought you needed to read something more serious than cartoons,' recalls Martin's cousin Roslyn Sharp.

Like many men of his era, Henry was not a demonstrative father. He enjoyed quiet, solitary pursuits, such as reading and sailing his boat on Sydney Harbour. But Martin's parents shared a love of popular music. Henry played the piano, sang Gilbert and Sullivan and music hall songs, and played the latest 78 rpm records on his radiogram. And they shared a love of animals. Dogs were always part of the household, including several red setters. One of Martin's first images was a plea to preserve Australia's flightless bird. Above a painting of the creature, he hand-lettered the words 'Don't Harm Emus'.

Martin was nine when his mother took him into the city to the Mark Foy's building in 1951 to see his first art exhibition. It was the inaugural Blake Prize, an annual award for religious art. Martin was captivated by the blaze of colour in the winning painting, Justin O'Brien's triptych *Virgin Enthroned*.

The Cadillac pulled out of Cranbrook Lane. With its gleaming metal grille, elongated bonnet and bumpers resembling artillery shells, the vehicle glided towards the city. It passed Sydney's wealthy harbour-side suburbs of Double Bay and Rushcutters Bay, skirted the fringes of scruffy Kings Cross and entered Elizabeth Street. At the wheel was the Ritchie family's chauffeur. In the rear were two excited boys. It wasn't the first time Martin and his friend John Gregory-Roberts, who lived next door, had gone on outings together, usually accompanied by Martin's nanny. This day, the destination was the city's upmarket department store, David Jones. The goal was to buy fireworks. The boys made their selection and returned to Cranbrook Lane, where they set them off on Martin's lawn.

Martin was four when the Gregory-Roberts family moved next door. John was six months older than Martin and the pair became inseparable. A gate was installed between the two properties so the boys could more readily play together. The family dog Hippy and later Rusty, a red setter, followed at Martin's heels.

They met most evenings to listen to the children's program *The Argonauts Club* on the radio. Broadcast during *Children's Hour*, it was a popular segment among a pre-television generation of children, whose imaginations were fed by listening rather than watching. Martin was part of the last generation of kids for whom radio would be the dominant mass media. Each day, various *Argonauts* characters talked to the young listeners about different subjects. Tom the Naturalist spoke about wildlife, Antony Inkwell about writing and Phidias spoke about art and painting. The jolly, erudite Phidias was actually the artist Jeffrey Smart. Through his 'Art Gallery of the Air', Smart encouraged children to pick up a brush and send in their work. Martin got some of his earliest art instruction from Phidias.

John's father was an eye doctor and Martin was fascinated by Dr Gregory-Roberts' eye charts that tested for colour blindness. Martin was already experimenting with altered perception. He spent hours in his father's upstairs study, looking through his microscope studying slides and specimens, admiring their abstract patterns. He gazed through Henry's large Japanese army binoculars mounted on a tripod in the room with its harbour view. The lenses were powerful enough to see the detail of people sailing around Rose Bay.

Martin kicked a football around the lawn with his other childhood friend Anthony Abrahams, who later played rugby union for Australia. The pair sat in the kitchen alcove, where there was a photograph of Olympic swimmer Murray Rose, Jo's hero; Martin struck matches to dispel the odours from Rusty, the flatulent red setter, while Jo fetched iced Milos.

Jo welcomed all Martin's friends. '[Jo] was winsome and a bit eccentric with a wry sense of humour … She was very warm and extremely fond of us all. You felt bathed in that warmth,' Anthony recalls.

Martin often wandered down to Rose Bay to swim or fish. When it was time to return home, Jo's cry for 'Maaaartin' echoed down the hill. After one such trip, Martin was walking up the hill towards his home when some writing on the pavement caught his eye. A single word was written in yellow chalk in a flowing copperplate script. He wondered what it meant, what it was doing there and who had written it. The ephemera of the powdery chalk, which would wash away in the first rain, was a contrast to the word itself: *Eternity*.

Martin scrambled onto the roof of the garage, carrying an umbrella. With his feet planted on the roof, he opened the brolly—and leapt off. He imagined himself floating down to the grass below, like Mary Poppins. He didn't. He plummeted back to earth like any other boy then walked away, shaken but uninjured.

When he entered the Peter Pan Kindergarten at Sydney's Point Piper, he hoped he might learn how to fly. Surely that was what he would be taught in a place named after J.M. Barrie's famous flying boy, the boy who never grew up: 'I did think you could fly.'

He was seven when he followed his father's footsteps and entered Cranbrook School at Bellevue Hill. The Anglican school educated the children of the elite—including the Packers and Fairfaxes—but was less sports-oriented than some of Sydney's other private schools.

He enjoyed his early school years and was thrilled when he received as a prize *The Happiness Box* by David Griffin. The tale is centred around three animal friends in search of happiness, including Martin the monkey who looked after a tree house. But Martin Sharp and Martin the monkey were very different characters. 'I was a very untidy boy, but Martin the monkey was very tidy,' he later recalled. He was moved by the book's backstory. Griffin, a former Cranbrook student, handwrote the tale while held as a prisoner of war in Changi, Singapore, in 1942. Fearing the book contained coded messages, his Japanese captors ordered its confiscation. Instead the book was secretly buried until Singapore was liberated in 1945, when Griffin brought it back to Australia where it was published.

Always fascinated by animals, Martin used to enjoy watching a couple of draught horses pull a mower and roller around the school's oval. But an incident at junior school cast a long shadow over his life. It was sparked by a pencil sharpener in a leather case his mother had given him as present: 'It was my pride and joy.' He accidentally knocked his pencil sharpener off his desk in class one day and got out of his seat to retrieve it. He was unsure why this so displeased his favourite teacher, Miss Beatrice Peel, but she asked to see him after class and sent him to the junior school's headmaster.

'He beat me with a big thick strap,' he remembered. 'I was completely shocked and outraged. I thought, that is so unfair. All I did was get out of my seat in class ... My relationship with Miss Peel was never the same.' He began, like Antoine de Saint-Exupéry's *The Little Prince*, to mistrust the world of adults.

———

The biggest upheaval in Martin's young life came when he entered Cranbrook School, aged twelve, as a boarder. He did so at the beginning of third term by which time the other boarders his age had settled into the daily routine and formed friendships. Martin felt an outsider. His first night in the dormitory was lonely and alienating. 'No one said, "Here, Martin, I'll show you around." I was not shown where the toilets were and I was too embarrassed to ask. I was a very shy kid. So without being told, I wet my bed.'

Martin's childhood home was just a few minutes' walk down the hill to Cranbrook School. And his maternal grandparents' home, Wirian, was even closer—it was a few metres from the school on Victoria Road. Despite this proximity, throughout his adolescence, Martin saw his home and family only on Sundays and during holidays.

Becoming a boarder was unusual for a boy who lived so close to the school. Most boarders were country boys. And many dayboys travelled across the city to attend. Martin believed his father was keen for him to board to encourage greater male influence on him after a childhood spent close to his mother. But there may have been other reasons. Martin was aware his parents' marriage was troubled. Boarding their young son may have been an attempt by his parents to shield him from their dissolving relationship.

'I think it was because I was an only child. I think it was considered I might have become a mother's boy. But maybe they just wanted to fight in private.' At times, the tension in the Cranbrook Lane home was palpable. 'I could feel it. We had a little nook where we used to sit for breakfast. My father would hide behind *The Sydney Morning Herald* and there was total silence at the breakfast table. So it was pretty heavy going.'

There were more than seven hundred students at the school, most of them day pupils. Less than two hundred were boarders. He shared his dormitory with about twenty other boys. But he did not fit easily into the structured morning routine of 6.30am bell, 7am roll call, then breakfast before classes began at 9am. Although he was not usually an early riser, on one occasion when he got up before the morning bell, he recalled being punished for doing so. There were shoe inspections and fingernail inspections; he had to make his own bed and prepare his laundry bundle. He cut a shambolic figure, his tie often askew and his socks usually at half-mast.

He was, however, good at sport. He was a member of the swimming team and he played breakaway in the school's rugby union team. Actor John Gaden, who was at Cranbrook at the time, remembers Martin's prowess: 'Breakaways were on either side of the scrum; their job was to spoil the opposition when they got the ball. Martin was a demon tackler, he was very fast around the field. He was a slight boy, he wasn't a big boofy bloke, wiry. He was lethal.'

Anthony Abrahams was also impressed with Martin's ability on the field: 'He really put in. I remember him scoring a try with that long, lean body at the side of the scrum on Hordern Oval.' Anthony recalls Cranbrook as being more tolerant of difference among its pupils than other elite schools of the time: 'For a school of that period it was nurturing. It had a reputation of embracing difference. It was once described in a review of schools as having a rollicking liberalism … there was less of an emphasis on outward manifestations of toughness. It was a better school for someone like Martin to go to.'

John Gaden agrees. But the school's emphasis on art, drama and debating meant it developed a reputation for producing 'sissies', and this prompted a chant by rival schoolboys: 'Tiddlywinks old man, get a woman if you can/If you can't get a woman, get a Cranbrook man.'

Martin frequently pushed the rules. He received detention regularly for what he considered minor misdemeanours. Sometimes he was detained—usually for one or two hours—on Sundays, the one day of the week he was allowed home to his family. An encounter with an older student while on detention one day was pivotal in shaping Martin's outlook. The boy, who was also serving detention, insisted he was a prefect. The older student carried an air of authority when he spoke to Martin.

The student told Martin to sit beside him. 'He said, "Open your fly" . . . He touched me and I didn't get excited, of course. I was absolutely horrified at his behaviour. Then, because I didn't show any stimulation, he just walked away. Then I noticed him behaving in a bullying manner to a lot of the small kids. I must say I took the initiative and started to talk to these people. Suddenly, from being oppressed, we became powerful because of our numbers. We reported him to the authorities.'

Although Martin did not report the sexual contact, he felt empowered by speaking up about bullying with the other boys. He learned it was possible to challenge what he saw as the misuse of power: 'That was my first political act, organising the weaker people together.'

The boy was disciplined. But Martin was appalled when a couple of years later the boy was made a prefect: 'He was given the very authority he was pretending to have and which he had abused.' Despite his growing wariness of hierarchies, Martin harboured hopes of becoming a prefect. These were not realised: 'I did want some kind of respect . . . I was keen to get some authority of some sort.'

When Martin first entered Cranbrook's art room, a new world opened before him. Inside was an exuberant realm of colour, imagination and creativity, a refuge from the discipline and formality outside its walls. Its centre was art master Justin O'Brien.

Unlike other classes, the boys were allowed to talk in art class, and they made the most of this. For some it was a muck-up class, and Martin wasn't beyond flicking clay across the art room at his classmate, the later artist Peter Kingston. 'There was a roar of noise and [O'Brien] would scream out, "Silence! I can't hear myself think,"' Martin later recalled.

O'Brien was an artist in his own right, who taught part-time at the school. He used jewel-like colours in works that usually had religious themes. Martin had been entranced by O'Brien's painting that had won the Blake Prize when he stood before it with his mother. Now he was about to be mentored by the artist himself. O'Brien's impact was profound; Martin would in later life refer to the painter as his 'art father'.

It took Martin a while to find his way to O'Brien's extra-curricular art classes—he was too shy to ask where to go. But when he did, he never left. O'Brien remembered his young student as eccentric and 'almost monosyllabic'.

Like Martin's father, O'Brien had known the horrors of war. As an Australian Army medical orderly in Greece, O'Brien nursed the wounded, and witnessed famine and mass burials. He spent nearly three years in a prisoner-of-war camp in Torun, Poland. There art became a refuge from the cruelties around him as he set up an art class in the camp and joined its theatre group. When O'Brien returned to Australia he saw out his service at Concord Hospital, as had Henry Sharp.

O'Brien joined Cranbrook in 1946, just two years after his traumatic wartime experience. As art master he created the conditions and environment in which Martin's artistic talents could emerge. As Martin explained: 'He provided lovely colours, jars of paint ... He didn't really tell you what to do, but he allowed you to do what you were interested in.'

Martin's interest was in portraits. When he was about fifteen, he painted in his art class a vivid series of characters, including a top-hatted toff, a cook, a dentist, a criminal and a wharfie. He was still inspired by the image of the toff nearly fifty years later, when he created an oil painting based on his schoolboy portrait.

O'Brien displayed the boys' work in their classrooms. But the best works were singled out for special treatment. Every two weeks, these were hung up in a staircase in the main building, where they were seen by all the school. It was rare when a Martin Sharp painting was not on show. Martin was thrilled when his work was on the walls of the staircase, especially when shown alongside other artistically talented students, including John Montefiore, whose work Martin admired.

Although drawn to portraiture, Martin did create a still life based on a Vincent van Gogh work. O'Brien had given his student a small book of the artist's paintings as a prize and suggested Martin copy one of the book's paintings. A 1957 still life is the first of Martin's many works that drew on van Gogh.

O'Brien oversaw the creation of theatrical sets for the school's annual play. Martin, too, lent a hand, painting sets for several productions. He also appeared in minor roles in *Sweeney Todd* and *The Prodigious Snob*, based on Molière's *Le Bourgeois Gentilhomme*, with John Gaden, later one of Australia's finest actors, invariably landing leading roles.

Martin's house tutor was mathematics teacher Terry Clarke, who later gained fame as a theatre director and composer, most notably creating the music for Nick Enright's *The Venetian Twins* and *Summer Rain*. He recalls Martin as paradoxically reserved yet assured, with his own take on the world: 'He was a confident boy, but a shy boy. He had a sense of self that you don't always see in schoolboys.'

As house tutor, Clarke's duties included conducting evening prayers. One night as he did so, the assembly was plunged into darkness. He ploughed on, reciting from memory the first evensong prayer that sprang to mind. He intoned, 'Lighten our darkness we beseech thee, oh Lord, and by thy great mercy defend us from all perils and dangers of this night.' As he uttered these words, the lights returned. The boys, and especially Martin, were much amused by this apparent demonstration of the power of prayer.

Sunlight streamed into the wood-panelled classroom where Martin stood by a wooden bookcase, cloth in hand. Once again, he had forgotten to bring his English books to class. And once again, he was polishing the teacher's bookcase as penance.

The punishment was more of a source of amusement than others he was subjected to. The man who presided over this book-lined classroom, Colin Aubrey Bell, was a formidable figure but one of the school's most respected teachers. Dubbed, ironically, 'Cheery' Bell by the boys, he was a man of a few words, given to long pauses, but pithy asides. Bell was Martin's housemaster and English teacher and his dry humour appealed to the schoolboy: '[Bell's class] was next to the physics lab, so if anyone farted he said, "It must be something coming from the lab."'

What Bell lacked in loquaciousness he made up for in his love of the literature on his bookshelves. Martin studied *Kidnapped*, R.L. Stevenson's boyhood adventure yarn, and Bell imparted his passion for poetry. Keats's 'La Belle Dame sans Merci', Coleridge's 'The Rime of the Ancient Mariner', and Malory's *Le Morte d'Arthur* were particular favourites. One poem especially lodged in Martin's mind: 'Australia', by radical poet Bernard O'Dowd, who wrote about national identity and what European culture needed to learn from Aboriginal spirituality. Martin loved the opening line of 'Australia' in which the great southern land is described as the 'Last sea-thing dredged by sailor Time from Space' and he committed the poem to memory.

Martin's first artwork to gain attention was a portrait of 'Cheery' Bell. The work began as an image of an English policeman, before Martin realised the picture unintentionally resembled his English teacher. He reworked the portrait to depict his pipe-smoking master in academic gown and glasses in his classroom with the boys in the background, including one polishing the bookshelves.

Justin O'Brien was so impressed with his student's work he singled it out for special treatment. He placed it in prime position in the fortnightly exhibition, midway up the staircase in the main building. It was the first time any of Martin's work had been hung in the coveted spot. 'If you got one there ... it was like winning the Archibald,' Martin exulted. The work created a buzz as the boys crowded around the audacious portrait on the stairs. 'It was considered quite cheeky ... no one had ever painted a teacher before, let alone [of Bell] who was the most severe teacher in the school.'

Bell asked for and was given the work: 'I don't know if he liked it or wanted to get it out of sight.' The reaction to the portrait was transformative for Martin: 'I realised [for the first time] that my art could have an impact.'

At fifteen, Martin was impressing with his art, but he was at best an average student in other subjects, including English, ancient and modern history, geography and Latin. But in maths, especially, his performance was dismal. 'An indefensibly bad exam—shameful,' maths teacher Terry Clarke wrote. 'His work has been unsatisfactory: he has prematurely resigned himself to failure in General Maths in the LC [Leaving Certificate]. Were he to apply himself next year he could achieve a pass standard comfortably.'

His chemistry teacher was more diplomatic about Martin's poor performance: 'He has the ability but so far we have not fired him with enthusiasm or confidence.' Only art teacher Justin O'Brien praised his student: 'Martin has been very busy again this term and painted some excellent pictures.'

Martin was an intelligent, capable student but unwilling to put his energies into subjects that did not appeal. His housemaster summed up: 'He is coming on and developing quickly but is much too ready to be put off by spirits which he feels are not kindred spirits—those of mathematicians and chemists. I wonder how he would react to the discipline of the great artists and if he in fact is ready to learn from them yet.' His end of year report would have brought little joy to his parents. But by then they faced troubles of their own.

Keith Hollingworth was a beatnik with a passion for the blues. He worked around the Rose Bay waterfront where he maintained sailing boats, including Henry Sharp's. Henry hired him to do jobs around the Cranbrook Lane property and he moved for a while into a room above the garage.

Martin liked the cool, free-spirited figure and his collection of Bessie Smith records. Jo liked him too. She liked him very much. She began an affair with the young handyman, who was about ten years her junior. The affair had echoes of D.H. Lawrence's *Lady Chatterley's Lover*, then banned in Australia, in which an upper-class woman, physically and emotionally distant from her husband, embarks on an affair with her gamekeeper.

Martin knew his parents' marriage was unhappy. He had heard their arguments and the lengthening silences between them. They had different natures—Henry reserved and cool, Jo demonstrative and demanding. They had drifted apart for years, almost from the outset of their marriage. Martin maintained that his father had been transformed by his wartime experience. And he believed his father had a number of affairs, conducted with his mother's tacit approval. 'My father had been given a certain leniency because of the war by my mother,' he said. Henry's liaisons were tolerated, provided the facade of the marriage was maintained.

But Jo's affair with Hollingworth cracked the facade and was the catalyst for the end of the marriage. For Jo, the relationship was more than a below-stairs dalliance. She fell passionately in love, and Martin was convinced her feelings were reciprocated.

Martin recalled his father telling him the marriage was over while he was still at school. 'I've had enough. I'm getting out of here,' Henry told Martin when they were alone together one day. Nonetheless, Jo and Henry did not officially separate until March 1960, a few months after Martin left school.

Martin sided with his mother: 'My mother wasn't the first one to leave the marriage. He was the first one to leave the marriage. But then she was blamed for, punished for, the sin because she fell in love.'

Jo became pregnant to Keith. Although Jo had wanted more children during her marriage, she did not continue with the pregnancy. She had an abortion, a procedure then illegal. Jo would have no other children; her hopes for the future rested with Martin alone.

Jo's parents were distraught at the breakdown of her marriage and furious when they learned of her affair with Hollingworth. They worried Hollingworth was a fortune-hunter and for their daughter's reputation. Stuart Ritchie demanded Jo end the relationship. He refused to see his daughter—his only child—until she had. Jo continued to see her mother, but was shunned by her father.

'And she did give Keith up. It broke her heart but she did. But her father didn't believe her ... It destroyed her, I think. It was like the male world was against her,' Martin said.

Stuart Ritchie continued to live just a kilometre away from his daughter. But they might as well have been continents apart. He remained implacable. He never saw his daughter again.

Martin repeated his final school year in an effort to improve his Leaving Certificate performance, but with little effect. He scraped through. With no demonstrated aptitude for maths and chemistry, following his father into medicine was not an option. Nor was he likely to follow grandfather Ritchie into industry.

Martin was unsure of his next step. 'It was Justin's suggestion that I go to art school, because I didn't know what to do. I suppose then my father had to hand me over to what would have appeared to him as the extremely dubious world of the art world. Because he was hoping I'd become a professional of some sort … Art school at that stage was just for people who couldn't fit in anywhere else.'

He spent a year at the National Art School, then known as East Sydney Technical College, before changing direction.

CHAPTER 3

ART VERSUS ALFS

With its manicured lawns, gothic towers and grimacing gargoyles, Sydney University pays wistful homage to Oxbridge's dreaming spires. When Martin enrolled as an architecture student in 1961, Australia still looked to Britain with unqualified deference and admiration.

Britain's monarch was our monarch. A republic was not even a whispered possibility at a time when Australia's cinemas played 'God Save the Queen' before the main feature, and Sydney University's carillon peeled the anthem each lunchtime from the clock tower. Such was the esteem in which the monarchy was held that when the newly crowned Queen Elizabeth visited Sydney for the first time in 1954, more than half the city's population of 1.8 million turned out to see her. Onlookers crammed the harbour, including Taronga Zoo where the shells of its giant tortoises were painted with Union Jacks.

Shiploads of migrants arrived from central and southern Europe in the postwar years; many headed to the belching steelworks of Newcastle, Port Kembla and Whyalla or to the Snowy Mountains irrigation scheme. But overwhelmingly, migrants came from the United Kingdom. They were dubbed 'ten-pound Poms', after the subsidised fare they paid to emigrate under the Australian government's populate-or-perish Assisted Passage Migration Scheme.

The racist White Australia policy—which effectively excluded Asian, especially Chinese, and other non-white migrants in the first half of the twentieth century—was still in force. Australia was a white-bread country, its tastes and traditions were Anglo, and its dreams as modest as a suburban bungalow on a quarter-acre block. Its culture was conservative and conformist and reinforced by a government that brooked little dissent.

Prime Minister Robert Menzies, an unabashed Anglophile, retained his grip on power throughout the 1950s and well into the 1960s, ultimately for eighteen years. He had successfully appealed to what he called the 'Forgotten People'—the frugal, hard-working souls he argued were taken for granted by political parties. Truly forgotten were Australia's indigenous people. Their voices were little heard, their right to vote restricted and their children forcibly removed from their families.

The opposition Labor Party was too busy ripping itself to shreds to offer a credible alternative vision. The breakaway Democratic Labour Party—founded in 1955, conservative, Catholic and virulently anti-communist—helped keep the Liberal-Country Party coalition in power for another decade. As the Cold War took hold, the Red Menace became the postwar bogey, even though Menzies had tried, and failed, to ban the Communist Party.

Other bans were effective though. Books, high- and low-brow, had long been scrutinised in Australia for their unsavoury content and were routinely prohibited. Among those banned in the 1950s were *The Catcher in the Rye*, *Lady Chatterley's Lover*, Norman Lindsay's *Age of Consent*, Gore Vidal's *The Judgment of Paris* and a host of bodice-rippers and pulp fiction novels with racy covers. Customs officials regularly scoured the bags of new arrivals to Australia in search of such contraband.

Among the bags searched were those of Sir Eugene Goossens, the British-born conductor of the Sydney Symphony Orchestra, when he flew back from Europe in 1956. Customs officials at Sydney airport found what were considered pornographic photographs and other material, including three rubber masks and some sticks of incense.

When his affair with Rosaleen Norton, the so-called 'Witch of Kings Cross'—an artist with a taste for erotica, bondage and the occult—became public, he was hounded from Australia and his reputation shredded.

The fifties were not encouraging times to be an artist in Sydney. Even when not being chased from the country, an artist's life was viewed with suspicion. As artist Colin Lanceley, one of Martin's mentors, described it: 'There was no art world in Sydney. You couldn't think of making your living as a visual artist. It was very myopic and provincial. Everybody wanted to go away ... Parents were genuinely concerned when a son of theirs wanted to be an artist. It was too dodgy, too risky, and it wasn't respectable.' Little wonder many upped and left the country, invariably for Britain.

Suburban Sydney, red-roofed and liver-bricked, seemed little changed from the 1920s, when D.H. Lawrence had written: 'Great swarming, teeming Sydney flowing out into these myriads of bungalows, like shallow waters spreading, undyked. And what then? Nothing. No inner life, no high command, no interest in anything, finally.'

Well, no interest in anything except sport. But the decision to build an opera house at Sydney's harbourside Bennelong Point provided a glimmer of hope for those who dreamed of a creative life in Australia. Young Danish architect Jørn Utzon won an international competition to design the building in 1957, and work was underway three years later when singer and activist Paul Robeson sang 'Old Man River' and 'Joe Hill'—the first unofficial performance at the site—to an audience of construction workers.

In 1960 more than a third of the Australian population were under eighteen years, and some were hungry for change. Youth culture had begun to emerge through the 1950s, including bodgies and widgies, Australia's version of Britain's teddy boys or America's greasers. Bodgies wore their hair long and their trousers tight and hung around the milk bars of Sydney's Kings Cross and Darlinghurst with their widgie girlfriends, in pencil skirts and fitted blouses, jiving to the new rock'n'roll. Drawn mainly from working-class kids, bodgies and widgies were frowned upon in the press and courts as an unhealthy and unsavoury cult and a breeding ground for crime and licentiousness.

A different group of young people was drawn to Sydney University, the country's most prestigious university, in the early sixties. They were a precociously talented group of students who included Germaine Greer, Clive James, Robert Hughes, Bob Ellis, Richard Walsh, poet Les Murray, actors John Bell, Arthur Dignam, John Gaden and filmmaker Bruce Beresford. Some would go on to international careers; all would shape Australia's cultural life.

Greer, James and Hughes and others were associated with the Sydney Push, an anarchic group of writers, intellectuals, drinkers and gamblers. Their guiding light was a flame-haired Scot, the free-thinking John Anderson, professor of Philosophy at Sydney University. Their stamping ground was Sydney University and their watering hole the Royal George pub in Sussex Street in the city. They scorned all that the conservative Menzies era stood for: respect for authority, the family and sobriety. They sneered at careerism, advocated sexual freedom, opposed censorship and labelled as 'Alfs' those who slavishly accepted society's stultifying mores.

The student newspaper *Honi Soit* provided a creative outlet for some of those talents. More literary than political, the magazine published poems by Clive James and articles by Mungo MacCallum, Laurie Oakes and Bob Ellis. It reviewed student theatrical productions—from *The Mikado* to university revues—ran stories on a visit to a local strip club, covered fledgling student director Bruce Beresford's struggle to make his first film and, between adverts for cigarettes and pipe tobacco, grumbled about the quality of campus coffee. Only occasionally did the outside world—such as South Africa's Sharpeville massacre—intervene.

After dropping out of art school, Martin enrolled in architecture at Sydney University in an attempt to please his father. Henry Sharp was keen for his only son to attend university and embark on a career, as he had done. But Martin quickly found the company of the campus's brighter fellow students and extracurricular activities more appealing than attending architecture lectures.

He began contributing cartoons to *Honi Soit*. Some were essentially illustrative, but in one of his first, the former private schoolboy sneered at the working-class bodgies. The cartoon, which depicted a pimply-faced bodgie with quiffed fringe, had the punchline: 'I wear's me hair long to keep me brain warm.'

Martin soon set his sights on bigger targets than bodgies. By mid-year, he weighed in on a controversy that embroiled the city and especially the university. The fracas began when the Anglican Primate of Australia, Sydney's archbishop Dr Hugh Gough, attacked university philosophers—essentially Sydney University's John Anderson—for 'immoral' teachings that decried marriage, advocated premarital sex, free love and self-expression. In a sermon to international lawmakers in Sydney, Gough urged the government to take action against the decline in morals.

The sermon, which prompted heated debate in the press, was based on an until then little-known pamphlet written three years earlier by a retired Sydney Catholic doctor, V.J. Kinsella. *Honi Soit* devoted pages to the ongoing debate. Martin produced a cartoon of a relay race in which Dr Kinsella, in a runner's shorts and singlet, hands a torch to a dog-collared Archbishop Gough.

At the time, Martin was living on campus at the Anglican college St Paul's, the same college his father had attended. In contrast to his father, Martin was deeply unhappy there. After years at boarding school, he was again in an all-male institution. And again Martin did not fit in: 'College was like going back to boarding school . . . I couldn't stand the bullying, the hierarchies.'

He disliked its blokey culture with its emphasis on sporting prowess and drinking. Throughout his life he rarely drank alcohol—tobacco and dope were Martin's drugs of choice: 'I stopped going to breakfast, then I stopped going to lunch. There was a lot of drinking there and I wasn't a drinker at all. At the football dinner, everyone would have big jugs of beer on their table and I had a jug of orange juice. The only one in the whole dining hall.'

Nor was he happy with his studies. He had little interest in architecture. Only the art classes by Lloyd Rees, who taught at the faculty for forty years, had any appeal. Martin quickly decided this profession was not for him: 'I took one look at the building, which was designed by the dean of the architecture faculty, and I realised I wasn't going to get taught any architecture there and it was boring.'

Martin's attempt to please his father by studying architecture was short-lived. After two terms, he abandoned Sydney University and his attempt to follow someone else's wishes. From then on, he would chart his own course.

The gallows once stood outside the forbidding circular entrance pillars of the convict-built Darlinghurst Gaol. Poet Henry Lawson, bushranger Captain Moonlight, and Aboriginal tracker Jimmy Governor were among those who had been held within its sandstone walls. The prisoners had long gone and the former jail housed art students by the 1960s.

Martin was back at East Sydney Technical College for third term. He was again in the company of artists, including his teachers John Coburn and John Passmore, both abstract artists, and William Salmon. Soon Martin began to produce abstract works.

He held a small student show of them at the Ensemble Theatre in North Sydney. A Catholic priest with some friends stood laughing at the work on display. Whether it was their ridicule or his nerves, Martin fainted at the opening. It was hardly an auspicious start to his artistic career. He later destroyed much of this work, believing it to be a failure.

He abandoned abstracts and turned his attention to creating posters. His first was for the annual Artists' Ball. The theme was Moulin Rouge and the poster depicted a Toulouse-Lautrec-like figure at his easel in a black and white image evocative of the work of American Ben Shahn.

The fancy dress ball was held for several years at the Trocadero, a glamorous Art Deco dance hall on George Street. These were the most raucous events held at the Troc, as it was known, and drew bohemians, artists, their models and drag queens, the latter a relatively rare sight in Sydney at this time. For Martin the balls were the high points of the three years he spent at art school, where he claimed he learned nothing other than how to crosshatch. He dressed as a sea monster at one of them, where the drag queens arrived in a truck because their outrageous costumes were too big to fit in a car.

The Artists' Balls were more exuberant affairs than the other annual ball on the social calendar, the high-society Black & White Ball. But Martin attended one of these with a young woman he had recently met at St Paul's oval.

Louise Ferrier had little recollection of that first encounter, so she was taken aback when he telephoned her home. As she recalls: 'He said, "Oh, it's Martin Sharp here." Then there was this deadly silence.'

Martin would never rush to fill a telephone silence, a habit that disconcerted many over the years. Louise let the silence hang. 'I was pretty shy myself. After about a thirty-second silence, I just said, "Who are you?"' Nonetheless, she agreed to go to the ball, unaware of the strict black and white dress code. Louise stood out in a bright orange dress.

At art school, Martin found the early promise he had shown in his Cranbrook portraits vanished and he lost his ability to paint. But he drew cartoons instead. He became friends with fellow art student Garry Shead. They began contributing cartoons to *The Bulletin*. Martin was impressed with Garry's skills, and his cartoons were often given a full page. One of Garry's early cartoons depicted a man carrying a peace banner staring down at the word *Eternity* written on the pavement in copperplate script: 'I always remember Martin looking at that and he thought it very good. He ran with the ball after that.'

Garry Shead was keen to produce a student magazine aimed at art students since no local publications catered to their interests. *The Arty Wild Oat* appeared in April 1962, with him as editor and Martin as assistant editor. The title meant 'pretentiously artistic', its editors announced, but they added: 'We intend to publish no article smacking of pseudo intellectualism.'

For the magazine's lead article, Martin interviewed a young Robert Hughes about Sydney's Art Gallery of New South Wales. Hughes, who would become one of the most influential international art critics of the late twentieth century, took aim at its incompetent trustees, its collection and the building itself. He wanted it demolished and rebuilt on the site of the then run-down Queen Victoria Building, which he also wanted to see fall to the wrecker's ball.

Martin also contributed a couple of cartoons to *The Arty Wild Oat*, including one based on Sidney Nolan's *Leda and the Swan*: 'Psst Leda, don't look now but I think that artist is spying on us again.' It was one of the first times he took art itself as his subject.

Several prominent artists contributed to the second issue in July, including Colin Lanceley and Ross Crothall—part of the avant-garde Annandale Imitation Realists collaborative group—and Norman Lindsay. The issue also reflected a fascination with Sydney's demimonde and included a lengthy unsigned article on a visit to a local prostitute, accompanied by a piece on Toulouse-Lautrec titled 'Painter of Prostitutes'. Martin's most visible contribution was a cartoon strip, in which a bouffant-haired society dame attempts to tell her daughter about the facts of life, only to learn her efforts are too late—the young woman is pregnant.

The magazine was short-lived—the second issue was the last. But Martin had picked up layout and design experience and honed his cartoon skills.

Martin was tall and lean, with sparkling sapphire eyes, a patrician nose and thick, dark hair. He invariably held a French cigarette between his long elegant fingers, trailing a cloud of pungent smoke. He resembled a young Jean-Paul Belmondo. His looks and talent drew many young women into his orbit.

Fashion student Jenny Kee was captivated when she met Martin at East Sydney Tech: 'He just was a total romantic—the Gauloises out of the mouth, red and white check trousers like a lot of chefs wear. You'd fall under his spell.'

Martin's first serious girlfriend was a Brigitte Bardot lookalike, with long blonde hair, at times coloured purple, kittenish features and a style ahead of the times. Anou Kiisler made her own minidresses in gingham and corduroy long before British model Jean Shrimpton scandalised prim Australia by appearing in an above-the-knee shift at Melbourne's Flemington racetrack in 1965.

Martin had been friends with Anou since they met at a high school formal. After leaving school Anou, who was of Estonian background and lived in the Eastern Suburbs, enrolled in medicine at Sydney University. Her radical style brought her to the attention of *The Australian Women's Weekly*. The magazine photographed the eighteen-year-old on campus in what it called her 'way-out wardrobe', including thigh-high black leather boots over blue jeans, and a series of minidresses she ran up 'whenever there's a party on that night'. One male student told the *Weekly* that she caused a sensation each time she arrived late for lectures.

Martin and Anou were a glamorous and photogenic pair when they appeared in an early experimental black and white film by Garry Shead. In it, Anou stands self-consciously on a plinth in a Sydney park before Martin rescues her and they mount a bronze statue of a horse, like a knight rescuing a damsel in distress. The mood is as exuberant and carefree as the film's title, *Ding a Ding Day*.

Anou later caught the *Weekly*'s eye again when she was photographed in a pink minidress and pink stockings on which she had sewed pink flowers. She was about to be an usher for Sydney University's 1965 revue, *First, No Pinky*. Martin's design work for this show included creating mask-like smiles on sticks, an image that he would return to for years.

In the revue, he heard a song about an eccentric who chalked the word *Eternity* on Sydney's streets. Arthur Stace was a reformed alcoholic who, inspired by a preacher, had written the word in yellow chalk on the city's pavement. He kept on doing so. Martin had seen the word, always in copperplate script, on pavements around the city a number of times after he first encountered it near his childhood home. So had most Sydneysiders. By the time Stace died in 1967, he had chalked it on pavements about half a million times.

Few university students had their own cars in the early 1960s. The lucky ones might have occasional access to the family's EJ Holden. Martin not only had his own car but it was a sporty Triumph Herald, which his Ritchie grandparents bought him soon after he left school.

But it was not to Martin's taste. He wanted a convertible. John Weiley was among several friends he recruited to take off the roof with hacksaws. They hacked and sawed away and eventually decapitated the car. But the vehicle began to sag. 'I was driving with Martin and the car felt very weird. The roof had been important to the car structurally. The doors wouldn't shut properly,' John recalls.

The sports car was replaced by a Renault 4. The vehicle had impressed Martin when the salesman took him for a test drive. As they sped along Cowper Wharf Road at Woolloomooloo, the salesman attempted a U-turn and the car tipped over. After the occupants had exited through the windows, Martin bought the car, impressed that the vehicle had simply tipped over rather than rolled. Perhaps he realised his abilities behind the wheel would require a robust vehicle.

Alex Popov, an architecture student and friend, shared a hair-raising ride back from Palm Beach on Sydney's northern beachside one day: 'He kept touching the gutter all the time. He said, "Oh, I haven't got my glasses." He was just making sure the road was there.' Martin's misplaced glasses—he was short-sighted and frequently lost them—wasn't the only thing that made driving with him hazardous. 'He never thought to put oil in it or service it.'

Martin often drove his friend and fellow art student Peter Powditch home from classes. It was a mixed blessing. Martin was so fond of detours—to visit Anou, Justin O'Brien or a strip club—that Peter often didn't get home until after dark.

Martin spent many evenings at Vadim's, one of the city's few late-night venues. The Kings Cross coffee house and restaurant, on Challis Avenue near Macleay Street, was basic—about a dozen tables in a neon-lit two-storey building. But its tables drew actors, writers, intellectuals, poets and artists, among them Barry Humphries, Robert Hughes, Les Murray, Margaret Fink and Germaine Greer. *The Sydney Morning Herald*'s influential theatre critic Harry Kippax had his own table at which he wrote reviews after opening nights. Visiting celebrities—Rudolf Nureyev, Margot Fonteyn and Vivien Leigh—dropped in.

Overseeing this Kings Cross salon was Vadim Steven Kerr. Born Vadim Kargopoloff in Shanghai, where his Russian parents had fled the revolution, he arrived in Australia in the late forties, fleeing Mao. At his Challis Avenue restaurant he served borscht and stroganoff, exotic fare for a generation raised on silverside and boiled vegetables. And he surreptitiously served alcohol in white coffee cups at a time of strict licensing laws.

Despite the generally conservative climate of Sydney, shoots of youthful optimism were beginning to appear. Martin, together with John Weiley, believed there were aspects of Australia's past worth celebrating. And they believed the times were changing—for the better—and they could be part of it. They began making a film together based on Australian imagery found on posters outside pubs. When John read a poem one day that resonated with him about the country's spirit, he rushed around to Martin's to show him. It was Martin's favourite childhood poem, 'Australia' by Bernard O'Dowd.

'We wanted to celebrate everything that was traditionally Australian. The Australia of King O'Malley, Bernard O'Dowd, the founders of the nation, and the idea of a Commonwealth. Those things really spoke to us, we were passionate about it,' John Weiley recalls. And because of their faith in Australia, the pair made an unusual vow: 'Martin and I made a blood oath that we would not be like everyone else and leave Australia and go to England.'

At the red-brick University of New South Wales in Kensington, its student paper, *Tharunka*, had just acquired a new editor in March 1962. Richard Neville was an arts student determined to make a splash. A stint as an advertising trainee at a city department store had equipped him with print production skills and fed his instinct for publicity. He had already been involved in a student prank, helping 'kidnap' Brian Henderson, the host of pop music TV show *Bandstand*, and spiriting him away to the New South Wales central coast for a late-night party.

Like Martin, Richard was a former private schoolboy and no stranger to corporal punishment. The school's harsh discipline was the reason Knox Grammar's colours were black and blue, he quipped.

His father had been a colonel and managing director of *Country Life* magazine, his mother a newspaper columnist.

In the small world of alternative publications, Martin and Richard's paths soon crossed. Neville was as garrulous as Sharp was reserved, but they began to hang out together. Both of them appeared in Garry Shead's *Ding a Ding Day*, which captures their different characters. In it the pair walk along a city street, Richard clowning to the camera, Martin quietly amused and smoking a cigarette behind his extrovert friend.

Meanwhile, at Sydney University, the editors of *Honi Soit*, Richard Walsh and Peter Grose, were about to be sacked by their masters, the Students' Representative Council. The SRC, long an incubator for aspiring politicians, had taken umbrage over the paper's irreverent reports about its activities. The pair had been reinstated by the time a student editors' conference was held mid-year in Adelaide and they drove down to it in the company of Alex Popov and Richard Neville. En route, talk turned to the possibility of joining forces and creating a new satirical publication free of the dead hand of SRC control.

Richard Walsh, too, was a former private schoolboy, having attended Barker College on Sydney's upper North Shore. His school days had been miserable. He had been beaten and bullied, and he detested the school's emphasis on sporting prowess. The son and grandson of accountants, Walsh's background was more staid than Sharp's or Neville's. As well as editing *Honi Soit*, he was enrolled in medicine at Sydney University and was the most studious and industrious of the three. He was paying his own way through university and could not afford to fail.

Richard Walsh was struggling with zoology assignments around the time he met Martin. Zoology required an ability to draw, a skill he lacked. Anou was also studying the subject, so Martin would sometimes tag along on zoology excursions when his girlfriend and Richard sketched the legs of a giraffe at the zoo or he would observe them dissecting a frog. Richard's assignments showed much improvement after such occasions: 'I was getting terrible marks and then every so often I'd shine ... because Martin would do the frog or the giraffe. My zoology prac book was full of the most terrible drawings, but occasionally there was a real little highlight.'

Martin made a number of trips to Melbourne, where he became friends with Georges and Mirka Mora, both of them originally Jewish immigrants from Paris. Georges was a former resistance fighter who became an influential Melbourne art dealer and businessman, Mirka was an artist; as a girl, she and her mother had narrowly escaped being transported to Auschwitz. En route to Pithiviers, a transit camp to Auschwitz, Mirka's mother had written down the names of the stations they passed on a piece of paper and put it in a stampless envelope. Mirka's slender fingers slipped the letter addressed to her father between the cattle train's slats. Somebody found the envelope and put a stamp on it. Her father, also in the Jewish resistance in Paris, received it and secured their release. He handed over many gold coins to do so, he later told Mirka. She never forgot the kindness of the stranger who had helped deliver her mother's letter.

Sleepy, sedate Melbourne in the 1950s was a refuge for the couple, who created around them the aura of Paris's Left Bank. Their *joie de vivre* and bohemian lifestyle became magnets for artists, writers and thinkers in an otherwise bland and provincial Melbourne.

The Moras rented space at 9 Collins Street; Mirka's studio there had previously been used by artists Arthur Streeton, Tom Roberts, Frederick McCubbin and Sir John Longstaff. At that time, few people lived in the centre of Melbourne and artists, musicians, journalists and politicians would drop by Georges and Mirka's welcoming inner-city home. One day Martin arrived on the doorstep. Mirka recalls: 'I remember his first visit ... 9 Collins Street had such a great atmosphere because of the history of it.

And Martin was like a cat, he could feel the atmosphere. Martin found us. He presented himself one day at 9 Collins Street and he never left.'

The Moras were the first truly bohemian family Martin had met. He had grown up amid great material wealth, privilege and conservative values. The Moras and their three sons were from a different, creative world; it was one Martin was keen to embrace.

'Martin was a big part of the Mora family. He loved the way we lived and everything we did … He wanted to be part of the family. He could not stop saying it. I would say, "But you are, you are my son number four,"' Mirka continues.

The Moras opened three celebrated café-restaurants: the Mirka Café, Café Balzac—Melbourne's first restaurant licensed to serve alcohol after 10pm—and the Tolarno. They fed a generation of artists as well as such visiting celebrities as Katherine Hepburn, Maurice Chevalier and Marlene Dietrich. Martin found Melbourne a less philistine city than Sydney, largely because of the Moras.

Martin helped Mirka with the interior of the Tolarno before it opened in 1965; he painted leaves and roses on its doors and windows. For Martin, as for the exuberant Mirka, a blank wall, door or window was a space to be filled. Among her wide range of friends he met art patrons John and Sunday Reed and visited their home Heide, east of Melbourne, where many prominent artists—including Sidney Nolan, Albert Tucker and Joy Hester—had worked and played. And through Mirka he met Melbourne-based photographer Robert Whitaker.

British-born Whitaker arrived as a ten-pound Pom in 1961 and settled in Melbourne, where he did fashion shoots and worked for the ABC. He was handsome and gregarious, and he and Martin became friends. 'We got on like a house on fire,' Robert recalled. Martin later used a portrait Whitaker took of Mirka as a cover for *Oz*, a grotesque image in which her face is covered in zinc cream and mascara.

Martin stayed at the Moras' beach house at Aspendale, about thirty kilometres from Melbourne. He took Anou on one visit and Robert photographed them on the beach with the Mora family. Martin, in stovepipe jeans and a pair of binoculars around his neck, stands with his right arm raised like a mock muscle man. Anou holds a sign that reads: 'God bless thee and keep thee ... Aspendale 1964'.

It was a farewell photograph. Robert Whitaker had just had an astonishing break. He had met The Beatles' manager, Brian Epstein, in Melbourne during the band's Australian tour. He had photographed Epstein for the *Australian Jewish News*, superimposing peacock figures on the portrait: 'I put peacock feathers around him, because I thought he was a bit of an emperor.' Epstein was so impressed with the image, he asked Whitaker to return to the United Kingdom and become The Beatles' in-house photographer. The band was at the epicentre of the pop universe and Robert was being offered unparalleled entree: 'And off I went.' So another friend went where Martin vowed never to go.

CHAPTER 4

THE TRIALS OF MARTIN SHARP

Sydney slumbered through its summer break, punctuated by the reassuring thud of leather on willow and test-match cricket commentary. Meanwhile, Martin and a group of students were working on a project that would shake Australia out of its long cultural somnambulance. The idea of a satirical magazine had gathered pace since the mid-year student editors' conference. The initial idea for a one-off annual issue had widened to the possibility of a monthly magazine that would appeal beyond university campuses. Undergraduates had spent long enough simply talking to themselves through their student papers. It was time to make an impact on the wider world.

With his cartoons, graphic eye and experience on *The Arty Wild Oat*, Martin's talents were in demand for the new publication. Martin, Alex Popov, Peter Grose and Richard Walsh were among those who gathered during the long university holiday at the Mosman home of Richard Neville's parents on Sunday, 6 January 1963.

The magazine needed a name. Martin favoured *ASP*—the *Australian Satirical Paper*. Richard Walsh disagreed; he thought the venomous acronym clunky. He wanted *Oz*—it was snappier and typographically stronger. With little money for advertising, the magazine needed to stand out visually. At the time the word Oz was associated with the movie *The Wizard of Oz* and its Yellow Brick Road, rather than a shorthand for Australia: 'It didn't occur to anyone that it was the first syllable of our native land ... for a long time it was a great mystery that we had called it *Oz*,' Walsh says.

Martin disliked the name, but *Oz* won the day. Fifty pounds was raised, and a printer in suburban Hornsby was lined up. The father of one of the editorial team, Gina Eviston—a fellow student, part-time model and later an investment guru—made available a carpentry workshop in The Rocks that they could use on Sundays. This Harrington Lane office had once been the stables of Britain's regal representative, Governor Arthur Phillip—appropriately enough for a magazine about to hurl manure at the monarchy.

The magazine launched on April Fool's Day 1963, when about forty female student volunteers took up their positions on Sydney streets with copies of the first issue. Grose, Neville and Walsh were editors of the sixteen-page publication, Martin was among its artists, and its editorial assistants included Garry Shead and Alex Popov. '*Oz* is a new magazine,' the cover announced. Its front-page image featured a cartoon Queen Elizabeth and a scantily clad male with a padlock over his privates. The Queen had just visited Australia, and the paper poked fun at some of the more fawning press coverage—and at that time there was little else—including Prime Minister Robert Menzies' infamous brown-nosing comment: 'I did but see her passing by, and yet I love her till I die.' The feature was accompanied by Martin's cartoon of the monarch grinning like a Cheshire Cat.

Sexual repression was a dominant theme in the first issue, perhaps not surprisingly: as poet Philip Larkin memorably observed, sexual intercourse began in 1963. A feature on chastity belts was accompanied by Martin's drawing of an alarmingly spiked device. There were interviews on abortion, including with an abortionist. Abortions were illegal and were often being performed under dangerous conditions by unqualified 'backyard' operators.

'Everybody is talking about *Oz*!' the paper announced—perhaps only a little prematurely—beneath Martin's prescient cartoon of a tree branch on which sat three vultures and a clergyman, eagerly waiting to swoop. The first issue sold about 7000 copies, some of which were torn up by irate buyers.

Oz and other alternative shoestring magazines that sprang up in Australia and overseas around this time—*Village Voice* had begun in Greenwich Village in 1955 and *Private Eye* launched in Britain in 1961—were aided by changes in printing technology, including offset printing. By the early 1960s, anyone with a typewriter, scissors, Letraset and pot of paste could produce a magazine. *Oz* had most in common with the satirical *Private Eye*, with its mix of undergraduate cheekiness, ridicule of the powerful and sensational stories that the mainstream press dared not touch.

A bigger target than the Queen was the focus of *Oz*'s second issue. An interview with God was accompanied by Martin's cartoon depicting a cigar-smoking tycoon, with angel wings and a halo on a peg behind him, seated at his desk before three trays marked Heaven, Purgatory and Hell. Martin in later life would become a defender of the monarchy and deeply religious, but there was no sign of this in his early *Oz* work.

Martin's cartoons grew in strength and prominence with each issue. By the third—when he was listed in the staff box as 'Beautician'—a whole page was given over to his main cartoon. It was a narrative-style monologue, and this full-page format became the hallmark of his most popular early cartoons. *The Portrait of the Artist as a Young Man* satirised the faddishness of the art world. It traced a hapless young artist trying to carve a name by appearing at the right openings, drinking at the Windsor Castle (then a popular Paddington artists' watering hole), winning critical acclaim and a trip to London. There the critics turn on him, his art fails to sell and he returns crestfallen to Australia, where he passes unrecognised in the Windsor Castle. Even as a 21-year-old, Martin had few illusions about the capriciousness of the art world.

The third issue continued to provoke. With homosexuality not just a crime but 'Australia's greatest menace'—according to former New

South Wales police chief Colin Delaney—a letter writer suggested homosexuality could be harnessed for the good of the country. The correspondent advocated filling the military entirely with gay couples: '"Army camps for army camps" would be our slogan and "God Save the Queens" on every lip.'

The cover alluded to the mysterious deaths of physicist Dr Gilbert Bogle and Margaret Chandler, whose partially clad bodies had been discovered in a lovers' lane beside the Lane Cove River after a New Year's Eve party that year. Bogle was an eminent CSIRO scientist, Chandler the wife of a scientific photographer also employed at the CSIRO. The case gripped Sydney for months, eliciting tabloid coverage with salacious tales of North Shore wife-swapping, drug-taking and conspiracy theories. Above a photo of the Chandlers together and dressed up there was a speech bubble—a form of satire familiar to readers of *Private Eye*—with the words: 'Apart from that it was a good party.'

But the magazine was by then in trouble with the authorities. The editors were charged with publishing an obscene publication. In the fallout, advertisers cancelled their contracts, except for a loyal hamburger bar, Binkie's Burgers. Hours before the fourth issue was poised to go to press, the Hornsby printer got cold feet. The issue had been typeset, but its editors scoured Sydney for three days to find a printer willing to put it on his presses. A saviour came in the eccentric, ebullient form of Francis James at the Anglican Press.

James had been a religious correspondent for *The Sydney Morning Herald*, where he made his office in the back of a Rolls-Royce parked beside the newspaper's offices. Colleagues got his attention by dropping paper clips onto the vehicle's roof. An air of mystery and panache surrounded James, heightened by his fondness for sunglasses and a broad-brimmed hat. Flamboyant as his sartorial style undoubtedly was, it also served to shield his eyes, which had been damaged when his Spitfire was shot down over France in World War II.

James had been at the centre of an infamous media dust-up in 1960 when a young Rupert Murdoch was competing with rival media baron Sir Frank Packer to take over the Anglican Press. Alerted that Sir Frank's sons, Kerry and Clyde Packer, had broken into the offices of the little printing and publishing house in an effort to gain control, James appealed to Murdoch for assistance. The *Daily Mirror*'s knockabout sports columnist Frank Browne, a former professional boxer, duly turned up with four burly men to confront the Packers holed up inside the building. A brawl ensued, in which the Packer boys came off second-best. 'Knight's Sons in City Brawl', Murdoch's *Mirror* screamed the next day and carried a front-page photo of the scrum.

The larger-than-life Francis James is said to have later claimed to have simply been studying Psalm 35 with Browne. In a sense he was. The psalm advocates taking up spears and swords against one's enemies.

After James rolled the presses on the fourth issue of *Oz* in July, publication was suspended until the obscenity matter was resolved. Neville and Walsh, together with Grose—who had by then left *Oz* to become a mainstream journalist—did not defend the charge when it went to court in September. They knew a criminal conviction would have serious consequences for young men with their careers ahead of them. Instead they pleaded guilty in the hope that, as first offenders, they would get a smack over the wrists but no conviction would be recorded. They were each fined twenty pounds.

Martin was unimpressed that the three had pleaded guilty rather than take a stand. In particular, he satirised his friend Richard Neville in a cartoon depicting him as full of bravado ahead of his court appearance before buckling to pressure, getting a haircut, borrowing a suit and meekly pleading guilty. Martin, of course, had rather less at stake. He had family money behind him and the independence this brought. He was untroubled by the need to earn a living. And controversy never did an artist any harm.

Neville and Walsh seemed only slightly chastened when, with their university exams over, the magazine reappeared in December 1963. 'We think you will find that six months has not dampened our vigour nor court appearances tamed our thoughts,' they declared. But they acknowledged the first issue had sailed close to the wind, and added 'we are unlikely to sail so close again'. How wrong they were.

Over that summer, Martin and John Weiley drove up to Palm Beach, on Sydney's northern coastal fringe, to work on a film and take photographs. Their girlfriends, Anou Kiisler and Denise Ropert, accompanied them. After a swim at the beach they stopped for a drink at the Newport Arms, a local watering hole popular with the boozy, surfie tribes of the northern beaches. The seething hostility directed their way in the pub alarmed them.

'We were intimidated by the incredible animal-like crowd there and left,' John wrote in his diary. He still recalls the aggressive atmosphere, and the effect their female companions had on the inebriated crowd: 'The beer garden was full of beery half-pissed blokes when we arrived—two long-haired scrawny boys with two beautiful girls. We had just come from a swim, and bikinis that had seemed unremarkable at the beach suddenly seemed very skimpy at the pub. Some of the more aggressive drinkers pushed in close, ogling the girls and coming up with seductive lines like "What are you doing with these poofters, love?" It got quite heavy.'

Shortly after, Martin created another of his monologue-style cartoons. In this one the speaker damns himself from his own mouth. Known as *The Gas Lash*, it was published on the back page of the orientation week issue of *Tharunka* in February 1964. In the cartoon, a student narrates in bar-room slang how he picked up a buxom young female of easy virtue at a student formal and plied her with booze.

But his attempts to seduce her were foiled when she, having drunk too much, 'chucked all over me tux'.

Soon it was the authorities who were spewing. And Martin was front-page news. Eastern Suburbs police had been inundated with complaints about Martin's cartoon, *The Sydney Morning Herald* reported. 'They have described *The Gas Lash* as pornographic, obscene and depravity plus,' an unnamed detective said. The vice squad had been called in. The university's vice-chancellor, Professor John Baxter, was not about to go in to bat for the student magazine. 'The university is extremely concerned at this publication … this issue of *Tharunka* was published before we could have confiscated it,' Baxter said.

It was a big day for moral outrage. The article appeared alongside a story about the Victorian vice squad banning striptease shows in Melbourne. Martin hit back, penning a letter to the *Herald*'s editor. His cartoon had been misunderstood. Had he used conventional language, rather than slang, there would have been no fuss and possibly been praise, since he had highlighted the 'undesirable type of student that the more conventional critics, such as the church and university authorities, are constantly inveighing against'. The cartoon's language was colourful, but not indecent, he argued. 'Either critics are too unperceptive to understand the satire (which was aimed at and produced for university students) or have their necks buried so far in the sands as not to know what their kiddies are up to. *The Gas Lash* was written as a warning to freshers.'

Martin soon acquired a bad-boy image in the tabloid press. He was dubbed the 'angriest young man in the Sydney art world' when he took part in a group exhibition soon afterwards. A press report described him swanning into the exhibition, casting a contemptuous gaze over it and dismissing the show as 'sick, sick, sick'. The photograph tells a different story—a beaming Martin happily poses with his own contribution to the exhibition, a large assemblage sculpture that is topped by a dressmaker's dummy.

The assemblage, which he titled *Nature Key to Beauty*—but he had originally intended calling it *White Goddess of Moral Indignation* as a nod to the obscenity-hunting guardians of public decency—was reminiscent of work by his mentor Colin Lanceley. Martin had abandoned East Sydney Tech before finishing his course and instead was now attending the Mary White School of Art in Edgecliff where Lanceley taught. The school also counted John Olsen and Robert Klippel among its teachers. Martin became friends with Colin and they saw each other frequently, including spearfishing together several times a week.

When he wasn't spearing fish, Martin was spearing hypocrisy. He soon produced another monologue. It began, 'The word flashed round the Arms ...' The Arms was the pub where inebriated patrons had so unsettled Martin when he had stopped for a drink with his friends over summer. In his monologue, a yobbo narrates how he and his drunken mates from the Newport Arms gatecrashed a party and gang-raped a young woman. Once again it was a tale told in the vernacular. It appeared in the February issue of *Oz*—around the time *The Gas Lash* was rolling off the presses. Martin's hand in that month's *Oz* was considerable. He drew at least nine works that satirised the media, religion and even The Beatles. He created a board game about police corruption entitled *Coppers' Snakes and Ladders*, with the instruction that the game should be played with loaded dice.

The cover photograph was of a fountain in which three young men appeared to be urinating. The fountain, created by sculptor Tom Bass, had just been installed into the wall of the Sydney's P&O building on Hunter and Castlereagh streets, near *Oz*'s new Hunter Street offices. With its resemblance to a public pissoir, the fountain was ripe for a piss-take.

Beneath the photograph, Richard Walsh's extended caption punned on the building's name: 'This is no ordinary urinal. It has a continual flushing system and basins handily set at different heights. There is a nominal charge, of course, but don't worry, there is no need to pay immediately. Just P & O.' It would be the *Oz* team who would be made to pay.

———

The stern sandstone face of the Liverpool Street courthouse has stared down at all who have come before it for more than a hundred years. With its carved coat of arms, sturdy entrance pillars and chequerboard tiled foyer, it reeks of unyielding colonial authority. A nineteenth-century print of *The Worship of Bacchus*—a depiction of revelry, gambling and intoxication against a Sydney backdrop—hangs today on the foyer wall. It is an incongruous image for a courthouse, a warning perhaps to modern-day bacchantes.

In its dock once stood the former soldier who infamously upstaged the opening of the Sydney Harbour Bridge. Mounted on horseback in his military uniform, Francis de Groot had charged forward ahead of the controversial Labor premier Jack Lang, and cut the ribbon with his ceremonial sword. The power of the pen, not the sword, however, was at the heart of two consecutive cases within the Central Summons Court in July 1964. The common factor was Martin Sharp.

First up was *The Gas Lash* case, in which obscenity charges were brought against Martin, *Tharunka* editor Alex Popov, fellow University of New South Wales students Russell Conyngham and Michael Robertson, and printer Francis James, the Anglican Press printer who also printed *Oz*.

As the case was about to begin in the hushed courtroom, a young law clerk was outside, nervously looking at his watch and scanning Liverpool Street. There was no sign of his client, Francis James. The law clerk was Martin's former school friend John Gaden, who was then employed by his father's law firm. John had spoken to the eccentric James ahead of the case and advised him about how to behave in court. 'Francis was a bit of a loose cannon,' John recalls. 'I remember saying, "Francis, the important thing in these cases is that you just appear respectable because the law is against you."'

But as John paced outside court, he wondered whether his client would even appear at all: 'At about one minute past ten, a very old green Rolls-Royce pulled up with a driver. Francis got out wearing a large black hat and black cape [and asked], "Will this dooooo?"'

John Gaden hurried James into the courtroom where exhibit one was Martin's cartoon *The Gas Lash*. Legal argument ensued over Martin's use of the phrase 'pissed as a fart'. Would the use of less vulgar words have made the cartoon less successful? 'Yes,' said a lecturer in English at the University of New South Wales, Ernest Coleman. Did new students know about copulation, contraception and drunkenness, asked police prosecutor Sergeant Ellis. 'I should say without exception that they know a great deal a great long time before they get to the university,' replied an associate professor of Clinical Psychology at the University of New South Wales, Reginald Martin.

Artist John Olsen was loquacious in his defence of the cartoon's artistic merit, comparing the work to Hogarth and treating m'learned friends to a brief history of nineteenth century cartooning. Martin's lawyer, Neville Wran, later premier of New South Wales, summed up: *The Gas Lash* might disgust, bore and bewilder, but would not affect the morals of young people, he argued. The magistrate adjourned to consider his verdict. But *The Gas Lash* case was merely a dress rehearsal. A more far-reaching courtroom drama was about to unfold.

Martin crossed the echoing courthouse foyer on 23 July and entered the wood-panelled courtroom, with its creaking floorboards, hard church-like pews, and steps that led down from the dock to the cells beneath. This time he was joined by *Oz* co-editors Richard Neville and Richard Walsh. Young law clerk John Gaden was again in the courtroom, for *Oz*'s printer Francis James was facing charges.

Also in court was police prosecutor Sergeant Ellis. He had barely drawn breath from summing up in the *Tharunka* case earlier that morning. Now he had a more significant obscenity case to prosecute. *Oz* magazine had a much larger circulation than *Tharunka*, and its readership was not confined to a bunch of fresh-faced first-year university students who had picked up a free copy on campus. *Oz* was sold to the public in Sydney, Melbourne, Adelaide and Canberra.

On the raised wooden bench, the florid face of magistrate Gerald Locke glared down through steel-rimmed spectacles. He had grey hair, cut short back and sides. No flicker of amusement ever troubled the firm line of his unsmiling mouth. Although Locke was about to preside over Australia's most high-profile obscenity case, it is likely he did so without any legal background. Many older magistrates did not. Only those appointed after 1955 needed legal qualifications.

Martin, the two Richards and Francis James stood before Locke charged with obscenity after the vice squad had seized 140 copies of the February issue of *Oz* from a Kings Cross newsagent. 'Obscene' was defined as 'unduly emphasising matters of sex, crimes of violence, gross cruelty or horror' under the Obscene and Indecent Publications Act of 1955. Central to establishing obscenity was a publication's tendency to deprave the morals of readers. But the act allowed exemptions for works of artistic merit. Much of the case revolved around Martin's monologue, *The Word Flashed Round the Arms*.

Methodist minister Reverend Roger Bush was among the first to take the stand. Bush was a popular radio broadcaster who had interviewed and recorded the conversations of young people for use on his shows. 'I don't let them know who I am until it is over,' he told the court, although no one quizzed his dubious practice.

As an expert on youthful slang, Bush's role was to 'translate' the vernacular of Martin's monologue for His Worship's edification. And so the cartoon's first lines—'The word flashed round the Arms that there was a GAS turn up at Whale Beach Rd so we piled into the Mini Coopers and thrashed over . . .'—in Bush's rendition became: 'The word passed quickly around the hotel at Newport that there was a mighty party in progress at Whale Beach Road.'

Bush plodded on. And so Martin's words 'Then the old lady of the bird who was having the turn said she'd ring the Johns so Sid chucked all over her and she got hysterical so Dennis belted her and then Phil did his King hambone on the kitchen table and ran around the house in the raw ripping the gear off all the birds . . .' in Bush's rendition became: 'Then the mother of the girl who was having the party said she would ring the police so Sid vomited all over her and she got hysterical. So Dennis hit her and then Phil did his mighty striptease on the kitchen table and ran around the house in the nude ripping the clothing off all the girls.'

The *Oz* team lined up a stellar array of witnesses to help defend their case, including academics, editors, artists and critics, as well as a psychiatrist and criminologist. First up was Sydney University literature scholar Dr Harry Heseltine, an editor of the literary journal *Meanjin*. Satire was a form as old as classical Rome, he explained. Martin's cartoon was not the author speaking but the words of a character he had created. And that character's violence and sadism would be 'repugnant to any normal person'. Heseltine regarded the piece as 'satire of considerable merit'.

The scholar was quizzed on specific phrases: Did he know what a 'King hambone' meant? Yes, it was a male striptease. Did he know what 'this little dago crap' meant? 'It suggests disapproval of a young Italian.' And did he know in particular what 'crap' meant? 'It suggests scatological disapproval. Human excrement is the usual meaning for crap.' Magistrate Locke turned puce. 'I thought he was going to explode,' John Gaden recalls.

Another churchman took the stand after lunch. Reverend Peter Bennie was warden of St Paul's, Martin's former college, and knew the young artist. Bennie was a liberal who admired satirist Alexander Pope. As long as literature had existed, it had been used to castigate behaviour, Bennie told the court: Martin's work was 'a very intense satire of the behaviour that it describes, written with revulsion and vehemence'. Did the cartoon have any tendency to corrupt or deprave people? 'No, the very reverse,' said Bennie. Could it injure people's morals? 'It doesn't corrupt people's morals learning the facts. The most moral figure I can think of is certainly not an ostrich with his head in the sand.'

After lunch, it was the turn of John Olsen. The artist was among several defence witnesses called in the *Oz* case who had appeared earlier that week for *Tharunka*. Olsen's encore performance was among the wittiest of the entire *Oz* case. Asked whether he still taught university students, Olsen replied: 'I try and avoid it if I can.' He revealed why when quizzed about Martin's cartoon. 'What Mr Sharp is endeavouring to do in this particular case is to follow the mind of the particular nitwit that he happens to be trying to portray. In other words, this writing is like the writing of a teenager in a hurry. I know this in particular because I have happened to correct, or rather had the misfortune to correct, architectural papers from university students who were not particularly bright and this, to my mind, is just the kind of writing that they would do.'

The Word Flashed Round the Arms was not the only one of Martin's cartoons raised in the obscenity case. So, too, was a cartoon strip depicting a long-haired folk singer strumming a guitar and captioned 'Get folked'. Several witnesses acknowledged the double entendre, while Olsen explained: 'I believe it is a colloquial saying amongst folk singers.' He had even heard the phrase used at a Bellevue Hill party.

While the caption 'Get folked' attracted much attention, the cartoon strip itself was largely overlooked. It was an astute piece, in which a folk singer tells her audience how she travels the world picking up songs: 'One of the most beautiful of these traditional songs, one which so captures the country from which it came is this song from Australia.' The singer then performs 'God Save the Queen'. Only one *Oz* witness noted that this was a satire on the 'quaint Australian custom' of performing the national anthem on occasions when not even Britain itself did. Other witnesses likened Martin's work to such satirists as Pope and Juvenal.

If Martin preened at hearing such comparisons, he would have been crestfallen to hear the assessment of eminent art critic Elwyn Lynn. Martin's cartoons in *Oz* number 6 varied from 'quite good to mediocre' while The Beatles cartoon strip was 'rather feeble', Lynn told the court.

Among the parade of top-drawer witnesses, the woman who took the stand next morning was the star turn. Betty Archdale was the British-born headmistress of the exclusive Abbotsleigh School for girls on Sydney's upper North Shore. She gave a performance to match her pedigree. Archdale was an early feminist, the goddaughter of English activist Emmeline Pankhurst and had captained England's women's cricket team. She had a legal background and a quick wit. Asked whether her pupils came from the 'better class homes in our community', she replied: 'They like to think so.' She preferred her girls not to read *Oz*, but if they did, she doubted they would understand Martin's cartoon. 'There are a lot of things I would not like them to read, but that does not mean they are legally obscene,' said Archdale, who was a member of the British bar.

Altogether seventeen high-profile defence witnesses were called over two days. Two questions were asked over and over, and elicited unanimous answers. Did the work have literary or artistic merit? Yes. Could it harm morals? No.

The case was interrupted at times by Francis James, who retained his sartorial style of black-brimmed hat and cloak, and a habit of flouncing in late. As he sat in court, he frequently and theatrically removed his contact lenses. His performance transfixed Locke's steely gaze. Francis regularly interrupted proceedings by seeking to be excused because he needed to rehydrate his war-damaged eyes. They had become as dry as the legal argument.

Perhaps Martin's cartoon should have carried a moral warning for young people, the prosecutor suggested to one academic. 'You can't write a satire and head it "Beware, this is written to warn you"', the scholar replied. Parts of the testimony may have amused some in the courtroom, although not the unsmiling Locke. Stephen Little, an English lecturer at Sydney University, ventured that when he saw Tom Bass's sculpture, he had the same reaction to that depicted on the cover of *Oz*. Surely Mr Little hadn't urinated in the fountain, Sergeant Ellis asked? No, he hadn't.

At times, Locke had questions of his own. Questions that made John Gaden suspect the magistrate had already made up his mind: '[Locke] was prosecuting as much as the prosecutor. He cross-examined witnesses in a bullying manner.' After two days, the matter was adjourned twice and it was early September when the police prosecutor gave his closing address.

Ellis was barely on his feet when Locke interrupted. This time it wasn't Francis James fiddling with his contact lenses that caught His Worship's eye. 'There is a lady sitting in the back of the court taking notes and I want to know why,' Locke demanded. The woman was a reporter for the Australian Broadcasting Commission, a sight so rare in a courtroom in 1964 as to bring proceedings to a halt.

Ellis told the court the magazine went downhill from the front page and sank to its lowest depths with *The Word Flashed Round the Arms*. Witnesses had made 'clumsy' attempts to show how the magazine had literary or artistic merit. He singled out John Olsen for special mention, suggesting the eminent artist's claim to have heard the phrase 'get folked' used at a party was nonsense. Locke reserved his judgment.

Meanwhile, the magistrate in the *Tharunka* case had made up his mind about Martin's *Gas Lash* cartoon. In August, Magistrate Gibson found it unduly emphasised sex and that Martin, as its author, and James, as printer, carried greater responsibility than the three other students. He fined Martin and James ten pounds each and the three others five pounds. An appeal was lodged.

CHAPTER 5

'FILTHY AND DISGUSTING'

Martin resumed his artistic life. He began painting vivid black and white murals on the glass windows of a new music venue about to open at the raffish end of Elizabeth Street next to Binkie's Burgers, near Central Station. He had also designed an advertisement for this venue, which was published in *Oz* magazine.

Its name was The Gas Lash and it opened just two weeks after Martin's *Gas Lash* cartoon had been judged obscene. Beneath a ceiling hung with hessian, about two hundred patrons sat on barrels to hear folk singers and other musicians perform, or else they hit the small dance floor. It drew an arty crowd, including Margaret Fink, Bruce Goold and Jenny Kee, who also waitressed there. And it occasionally drew some high-profile musicians. Heads turned the night Kee swanned in with Mick Jagger and Keith Richards during the Rolling Stones' first Australian tour.

Billed as Sydney's first discotheque, its young patrons were vastly different from the inebriated revellers depicted in Martin's *Gas Lash* cartoon, as was quickly discovered by the venue's operator, Ron Murphy, who also ran Binkie's Burgers. Murphy provided tea and coffee, but stopped selling alcohol in the disco: 'They drank so little it didn't seem worth bothering. We'd sell less than a bottle of beer in a night.'

As he awaited Locke's decision over the *Oz* case, Martin went to the Art Gallery of New South Wales to see his friend and mentor Colin Lanceley awarded the prestigious 1300-pound Helena Rubinstein travelling art scholarship that would see another artist embark for London and brighter artistic horizons.

Martin and Richard Walsh wore their old school uniforms and ties when they arrived at court on the morning of 23 September 1964 for Locke's verdict on *Oz*. Neville was not with them. He had gone to New Caledonia earlier in the month and a flight delay meant he couldn't return until the following day.

Locke took the bench and reluctantly acknowledged the magazine had artistic and literary merit. But any hopes that he might dismiss the case evaporated as he rejected the evidence of the eminent defence witnesses as an 'affront to the court's intelligence', before dissecting the magazine from cover to cover. The 'Get folked' cartoon contained a 'smutty pun', he said. 'Smut with humour is the literary device of the gutter, it is usually found on the walls of latrines. Smut remains smut even when satire is used.'

The cover would attract the 'immature and unhealthy-minded'. One article was 'a disgusting piece of blasphemy', another 'childish' and 'an obscene libel'. Martin's *The Word Flashed Round the Arms* was 'filthy and disgusting'. Polluting the minds of the young was a serious matter and it was high time the publication of 'this stuff' was stopped. Locke intended to make an example of the young defendants: 'Those of us who have worked in these courts, as I have done for more than thirty years, know only too well the tragic effect that wrong treatment of matters of sex has on the minds of immature and weak-minded adults. In all I am satisfied that salutary penalties are called for and I propose to inflict such penalties,' he said.

He sentenced Sharp to four months' jail, Walsh and the absent Neville to six months' jail; all three sentences were 'with hard labour'. Francis James received a fifty-pound fine. Martin and Richard Walsh were escorted to the police cells underneath the court. The possibility of being jailed hadn't occurred to either of them so they had arrived at court empty-handed. 'We didn't have a toothbrush, we certainly didn't have a bag packed, we were just in our suits,' Richard recalls.

They were fingerprinted and their mug shots taken before being placed in a dank holding cell behind a metal door that clanked shut. They weren't alone. Several shabby men sat on the sopping concrete floor. They stared up at the two well-scrubbed young men in the uniforms of Sydney's elite private schools. Martin and Richard stood in the cell. 'We weren't going to sit on the floor and get our bloody suits wet,' says Richard.

Just before lunchtime, a hatch at the bottom of the door opened and through it came some empty mugs. The hatch opened again and a tureen of soup was pushed through. The cellmates grabbed the mugs and sloshed them into the tureen. 'I remember Martin saying, "Are you hungry?" And I said, "I think I've lost my appetite"', Richard continues.

John Gaden went down to the cells to tell the two of them that an appeal was about to be lodged: 'They were standing there against the wall. And above them in big graffiti was "fuck all cops".'

Martin's father, Henry Sharp, arrived to bail out the pair. But Richard's parents, already distraught after their son's previous court appearance and fine over *Oz*, were still in the dark about the morning's events. Richard telephoned them to break the news that he had been jailed, was about to be bailed and that the case would likely be in the afternoon's papers. Sorry. The front page of the tabloid *Sun* screamed: '3 gaoled: "filthy paper".'

As the appeal was lodged for *Oz*, Martin received a telegram of support. It came from Melbourne arts patron and publisher John Reed. The cable struck a triumphal tone. In the unpunctuated style of such communications, it read: 'Congratulations to all regard as dramatic victory to be pursued strongly hope appeal against conviction as well as sentence my support available if required.'

Reed had previously faced his own court dramas as publisher of the modernist literary journal *Angry Penguins*, which championed the avant-garde. That magazine had been at the centre of an obscenity case in the 1940s over poems it published by an 'Ern Malley'. But Malley and his poems turned out to be a fiction concocted by writers James McAuley and Harold Stewart, keen to dupe the magazine's editor Max Harris. The Ern Malley hoax remains Australia's best-known literary scam.

Meanwhile, Martin and the *Oz* editors began writing scripts for a satirical television program. *The Mavis Bramston Show* premiered in November, with Martin and Richard Walsh credited as writers, and Richard Neville joining later. The program presented a segment entitled 'From the *Oz* Newsdesk'. Influenced by the British satirical television series *That Was the Week That Was*, *The Mavis Bramston Show*'s cast included Gordon Chater, Noelene Brown, June Salter and Carol Raye, and became one of Australia's most popular during its three-year run.

The cast of *The Mavis Bramston Show* was among those who performed at an *Oz* benefit concert at Sydney University four days after the television show premiered. They were joined by The Missing Links, who were at that time the bad boys of rock'n'roll, plus Martin's folk-singing friends Tina Date and Garry Shearston as well as actor Leonard Teale, the star of the popular TV show *Homicide*, who recited 'Clancy of the Undertow', a surfie version of Banjo Paterson's classic poem. A young law student, Geoffrey Robertson—later an international human rights lawyer—spoke in defence and donated his schoolboy allowance to the cause. Others, too, rallied behind *Oz*, with protests held on most campuses around Australia.

The Australian Journalists Association offered moral support and invited the *Oz* trio to their fancy dress ball at the classy Chevron Hotel in Macleay Street, Kings Cross. Martin threw himself into creating costumes. Dressing as the Royal Family seemed perfect for a publication that constantly lampooned the monarchy. He raided his mother's ball gowns and high heels to transform Richard Walsh into the Queen. Martin created a tiara and painted an *Oz*-style ear-to-ear smile in red lipstick on his friend. Martin's art teacher Colin Lanceley dressed as Prince Philip.

Unable to find a parking space near the Chevron, the regal couple and their retinue traipsed through Sydney's red-light district. Even on Sydney's more raffish streets, the real Royal Family enjoyed considerably more popularity than in the offices of *Oz*. Offended locals booed the regal parody. The ballroom, full of knockabout journalists, was barely more appreciative. Few had even bothered with fancy dress. When Richard teetered into the ballroom on Colin's arm, they faced a sea of aghast faces.

The *Tharunka* appeal was successful and in November the convictions against Martin, Alex Popov, their fellow students and printer Francis James were quashed. *The Canberra Times* hailed the result as 'one of the most liberal and sensible judgments to have been delivered in the courts of Australia'. In lieu of legal fees, Martin gave his lawyer Neville Wran the original of *The Gas Lash*. The owner of The Gas Lash nightclub might even have sold an additional bottle of beer that evening.

As trees were decked with baubles in the run-up to Christmas, the *Oz* appeal began in the Quarter Sessions Appeals Court on 14 December 1964. By then Martin was sick of musty courtrooms. He told journalist Craig McGregor: 'It smells as though the air's been locked up here for centuries, with none but old men to breathe it.'

John Kerr QC, later the country's most controversial governor-general, was part of the all-star legal cast who appeared for Sharp, Neville and Walsh. Edward St John QC, who would become a controversial Liberal politician and ultimately an independent in the federal parliament, appeared for Francis James. Neville Wran also represented Martin.

The greatest stroke of good fortune was that the appeal was presided over by Judge Aaron Levine, who had just quashed the *Tharunka* convictions. Levine was a vastly different figure from Locke. New York-born, Levine's family had fled Russia's anti-Jewish pogroms. As a young law student at Sydney University in the 1930s, Levine had been drawn to liberal causes. He wanted to join the International Brigades and fight in the Spanish Civil War, until his mother persuaded him to finish his studies. A student at the time when Hitler and Mussolini were on the ascendant, Levine became involved in publishing anti-fascist material.

Levine loved music and the arts. He married a violinist who performed with the Sydney Symphony Orchestra, and his friends included the artist William Dobell, whom he came to know during family holidays at Wangi Wangi on Lake Macquarie. Levine had a son and daughter about the same age as the three young men before him. He was interested in the ideas of young people and sometimes sought his children's views on issues. His children were a sounding-board for the opinions of a younger generation.

Several *Oz* witnesses from the original case made encore appearances at the four-day appeal, including Reverend Roger Bush, Betty Archdale, journalist Mungo MacCallum (senior) and artist John Olsen. Some new faces also entered the witness box, including novelist Morris West, cartoonist Les Tanner and Harry Kippax, *The Sydney Morning Herald*'s theatre critic and habitué of Vadim's. Indeed, Vadim's proved a fertile recruiting ground for witnesses, many of whom had come to help Francis James. Also among the witnesses was the larrikin behind the Ern Malley hoax, James McAuley. By then McAuley was professor of English at the University of Tasmania and he told Levine that *Oz* contained 'genuine, spontaneous bright thought'. Sculptor Tom Bass, the artist who had created the 'urinal' pictured on the cover of *Oz*, also took the stand: 'It is a lurking fear of civic sculptors that their sculpture will have implications they did not foresee. I didn't premeditate on the magazine's implied comment. It is, however, fair and apposite comment, although not the type I would prefer,' said Bass.

John Kerr argued that nothing was immune to satire, not even sex. The case raised the right of legitimate satire to exist. Edward St John said Australians could be insular, isolated and narrow. 'It does us no harm when our pretentiousness, pomposities, and self-pieties are exposed . . . Satire is a cleansing breath through society.' Martin was particularly impressed with St John's arguments in this David-and-Goliath battle. But he was appalled that Kerr—who he later recalled was the only lawyer who accepted a fee—soon after the *Oz* case defended a Goliath. Kerr represented landowner Lord Vestey, owner of the Northern Territory's Wave Hill cattle station, against the Aboriginal stockmen. Martin never forgave him for that.

With defence arguments over, it was the Crown's turn. Martin's cartoon was a well-written account of gross immorality which, if unpunished, could open the floodgates. For if *Oz* was allowed to write in such a fashion, so were the newspapers. Judge Levine reserved judgment.

While the threat of a jail sentence hung over the three young men all summer, another student activist was challenging the status quo. Young Aboriginal leader Charlie Perkins spearheaded a Freedom Ride through country New South Wales to draw attention to the racist discrimination under which Indigenous people lived. Violence erupted in the town of Moree as the Freedom Riders tried to enter a swimming pool from which Aboriginal people were banned.

In was late February 1965 before Martin and the two Richards returned to court to learn whether they would go to prison. When Levine took the bench, he cut to the chase: the magazine had literary merit. He accepted McAuley's evidence that *The Word Flashed Round the Arms* did not glorify the criminal behaviour of the gatecrashers, and Betty Archdale's testimony that neither the cartoon nor the magazine had a tendency to deprave or corrupt. Nor did the cover image encourage public urination. He intended to quash the convictions.

Outside the court, Sharp, Neville, Walsh and James raised their hands in V-for-victory signs for the cameras before adjourning to Vadim's. Neville and Walsh wrote a piece for the next day's edition of *The Australian*, insisting *Oz* would continue to publish. 'After all, who could resist the temptation of editing a satirical magazine in a country where … non-whites are still deported, men are still hanged, best-sellers are still banned and people still stand up for God Save the Queen?' To accompany this manifesto, Martin drew a cartoon of himself and his two colleagues as the three wise monkeys.

In the wake of the high-profile case, Martin received a letter from his much-loved art teacher Justin O'Brien, who was living in Rome, asking what his former pupil's plans were. O'Brien watered a seed that had yet to take root when he wrote: 'Perhaps it would be a good idea to come over here for a year or two. You sounded rather like Hamlet in your last letter—not being able to make up your mind. Anyway, you'll never know until you make the move whether it was worth it or not.'

A legal hitch (the Crown appealed against Judge Levine's decision, ultimately unsuccessfully) meant the *Oz* case wasn't fully resolved for another year. During that time Martin was snapped up by *The Sydney Morning Herald* as a contributing cartoonist. The notoriety that followed the obscenity conviction and high-profile case added to his appeal as a controversial artist. Which is no doubt why, when Levine's judgment was officially endorsed in February 1966, Martin questioned whether it was an unqualified victory for himself and the young *Oz* editors.

The Sydney Morning Herald reported the conclusion of the case, after the Crown appeals had been set aside, on the same page as Martin gave his satirical take. He sketched himself and the two Richards with a speech bubble: 'Fancy Levine white-washing us ... our careers are ruined.' Levine, who kept clippings of the cases he sat on, pasted a copy of the newspaper report and Martin's cartoon into his scrapbook.

In his final judgment, Levine acknowledged times had changed: 'We are living in times when great freedom of expression on matters of sex is accepted by the community. Indeed, even a casual glance at the current newspaper topics and advertisements, the nature and types of magazines available and the films shown on television and in theatres clearly indicate that the community accepts today an open discussion of matters of sex which would never have been tolerated by our Victorian forebears.'

The *Oz* decision was hailed as a victory for common sense and a sign of liberalism after one of the busiest periods for Australian censorship since the mid-1950s, according to *The Bulletin*. For 1964 had also seen the launch of pro-censorship organisations and the use of increasingly draconian techniques of censorship, including action against Nabokov's *Lolita*. But while the *Oz* prosecutions had set a new level of severity in penalties, Levine's decision heralded a lessening of the censorship drive.

The case was a watershed, lawyer Edward St John would later reflect: 'That was really a turning point in the law relating to censorship and obscenity in Australia, because our laws and our courts had adopted a very repressive attitude. A new wave was building up and the police took it upon themselves to nip it in the bud by prosecuting the *Oz* magazine and *Tharunka* magazine ... I think it was very fortunate for us we came before Levine because he took a very liberal view, which I think few of his colleagues would have taken ... It was really a significant turning point because, from then on, the law didn't change but the administration of the law became less repressive in relation to what was regarded as permissible and what was not.'

But *The Gas Lash* and *The Word Flashed Round the Arms* remained controversial. When a best-of book of Martin's cartoons was published two years later, the two cartoons were conspicuously absent. And it was not as though obscenity cases became a thing of the past. Indeed Gerald Locke sentenced another artist, Mike Brown, to three months' jail over works the magistrate described as grossly indecent in depicting 'exaggerated' sex organs and orgies. But again Levine took a more liberal view, reducing Brown's penalty to a fine.

Wowserism and liberalism continued to compete. While Levine would go on to transform the lives of New South Wales women with a landmark 1971 ruling that opened access to safe, legal abortion, Martin would immortalise Locke in a savage caricature. He drew the magistrate precariously balanced on a plinth, at which a cartoon Martin takes potshots. If you turn the cartoon upside down, the grotesque shape of Locke's head and nose reveals something more. It is composed of a hairy, wrinkled scrotum and penis.

Whether obscenity was the sole reason *Oz* magazine was so vigorously pursued remains an open question. It was an era of hypocrisy and pursed-lipped prudery, but *Oz* weighed in on more controversial terrain than sexual licentiousness and boozy parties. It took on the mainstream press, including over its role in the death of a Sydney schoolboy named Digby Bamford.

The tragic tale began when Rupert Murdoch's *Daily Mirror* ran a front-page story in March 1964 headlined 'School Sex!' about promiscuity among schoolkids at a local high school. The story was based on the diary of a schoolgirl. A girl and a boy named in the diary were suspended from school. A couple of days later, the *Mirror* reported that a thirteen-year-old boy had been found hanging from the clothesline of his Redfern backyard. It did not report that this was the boy who had just been expelled from school. But *Oz* did.

Geoffrey Robertson alluded to the case years later when Murdoch, by then a global media baron, was at the centre of the schoolgirl Milly Dowler phone-hacking scandal in England. Robertson drew a line that began with the Digby Bamford case and the invasion of privacy in publishing the diary of a schoolgirl through to the hacking of the phone of a thirteen-year-old murder victim.

Oz also weighed in on police corruption and organised crime. With the innocence and invulnerability of youth, they were more naïve than brave in the material they published at times, Martin recalled: 'We were treading on toes that we didn't even know were toes. They were just names to us, you know. So we probably published things which no one else would publish.' A case in point was 'The *Oz* Guide to the Sydney Underworld', which lifted the lid on the city's criminal underworld and included a top-twenty list of crims. The number-one spot was left blank—'there isn't any'—but in second place was 'Lennie'. The story referred to Lennie as a fizzgig, or police informer.

Lennie McPherson was the Mr Big of organised crime, a standover man, murderer and racketeer. He was not a guy to mess with. Typical of the stories that swirled around him was his arrival at the home of his mother, from whom he was estranged, on her seventieth birthday. He was carrying a white rabbit. Angry that he had not been invited to her party, he ripped off the rabbit's head and threw the bloodied, twitching remains at his mother's feet.

Lennie was not amused by the *Oz* article, although whether he was more upset at being called a fizzgig or not making the top spot is unclear. He paid Richard Neville a visit, arriving on his Paddington doorstep (without a rabbit). McPherson insisted he was no fizzgig and offered Neville a ride in his car, during which the standover man drew attention to its shotgun-riddled interior.

By then Robert Askin was premier of New South Wales, having ended nearly a quarter of a century of Labor rule in May 1965. McPherson thrived on Askin's watch, as rumours of bent cops and politicians in the pockets of crime bosses increased. The rumours of systemic corruption went to the top. But it was not until the day of Askin's funeral in 1981 that the mainstream *National Times* published details in an explosive story headlined 'Askin Friend to Organised Crime'.

Prime Minister Robert Menzies, ever ready to commit Australian troops to foreign conflicts, signed up for another—this time in Vietnam. This entry into a civil war in the former French colony played on Australia's long-standing fear of the communist menace. The countries of South-East Asia were poised to fall like dominoes, before communism leapt the water and spread across our wide brown land—or so the hawks feared.

Martin's strength as a cartoonist was in social observation rather than political insight. But with Australia's entry into the Vietnam War, he produced a series of telling cartoons on the subject. A couple of days before Christmas, 1965, and with the war escalating, his *Herald* cartoon depicted a bomb in a Santa sack with a gift label that read 'For Vietnam. Season's Greetings. Lyndon'.

Menzies reintroduced conscription before finally exiting the political stage in January 1966, saying he was old and tired. But anyone hoping for a fresh political vision had those dreams dashed. Menzies handed power to Harold Holt, who jetted off to Lyndon Johnson's White House and announced Australia was 'All the way with LBJ'. It was a bit of brown-nosing every bit as execrable as Menzies' past toadying to Britain. Martin lampooned it in an *Oz* cartoon in which a tiny Holt dances to the United States president's tune.

CHAPTER 6

THE WHITE-ANT OF BELLEVUE HILL

Wanted nude girl to model for photos to be used in collage for coming Sharp exhibition—lovely figure, good pay (optional). Martin placed the advertisement in *Oz* magazine. It ran in October 1965, without an eyebrow raised or a visit from the vice squad.

Among those who answered the advert was a seventeen-year-old Sydney schoolgirl, Linda Gumbert. She was a keen *Oz* reader, and thrilled at the prospect of being in one of Martin's collages. She arranged to meet him and *Oz* photographer Mike Molloy at a city studio: 'I took my clothes off and they took a lot of photos and then they took me out to lunch and they gave me twenty quid and I went home. It was all jolly good fun.'

Martin was preparing for his big break, his first solo gallery show. Friends gathered to assist. Molloy took photos for collages while others wielded paintbrushes, or helped him cut images from magazines. Photographer Greg Weight recalls being an early studio assistant, helping him work on paintings, sculptures and with framing. Throughout his artistic life Martin had help from friends. He worked collaboratively and was never an artist who required quiet and solitude. He painted in a swirl of chaos, with music playing, dogs around his feet, people coming and going, oblivious to the distractions. That pattern was evident as he prepared for his first show.

John Weiley photographed Martin as he knelt over one piece of artwork on the ground outside the French doors at his Cranbrook

Lane home. Martin has a felt-tip pen in one hand, a half-smoked cigarette in the other. He is absorbed in his work, seemingly unaware of the camera. '[Martin's] ash kept constantly dropping on the painting, so I had to go round with a silver paintbrush redoing all the edges to cover the marks,' John says. John helped cut images from a range of magazines—everything from girlie magazines to a dental equipment catalogue: 'We cut out a head, then we made a painting out of eyes, we cut eyes out of everything we could find—old *Playboy* magazines—and made them into little flowers on stalks, and Martin painted the vase and we stuck the eyes on as the blossoms.'

Having lost his creative confidence at art school, Martin regained it through cartooning. He had learned to work quickly and to deadline, so his output was prolific. He created many collages for *Oz*, but he wanted to develop his art further. So he stayed home, painted and worked towards his exhibition, to be held at Sydney's Clune Galleries at 59 Macleay Street, Potts Point. Terry Clune and his mother, Thelma, had established the gallery in the 1950s with Frank McDonald as its manager and it represented many leading Australian artists, including John Olsen, Sidney Nolan and Arthur Boyd.

It was a quirk of timing and good fortune that resulted in this distinguished gallery hosting Martin's first exhibition. Martin drew many of *Oz*'s tongue-in-cheek ads and he had initially visited the gallery to attempt to convince them to advertise. The gallery's discerning manager was overseas when Sydney's most unlikely salesman arrived, so Martin spoke with an assistant. 'Terry White was in charge of the place while Frank was away. Terry said you can have a show here. [When he returned] Frank McDonald was horrified,' said Martin.

He created an invitation for the opening which played on his infamous cartoon. It featured a collaged Mona Lisa with a thought bubble: 'The word flashed round the Windsor Castle that there was a Gas exhibition up at Terry Clune's . . .'. *Art for Mart's Sake*, which opened on 8 December 1965, included cartoons from *Oz*, *The Sydney Morning*

Herald and *The Australian*, plus collages, paintings and combinations, including one titled *Norman Normal*. That name had frequently appeared in *Oz* and almost superseded Alf as a paragon of dreary, closed-minded, lawn-mowing suburbia. Martin thought the work—a fleshy figure with eyes in odd places—was one of his best in the exhibition, although it did not sell.

Norman Normal and other works featured cut-out smiles snipped from *Vogue* magazines. The sinister gap-toothed smile would recur in Martin's works, in *Oz* and elsewhere. It may have been a nod to Albert Tucker's savage 1940s *Images of Modern Evil* series, which is peopled with grotesquely grinning figures. In a brief reference to the show, *Art and Australia* described Martin's work as skilful and 'lying between humour and mild horror'.

Only one of Mike Molloy's photographs of the young women who had responded to the *Oz* advertisement actually made it into an artwork. An eye-catching red headless female became part of one of Martin's most compelling and prescient early works, *Seventeen Minutes to Four*. With its psychedelic whirl of eyes, heads, torsos and flowers against a starry universe, it seems to evoke a drug-induced reverie. 'But it was before I knew anything about psychedelics,' said Martin. 'It was sort of Monty Python ... it was before I'd smoked a joint.'

Marijuana was not part of the early sixties scene in Sydney; the drug was hard to find. It would be a few more years before marijuana became a groovy party drug. John Weiley recalls: 'Marijuana was something that lascar seamen smoked. Drugs were hardly an item. We drank a huge amount of alcohol ... if you wanted hashish, you had to know somebody who knew somebody to get some, who had brought it in on a boat from Indonesia or India.' So there was no marijuana at Martin's opening, although there was music, especially by Bob Dylan, who Martin had constantly played as he prepared for the exhibition.

The show drew a hip crowd, and Martin was at its centre. 'If one had to choose a representative for the in-group of young people who orbit around *Oz*, *Tharunka*, *Honi Soit*, East Sydney Tech, and The Gas Lash discotheque that representative would probably be 23-year-old Martin Sharp,' *The Sydney Morning Herald* proclaimed. With his affluent background, the paper described him as the 'white-ant from Bellevue Hill'.

The show was reviewed positively by the *Herald*'s critic, artist Wallace Thornton. 'It can be rough, raw, garish or subtle. Take it or leave it, like it or reject it, it cannot be ignored ... Sharp has made his mark. The surreal, the unexpected, the strange or the abruptly shocking are slated in political, social or general comment that is made with no punches pulled. It is a developing expression, particularly in the painting—but Sharp is emerging with a forthright style.' Martin noted years later that his first gallery exhibition turned out to be his most successful.

As Martin prepared this exhibition, his parents were in the midst of ending their marriage. It was a time when divorce proceedings were public matters, when private detectives gathered evidence and the salacious details of high-profile cases filled the yellow press. No-fault divorce was still a decade away; it would introduce 'irretrievable breakdown of marriage' as the sole grounds for divorce.

Henry filed for divorce on the grounds of separation. Jo and Henry had experienced 'unhappy differences' for some time. Eventually Jo asked Henry to leave, which he did on 27 March 1960, according to court documents. Since then they had not seen each other and had lived separately: 'There is no reasonable likelihood of cohabitation being resumed.' The stress took its toll on Henry, who had been experiencing irregular heartbeats. He submitted a note to the court from his medical specialist, urging a swift resolution. The divorce was finalised on 7 January 1966. Jo received the Cranbrook Lane house in the settlement.

In the vacuum of a fractured family, Martin drew around him a group of creative friends, many of whom he would remain in contact with for the rest of his life. They included Lin Utzon, daughter of the Sydney Opera House's architect Jørn Utzon. Lin was seventeen and studying at East Sydney Tech when Martin arrived at a noisy Paddington party around the time of the *Oz* case, with Anou Kiisler, Richard Neville and Alex Popov: 'I was in awe of them because there was this whole court case ... They emanated this special intelligence and charm and roguishness.'

She helped Martin work on the dressmaker's dummy sculpture for his early group show; he came to Palm Beach, where her parents lived; they went to parties together. She enjoyed his originality: 'Martin was like a flame of intelligence. He was so illuminated in a way, so different from everybody else. All his thoughts and ideas were so incredibly original and different.' Even his approach to a fancy dress ball at Paddington Town Hall was unique, she recalls: 'Everybody was trying to be outrageous and Martin came as Mr Goldfinger. He wore his suit and had a gold finger.'

After living briefly in a studio in Paddington, Martin had returned to his mother's house in Cranbrook Lane at her request around the time of the *Oz* case. The house was invariably full of his friends, and Jo welcomed their presence. She continued to host high-society Melbourne Cup parties and charity events at her home, but it was the company of young people she particularly enjoyed. 'She was very supportive of [Martin], and accepted all of us, his friends, to come and go at all hours of the day. She was a very slight woman. I always remember her as being in a pink mohair sweater, with her cocktails, gin and cigarettes,' says Lin. 'She was very feminine ... She was the ultimate model of a woman for him. And complicated.'

Jo's affinity with, and enjoyment of, young creative people was not surprising. The adult world had not treated her well. Martin told interviewer Helen Topliss: 'Her own age group were pretty shitty to her.' Jo's broken marriage and estrangement from her father no doubt left deep scars. She became a confidante to Martin's friends, Alex Popov recalls. 'She was the kind of person whom we would all go to and tell her our problems ... [Martin's house] was the focus of all the intellectual groups in Sydney because his mum was so welcoming to us all.'

There was witty banter between Martin and his mother—she would chastise him and he would send her up. Alex Popov recalls Martin deciding to play a trick on his mother. He dressed as a girl and put on makeup to visit the Double Bay café he knew Jo had gone to. He sat at a table near her in the café. 'She was staring, she wondered if it was him. Eventually she said, "I knew it was you all the time. How could you do this, Marty, you naughty boy?" She adored him ... There was always a game between them,' Alex says.

Jo had strong opinions and didn't hesitate to share them. She could have stepped from a Patrick White novel, according to theatre director Jim Sharman. She had a dash of *Riders in the Chariot*'s eccentric heiress Miss Hare and a dash of Judy Garland. 'She had the slacks, the shirt and would say, "Get me another wikey [whisky], darling,"' Jim says.

There was no shortage of young women dropping in to Cranbrook Lane. In mid-1965, Martin's romance with Anou Kiisler had been in trouble, as Weiley noted in his diary: 'Martin and Anou are going through turgid times. Martin wants out, but it won't happen at any price. Seriously difficult.' Other women began entering Martin's life, including a dark-haired beauty called Leondra Kunemann. She accompanied Martin when, with John Weiley at the wheel of his open-topped Jaguar, they drove to Faulconbridge in the Blue Mountains to visit artist Norman Lindsay. Martin was overjoyed to meet Lindsay—and his wife and former model, Rose—and to walk through the elderly artist's garden with him.

One evening there was a birthday dinner in Sydney for Lin Utzon. It was a gloriously carefree time, as John Weiley noted: 'Went back to Martin's afterwards and danced and danced. Lin played Beethoven on

Martin's grand piano ... We are all so happy that I am afraid of being struck by lightning.'

Days were spent sunbathing, swimming and spearfishing. Nights were filled with parties, talking, dancing and listening to Dylan. Writer and former Cranbrook student Craig McGregor recalls being at a house party with Martin and a group of his friends. Martin put Dylan's newly released 'Mr Tambourine Man' on the record player and danced—under a diamond sky—to the song, acting out its ecstatic lyrics until its poetic conclusion, when he 'danced and danced with his arm up waving, not parodying, a performance of the whole song'.

Martin was captivated by Dylan, particularly 'Ballad of a Thin Man', released on his *Highway 61 Revisited* album in August 1965. The song, about a generational and cultural divide, conjured an image of a man—Mr Jones—every bit as uncomprehending of the times as the Alfs Martin had long lampooned: 'It was an amazing song. I loved Bob Dylan. I loved The Beatles, but I loved Bob Dylan more because he was really singing about things, not just boys and girls.'

Martin's off-again, on-again romance with Anou was back on by the end of 1965, when they celebrated New Year's Eve at a party with, among others, Richard Neville, Di Morrissey, Craig McGregor, Mike Molloy, Garry Shead and John Weiley, Martin's blood-oath partner who had decided to leave for England. The mood was optimistic as the new year dawned and Weiley wrote in his diary: 'Walking up Mart's driveway—poplars against light sky, air just cool enough to feel—happy and full after drowsy conversation with Mart about plans to go to Europe. Happiness ... The sun is up, the birds are actually chirping. 1966 is going to be our year.'

Each time he drove from Cranbrook Lane to the city, Martin could see the arched ribs of the Sydney Opera House taking shape on

Bennelong Point. With its stepped base inspired by ancient Mayan and Zapotec temples, this secular temple had until recently been a tram depot. With a curved, fan-like roofline that evoked sails or shells, the structure seemed to defy belief. It was the realisation of a seemingly impossible dream.

The idea of an opera house had been sparked by the Sydney Symphony Orchestra's former conductor Eugene Goossens who, eager for a centre for opera, ballet, theatre and concerts, searched the city for a site. He convinced then New South Wales premier Joe Cahill of the need for a venue to enrich the city's cultural life. Cahill, a former railway worker more familiar with the 'Londonderry Air' than *Lohengrin*, was an unlikely champion of an opera house. Cahill convinced his sceptical Labor Party and the public of its value.

It was an enormous gamble: when the idea was first floated Australia didn't even have a full-time opera company, and the other art forms that would eventually use the venue—classical ballet, contemporary dance and theatre—were embryonic or non-existent. But it was a dream of a more creative future, of a nation that could aspire to more than sporting prowess and booming steel production. At a time of cultural cringe, it signalled a shift in values: that artists had a place and were valued.

In Denmark, Lin Utzon was ten years old when she answered the phone to discover Australia was on the line. She got on her bike and pedalled after her parents, who had gone for a morning walk. Her father had won the international design competition. The architect recognised the special qualities of Bennelong Point, which juts like a pointed finger into Sydney Harbour. Any building on its fingertip would be visible from all aspects, including from the elevated Sydney Harbour Bridge to the west and sloping Botanic Gardens to the east. Utzon, a keen sailor, saw similarities between Bennelong Point and a peninsula around which he sailed in the Danish city of Elsinore, with its castle immortalised in *Hamlet*.

Some scoffed at the premier's grand dream, dubbing it the Taj Cahill, and resented money being spent on it—even if it was to be funded by a lottery. Cahill was undeterred. Martin poked fun at the naysayers in a cartoon that depicted a woman wearing a large hat resembling the Opera House: 'You wouldn't catch me buying a lottery ticket to build that monstrosity. It's a waste of money if you ask me.'

Utzon arrived to a hero's welcome when he moved his family to Sydney to live in March 1963. Even the Queen, in Sydney at the time, wanted to dine with him. Within an hour of touching down at Mascot airport, Utzon was aboard the royal yacht *Britannia* on Sydney Harbour. The lunch party included swimmer Murray Rose, as well as author Patrick White. Utzon offered to show White around the site. White did so a few days later and was thrilled: 'It has made me feel glad I am alive in Australia today. At last we are going to have something worth having.'

Yet by the time of Utzon's arrival, the Opera House had lost its most powerful champion with the sudden death of Cahill. The building had previously seen the departure of its initial supporter when Goossens was hounded from Australia in the wake of the 'pornography' scandal. Soon a gathering political storm would knock the wind from the Opera House's sails. The troubles escalated with the election of Robert Askin and his Liberal-Country Party coalition government. Askin had made the Opera House an election issue amid allegations of delays and cost blowouts; he vowed to rein these in. To do so, he appointed Davis Hughes as Minister for Public Works.

Hughes had the architect in his sights. At an election-night dinner, Hughes's daughter boasted that her father would soon sack Utzon. Months of mounting tension followed. Hughes starved Utzon of funds and forced a showdown. Utzon met Hughes in his office on 28 February 1966 and warned that, without the money, he would be forced to quit. Hughes called a press conference and announced that Utzon had resigned and the job would be completed without him. It would be finished by a committee of architects, without departing from the spirit of Utzon's original conception.

The claim was quickly dismissed as nonsense by many Utzon supporters. The political storm seemed to lash the building itself. As Hughes was drawing up a list of architects to replace Utzon, one of the Opera House's roof arches collapsed, narrowly missing six riggers.

Patrick White and architect Harry Seidler led a demonstration of 3000 architects and students. They marched from the Opera House and along Macquarie Street to State Parliament. They demanded Utzon's reinstatement and petitioned Askin, stating that the only architect who could finish the building in the spirit in which it was conceived was Jørn Utzon.

Martin ridiculed Hughes and his myrmidons in a series of cartoons for March *Oz*. In one, the minister rails against Utzon: 'Brilliant move forcing that Danish prima donna to resign, he'd want to sing his own bloody operas if we'd let him stay . . . We have some of the world's greatest architects right here in Australia … I've even drawn up a few plans meself.' Martin's cover depicted Boofhead—the dull-witted cartoon character who would reappear in his art—insisting: 'But I don't give a stuff about Opera!'

As the pressure on Utzon mounted, Martin was preparing to see *Oz* migrate from print to stage. Young director Jim Sharman explored doing so in a series of unconventional meetings. These including joining Neville at a swimming pool where the young *Oz* editor was surrounded by bikini-clad girls. And riding up and down in a manually operated elevator with Walsh, who worked shifts as a lift operator. *On Stage Oz* opened in March and included a dramatised version of Martin's narrative cartoon *The Word Flashed Round the Arms*.

'On the practical level [Martin] was the one who contributed most to the review because he was the cartoonist, he was the satirist and he understood the theatre,' says Jim Sharman, who would become a leading director of theatre, opera and musicals, including the original

London production of *The Rocky Horror Show*, and the later film version. *On Stage Oz* drew a young audience and played to full houses in makeshift venues for more than a month with a cast that included John Krummel and Ross Thomson. 'Although the material is never obscene, the audience can expect to be shocked by its merciless directness,' the *Herald* reported.

The lobbying for Utzon's reinstatement continued. But to no avail. Utzon made plans to leave Australia. Utzon, his wife and their three children secretly made their way to Sydney airport. They were the last passengers to board a flight bound for San Francisco on 28 April 1966. Lin was nineteen and distraught at the prospect of leaving the city and friends she loved.

The timing of their departure caught the government off guard. No one—neither Utzon's staff nor Harry Seidler, who had tirelessly advocated for Utzon—knew Utzon was about to leave Australia. Only two people close to the Utzon family knew of their imminent departure: Martin and Jo Sharp. The well-connected Jo arranged to get the family onto the plane and evade the press. Lin recalls: 'Martin's mother organised our departure. They were, in fact, the only ones who knew we were leaving. She organised with Qantas that we could get onto the tarmac to the plane . . . My father was hounded by the press at the time. And it was terribly emotional for me to leave my friend Martin, my friends, everyone.'

For Martin, the treatment of Utzon was the final straw. The March issue of *Oz*, with Martin's Opera House cartoons, was his last as the magazine's art director. He was poised to go overseas. He and John Weiley rescinded their mutual vow, prompted in large part by the continued harassment of Utzon. 'That was such a blow to our hopes,' says John. '. . . I just thought, this country is fucked. We are killing ourselves, there is no point in hanging on here ... Stuff it. We will rescind our oath.'

Utzon's bold dream had turned into a nightmare. It had become a symbol of all that was wrong with Australia—narrow, provincial, without vision. The Alfs had won. England had never looked so appealing. And London was said to be swinging.

Martin looked down awestruck at the vastness of the continent. He always sought a window seat in an aeroplane—he loved to watch the clouds. But this was his first flight over central Australia and it was the land itself that moved him, impressed by 'the enormousness of it, just a little glint of a roof here and there'. Martin was bound for Singapore with Richard Neville. The pair planned to travel in Asia before heading to London.

The overland hippie trail was a phrase yet to be coined when they packed their rucksacks. Before gap years became mandatory and *Lonely Planet* guides and TripAdvisor colonised the world, an Asian overland trip was an exotic adventure. And it was one of sufficient interest that *Oz* and *The Sydney Morning Herald* agreed to publish Martin and Neville's despatches.

Martin's *Two Innocents Abroad* cartoon for *Oz* depicted himself and Neville—*Oz*'s 'foreign agents' as the magazine dubbed them—arriving in steamy Singapore in leather jackets and duffel coats. Not that they began their trip as scruffy backpackers—they spent their first night in Singapore's famous Raffles Hotel.

Nonetheless, Martin soon had culture shock. In Australia, he had been in the majority, surrounded by other Anglo faces. For the first time, he was in the minority. 'Suddenly to be plunged into Chinese, Indian all sorts [felt] very interesting.' After the luxury of Raffles, he and Richard moved into a guesthouse run by a Chinese family.

'Unfortunately with my first meal in a street corner café I picked up dysentery, which plagued me for some long time.' He missed Binkie's Burgers and drew an advert for *Oz* indicating as much.

The *Herald* promoted their itinerant correspondents in a front-page story: 'Richard Neville, young Sydney writer, and cartoonist Martin Sharp are on a hitch-hiking world tour.' In his first *Herald* article, Richard railed against the censorship in Lee Kuan Yew's Singapore and a local population addicted to spy films. The pair had an uncomfortable reminder of home when they encountered Australian soldiers who greeted them with, 'Look … bloody poofters.'

After ten days in Singapore, they headed up the Malay peninsula to Kuala Lumpur. Along the way they became friends with a Muslim taxi driver, who took them to his east-coast village. Martin watched a wedding ceremony underway there and admired the village's wooden houses, while Richard recited Shakespeare to perplexed villagers. At the Thai border the pair caught a train north and, after a thirty-hour trip in a third-class carriage, finally arrived in Bangkok.

They walked out of Hua Lamphong railway station and into a guesthouse. The Thai Song Greet was crowded but cheap. It was a far cry from Raffles, but it was one of the few budget places on offer—apart from the railway itself or a Buddhist monastery floor—until Khao San Road cornered the Bangkok flophouse market in the 1980s. The Thai Song Greet had a hole-in-the-wall Chinese noodle shop downstairs and dark rooms with ceiling fans and mosquito nets upstairs; Martin and Richard shared a room with about six others for $1.50 a night. The hotel was also a brothel and a meeting place for young foreigners at a time when the main source of travellers' tips was by word of mouth. 'It was a great place to stay. I did a lot of drawing while I was there,' Martin said.

It provided inspiration for a cartoon. He drew a crowd of young tourists in the guesthouse, passing on travellers' tips ('Yer can sell yer blood for $10 a pint in Kabul'), writing home for more money and suffering heatstroke. A bearded Scot bemoans: 'Ach mon, it's a wee bit hot. Me singlet's as wet as Loch Ness.' Martin, meanwhile, appeared to be missing more sophisticated fare than Binkie's Burgers. He featured in the centre of the cartoon, lamenting, 'Oh for a nice filet steak.' Because of the repeated stomach upsets he was suffering, food frequently seemed on his mind.

Along the way he drew black and white illustrations for friends' books—Peter Draffin's *Pop* and Craig McGregor's book of essays *People Politics and Pop*. The latter contained more than a dozen of Martin's drawings, including an early Bob Dylan image and the 'dickhead' cartoon of *Oz* magistrate Locke.

In Bangkok, he discovered marijuana. 'You'd buy grass off the street then, already rolled up in cigarettes. I wasn't so sure what they were, but they were very thought-provoking.' The combination of dope and music, which he always played when he painted, proved transformative. 'Suddenly I was inside the music. And that was an eye-opener to me.' Elvis Presley and Dylan were among the musicians he listened to in Thailand.

In Cambodia, he again encountered the strange cigarettes. He smoked some on a bus travelling through the countryside and, at roadside stops along the way, amused local villagers by performing Donald Duck impersonations. He and Richard travelled to the ancient Khmer capital of Angkor and wandered through the stone temples of Angkor Wat and the Bayon. He marvelled at the weathered sandstone towers carved with four-faced deities and the giant fig trees growing out of stone temples and sculptures. He thought Angkor the most beautiful place he had ever seen. And he would draw on images of its temples when he reached London.

Martin could hardly have seen Angkor at a better time—before mass tourism brought swarms of visitors to the sacred site and before Pol Pot's murderous regime decimated the country and left a quarter of the population dead. They wandered the streets of the cosmopolitan capital Phnom Penh where chic cafés still served aperitifs and crème caramels, a legacy of the French, and bookstores sold Chinese newspapers and the writings of Mao Zedong.

Marijuana was not the only drug they consumed in Cambodia. Martin and Richard, attired in sarongs, lay on the floor of a blue-lit room smoking pipes of opium. 'It was a harmless experience. We enjoyed the illusion of depravity without suffering the discomfort of addiction,' Neville told his *Herald* readers.

After a dispiriting trip to the Lao capital Vientiane, with a 'mood of uncomfortable gloom', as Neville described it, they returned to Thailand via the Mekong. While Richard turned his scorn on the French colonial types waterskiing on the river, Martin turned his satirical eye on his travelling companion. He drew Richard staring at a speedboat on the Mekong and thinking: 'Damn tourist, spoiling our natural beauty.' Meanwhile a local looks at Richard and thinks the same.

From Bangkok they flew to Burma, on their way to Calcutta. When monsoon rains twice delayed their departure from Burma, they stayed for free at the Raj-era Strand Hotel in Rangoon. The grand hotel that had once sheltered Rudyard Kipling and Somerset Maugham was by then crumbling in post-independence neglect. The pair rattled around the nearly empty hotel but, being tieless, they struggled to be served in its dining room. The golden spires of the Shwedagon temple were consolation.

Martin was plagued by repeated stomach problems throughout the trip. By the time the pair reached Nepal in July, he'd had enough. Not even the legal dope shops around Kathmandu's Freak Street were enough to detain him. Martin was eager to get to London, while Richard wanted to walk in the Himalayas. 'I was too sick to do that,' said Martin. 'I was keen to get to England, see Bob Whitaker and experience the pop scene.'

CHAPTER 7

SWINGING LONDON

England was being transformed as Martin arrived. Although the scars of World War II were still evident in the bombed-out sites around the capital, the years of grey, grim postwar rationing and austerity were over. The mood was euphoric, and not just because Britain was basking in glory in the summer of 1966, having defeated rival West Germany to win football's World Cup. Traditional class boundaries were breaking down. Labour had swept to power in 1964 after more than a decade of Tory rule. In Harold Wilson, the country had a prime minister with a Liverpool seat and a northern accent. *Time* magazine had just declared London the 'Swinging City'.

It was a time of possibilities and rapid social change. Mass media and youth culture were emerging, and fashion, music and art were an integral part of this change. The boundaries between high and low culture, too, were dissolving. As hemlines rose and prices fell, fashion was no longer the preserve of the wealthy. It was the beginning of the electronic age. Portable transistor radios, movies, vinyl records and television became affordable, available and their influence pervasive. The airwaves were dominated by the Rolling Stones, The Kinks, Manfred Mann and especially by The Beatles. Teenagers tuned their transistor radios to pirate station Radio Caroline and their TV sets to *Ready Steady Go!* and *Top of the Pops*. Even in the United States, long the home of popular music, British bands filled their music charts.

And visual artists were embracing and reflecting the change underway. Pop art—the defining art movement of the sixties—was born in Britain. More than a decade before Andy Warhol's *Campbell's Soup Cans* appeared, Britain's Richard Hamilton had created his collage of a living room filled with the new consumer goods in *Just What is it That Makes Today's Homes So Different, So Appealing?* Generally seen as the first pop art work, it had a framed *Young Romance* comic on a wall, an advertisement on the television and a semi-naked bodybuilder holding a paddle emblazoned with the word 'pop'.

Hamilton's groundbreaking collage featured on a poster to advertise the *This Is Tomorrow* exhibition at London's Whitechapel Gallery. The 1956 show was a watershed in British art and sowed the seeds of pop art. Pop art, Hamilton wrote, was: 'Popular, transient, expendable, low-cost, mass-produced, young, witty, sexy, gimmicky, glamorous, and big business.' Intertwined with the emerging pop culture was a youthful underground or counterculture that encompassed music, art and literature, and embraced psychedelia and hippie culture.

A number of Martin's Australian friends and associates were already in London when he arrived, including Jenny Kee, Richard Neville's girlfriend Louise Ferrier and John Weiley. Barry Humphries was lampooning the beer-drinking ocker in the Barry McKenzie cartoon strip for *Private Eye* and Robert Hughes was writing for British broadsheets.

Robert Whitaker was Martin's first port of call when he arrived in England. Whitaker had toured the world with The Beatles since he left Australia. And he had photographed Epstein's stable of mostly Liverpudlian musicians. Thanks to the genius of the Liverpool-born impresario, the Mersey sound dominated the pop charts—Cilla Black, Gerry and the Pacemakers and Billy J. Kramer were among those Whitaker had trained his lens on.

He had shot the controversial 'butcher' cover for The Beatles' album *Yesterday and Today*. The image featured the band dressed in white butchers' coats, and draped with raw meat and decapitated dolls. The album was released only in North America, and contained material from their first two British albums that had not yet been released in the USA, but it was recalled and the cover replaced after an outcry. Whitaker had also shot some of the images used in the collage for The Beatles' *Revolver* album, created by the German artist Klaus Voormann, who was also Manfred Mann's bass player.

But Martin was disappointed to discover his celebrated photographer friend was not living in an elegant studio in the centre of hip, dionysian London. Rather, Whitaker was ensconced in a modern flat in suburban Chiswick. 'That wasn't quite the excitement I'd been hoping for. I suggested we try and get a place in Chelsea or somewhere,' said Martin.

Meanwhile, he shifted around London. He stayed for a time with Robert Hughes, who tossed him out after he trashed his kitchen. Martin was never a domesticated houseguest. He stayed with Colin and Kay Lanceley. They had rented an eight-room flat in Hanover Gate Mansions on the edge of Regent's Park. It was a gracious building with high-ceilinged rooms and liveried doormen, but something of a crash pad for expat Australians. The Lanceleys had a full house and no spare bed when Martin arrived. Undeterred, Martin slept in the hallway. But, having grown up with servants and a well-stocked larder, he soon complained there were no cans of tinned peaches or packets of Kellogg's cornflakes.

He stayed with Richard Neville's sister, writer Jill Neville, in her basement. When Richard joined him there after his Himalayan trip in September 1966, an idea that the pair of them had tossed around in Asia, to create a London version of *Oz*, took shape. Neville told the *London Evening Standard*'s Mary Kenny about this plan in an article which ran with a photo of Richard and Louise Ferrier. London *Oz* was to be a follow-on from Sydney *Oz*, a satirical magazine rather than a psychedelic or underground publication (one such underground magazine, the *International Times*, or *IT*, was already poised to launch in London in October). Seated at a dinner party next to Paul Johnson, the then influential editor of the *New Statesman*, Richard boasted that he would produce 'something between *Private Eye* and *New Statesman*'.

Martin's image of a sinister gap-toothed grin was on the cover when London *Oz* launched in January 1967. Inside, Germaine Greer wrote a column titled 'In Bed with the English' about the shortcomings of the English male. The issue was disparaging of the hippie scene, not least in Martin's illustrated monologue *The Somewhat Incredible Turning on of Mervyn Limp, Bank Clerk*. After smoking a joint, the hapless Limp transforms into a beat poet, hits the hippie trail and lands in Kathmandu, where he dies of dysentery: 'Turned on. Tuned in. Dropped dead.' The cartoon used photos of Martin and Neville shot in the alternative bookstore Indica. The strip was also published three months later in Sydney *Oz*, to which Martin continued to contribute.

The most arresting aspect of the first London *Oz* was Martin's image *The Madonna of the Napalm*. It depicted US president Lyndon B. Johnson as the Madonna, with a halo of rifles, cradling a bomb and South Vietnam's ruler. Above him, like a cherub, was a kangaroo with the face of Australian prime minister Harold Holt, who had famously declared that he was 'All the way with LBJ'. Years later, Robert Hughes praised the work as a 'one of the classics of sixties anti-war cartooning'.

Robert Whitaker found a light-filled flat in Chelsea's Jubilee Place, and he and Martin moved in. Named after the nineteenth-century artist and interior designer Amédée Joubert who created it, Joubert Studios was entered through a make-shift kitchen area, a glass corridor like a greenhouse, that opened onto a large wood-panelled studio. Beautiful as it was, the studio was not ideal for two people as it lacked bedrooms. '[Whitaker] turned the big main room into his bedroom, so I just built a tent in the kitchen area ... with blankets and stuff hung up,' Martin said.

Still, the studio had other attractions, Robert recalled: 'It was right off the King's Road, which is where we used to watch all the girls going by wearing miniskirts.'

The three-kilometre King's Road had been an exclusive strip since Charles II established it as his private thoroughfare. Here Thomas Crapper later sold water closets and Thomas Arne composed 'Rule, Britannia!'. Running from ritzy Sloane Square to run-down World's End, by the mid-sixties King's Road was the epicentre of swinging London, a mecca for the young, hip, fashionable and some of Britain's more bohemian bluebloods. Designer Mary Quant, who named the miniskirt, set up shop there. Michael Rainey and his then wife, Jane Ormsby Gore, Lord Harlech's daughter, opened Hung On You on King's Road, where Australian John Crittle (later the estranged father of prima ballerina Darcey Bussell) sold threads. Artist Nigel Waymouth had just opened the psychedelic boutique Granny Takes a Trip when Martin arrived.

Whitaker wasn't flush with cash, despite his high-profile work. 'Martin always had pockets full of money and I never had huge amounts.' What the photographer did have was access to the pop elite. 'So many people—like Cream, The Beatles, The Stones—I knew. So when it came around to parties and things, we were right in the middle of it. And we were both cute kids,' said Whitaker.

Martin likened London to his university and Chelsea to his college. His time in Chelsea was one of the most creative periods of his life. In his studio with Whitaker, Martin was prolific. He was busy with London *Oz* and he continued to do cartoons for Sydney *Oz*, lampooning swinging London's upper-class trendies.

Martin took his first acid trip in London. Until the mid-sixties, Lysergic acid diethylamide, or LSD, was known primarily to psychiatrists and military scientists. The US Central Intelligence Agency secretly experimented with it, dosing unwitting Americans. The military considered LSD a possible tool for mind control and brainwashing. At the same time, a vastly different group became aware of the drug, drawn to its potential to expand consciousness.

Thanks to Aldous Huxley, author of *The Doors of Perception*, and former Harvard psychologist Dr Timothy Leary, who promoted 'turn on, tune in and drop out', the use of the drug had grown. After introducing Leary to LSD, British psychedelic researcher Michael Hollingshead returned to Britain from the United States in 1965, and opened the World Psychedelic Centre in Chelsea to evangelise its use.

Long before Apple co-founder Steve Jobs described taking LSD as 'a profound experience, one of the most important things in my life', advocates claimed the drug could transform human consciousness, producing euphoria and spiritual experience. Taken in the right environment—and the effects of LSD, more than other hallucinogens, appear to be susceptible to the surroundings in which the drug is taken—it could intensify colours and sounds and produce synaesthesia. Not surprisingly, artists and musicians were among a young generation who began dropping acid. And the impact was seen in the emergence of psychedelic music and art—at the same time as the drug became illegal in Britain and the States, in 1966.

In Britain, the premier psychedelic band was Pink Floyd. With their experimental sound, meandering improvised instrumentals and light shows, they were leaders of London's underground music scene. Their line-up included a charismatic frontman and singer-songwriter, Syd Barrett, when they became regulars at London's UFO Club, the short-lived basement club on Tottenham Court Road that was psychedelia central.

The Incredible String Band, The Crazy World of Arthur Brown, and Procol Harum were among the psychedelic musicians who cut their teeth at the club run by John Hopkins, founder of the alternative newspaper *International Times*. But it was Pink Floyd and the visionary but troubled Syd Barrett who most captured Martin's attention. 'I admired Syd Barrett immensely. I thought [Pink Floyd] were the most modern group I saw at the time, because of the light shows they had and the UFO concerts they had. Floyd were the main band there,' Martin said.

Martin took his first acid trip watching Pink Floyd at the UFO Club. 'Another dimension of reality was revealed. I attempted to express that within my art,' he said. But he found taking LSD and working incompatible: 'I didn't draw under its influence. I don't believe one can. Worthwhile art takes a lot of discipline.'

Today, the use of LSD is tempered by fears it may trigger or aggravate mental health problems. And Syd Barrett, who left Pink Floyd after the album *Piper at the Gates of Dawn* and retreated to Cambridge, has been singled out, rightly or wrongly, as one of acid's most high-profile casualties. But Barrett was at the height of his talents when Martin became a regular at Pink Floyd's UFO gigs.

Despite his attraction to acid-inspired music, Martin retained his love of popular songs from an earlier era. So he was delighted by a dawn encounter as he returned late from seeing Pink Floyd at the UFO. Martin had forgotten his studio keys and, unwilling to wake Whitaker so early, was killing time in St James Park when a man asked him for directions. It was Bing Crosby. The pair chatted about horses—Crosby was a great horse lover—before Martin wandered off to see if Whitaker was awake.

Martin was at his desk in his greenhouse-like studio working on what would become the best-known image of his career: a poster of Bob Dylan, *Mr Tambourine Man*. Martin's Finnish-born model girlfriend, Eija Vehka-aho, was helping him. She was drawing with a compass hundreds of swirling circles that became Dylan's hair. They worked quietly; Eija was meticulous and reserved, not given to chatter.

Their silence was punctured by a knock on the door. Two men entered the studio. Martin had not met the clean-cut, middle-aged man with a comb-over who overshadowed his more fashionable younger companion. It wasn't just his prize-fighter energy, flared nostrils or thin-lipped slash of a mouth that made the older man impossible to ignore; it was the tsunami of words that came out of that mouth. His name was David Litvinoff.

Litva, as Martin called him, was mercurial, gay, witty and fiercely intelligent, with an aura of dangerous glamour. He was a mysterious, mesmerising figure, about whom fact and fiction were frequently indistinguishable. He was an East End rogue and an associate of notorious London gangsters Ronald and Reginald Kray, the murderous twins who dominated the capital's criminal underworld in the fifties and sixties. Litva's mouth had been sliced to the ear—possibly after a fallout with Ronald Kray. Plastic surgery did not erase a scar on the left side of his mouth and another across his right cheek.

Litva moved nimbly between art, pop and criminal worlds. Born in 1928 of Russian Jewish background, the son of an East End tailor, Litvinoff modified his working-class cockney accent listening to recordings of Laurence Olivier. He was a familiar figure around Soho's jazz and gambling clubs in the 1950s, and rumoured to procure boys for Ronald Kray. By the 1960s, he had moved into more bohemian and artistic circles.

He knew Lucian Freud, whom he resembled so closely that Litva used to pass himself off as the artist in London bars. But the pair fell out after Freud painted a portrait of Litva known as *Man in a Headscarf*. It wasn't the bent pugilist's nose or downcast expression that offended Litvinoff but the famous portrait's disparaging alternate title, *The Procurer*.

Litva was rumoured to be the inspiration for the Rolling Stones' 'Jumpin' Jack Flash', a myth he helped fuel. He certainly crossed paths with the Stones, and Keith Richards has described him as a man 'on the borders of art and villainy'. Indeed, the underground and underbelly of sixties London met in the figure of David Litvinoff.

When he erupted into Joubert Studios, his timing was impeccable. He did so as Martin had become dissatisfied with the space he shared with Whitaker. After nearly a year, sleeping in the kitchen had begun to pale. Martin said: 'It became apparent two couldn't really live there because of the design of the place. It was a bit like the Yellow House in Arles, where Gauguin had to get to his room through van Gogh's bedroom. So it wasn't a suitable arrangement.'

Amid Litvinoff's wall of chatter, he had some news that commanded Martin's attention. A better place was about to come up for rent nearby. Litva may well have described it as a 'gas', as he frequently described anything that enthused him—and further consolidated the myth of 'Jumpin' Jack Flash'. The studio he alerted Martin to would become the epicentre of the sixties creative explosion.

The Bob Dylan poster Martin was working on when David Litvinoff burst into his life was the first he had done since his posters for Sydney's art school balls. 'I wanted to do a tribute poster of him ... no particular reason, just a tribute,' said Martin.

He enlarged a photo of the singer wearing sunglasses for the central image. His hair is a mass of swirling circles, hardly any two alike. The circles were influenced by Leonardo da Vinci's knot design and by the nineteenth-century Art Nouveau illustrator Aubrey Beardsley, who was undergoing a revival. Indeed, Beardsley posters, paintings and book illustrations, full of swirling, erotic, decadent imagery, had been the subject of an exhibition at London's Victoria and Albert Museum when Martin arrived in London.

Eija recalls working at times on the studio floor, drawing the hundreds of tiny circles. Unlike Martin, Eija was fastidiously precise, which may be why Martin asked her to help. 'Martin was really messy, he was always dropping his ink bottles on drawings that he had already done ... He knew that I was neat,' she says.

Dylan's carnivalesque song 'Mr Tambourine Man' was among Martin's favourites. But the image also referred to another seminal Dylan song. With an inverted letter in Dylan's sunglasses, Martin changed 'Blowin' in the Wind' into 'Blowin' in the Mind'—and captured the psychedelic spirit of the era. At the bottom he superimposed an image of Dylan in profile, placing it over his lettering of 'Mister Tambourine Man.' Whether by accident or design it appears to read 'Mister Urine Man,' something which, in later life, embarrassed Martin.

He took the image to his friend Peter Ledeboer, whose Big O Posters produced psychedelic posters. Martin wanted the poster printed in purple and black on silver, instructions Ledeboer conveyed to the printer. It came back red and black on gold. A happy accident, perhaps. The poster became a bestseller, Martin's best-known work and a seminal image of the sixties.

Eija Vehka-aho arrived in London in 1966. She was a striking, ethereal presence—tall, lean, blonde, alabaster skin, with a penchant for floating chiffon and red lipstick used as eye shadow. She was often silent around Martin's friends, reluctant to talk until she had perfected her English. Eija recalls meeting Martin on a dance floor. 'I saw like an aura around him and that was it. We started dancing. Well, he didn't really dance—we were in front of each other, his way of dancing was kind of dreamy. He was dancing in a bubble ... We just started being together, but he was very bohemian and so was I, so there weren't any rules about anything.' Martin's relationship with Eija would become the most significant, but turbulent, romance during his time in London.

The dance floor where they met was the Speakeasy Club, an exclusive, late-night venue in Margaret Street behind Oxford Circus. It stayed open until 4am—rare in London at the time—and styled itself on US prohibition-era illegal drinking dens, with a brooding image of Al Capone presiding over the bar. The entrance foyer to the basement club was a fake undertaker's parlour. The cash desk was a coffin on which members handed over their entrance fee before passing through a mirrored wardrobe door to the bar. The club opened in December 1966 and soon became the hippest in town.

Musicians and record industry people were drawn to its live music and impromptu jam sessions. The Byrds, Soft Machine and The Beatles were among those who performed at or frequented the club. It was a place of improbable encounters. None more so than the night Martin went to the Speakeasy, around April 1967. He had gone to the club to see his Sydney friend Jenny Kee, with whom he had had a fleeting romance, who was waitressing there. The only other person he recognised inside was a young French model he had previously met at Bob Whitaker's studio, Charlotte Martin. She was seated with two men and Martin asked if he could join her table. 'I didn't know anyone there, so I was just sitting down talking to a couple of guys. I gathered they were musicians. And I said, "Oh, I've just written some lyrics,"' Martin said.

Charlotte's guitarist boyfriend said he had just written some music. Martin wrote out his lyrics and address on a serviette and handed them to him. Martin didn't recognise his name: Eric Clapton. Or his band, Cream. 'A couple of weeks later—[Cream] were recording at the time, I hadn't even heard of Cream, I didn't know who [Clapton] was—he turned up with a copy of the record.' The 45 rpm single was 'Tales of Brave Ulysses' and it was the B-side of Cream's 'Strange Brew', which entered the UK charts in June 1967. The Speakeasy meeting was the beginning of a long friendship and occasional collaboration with Clapton.

Martin wrote the lyrics after visiting the Balearic Islands, off the east coast of Spain, where he had gone during his first English winter.

He had island-hopped from Ibiza to the more remote Formentera, a smaller island off Ibiza's southern tip. He later learned that the Balearic Islands were where Ulysses, the hero of Homer's *Odyssey*, was said to have heard the sirens sing.

Ulysses had been warned about the Isle of the Sirens, where maidens sang enchanted melodies that lured seamen to watery deaths. As Ulysses approached, he plugged his sailors' ears with wax and tied himself to his ship's mast. Although the sirens' song prompted an overwhelming desire to throw himself into the sea, Ulysses had instructed his men to ignore his pleas to release him. And so he heard the sirens call without falling under their fatal spell.

Ulysses' tale was the starting point for lyrics that, like Martin's visual art, are many layered. There is a painterly quality to the poetic words, with their images of purple fishes, turquoise waters and a girl with sun-browned skin. His lyrics recalled how the purple fishes had danced between his fingers on the island—an image that echoes his boyhood fascination with Telford's blue groper. With its red soil and eucalyptus stands, Ibiza may have reminded him of his sun-drenched Australia. And back in the 'leaden winter' of London, he acknowledged he had felt homesick.

Martin had been nostalgic, too, for his Sydney girlfriend, Anou Kiisler. 'Tales of Brave Ulysses' is a song of erotic yearning, for a sun-browned girl he longed to take to the 'hard land of the winter'. Martin told his friend Peter Hannan—who later married Anou—that he had dedicated the song to her. Yet the temptations of other beautiful women are apparent in the song. In many ways, 'Tales of Brave Ulysses' encapsulates Martin's enduring romantic conflict: he would never commit to a long-term relationship and his head was constantly turned by beautiful young women.

The recording, with Clapton's wah pedal and Ginger Baker's thumping drums, was a vastly different interpretation to what Martin had conceived. He had written the lyrics as a folk rhythm based on

Leonard Cohen's *Suzanne*. He initially offered the lyrics to his Sydney folk singer friend Tina Date, who had been recording in London. To Martin's ultimate good fortune, she had not used them.

Robert Whitaker had been photographing a number of models at his studio when a pair of identical twins arrived. Michelle and Nicole Aloszko were tall and leggy, with long blonde hair and heavy fringes. 'The twins walked into the studio, they were sixteen or seventeen years of age and stunningly good to look at,' said Whitaker. The pair had grown up in a north London council house and, after leaving school, had worked at London's fashionable Biba boutique, danced at the Speakeasy and turned to modelling, including for Murdoch's tabloid *The Sun*.

Whitaker recalled: 'One day we took them out onto a golf course, near Ascot I think it was, and off came their clothes and on went the flowers and we clicked away for hours on end and came back to the studio. I processed all the film and then made a whole series of prints that Martin promptly cut up and started making into this fabulous collage, which is one of the great pieces of the sixties … Martin and I are in the picture, but you've got to hunt for us.' As Martin worked on the collage, Richard Neville visited the studio, where he encountered not just the twins, according to his memoir *Hippie Hippie Shake*. Martin spiked Richard's tea with LSD, his first encounter with the hallucinogen. 'You aren't hip till you trip' was the philosophy of the time.

Martin's collage became the day-glo poster *Plant a Flower Child*. The poster is filled with exuberant images of the naked twins as they peek enticingly at the camera and leap about, garlanded and crowned with daisies. There's an innocence to the image that encapsulated the heady perfume of the Summer of Love. The image ran in London *Oz* number 5 in July 1967 and, after struggling to find its feet, helped turn the fortunes of the magazine.

Police raided Rolling Stones guitarist Keith Richards' Sussex farmhouse Redlands in February 1967. Also caught up in the bust were the band's lead singer, Mick Jagger, his girlfriend, Marianne Faithfull—famously naked and wrapped only in a fur rug—former Etonians and leading Chelsea-set figures Robert Fraser and Christopher Gibbs, as well as a hanger-on called Nicky Kramer. In the ensuing court case, Jagger was sentenced to three months' jail for possessing amphetamines and Richards to a year's jail for allowing cannabis to be smoked in his home. The sentences were harsh and shocked not just the counterculture. Even *The Times* editor William Rees-Mogg weighed in with an editorial headed 'Who breaks a butterfly on a wheel?'.

The case became a cause célèbre in the summer of 1967 and a lightning rod for tensions between a punitive, authoritarian order and those advocating more liberal values. Pop artist Richard Hamilton was among those who signed a full-page advertisement in *The Times* that stated that the law against marijuana was immoral and unworkable. He created a series of images around the case, including one of Jagger and Fraser, who was Hamilton's art dealer and friend, handcuffed together in the back of a police van, attempting to shield their faces from the press. Hamilton called the series *Swingeing London*. The pun on swinging London was also a reference to the judge's comment in the case that a 'swingeing sentence can act as a deterrent'.

In the wake of the high-profile case, a Legalise Pot rally was organised for London's Hyde Park on 16 July. To advertise the rally, Martin created a poster, *The Putting Together of the Heads*. The wittily titled poster, filled with the heads of South American Indians taken from nineteenth-century ethnographic engravings, was printed in black and orange on gold foil.

Oz associate Peter Ledeboer printed six hundred copies and hired a man to paste them around London. But a couple of weeks before the rally, Martin realised none had appeared on the streets. The bill poster had sold them instead to a US poster distributor. Ledeboer arranged to have them reprinted, but the rip-off prompted him to realise the demand for posters. As a result, he set up Big O Posters, which printed some of Martin's early posters, including *Mr Tambourine Man*.

Robert Whitaker photographed beat poet Allen Ginsberg at the rally where he recited poetry and played an Indian squeezebox. Tripping on acid, Australian Jim Anderson, who would later become a co-editor of *Oz*, first met Richard Neville at the rally selling copies of *Oz* around Hyde Park Corner.

While flower children at the rally held signs advocating love, love, love, David Litvinoff played a violent bit-part in the aftermath of the Keith Richards drug bust. When suspicion fell on the hanger-on, Nicky Kramer, that he had informed on the musicians, Litva and a London underworld tough named John Bindon attempted to find out. They beat up Kramer, before dangling him out of a window by his ankles.

CHAPTER 8

THE PHEASANTRY

The Pheasantry was a grand Georgian red-brick and stucco house at 152 King's Road. Pheasants for the king's table had once been bred on the site, hence the name. Set back from the Chelsea street, the three-storey building was entered through a triumphal arch supported by a pair of Grecian caryatids—the flamboyant flourishes had been added by the interior designer Amédée Joubert, who had based his business there in the late nineteenth century. Through the twentieth century creative people had been drawn to the Pheasantry. Dancers Alicia Markova and Margot Fonteyn trained at a ballet academy run there by Leo Tolstoy's great-niece Serafina Astafieva. In the 1930s its basement had become a bohemian club, drawing artists, writers and actors, including Dylan Thomas, Francis Bacon and Anthony Hopkins.

The Pheasantry was ramshackle by the time Martin moved in and was divided into a rabbit warren of studios. But the group of artists who had studios within it in the late sixties helped define the era. Germaine Greer, whom Martin had met in Sydney, moved into a downstairs studio, where she worked on *The Female Eunuch*, which became a pivotal feminist text and an international bestseller. Writer, cartoonist and socialite Anthony Haden-Guest, who has written about the art world for *The New Yorker*, *Vanity Fair* and *The Observer*, had a studio in the Pheasantry at this time, as did artist Timothy Whidborne, where he worked on his 1969 portrait of the Queen on horseback.

Martin rented the top floor, which cost him fourteen pounds a week. It had three bedrooms, each with dormer windows and a balcony, and it overlooked King's Road. The bedrooms opened onto a big main room, which became the studio. A minstrel's gallery around the main room was too small to stand up in, but visitors often slept there. And there were plenty of visitors. He was frequently joined by his girlfriend, Eija Vehka-aho, although she kept her own flat nearby.

Martin set about painting the studio's interior, which became a work of art in itself. He painted the walls of the winding internal staircase up to the flat in orange with white curlicues. On a hallway ceiling, he pasted a poster of a baroque cathedral ceiling. The kitchen door was green with orange swastikas—a nod to the auspicious Hindu symbol, not to the Nazi emblem.

Martin had become friends with Eric Clapton. After the musician returned from America, where *Disraeli Gears* was recorded in May 1967, Martin invited him and his girlfriend, Charlotte Martin, to move into the Pheasantry with him. '[Martin and Clapton] really clicked,' recalls Charlotte.

Martin's eighteen-year-old friend from Melbourne Philippe Mora arrived some months later and moved into the remaining room with his Australian girlfriend, Freya Mathews. The Pheasantry would set the pattern for how Martin lived for the rest of his life. He would live and work communally—there would always be people around—but they would be there at his invitation.

Philippe's first night at the Pheasantry was interrupted by a blood-curdling scream. Fearing someone was being murdered, he went in search of his flatmate. Relax, Martin told him, it was the midnight horror screening at the Chelsea Classic cinema next door.

Philippe's other first impressions of London were more welcome. He was struck by the different attitude towards the Vietnam War that prevailed in Britain. Unlike Australia's Harold Holt, Britain's prime minister Harold Wilson was not prepared to go 'All the way with LBJ'.

His ruling Labour government and the British public opposed the war, and Wilson rejected Washington's request for troops. In addition, Britain no longer had compulsory military service. Conscription, introduced at the outbreak of World War II, was abolished in 1960.

'Martin and I were amazed. You could read all the papers, and it was actually okay to be against the war in Vietnam … You could legitimately say, "This war is wrong."' The dissenting opinion in Britain meant Martin focused his attention elsewhere. 'The fury turned down in London, and Martin got more into aesthetics, with psychedelic artwork,' says Philippe.

Nonetheless, Martin created several anti-war cartoons for *Oz* in London. Among the most searing was his blood-spattered cover based on an image of South Vietnam's national police chief shooting a bullet into the head of a Vietcong man. The summary execution was captured by Associated Press photographer Eddie Adams. 'The Great Society blows another mind,' Martin wrote beneath Adams' photograph. The cover appeared the same month that, away from the cameras, the bloodiest atrocity of the Vietnam War unfolded when US soldiers killed up to 500 unarmed civilians in what became known as the Mỹ Lai Massacre.

At the Pheasantry, Martin began working on the cover for Cream's seminal album *Disraeli Gears*. Martin said: 'It was Eric being a friend and just saying, "Oh well, you do the designs." Previously it would have been commissioned by the record company. But suddenly the middleman was gone and it was just artists dealing with other artists … they had the say, they chose the album covers, not the record company.'

Martin took an image of the three Cream members—Clapton, Jack Bruce and Ginger Baker—from a publicity photo. Beneath their portraits he added a pair of outstretched wings from a woodcut by German

Renaissance artist Albrecht Dürer. He also used cut-out images of a camera and a watch from early Army & Navy Stores catalogues. The day-glo pink and yellow reflected the band's warm electric sound. 'Fluorescent paints were available then, and somehow I managed to use them,' he said. Martin rarely did preparatory drawings beyond a doodle. He worked fast and often to size, including for *Disraeli Gears*.

The album cover's reverse side was a collage of Bob Whitaker's photos of the band taken during a road trip. Whitaker said: 'I went off with Eric Clapton, Ginger Baker and Jack Bruce around Scotland. We were on LSD most of the time, even climbing Ben Nevis—in full stage costume.'

Disraeli Gears was the album with which Cream took flight. The band's second album was released in November 1967 and reached number five on the UK album charts. Its standout tracks included 'Strange Brew', 'Sunshine of Your Love' and Martin's 'Tales of Brave Ulysses'.

Martin drove to Heathrow airport in a yellow Mini Moke. With a rag top and open sides, the vehicle was less than ideal for the English climate, but it was the height of cool. He was no more attentive to his Moke than he was to his cars in Australia, as Martin's Sydney photographer friend Mike Molloy discovered when Martin arrived to collect the latest of the Australian exodus.

Oblivious to parking restrictions, Martin left his Moke right outside the terminal. When he returned with Mike, Martin was astonished to find that the vehicle had vanished. It had not occurred to Martin that the car would be impounded. Mike moved into film work in Britain, becoming a cinematographer and working with Stanley Kubrick, Nicolas Roeg and Jeremy Thomas. But when he arrived in London, he was just one of a number of Martin's Australian friends who stayed at the Pheasantry.

So, too, did young architect Alex Popov, the former *Tharunka* editor who shared the court bench with Martin. Alex was en route to Copenhagen to join his girlfriend, Lin Utzon, who he later married. Lin had returned to Denmark after her father's departure from the Sydney Opera House.

Martin and Alex were eating near the Biba boutique one day when a tall woman with platinum hair approached their table. She handed Martin a book of Salvador Dali's paintings. Amanda Lear was Dali's muse and part of London's demimonde. The French model and musician was a figure of mystery and speculation, including about her gender. Dali was rumoured to have paid for her sex-change operation. This was a myth engineered by Dali for publicity, Amanda later said. Linked with the Rolling Stones' Brian Jones, David Bowie and Bryan Ferry—and featured on the cover of Roxy Music's *For Your Pleasure*—she was just one of the colourful figures who floated around Chelsea and across Martin's life.

When black jazz musician Jimmy Smith, who popularised the Hammond organ, came to London, a jam session was arranged with him and Cream at BBC studios. Smith had challenged the band to play with him, sceptical that a bunch of white guys could cut it—despite the fact that they had by then earned the admiration of composer Leonard Bernstein. Manfred Mann, the keyboard player with the eponymous band, drove Martin and Popov along to hear it.

'Jimmy started playing that slow *doo, doo-doo*, and Eric started playing with him. And Jack Bruce followed and he [Smith] tried to lose them. It was fantastic. And he had to acknowledge that these guys knew how to play,' says Alex.

Manfred Mann and Ginger Baker were among the musicians who visited the Pheasantry. George Harrison jammed with Clapton in the main room, and arrived one day with an acetate of what would become The Beatles' double LP *White Album*. Litva was often around the Pheasantry, and dropped by with unreleased recordings to the astonishment of the flatmates. No one knew how he got his hands on them, including what became known as Dylan's *Basement Tapes,* which were not released until 1975. 'Through David Litvinoff, somehow we were able to listen to tapes and music that hadn't been yet released,' says Charlotte Martin.

Much as she enjoyed his tapes, Litva unsettled Charlotte. She recalls: 'He was scary, he was just completely over-the-top in a kind of theatrical way ... He was interested in talking to Martin and Eric, he certainly wasn't interested in acknowledging me at all. I found him quite intimidating at the time. But he was so larger than life and I can see the effect he had on young guys. He came from such a seedy world and he had so many tales to tell, which was really captivating for the boys.' Litvinoff was probably Martin's first encounter with a portal to a criminal underworld whose operations Martin would, years later, forensically dissect.

Artists and performers were drawn to the Pheasantry's unusual salon, including artist Eduardo Paolozzi, a seminal figure in pop art. Members of the experimental Living Theatre came to stay. Their notorious 1968 work *Paradise Now,* which involved reciting a list of social taboos while disrobing, led to arrests for indecent exposure. At times so many of the troupe dossed at the Pheasantry that they had to sleep on the staircase.

Radical anti-psychiatrist R.D. Laing visited. Laing rejected traditional definitions of mental illness and treatment methods. He thought mental hospitals were no place for schizophrenics and that insanity was a sane reaction to an insane world. Laing, whose iconoclastic and LSD-inspired *The Politics of Experience* and *Knots* graced the bookshelves of all well-read hippies, spent several days at the Pheasantry observing its inhabitants. He sat in a chair watching Martin and Philippe paint and Eric play. He noted every detail, including when Martin went to the bathroom. The Pheasantry's inmates took Laing's theories to heart, welcoming artists, eccentrics and at least one psychotic.

The studio door was rarely closed at any hour—apart from one night when Anthony Haden-Guest walked up the Pheasantry's winding staircase accompanied by a glamorous woman. He wanted her to see Martin's studio. Anthony knocked but got no reply. Martin was busy and in no mood for visitors, so he did not answer. Anthony met Martin the next day and referred to his evening visit. He thought Martin would have enjoyed meeting French movie goddess Brigitte Bardot. Martin never again failed to respond to a knock on the door.

Martin's days began and ended late. He often worked until 4am, rose at midday and wandered across the road to the Picasso Café for strong coffee and a toasted cheese and tomato sandwich. Little cooking occurred at the Pheasantry, apart from custard. Martin always had money—for art supplies, clothes, meals and nightclubs. Much of it came from his grandfather Stuart Ritchie, who had given Martin more than three thousand dollars towards his trip. It meant he did not need to take paid work in London. Nor was Martin ambitious in any orthodox way. He did not seek to become part of the established art world. Consistent with the ethos of the era, Martin looked disparagingly on careerism. Part of the appeal of creating posters was that they were available to anyone, not just the elite.

He bought expensive art books from Zwemmer's bookstore on Charing Cross Road, which he took to with a Stanley knife and scissors to create collages. Friends lent a hand—Eija with the Dylan poster, John Weiley helped paste up some of the *Disraeli Gears* artwork and Philippe Mora helped with *Oz*. 'We were working really hard all the time. Martin always had a pen in his hand, I always had a brush … Eric was always playing guitar. We were conscientious young artists—I wouldn't say ambitious, it was just what we were doing. We were kind of driven,' says Philippe.

Charlotte Martin recalls Martin working constantly amid mess and chaos: 'I certainly remember him at work with a fag in his hand, a roll-up. And paper everywhere—collage paper, foil paper, different types of paper and cuttings, books being ripped open and images and stuff that he needed to construct all his amazing images ... It was just spread everywhere on the floor, at the table, in our main room.' Martin drew people to him, but the chaos could be overwhelming. 'It's like he danced through life; there was a kind of lightness about him. Because he was very inviting, one knew you could just pop in and be well received ... I just wanted to be with my boyfriend.'

At the same time as he surrounded himself with people, paradoxically he craved solitude, says Eija. 'Martin was very introverted, which you wouldn't actually think when you met him. But lots of times he wanted to be alone and do his work and lots of people around were disturbing him.'

But there was little solitude even at night, not just because of the visitors and music within the studio. Freya Mathews recalls: 'You couldn't sleep because of this awful, wretched Pheasantry Club in the basement. *Boom, boom, boom, boom*, all night till about 4am, shaking the whole building. Then Martin was coming back all night, going out to nightclubs, and coming back, and then going out again, coming back, and bringing people home. It was like the night was the living time.'

Freya, now an environmentalist, philosopher and author, appreciated Martin's generosity in putting a roof over her head. He didn't know her, she had no income and she lived at the Pheasantry only because she was Philippe's girlfriend. Martin didn't flinch when she acquired a couple of cats and put their stinky litter tray at the top of the staircase. Knowing she wanted to write, he offered her a small room to do so. Throughout his life, Martin provided spaces under his roof for people to create.

Eric Clapton became a musical star with Cream during this time. Freya was at the Pheasantry the day this hit home. 'I remember him on the phone talking to his manager and putting the phone down and saying, "I'm rich,"' she says. A Rolls-Royce drew up outside the Pheasantry for Eric soon after. 'We all got in and then drove around the block.'

Martin wore tight pants that were striped red, white and blue, like a Union Jack, and an embroidered Afghan vest. In front of his face he carried, like a lollipop, a smile on a stick. As he went, he bowed to passers-by. Even on the King's Road, he stood out.

Birgitta Bjerke, a fabric artist who later created the costumes for the movie *Dances with Wolves*, saw Martin frequently at this time. She had first met him at Joubert Studios, where she had been one of Whitaker's lovers. Later she occasionally stayed at the Pheasantry, where she painted a series of watercolours of the dramatic coloured rooms Martin had created. She would also bump into him across the road in the Picasso Café. With its outdoor tables, it was a meeting place for the in-crowd to gather and watch the passing peacock parade. Birgitta recalls: 'It was the greatest show in the world, King's Road on Saturday afternoon. There was nothing to beat it. You just sort of dressed up to walk on King's Road.' The King's Road was for the hip elite, much more so than Carnaby Street, in scruffy Soho, with its racks of mass-produced kipper ties and paisley shirts.

Birgitta often ran into Martin and Eija at the Chelsea Antique Market, another favoured haunt for musicians, artists and bohemians. The covered market was full of old wares, clothes and exotica. Martin had drawn an advert for the market and it had appeared in the first issue of London *Oz*. One of the market's most distinctive stalls was operated by Australian Vern Lambert. Melbourne-born Lambert had introduced his friend, the Italian fashion doyenne Anna Piaggi, to vintage clothes; he had a discerning eye and an ability to put together disparate pieces. Accompanied by Piaggi, he trawled the street markets of Portobello Road and Petticoat Lane and the country homes of the landed gentry in search of vintage gems.

Aristocratic attics were being emptied of their mothballed treasures. The cast-offs of the upper-class became high hippie fashion. Edwardian military jackets, white bell-bottomed sailor pants, Victorian nightgowns and collarless grandpa shirts were all suddenly sought-after items, often dyed in bright colours. There were ethnic fabrics—silks from Tunisia, hand-printed Indian cottons, Afghan coats—and a lot of crushed velvet.

Jenny Kee, who worked on Lambert's stall, watched musicians and their entourages scour the market for costumes, among them the Rolling Stones accompanied by Marianne Faithfull and Anita Pallenberg. Or she saw them in Bob and Pearl's café near her stall, eating toasted cheese sandwiches. (London might have become the centre of the fashion world, but British cuisine remained an oxymoron.) Humans were not the only exotic creatures on King's Road at the time. None was more exotic than the pet lion bought from Harrods by Australians Ace Bourke, who later became friends with Martin, and John Rendall. The pair exercised their young lion, Christian, in a churchyard near their King's Road flat.

The talk around Chelsea was about a hot new guitarist in town. Jimi Hendrix had arrived in London in September 1966, a few months after Martin, as an unknown American musician. Martin first saw him perform at a West End theatre and was transfixed by his music, energy and theatricality. 'While Eric was very modest on stage, Jimi Hendrix was absolutely full of show business,' said Martin.

No one played guitar like Jimi. He played it with his teeth, behind his head, between his knees; he even set it on fire. His movements were languid, his figure lean and his looks smouldering. His charisma was as electrifying as his music. Even before he recorded his first album, *Are You Experienced*, in early 1967, he had drawn an underground following. But 'Hey Joe', 'Purple Haze' and 'The Wind Cries Mary' propelled him into the UK top ten. By the time he recorded his searing version of Dylan's 'All Along the Watchtower', he was a star on both sides of the Atlantic.

Martin believed London was central to his success: 'Jimi Hendrix could only have happened in London ... London was so welcoming to people at that time. He dressed London. Everyone was a dandy then, everyone dressed in fancy clothes.' London was fertile soil for artists from elsewhere. Paris may have been the artistic mecca of the late nineteenth century and Berlin during the Weimar Republic, but by the late sixties London drew artists, musicians and photographers from Australia, South Africa and the United States.

Martin began working on an image of Hendrix while at the Pheasantry. He based it on a black and white photograph by Linda Eastman (later McCartney) of Hendrix, white Fender in hand, performing at a Central Park music festival in New York in July 1967. In it Jimi's eyes are closed, his arm outstretched, parallel to the guitar's neck.

Philippe Mora saw his flatmate create his Hendrix poster. As a filmmaker, Philippe was experimenting with cel animation at the time; it was a process used by Walt Disney, whereby an outline is drawn on plastic and coloured in from the back. Martin became intrigued by the process. 'I was working with Mylar plastic. I've always loved the clarity that plastic gives you,' Martin said. 'I laid a sheet of Mylar over it and traced the image ... I probably painted the red explosion from the guitar first.'

He splashed colour on the work, which he laid flat on the Pheasantry's floor—'otherwise the colour would have run'. The air around Hendrix appears to crackle. Blue streaks emanate from his head and shoulders, part halo, part force field. His guitar explodes with electric energy. 'I splashed that [paint] like a Jackson Pollock. It's completely influenced by Jackson Pollock, that style, radiating from him.'

Provocatively, Martin signed his name near Hendrix's groin. But along the way, the image of Hendrix was reversed. It meant Hendrix, who famously played left-handed, appeared to be playing right-handed when the image was first printed by Big O Posters. The poster was withdrawn and reprinted. By the time it appeared in *Oz* number 15, Hendrix was left-handed. The reversal was the result of the cel animation process, which requires working on the reverse side. Martin was mortified by his error, but knew he had captured Hendrix's essence.

'I know about music emotionally, but I don't know about it technically—hence my mistake of him playing the wrong way round,' Martin said. 'I didn't know whether he was right-handed or left-handed to tell you the truth. Apparently I did it the wrong way around in the original version … People in the music world wouldn't have taken it seriously. But the effect was it said Jimi Hendrix anyway.'

Martin created many variations of the image over the years. He edited out the microphone stand and he changed the colour of Hendrix's guitar—in some versions the instrument is white or pink or yellow. In others it almost vanishes in a blaze of colour. A few years before Martin died, he went back to the original negatives and reworked the image in perspex.

When John Lennon controversially commented that The Beatles were more popular than Jesus Christ, it was sacrilege to some, especially in the US. But to many under thirty it was a statement of fact. Musicians were at the pinnacle of Britain's new cultural order, their power unprecedented. So when Martin began taking musicians as his subject, in a sense he was doing what artists have always done, taking royalty and the aristocracy as subjects. Except he painted pop royalty. 'The groups ruled, they were the kings of the day,' said Martin.

By the late sixties, there was a brief, idealistic belief that music had the power to change consciousness and society. The Fugs captured the idea in their song 'When the Mode of the Music Changes, the Walls of the City Shake'. The title was borrowed from Plato and the band appealed to Martin. In the United States, musicians—Bob Dylan and Joan Baez among them—were identified with anti-Vietnam and civil rights movements. In Britain, where such issues had less immediacy, the music was less overtly political, yet more innovative. 'It was the turning of a page,' Martin said. Bands such as The Beatles and the Rolling Stones had drawn Martin to London. He loved their music, humour and attitude. But in London, the mode of the music continued to change. Martin arrived as Pink Floyd, Hendrix and Cream were poised to produce some of the most distinctive music of the era.

No music was more identified with the summer of 1967 than *Sgt Pepper's Lonely Hearts Club Band. The Times* critic Kenneth Tynan hailed it enthusiastically as 'a decisive moment in the history of Western civilisation'. It was certainly the soundtrack to the Summer of Love. The album was in tune with the times and yet peculiarly British. A concept album, it evoked cheap seaside holidays in the Isle of White, fairgrounds and brass bands. But it looked to the mystic east with Harrison's 'Within You Without You'. And 'Lucy in the Sky with Diamonds'—with its tangerine trees and marmalade skies—seemed to conjure an LSD trip, despite John Lennon's insistence that the song was inspired by his son's drawing. And by the time the album closed with the line 'I'd love to turn you on', many already had.

Artist Pete Blake's cover collage was a pop art pantheon. Cut-outs of Marilyn Monroe, Elvis Presley and Marlon Brando shared the cover with Carl Jung, Karl Marx and Lewis Carroll. The Beatles were attired in lolly-coloured military-style uniforms. 'A hallucination of an English childhood,' was how writer James Button later described it. With his nostalgia for childhood and immersion in psychedelia, little wonder Martin was transfixed when he first heard it at Robert Whitaker's Joubert Studios. He did so with Francis Bacon's model and muse Henrietta Moraes, with whom he had become friends. Moraes, a beauty and a hellraiser who battled drugs and alcohol, had been recently released from prison. She later became close to another of Martin's friends, singer Marianne Faithfull. Moraes contributed to June *Oz* a lengthy article critical of a quasi-religious organisation called The Process, a Scientology splinter group making inroads into the Chelsea and Mayfair sets with its brand of mind control.

Mind-bending and mysticism were in the air the summer The Beatles discovered the bearded Indian guru Maharishi Mahesh Yogi and his technique of transcendental meditation. Martin created a series of tarot cards for the June issue of *Oz*. He took the major arcana, the most significant twenty-two cards in the deck of seventy-eight, and created collaged images for them, including of the Fool, the Devil and the Sun. Martin's trademark wit was evident when he depicted the High Priestess as Mary Poppins and the Emperor as Timothy Leary.

By the end of the year, Martin's art and the counterculture that had helped spawn it belatedly caught the attention of the mainstream press. The up-market *Observer* newspaper's colour supplement dedicated an issue to London's underground scene, in which critic George Melly singled out Martin's Bob Dylan poster as outstanding. 'If such a deliberately transitory art form of the Underground poster could produce a work of permanent interest, this could well turn out to be it,' Melly wrote.

He described Martin as the chief designer of the underground, together with the design duo Hapshash and the Coloured Coat (artists Nigel Waymouth and Michael English), who created posters for the

UFO Club and were associated with *IT* magazine. But Martin's ideas were more original than Hapshash's, Melly argued. Also in Martin's favour, said Melly, was his connection with *Oz* rather than the more hippie *IT*, with its naïve confidence in mind-expansion as an answer to society's problems: 'Sharp's posters seem divided between a bitter political disillusion and the more agreeable if hackneyed universe of the Flower children.'

Melly argued that the underground was the first pop explosion to have evolved a graphic means of expression. While previous British pop movements had developed a visual style, these had been confined to clothes, hairstyles, and choice of scooter or transistor radio. In contrast, the underground had consciously evolved a graphic imagery to provide a parallel to its musical, literary and philosophical aspects, he argued.

Liverpool-born Melly, an eccentric polymath who was also a jazz musician, *The Observer*'s film and television critic and a lecturer on art history, became a champion of Martin's work. The colour magazine also carried a who's who of the underground, which included Richard Neville, along with DJ John Peel, The Beatles, John Hopkins—UFO Club and *IT* founder—and poet Pete Brown, who also wrote lyrics for Cream. Back in Australia, *The Sydney Morning Herald* reported that Martin's Dylan poster had 'exploded on to London's Underground scene'. The paper noted his inclusion in *The Observer* magazine and dubbed him the 'king of the kinky-poster makers'.

Australian Clytie Jessop opened her London gallery at 271 King's Road in 1967. The building was dilapidated when she moved in, but the peppercorn rent meant she could take a gamble on the artists she showed. Australians Philippe Mora, Michael Ramsden, Barbara Hanrahan and Jessop's brother-in-law David Boyd—married to her sister Hermia—were among those she exhibited. Every three weeks, Clytie had a new show. Her gallery was a lively salon and her openings legendary for the glamorous crowd they attracted and the free-flowing liquor. She recounts: 'Serving spirits ended up costing less than the usual cheap wine served at openings. We offered both but most people preferred spirits which they drank slowly, rather than guzzling down the vino.'

Clytie was also known for a spirit of a different sort. She appeared briefly but memorably as the ghost of Miss Jessel in the movie *The Innocents*, based on Henry James' *The Turn of the Screw*. The film and visual arts world also intersected at her gallery. Clytie was delighted when Richard Neville wandered in one day with Martin. Martin had impressed Clytie when she first encountered him at a party in Sydney in 1963, engaged in an argument with Bob Hughes and Colin Lanceley: 'Their friendly verbal fencing had me spellbound.'

With her gallery just a ten-minute walk from the Pheasantry, she continued to see Martin frequently. Jessop lived above the gallery; she remembers Martin being taken by her bright yellow walls and the icons on them. She witnessed his growing interest in van Gogh. They went together to a landmark van Gogh exhibition in 1968 at London's Hayward Gallery: 'He was so carried away by that exhibition.' And she recalls Martin reading van Gogh's letters: 'He was very taken with all the letters and became obsessed with van Gogh at that time.'

CHAPTER 9

'I NEED TO BE POSSESSED BY SOMETHING BIGGER THAN ME'

Pink clouds swirled against the turquoise sky. The plump orange ball of the Spanish sun paused just above the horizon before plunging into the sea. The gold rays faded to a black starry night, a diamond sky invisible in London. Martin strolled into the Fonda Pepe café on the island of Formentera, where the owner leaned against the bar, a cigarette dangling as always from his lips. Pepe, the owner of the café, wasn't much of a talker; he was wary of the beatniks and hippies who had increasingly come to his village. But Martin had begun to penetrate the owner's reserve.

Martin sat at a table as Judy Collins' 'I Think it's Going to Rain Today' played in the background. Martin had returned to the Balearic Islands that had inspired his 'Tales of Brave Ulysses' in autumn 1967 and was staying in the village of San Fernando. His skin was browned from trips to the beach where he spent his days diving and swimming. He swam slowly underwater like a fish. He had bought a flute and sat on cliffs high above the water, emulating the sound of the wild sea below.

He missed his London girlfriend Eija, to whom he wrote meandering, lyrical letters punctuated with drawings—of Pepe, fish and himself. He told her of his delight when he found a pair of brightly painted wooden statues of Mickey Mouse and Donald Duck in a local shop: 'Fancy meeting them here! … my heathen idols.' He enjoyed the quiet uncomplicated island life, even as he wondered if it might be too uncomplicated for him and sought a diversion. One night he wandered the island in vain for hours, in search of a party.

The evening darkened as he sat writing in the café and the starry sky brought to mind his favourite childhood book. 'There are so many stars one cannot imagine how many, there must be a star for every person who is alive now and who will [live] and who has lived. There are many for you and there is one where the Little Prince lives and waters his rose and shields her from the winds.' Martin had been reading other tales, too, by Antoine de Saint-Exupéry, who wrote lyrical works about flight in such books as *Wind, Sand and Stars*, *Flight to Arras* and *Night Flight*. Reminders of childhood filled Martin's sleep; he dreamed he was at his paternal grandmother's family Christmas party as she sang a song about the Little Prince.

He hadn't bothered with other women, he told Eija, largely because there were few around. He shared Pepe's reservations about the hippies, who abused the generosity of locals: 'They do not take too kindly to people like me—but my smile wears chinks in their armour ... I will do a cartoon about the Love Generation thieves, they spoil all they touch with their selfishness,' he wrote. He was about to return from Formentera to London in late October, but had missed the chance to speak to *The Observer*, which was preparing its hippie issue: 'I would have liked to talk to them—but perhaps it's best to let the posters talk instead.' He signed off as Sunshine Supermart with a whimsical cartoon of himself, flying back to London with wings and flippers, and holding an umbrella in his outstretched arm, like Mary Poppins. In the sea below, he drew a fish with a thought bubble: 'Glad he's gone.'

Eija Vehka-aho was not the only woman in Martin's life at that time. Many young women were drawn to the rich, talented artist with the rock-star looks. A parade of women made fleeting appearances at the Pheasantry. Eric Clapton recalled his flatmate's appeal in a later ABC documentary: 'He was a fantastic ladies' man, he had women queuing up, it was just wall to wall. Girls would be coming out of his bedroom and going home and ... half an hour later another would go in.'

Eija was aware of Martin's romantic dalliances. 'He wasn't hiding it ... he was kind of tasting this and that, different shapes, different colours, different nationalities ... they were always beautiful. They were beautiful bodies ... it was very important that they were like beautiful sculptures.' Although most of these encounters were fleeting, Martin remained in contact with Anou Kiisler, back in Australia. He had told Eija from the outset about Anou, the girlfriend who had inspired 'Tales of Brave Ulysses'. But in the spring of 1968, Anou was about to arrive in England. A distraught Eija fled to the home of Richard Neville and Louise Ferrier. Louise recalls: 'Eija left [Martin] about four in the morning and came over to our place. Then he met Anou at the airport ... Eija stayed with us for a while and she just cried and cried and cried.'

As Martin and Anou attempted to rekindle their relationship, Eija returned to her parents' home in Finland. Her departure threw Martin into turmoil. Many of his paradoxes and conflicts came to a head; he was paralysed by indecision, desperate for peace but drawn to chaos, and aware of his fear of intimate relationships.

The day Eija left London, Martin wrote to her full of remorse. He considered himself a cheat, a coward and a waster, aware for the first time of the pain he had caused her: 'I feel so clumsy with pearls cascading through my fingers ... now it is you who are away and she [Anou] who is here and what I fear is I will push her away because you are there and if you come I will push you away for her ... I played games which must have seemed crude to you ... [Anou] too offers her heart and it too is sore from my abuse.'

Although his actions had prompted Eija's departure, Martin was not about to let her go. He bombarded her with letters and even hoped their relationship would grow. Three days later he sat in the Picasso Café writing again to Eija. He planned to leave again for Formentera next day and wondered if he should abandon London for good. 'The distractions here are too great I rarely seem to find moments of peace—but still I seem drawn to it—avoiding peace until it becomes so necessary that for my own health I must have it.' Although Anou had only just arrived in London, Martin was about to travel to Formentera alone. And he was relieved at the prospect. 'Anou may come later but thank God I've been able to go by myself.'

When he reached Formentera, he stayed at the village of La Mola at the island's highest point. With just two shops and a church, La Mola was smaller and more remote than San Fernando where he had stayed the previous autumn. He sunbathed naked, gazed at the stars and dropped some acid he had brought from England. Yet he felt melancholic, confused and restless, unable to concentrate. He shared a house with his friend the Australian writer Peter Draffin, but found himself irritated by the clickety-clack of Peter's typewriter.

In London, Martin had been reading works by Carl Jung, the founder of analytical psychology, and the mystical German writer Herman Hesse, author of *Steppenwolf*; he hoped to read more on Formentera. He also wanted to immerse himself in the Chinese divination text *The I Ching*. But he found himself picking up and then putting down one book after another: 'I need to be possessed by something, something which is bigger than me because I am so small at the moment. Tiny Martin.'

He felt more peaceful a month later, sitting alone at sunset in a café near the port on Ibiza. He loved ports. He watched the clouds floating over the mountain tops and catching the last rays of the sun; the early evening light was a 'cocoon of blue'. He patted the dogs scavenging around the café's tables. 'London and all its confusion seems miles away,' he wrote to Eija. He had been riding around the island on a motor scooter and had seen horses ploughing the fields, the red earth, green fields and stone walls. 'The eye is very pleased here,' he wrote. Not least by the parade of young Spanish women, who captured his 'lusty eye' as they passed his waterfront café.

His letter to Eija is full of asides as one young woman after another rivets his attention. A woman without a bra—'bounce quiver'—and beautiful brown-skinned girls chaperoned by their 'ugly mothers'. 'More beautiful Spanish girls walk past—like a compass I swing …' The sirens were calling to Ulysses. He felt young and innocent, yet the darkness of the outside world intruded on his artistic and erotic reverie. News had reached him of an assassination. United States Senator Robert F. Kennedy had been shot dead earlier that month as he campaigned for the presidential elections: 'What can be done—what can be done … there is no escape.'

By July Anou had joined Martin on Formentera. But the attempt to reignite their romance quickly stalled. 'Getting very sick of Anou—plans for action—must be brave Ulysses. She is a nice girl but there is no magic—I need magic so much. No magic—no Martin.' He was buoyed by the surprise arrival of Richard Neville on the island. He had left Richard and Anou alone in the house: 'perhaps they will find TRUE LOVE!?'

Amid his crumbling relationship with Anou, the sea offered a release. He swam slowly under the silent water, rolling on his back and looking up at the surface. 'I feel free in the sea—it's flying slowly through the green—no voices—another world—I become a fish not wanting to spear them just to become one of them.' He had painted some small works combining van Gogh's images with his own. Paintings about paintings, he called them. He planned to do bigger versions when he returned to London.

In one of his most candid letters, he told Eija how he had been wrestling with his conflicted feelings, the impact on him of his parents and his fear of emotional intimacy: 'I must rid myself of my ridiculous guilt feeling which I have traced back to my mother's smothering and demands which resulted from my father's coldness which resulted from his mother's—etc, etc—stretching back to infinity—each generation handing on its hang-ups as heritage—If I can work it out and rid myself of it I will perhaps break the vicious circle. I'd really like to have some sort of LSD therapy with a very good psychiatrist to get to the heart of a lot of the problems I have—at least I realise they are problems now—that's one thing that has come into focus in the quietness here. I would like your ideas on the way I behaved. I have a ridiculous fear of involvement and yet I managed to get myself involved in this ridiculous relationship I've half kept going for years.'

His mood was dark and irritable by the time he returned to London in mid-July. He found the city dirty and crowded with sad grey people. He felt like a seagull lost in a city. Back at the Pheasantry, the telephone and the doorbell rang constantly. There were guitars, amps, newspapers and mess everywhere.

Letters were waiting from his mother and Mirka Mora. Both had written to him telling how they had met at an exhibition of Mirka's. But Martin was dismayed by his mother's description of the generous, exuberant Mirka—the woman who had embraced him as her own son—as 'quaint' with 'funny clothes'. Martin described to Eija his mother's response as: 'So Alf—it was a disturbing revelation to see both letters together and what they stood for.' In Martin's lexicon, an 'Alf' summarised all he could not abide: petty, narrow-minded and censorious.

With his relationship with Anou in tatters, Martin made overtures to Eija. He wanted to visit her in Sweden, where she had moved. As he made plans to visit her in August, he wrestled with his emotional immaturity, and Peter Pan-like qualities. 'The boy must become a man or forever remain a boy that grows old,' he wrote. He signed off another letter two days later: 'can this man boy be trusted, can he even trust himself.' And perhaps to underscore his dilemma, he drew beside his comment an image that would reappear in his art—a question mark sitting on the horizon.

———

Eric Clapton told Martin about an American singer he had come across in New York. The performer's name was Tiny Tim and he sang many of the old-fashioned songs that Martin enjoyed by the likes of Al Bowlly, Rudy Vallée and Bing Crosby, the music of his parents' and grandparents' era. Tiny Tim crooned his old-fashioned repertoire in a quavering falsetto voice, accompanying himself on a ukulele he pulled from a shopping bag. He looked as unearthly as he sounded. Long straggly hair, an enormous hooked nose and a powdered white face topped his lumbering 185-centimetre frame. He had taken his stage name from the crippled child from Dickens' *A Christmas Carol*, although he looked more like *Oliver Twist*'s scoundrel Fagin.

Tiny Tim had struggled for years, playing small New York clubs before he was spotted by Reprise Records boss Mo Ostin and landed a record deal. With a debut album, *God Bless Tiny Tim*, a high-profile appearance on Rowan and Martin's *Laugh-In* on American television in January 1968, and a hit single with 'Tiptoe Through the Tulips', Tiny Tim had quickly become an unlikely star. Tiny Tim was about to make his UK debut. He was mobbed by fans and streets were blocked off as he toured London in an open-topped Rolls-Royce ahead of his performance.

Martin dropped some acid and headed to the Royal Albert Hall on Wednesday, 30 October 1968, for a music concert that would change his life. Martin was not the only one in an altered state of consciousness when he took his box seat in an auditorium garlanded with flowers for the sell-out concert. As Marianne Faithfull recalls: 'We all went, a whole load of us, we were all friends. So me, Mick [Jagger], Martin and Eric, Eric's girlfriend ... The Beatles. Everyone went to see Tiny Tim at the Albert Hall. All on LSD.'

Tiny Tim emerged on stage in a cloud of dry ice. With his ukulele and a 45-piece orchestra, he worked his way through some oldies —'Welcome to My Dream', 'Brother Can You Spare a Dime' and 'As Time Goes By'. He chatted about how he had met Bob Dylan. And he sang the Sonny and Cher duet 'I Got You Babe', performing both parts—Cher's in a high falsetto and Sonny's in a baritone register. With members of The Beatles and the Rolling Stones in the audience, he sang 'Nowhere Man' and 'Satisfaction'. And he sang his hit single, 'Tiptoe Through the Tulips'.

Many of Martin's Australian friends were also at the concert, including Jenny Kee, John Weiley, Richard Neville and Louise Ferrier. No one was struck by the strange chanteur in the way Martin was. As Marianne Faithfull recalls: 'Martin had this blinding flash like you got on LSD ... and this blinding flash told him something like, Tiny Tim is God—or something like God—and all you must do for the rest of your life is paint Tiny Tim.'

Martin had encountered a musical Messiah. Tiny Tim was the 'one singer who is all singers, the Spirit of Popular music made flesh', Martin wrote shortly after the concert. On Formentera, he had yearned to be possessed by something bigger than himself. 'Tiny Martin', as he had called himself, was now possessed by Tiny Tim.

Herman Hesse was undergoing a revival. In his 1927 novel *Steppenwolf*, the protagonist Harry Haller is suicidal, torn between his savage animalistic self, which seeks isolation, and his spiritual self, which seeks humanity and love. Martin had read *Steppenwolf* at the Pheasantry and this conflict must have resonated with him, given his own competing desires for both solitude and society. As Harry Haller wanders an unnamed city, he sees a sign advertising 'The Magic Theatre—entrance not for everybody'. The Magic Theatre is for madmen only.

Martin now began work on what would become *Oz*'s most visually compelling issue, The Magic Theatre. Martin and Philippe Mora worked at the Pheasantry cutting, tracing and collaging images for the November issue. Beneath the front cover's red theatrical curtains, The Magic Theatre warns: 'Price of admittance your mind ... entrance not for everybody.' Beneath the curtains, there is a sinister gap-toothed grin on a stick and the back cover is dominated by a question mark that resembles his sketch in his letter to Eija, both recurring images in his art. Across the bottom are images from Eadweard Muybridge of a man running. Martin admired the pioneering photographer, who had been the first to capture the human figure in motion, and Muybridge's images reappear throughout the magazine.

The 48-page issue is a dense stew of colliding images, as news stories, cartoons, artwork and small ads create strange, and at times disturbing, juxtapositions. Starving children appear alongside an obese woman, naked runners sprout lines from Macbeth, and Tiny Tim's head is grafted onto the body of a muscleman, the singer's first appearance in his art. Images from van Gogh and Magritte bump up against astronauts, the Buddha, Mick Jagger, John Lennon and Yoko Ono, dwarves, freaks and savage beasts.

'It was drawn from all sorts of different sources, all images of the times and the past as well,' said Martin. 'I was just digesting all the stuff that was around. There are some wonderful pictures in there, some rather horrible.' Years later, he singled out an ethnographic photograph of a crouching man as among the most impressive. 'This figure struck me so much, and still does—the African man. He looks like he's a Neanderthal. He has an incredible dignity in his face ... He shines through as one of the most prominent images.' The crouching man appears opposite a colour page dominated by Martin's reworking of a van Gogh self-portrait and a quote from the Dutch artist: 'Life is probably round.' Martin conceived *Oz* number 16, The Magic Theatre, including its cover, as an endless circle. 'It's a circular magazine. The back goes into the front and keeps going around.'

The impact on Martin of van Gogh, which is apparent from this time, coincided with the opening of the Hayward Gallery's exhibition. Although Martin had already produced a sunflower yellow poster entitled *Vincent* for Big O, The Magic Theatre contains a small cartoon strip based on van Gogh's *The Artist on the Road to Tarascon*, a copy of which once hung in Martin's father's surgery. Martin would return to this image for decades.

Van Gogh is not the only artist whose influence is apparent in The Magic Theatre *Oz*. So, too, are Max Ernst and Francis Bacon as well as John Heartfield, a German political artist who used photomontages to protest against Nazism.

The all-graphic Magic Theatre issue received a mixed reception. No one had seen a magazine like it. Critic Robert Hughes was impressed: 'Sharp has assembled one of the richest banks of images that has ever appeared in a magazine; and if your response is to say it is not a magazine at all, you should rethink your categories. To my surprise, I find myself prepared to ignore the gaucheries, the illiterate Sharp spelling, the word balloons that sometimes read as if they were written by Andre Breton's bastard child out of Grandma Moses ... None of this will matter in a few years' time; what does matter and makes the Magic Theatre *Oz* the only first-class issue in the last sixteen, is that at last a magazine has broken the mould in a lyrical and decisive way. As a frequent non-reader, I can promise you that the readers *Oz* loses through such an experiment are no loss.' Years later, writer Jonathon Green singled out The Magic Theatre issue as 'arguably the greatest achievement of the underground press.'

Martin became increasingly involved in film in London. With photographer Bob Whitaker he created a gothic parody, *Darling, Do You Love Me?*, a three-minute tale about a woman who loves to death a little man. Its unlikely star is Germaine Greer, two years before *The Female Eunuch* made her an international name. In the film, a vampiric Greer—with kabuki-like white-powdered face, black eye shadow and a mane of dark hair—pursues, harasses and cajoles an unprepossessing man in a straw hat and glasses (Alistair Burg).

Martin is credited with writing the script, whose only spoken lines are 'Darling, do you love me?', which Greer operatically screeches throughout. It was based on a four-panel cartoon strip Martin had drawn a few years earlier. Martin's smile-on-a-stick makes an appearance in the film. The man ignores Greer's increasingly frenzied demands until she eventually strangles him. The film, funded by the British Film Institute, is a send-up of the clingy, demanding female.

Martin also became involved in the era's dark, iconic film, *Performance.* This crime thriller starred Mick Jagger, in his first screen role, as the jaded, reclusive rock star Turner. James Fox was an East End gangster, Chas. On the run from mobsters, Chas moves into Turner's bohemian house, where he lives in a ménage à trois with two women. Anita Pallenberg, then girlfriend of Keith Richards, is the decadently alluring Pherber and an androgynous Michele Breton plays Lucy. Amid a cocktail of drugs, sexual experimentation, rock'n'roll and mind games, Turner and Chas's roles reverse.

The film, by first-time directors Donald Cammell and Nicolas Roeg, shifts boundaries between reality and fantasy, on and off camera. It had a real rock star—Jagger was at the height of his powers as the Rolling Stones' dark, charismatic frontman—real bohemians and real underworld figures. These included John Bindon, who was a party with Litvinoff to the assault of Nicky Kramer in the aftermath of the Redlands bust. Bindon combined acting—including bit parts in the movie *Barry Lyndon* and the TV series *The Avengers*—with thuggery, and later faced trial for a gangland murder. He was dubbed 'Big John' for his twelve-inch penis and his pub party trick was threading this through the handles of five half-pint beer glasses.

Marianne Faithfull, then Jagger's girlfriend, has called the film 'a seething cauldron of diabolical ingredients ... a bitch's brew'. And Keith Richards has described the film's corrosive effect on his relationship with Pallenberg and pointed the finger at co-director Donald Cammell, whom he called 'a twister and a manipulator whose only real love in life was fucking other people up' and 'the most destructive little turd I've ever met'. A descendant of the Cammell Laird shipbuilding dynasty, visitors to his childhood home had included the notorious occultist and family friend Aleister 'The Beast' Crowley.

Performance was the first film produced by American Sandy Lieberson, who had been an agent, including for Peter Sellers, Richard Harris, Serge Leone and the Rolling Stones. Martin's underworld friend David Litvinoff was a consultant on the operations of East End gangsters. Lieberson recalls: 'David was very instrumental in helping us do the research for *Performance* and helped putting us in touch with the Krays, and that whole London gangster scene in the sixties.'

Through Litva, credited as dialogue coach and technical adviser, James Fox visited Ronnie Kray in jail to help prepare for his role. Aspects of the film seem to echo Litva's life. When Chas brutally shaves a character's head, it was a punishment Litva knew all too well. Litvinoff had once been bashed unconscious, his head shaved before being hung naked and bleeding from the railings of his Kensington High Street flat. Who was behind the walloping was unclear, but suspicion fell on Lucian Freud, who had a reputation for violence.

If Warner Bros, which funded the film, were expecting a Rolling Stones version of The Beatles romp *A Hard Day's Night*, this was far from it. Martin was drawn into the film, possibly through Litva. Sandy Lieberson, who became a long-time friend of Martin's, was an occasional visitor to the Pheasantry and recalls Martin's involvement: 'He

Henry Sharp and Joan Ritchie's Darling Point wedding in 1940 was a society affair. (Courtesy of the Estate of Martin Sharp)

Martin, aged 22 months, was an only child. (Courtesy of the Estate of Martin Sharp)

Martin, aged three on his Christening day, with his grandfather, industrialist Stuart Ritchie. (Courtesy of the Estate of Martin Sharp)

Martin at Sydney's prestigious Cranbrook School in 1956.
(Courtesy of the Estate of Martin Sharp)

Martin and friends farewell photographer Robert Whitaker, 1964. Left to right: (back) Georges Mora, Philippe Mora, Gail Bilu, Peter Burns, Anou Kiisler, Mirka Mora, Martin; (front) Gail Bilu's daughter, Peter Burns's daughter, Tiriel Mora and William Mora. (Photo: © Robert Whitaker)

(From left) Richard Neville, Martin, Richard Walsh and Francis James celebrate outside court after winning their Sydney *Oz* obscenity appeal in 1965. (Photo: © Mike Molloy)

Martin prepares for his first solo exhibition,1965. (Photo: © John Weiley)

Richard Neville (left) and Martin with their final issue of Sydney *Oz*,1966.
(Photo: © Robert Whitaker)

Martin and his Finnish girlfriend, model Eija Vehka-aho, c. 1967.
Martin wrote some of his most candid letters to Eija during their long correspondence. (Photo: © Robert Whitaker)

Martin (left) outside Dandie Fashions, King's Road, Chelsea, with friend, 1967.
(Photo: © Robert Walker, full credit details on page 324)

Martin made his first trip back to Sydney from London during the summer of 1968–69. (Photo: © Robert Walker, full credit details on page 324)

A question mark was among the recurring motifs Martin's worked on during his 1969 Sydney visit. (Photo: © Robert Walker, full credit details on page 324)

On the eve of the Yellow House opening in April 1971, Martin sits with the mercurial and bare-chested David Litvinoff, and friends. (Photo: News Ltd)

Martin presides at a Yellow House meeting, 1971. (Photo: © Greg Weight)

Martin in the Yellow House's Stone Room, where he and Brett Whiteley fought over their painted homage to Hokusai, 1971. (Photo: © Greg Weight)

Nell Campbell, who danced at the Yellow House, later appeared as Columbia in *The Rocky Horror Picture Show*. (Photo: Alamy)

'There's only possums up there', Jo Sharp told her religious son.
(Photo: Bernard Cumming, courtesy of *Quadrant*)

The Eternal Troubadour, Tiny Tim, held court at Wirian in the early 1980s.
(Photo: © William Yang)

Martin, in the early 1980s, had an intense relationship with artist Cressida Campbell. (Photo: © William Yang)

Artist Peter Kingston (left) and Martin worked to save Sydney's Luna Park. Martin restored the giant smiling face. (Photo: Martin Brannan, courtesy of Fairfax Media)

With her theatrical make-up and costumes, Yensoon Tsai, with Martin, was a mysterious presence at Wirian in the 1980s. (Courtesy of the Estate of Martin Sharp)

Martin's long friendship with Lin Utzon helped effect a reconciliation between her architect father, Jørn Utzon, and the Sydney Opera House. Martin (left), Lin and her husband Count Hugues de Montalembert in 2001. (Photo: Roslyn Sharp)

Martin reworked paintings for decades. Some lined Wirian's entrance hall in 2006.
(Photo: Quentin Jones, courtesy of Fairfax Media)

The Sydney Morning Herald

The Herald is made from recycled fibres

No. 52,941 First published 1831
MAY 26 – 27, 2007

WEEKEND EDITION

$2.20 (inc GST)
smh.com.au

LUNA PARK BLAZE Niece links Saffron to seven deaths

Michael Johnson, 13 | Jonathon Billings, 13 | Seamus Rahilly, 13 | Craig Godson, 4 | Damien Godson, 6 | Richard Carroll, 12 | John Godson

They weren't meant to die

Kate McClymont

AFTER almost 30 years of speculation, a niece of the late Abe Saffron has revealed that Australia's most notorious crime figure was behind the fire that killed seven people riding Luna Park's ghost train in June 1979.

"I don't think people were meant to be killed," Anne Buckingham told the *Herald*.

The daughter of Saffron's late sister and business partner Beryl Buckingham also confirmed that – despite years of denials by Saffron – her uncle sought control of the fun park after the fire.

Saffron, who was linked to seven other blazes, was the subject of a later National Crime Authority investigation into the fires. The NCA's final report noted that a Corporate Affairs Commission inquiry had failed to establish that Saffron became the owner, but the authority was scathing about the original police investigation.

While the trails had gone cold, the report stated: "Luna Park, it was alleged, had been coveted by Saffron for over 20 years and the fire in the ghost train had been lit as a trigger to evict the incumbent tenants and gain control of the park lease for himself."

Ms Buckingham said her uncle liked to "collect things" and the park was one of them.

When asked if she knew the identity of the person responsible for lighting the fire, Ms Buckingham remained silent. Her revelations emerged during an extended interview about her uncle for the *Herald's the (sydney) magazine*, to be published on Thursday. She laughed nervously when the subject of Luna Park was raised. "The fire at Luna Park – very strange that fire," she said before adding that no one was meant to die.

Ms Buckingham is contesting Saffron's will. Late yesterday she called the *Herald* to demand it not publish this story. It would not "advance" her cause, she said. She then sent a letter denying she had uttered the words attributed her, although they are recorded in a face-to-face, taped interview.

At 10.15 on the night of June 9, 1979, flames engulfed the ghost train at Luna Park. Six children and one adult were killed. They included four year 7 boys from Waverley College, Jonathan Billings, Richard Charles Carroll, Michael David Johnson and Seamus Rahilly.

The news of Saffron's suspected involvement was met with shock by some of the families involved. "We have always wanted a conclusion on our son's death," said the parents of 13-year-old victim Jonathan Billings, Sydney and Irene, in an email to the *Herald*. "Even though this knowledge has caused us shock and grief, we shall continue our journey with peace, whilst loving and caring for our children and our grandchildren."

Also killed was Jennifer Godson's entire family – husband John and their young sons, Damien and Craig. Clutching ice-creams, Mrs Godson, of Warren, had been waiting for them to finish their last ride on what was to

Continued Page 13

Linked to the tragic fire ... the late crime boss Abe Saffron. Photo montage.

■ FIREPOWER

Payments to players put heat on the Force

Gerard Ryle and Jacquelin Magnay

WALLABY players including Matt Giteau, the country's most expensive recruit, are entangled in secret payments that have the potential to rock the Australian Rugby Union.

A swag of cash and share inducements involving the controversial Perth fuel technology company Firepower were used to woo players to the Western Force Super 14 club in breach of ARU protocols.

The ARU has been concerned about these secret payments and offers to players by the Western Force to tempt them across the Nullarbor to join the two-year old Super 14 team.

The *Herald* has learnt that the chief executive of Western Force, Peter O'Meara, was directly involved in introducing the Firepower sponsor Tim Johnston to at least one player-manager. Under the protocols, no state union is to be involved in facilitating, procuring or arranging third-party deals as an inducement to sign any player without ARU approval.

Documents seen by the *Herald* refer to the possibility of tens of thousands of dollars in additional payments to players involving a potential arrangement with Firepower. Mr O'Meara's signature appears at the bottom of one of them.

But Mr O'Meara told the *Herald* that no offers had been underwritten and he had not facilitated any meetings between players or their agents and Firepower.

Mr O'Meara, who is touted as favourite to fill the vacant job of ARU chief executive, said he had no knowledge of any third-party deals.

"Any arrangement that Firepower has negotiated with sports people, Western Force, ARU or cricket or racing, they have all been done through that organisation, not through me," he said. "I haven't facilitated any of those

Continued Page 4

The Sydney Morning Herald linked the Luna Park fire to crime boss Abe Saffron in 2007. (Image: Fairfax Syndication)

Martin remained friends with Eric Clapton and caught up with his former flatmate after the musician's Sydney concert in 2009. (Photo: Angelica Tremblay)

Singer Marianne Faithfull, who attended Tiny Tim's London concert with Martin, visited him at Wirian in 2010. (Photo: Roslyn Sharp)

Despite failing health, Martin painted from his wheelchair in the months before his death in 2013. (Photo: Roslyn Sharp)

created quite a bit of the artwork that was on the walls in *Performance*. He was very, very helpful and very much a part of helping to create an atmosphere and mood in Turner's house.'

Turner's decaying mansion is a Moroccan-style fantasy. Martin's art is apparent in several scenes. His Dylan poster appears—with a few collaged additions—as does his image of Mick Jagger, a version of which appeared on the cover of *Oz*. And in Chas's bathroom scene, some of the early portraits Martin painted at Cranbrook appear. Martin had a number of the paintings sent over from Sydney for the film.

Although Martin is not credited in the film—he settled for payment instead—he spent time on set as Turner's house was being prepared for filming in autumn 1968. At the completion of filming, Martin wanted his paintings back and wrote to Eija from Sydney to try to get them from Donald Cammell's brother, David: 'Ask him for my Boyhood paintings, and the poster of Mick Jagger (called Turner and his Purple Orchestra) which I did for the film. The first are the most important.' But the portraits were never located and are now lost.

Performance received mixed reviews when it was released in 1970, but it has since undergone a critical reappraisal. Film critic Philip French has described it as encapsulating 'the culture of Swinging London at its most seductively corrupt'.

Freya Mathews was in the bath when she heard banging on the Pheasantry's staircase one morning. She thought the commotion was tradesmen carrying ladders up the winding stairs. She carried on soaking. Wrapped in a towel she eventually walked down the hallway from the bathroom and entered the main room. There she found Martin and her boyfriend, Philippe, in a room full of police.

As the police scoured the flat for drugs, across the road at the Picasso Café, American photographer Bob Seidemann was finishing a cup of coffee. Seidemann had been staying at the Pheasantry, sleeping on the mezzanine. He had arrived a couple of months earlier, when Clapton sent his Rolls-Royce to pick him up from the airport. The pair had met backstage at the Filmore Auditorium in California. Seidemann had previously produced iconic images of a semi-naked Janis Joplin and the Grateful Dead.

As Seidemann crossed the road and walked up the path to the Pheasantry, he heard a familiar voice shout out to him. 'It was Martin saying, "Run, Bob. It's the cops,"' says Seidemann. 'I did a quick right turn, but they [the police] pulled me over. I was the only hippie on the block. The detective said I was the only one running down the King's Road.'

The raid was led by Detective Sergeant Norman 'Nobby' Pilcher. The detective had been carving a career by busting rock stars. Pilcher's target at the Pheasantry was Eric Clapton. But the musician wasn't there; Clapton had been tipped off by Cream's drummer Ginger Baker that he was in Pilcher's sights and had gone away, not expecting his flatmates would be busted instead.

Martin, Philippe and Freya were taken to Chelsea police station where they were held in a filthy cell. Richard Neville and Clytie Jessop arrived and bailed them out. Clapton's manager, Australian Robert Stigwood, provided a lawyer when the case went to court. Martin acknowledged the dope was his and charges against his two young flatmates were dropped. Martin's lawyer told him to expect a small fine and advised him to express contrition to the magistrate.

But shortly before the bust, Martin had extolled the merits of marijuana smoking to a British government inquiry, chaired by Baroness Wootton of Abinger, whose report advocated more lenient penalties for cannabis. Although Martin was not about to change his tune, no one expected him to grandstand in court. Philippe cringed as Martin disregarded his lawyer's advice and used his court appearance to advocate the widespread use of cannabis—not least by His Worship. Instead of a rap on the knuckles, Martin was fined more than fifty pounds.

Detective Pilcher went on to bust the Rolling Stones, Donovan, George Harrison and John Lennon, who obliquely referred to the detective as Semolina Pilchard in 'I am the Walrus'. Pilcher was later disgraced and convicted of perjury.

Inspired by the Marx Brothers, Hollywood musicals and Bertolt Brecht, Philippe Mora decided to make a movie. *Trouble in Molopolis* was shot in the Pheasantry and around World's End on the leftover film, known as short ends, from *Performance*, and was funded by Eric Clapton and Australian artist Arthur Boyd.

Philippe convinced many of his Australian friends to appear in his first film. It included Martin as a mime, Germaine Greer as a cabaret singer, Richard Neville as a public relations man and Jenny Kee as Shanghai Lil, a Chinese prostitute. The script called for a madman in the role of the mayor. Philippe had an idea. Why not cast a real madman? Martin approved. Such was the atmosphere at the time—when definitions of madness and sanity were up for grabs, and real rock stars and gangsters appeared in films—that casting a madman seemed to Philippe a stroke of genius.

Fortuitously or not, the Pheasantry had a resident lunatic. John Ivor Golding, a Welsh vagrant, appeared at the Pheasantry through David Litvinoff. Golding had been in a mental institution and was on anti-psychotic medication when he began sleeping in the minstrel's gallery. He arrived with a strange pedigree: it was rumoured playwright Harold Pinter had based the tramp Davies in *The Caretaker* on Golding.

As he began filming *Trouble in Molopolis*, Mora realised he had trouble closer to hand with Golding. 'The first day of the shoot, the assistant director said, "We've got a little problem. He's just done a poo in the middle of the set,"' says Mora. It was not an isolated occurrence.

Martin's filmmaker friend John Weiley, who also worked on the film, recalls: '[Golding] hung around the Pheasantry all the time. His life was so busy he didn't have time to take toilet breaks, so now and again we would be filming a scene with John Ivor and he would shake the leg of his trousers and a turd would plop out onto the floor.'

Weiley, who was by then working for Granada Television and based in Manchester during the week, encountered Golding only on weekends. Freya found Golding—who had a fetish for nappies and Johnson's baby powder—a nightmare, even while she admired her flatmates' compassion in putting a roof over his head.

Martin created a full-page photomontage of Golding for *Oz* number 24, in which he is described as having gatecrashed George Harrison's home and the christening of Lord Harlech's grandson. Dressed in a suit, tie and broad-brimmed hat, he stares unsmilingly to camera. The image ran alongside an incomprehensible article by Golding entitled 'Urological Nurturement'. Ironically, after *Molopolis*'s release one reviewer singled out John Ivor Golding's performance as 'quite brilliant'.

CHAPTER 10

BACK AND FORTH

The dome of St Peter's Basilica dominates the Rome skyline. In front of it, the colonnades of St Peter's Square reach out like arms to embrace pilgrims. Martin entered one of Christianity's holiest shrines and artistic masterpieces. Inside, he saw Michelangelo's *Pieta*—then undamaged by the hammer blows inflicted on it in 1972 by the Hungarian-born Australian Laszlo Toth, who claimed to be Christ risen from the dead.

Martin walked down the central nave with its fluted pilasters and statues of the saints to reach the four bronze spiral columns that support the canopy over the high altar. Beyond it, he saw the dove of the Holy Spirit, like a golden window into heaven. Above, the dome cast its crepuscular rays. It was all 'so spectacular and over-decorated', Martin wrote to Eija. He climbed to the roof and sat in the winter sun looking out on the Eternal City.

He entered the Sistine Chapel and looked up at Michelangelo's ceiling, with its images from the Book of Genesis; on the wall behind the altar he saw *The Last Judgment*. A nun was inspecting the images with binoculars and Martin wished he had brought a pair. 'It was so much more than I thought it would be. Sistine Chapel [was] incredible though I could hardly take any of it in.' It was his first encounter with the great Renaissance and Baroque treasures that until then he had seen only in art books, and he felt overwhelmed. He had 'gorged on too many images I almost went blind—If I see another angel I shall faint with exhaustion'. He was amused at the coyness in covering some of the naked statues he encountered: 'All the statues have their cocks broken off and plaster fig leaves instead.'

He loved Rome; he found it soft and beautiful. He explored the Forum and observed the layers of the city's pre-Christian past, the 'pagan centre of Christendom'. And he was reunited with his former Cranbrook teacher, his 'art father', Justin' O'Brien. They exchanged letters over many years, and O'Brien also corresponded with Jo Sharp.

Martin and O'Brien stayed up talking until dawn. There had been much to catch up on. For Martin, 1968 had been a turbulent and creative year. He had finally parted from Anou and been reunited with Eija, who had returned to London in autumn, and he had encountered Tiny Tim. And O'Brien, who was gay, had news of his own. He told Martin about his Italian boyfriend. It was the first time O'Brien had broached the subject with Martin, who sensed his former teacher was relieved to discuss it.

Although gay rights had yet to come to prominence, Martin appears curiously naïve in his attitude to homosexuality. In a letter to Eija, he gives an almost ethnographic account, as though observing an exotic species. In later years, some of Martin's gay friends found him disapproving of homosexuality, yet his youthful attitude is open and non-judgmental. He wrote: 'I spent the whole time with homosexuals—the only people I know in Rome seem to be. So I listened and asked questions and found out quite a lot which I didn't know before. It seems to be a much larger society than I ever realised, especially in the Mediterranean countries ... It seems they are preservers of culture, victims of segregated education and a product of overcrowding, often very sensitive, whether because of their situation or because of their nature I'm not sure. Nature's contraceptive.'

Martin gazed down on rivers meandering to the sea, ploughed farmlands and paddy fields, as his plane descended over Burma and into Bangkok. He saw a golden pagoda glistening in the sun. 'It was so beautiful, I'm sure the Gods would not miss it,' he wrote to Eija mid-flight. His reverie was disturbed by a crying baby. He thought the parents cruel to ignore the infant's howls and threw a ball of paper towards them. He missed and the missile hit a passenger seated behind the parents. Martin ducked for cover. Otherwise, he passed the flight looking out of the window and smoking cigarettes offered by the air hostess, adding to the toxic cloud of tobacco smoke that hung in the cabin.

After his time in Rome, Martin was flying home for a visit in December 1968. He'd been in the air for almost a day: 'My wings are getting tired.' Before he dozed off, he drew in his letter an image of himself asleep in a winged shoe floating in the clouds above Australia. It was his first trip back.

While he had been in London, Martin's grandfather Stuart Ritchie had died. Stuart never reconciled with his daughter, Jo, Martin's mother, and died broken-hearted. Stuart did, however, leave her a modest allowance of two thousand dollars a year. But he left the bulk of his substantial $886,000 estate, including Wirian and Telford, to his widow, Vega. To Martin, he bequeathed $50,000—a considerable sum when men earned on average $3500 a year.

Martin rarely spoke of his father and few of his friends ever met him. But during his visit, Martin made an effort to get to know Henry, who had recently remarried. He had wed his secretary, Dorothy Muller, a few months earlier. 'Getting through to father as much as possible—well it's up to me and I should be ashamed to fail,' he wrote to Eija. He was happy with the progress they made over the Sydney summer: 'Had a few good discussions with my father. Like tentative lovers courting. We are getting closer. He sings old songs on his piano like a tone deaf Tiny Tim, but very nice.'

Dorothy and Henry Sharp lived at Shellcove Road in the Sydney harbourside suburb of Neutral Bay. With her fondness for plaid kilts, the former medical secretary was more *Dr Finlay's Casebook* than Judy Garland, but Martin developed an affection for his stepmother. Henry's boatshed beneath his waterfront house had become the venue for the annual Sharp family Christmas gathering, a tradition his mother, Bessie, had started. Martin, as the oldest of the Sharp cousins, helped hand out presents that year. But the house was a more restrained, conservative environment than at Cranbrook Lane. The curtains were often closed to keep the bright harbour light from fading the interior, including the dining room with its engravings of Napoleonic-era ships and naval battles. In the study, a writing desk was positioned with its back to the dazzling view.

Martin spent the summer working on lithographs and creating images of van Gogh, of suns and hearts and question marks on plastic. He had a welcome-home party at an inner-city club, Paddington RSL, and he spent time with his grandmothers, cousins, friends and his red setter. Martin enjoyed Sydney more than he had expected: 'A nice lot of heads have sprung up like flowers in the wilderness' since he had been away. But he was disappointed to see Sydney *Oz*, which Richard Walsh and Dean Letcher had continued to edit. 'The remnants of *Oz* is a bit sad—old eyes.'

Although Martin had continued to contribute intermittently to Sydney *Oz* from London, it had lost its graphic punch. Nonetheless it had broken some controversial stories, not least suggesting that Sydney's Archbishop Gough—the target of one of Martin's first cartoons—had suddenly resigned his post following an adulterous relationship on a cruise ship. While back in Australia, Martin worked on the final issue of Sydney *Oz*, number 41, which appeared in February 1969. He designed its cover—a psychedelic swirl of eyes and a smiling mouth resembling shark's teeth. Inside, he drew a double-page spread featuring a map of Australia across which Muybridge-like human figures gradually transformed themselves into kangaroos.

Back in London, German-born Sigi Krauss ran an avant-garde gallery in Covent Garden's Neal Street. Sigi was friendly with Philippe Mora and had visited the Pheasantry where he watched Martin cutting up expensive art magazines and making collages. Martin was reluctant to exhibit his work. Gallery shows seemed passé—just for the elite. Posters, magazines and album covers seemed a more democratic way to connect with an audience. But Philippe encouraged Martin to exhibit and suggested the idea to Sigi, who agreed.

Sigi was also a high-end picture framer. He framed work for the prestigious Marlborough Gallery and was familiar with the work of the German Expressionists and Dadaists who had shown there. He saw parallels with Martin's work and that of the earlier Dada collagists. Sigi recalls: 'When I saw Martin's work I thought, he's a modern Kurt Schwitters, he's a male Hannah Höch. It was impossible not to think of the Dada people.' Martin took iconic works by van Gogh, Magritte, de Chirico, Munch, Monet and others and combined them. 'It was amazing how they came together and they became something completely new,' says Sigi.

The collages needed framing before they could be exhibited, and Sigi had an idea. 'I suggested that instead of a mat, there should be a mirror.' And so each of the two dozen works was surrounded by mirrors. Around the distinctive mirror-mount each had a hand-gilded frame in white gold. Martin was thrilled with the result.

Just as he had done for his Sydney solo show, Martin created a witty invitation. His four-page invite for *Sharp Martin and his Silver Scissors* was part-manifesto, part-comic and part-artwork in its own right. 'Smart!' was the only word on the cover, which combined images of van Gogh's chair and bandaged head with Magritte's bowler-hatted men. Inside, Martin called himself a Smartoonist and his works Artoons. He sent up the hyperventilating language of advertising, describing his show as a 'breathtaking new move in the "art game"'. The exhibition opened on 6 March 1969 and showed until 18 April. Sigi recalls that although people loved the work, not one piece sold. If Martin was disappointed, he didn't appear so to Sigi: 'He said he liked them so much he might just keep them.' So the works returned to the Pheasantry.

Meanwhile, his cover for Cream's next album, *Wheels of Fire*, which included 'White Room' and was released in 1968, won the New York Art Directors' Prize for best cover in 1969. The front and back of the gatefold were black line drawings on silver aluminium foil. A three-headed figure on the back was inspired by the carved temple images Martin had seen at Angkor in Cambodia. The monochrome exterior contrasted with the swirling orange, yellow and pink within, with a pair of eyes the dominant image.

Martin also co-wrote another song with Clapton, 'Anyone for Tennis'. It is a jaunty ditty, redolent of Ringo Starr's 'Octopus's Garden'. Yet its cynicism and horrific images—of a Bentley-driving guru and a burning Buddhist monk—undercut the jolly tone and title. Released as a single in 1969, it appeared on later pressings of Cream's *Goodbye* album. The song never garnered the attention of 'Tales of Brave Ulysses', yet it is a lyrically complex and poetic work.

After Cream's demise, Martin designed the first album by Ginger Baker's Airforce, a band that included Steve Winwood (Blind Faith and Traffic) and Denny Laine (The Moody Blues). The image is similar to the cover of The Magic Theatre issue of *Oz*, with its theatrical red curtains, trademark grin and, on the rear, Muybridge's running men. The design marks a departure from the psychedelic style of the two Cream albums. By now Martin's art had become less decorated and was employing blocks of solid colour.

The shift from psychedelia is also reflected in a series of eight works he created at this time on plastic. Dubbed *Smartiples*—perhaps a combination of his name and the brightly coloured English sweets

Smarties—Martin may have intended the translucent works to have been illuminated from behind. Each had an arresting image and a witty title. Some of the images had earlier appeared as simple ink sketches in Martin's letters to Eija. They include a question mark entitled *Wot!*, an erect penis *Standing*, a UFO *Coming*, and a breast *Boo-Zoom*.

As Martin became more involved in film work, album covers and posters, he was less involved with London *Oz*. By then Jim Anderson and Felix Dennis were co-editors with Richard Neville. Dennis had initially been a street-seller for *Oz* before selling its advertising, reviewing record albums and learning from *Oz*'s designer Jon Goodchild. Anderson moved into Neville and Louise Ferrier's place in Princedale Road, Notting Hill, where *Oz* was put together in the basement. Anderson rarely saw Martin, who mixed in different circles and took his material straight to Goodchild.

Goodchild had been *Oz*'s designer from the outset, with Martin as art director. Martin's last *Oz* cover image was a grinning moon above a Mickey Mouse who juggles stars. It coincided with one of the decade's most dramatic events, the first moon landing, when Neil Armstrong and Buzz Aldrin stepped onto its surface. Martin hired a television set especially to watch the broadcast with Pheasantry residents and friends.

Martin argued with Richard Neville about including Tiny Tim in *Oz*. With his repertoire of vaudeville-era songs, Tiny Tim was hardly a hippie figure and unlikely to appeal to a readership then devouring The Doors, The Moody Blues and early prog-rockers Mott the Hoople. Nonetheless, Martin prevailed and created a double-page spread in December 1969. It coincided with the year's other remarkable televised event: Tiny Tim married a seventeen-year-old fan, Miss Vicki—Victoria Budinger—on Johnny Carson's *The Tonight Show* on 17 December. An estimated forty million US viewers turned in—the largest since the moon landing—as Tiny Tim promised to be sweet, gentle, kind, patient and 'not puffed up'.

Martin's *Oz* spread depicted Tiny Tim, icon-like with a halo, as 'The Spirit of Popular Song'. For Martin, the singer was indeed a Messiah. Richard Neville observed: 'Martin was reinforced and re-energised by Tiny at a time when he was getting a bit sick of the world and London and all the chaos and contradictions of the sixties. At the tail end of the sixties, when some of it was laid bare and people became too stoned or too selfish, Tiny represented an innocence.'

The topless bars and strip joints stretched the length of Sydney's Darlinghurst Road where prostitutes plied their trade. Neon lights flashed their tawdry promise of sex and sin at the Pink Pussycat, Les Girls and the Venus Room. The Vietnam War had been a boon for the saturnalia business in Kings Cross, which filled with American soldiers on R&R (rest and recreation leave). Opposition to the war was growing when Martin made another trip to Australia as the new decade dawned. Moratorium marches were being organised around the country and would draw 200,000 people. 'All the way with LBJ' had been replaced by a different chant: '1, 2, 3, 4—we don't want your fucking war.' Labor had a new leader in the reforming Gough Whitlam and, although his party was narrowly defeated in late 1969, the end of conservative rule was in sight.

Around the corner from the tawdry Kings Cross strip, the radical stage show *Hair*—a musical response to the Vietnam War—gave voice to the changing mood. It had full-frontal nudity and a tribe of free-loving, dope-smoking hippies. The show was directed by Jim Sharman, who had cut his teeth directing *On Stage Oz*. Martin was smitten with one of *Hair*'s tribe, teenager Victoria Cobden. He had encouraged Victoria to audition for the part. Martin had known the former private schoolgirl for several years, and their mothers were friends. Victoria was magnetised by Martin's aura of sophistication—with his latest London clothes, long hair, Camel plain cigarettes—and his circle of glamorous, exciting friends.

Victoria accompanied Martin and his rock critic friend Lillian Roxon to Sydney's Royal Easter Show, where Lillian, in a black kaftan and carrying a kewpie doll, pulled scary faces at the children. He introduced Victoria to Marianne Faithfull and Mick Jagger. And Martin gave her a leather jacket that had belonged to Eric Clapton. Not that Victoria knew initially who Clapton was when Martin, making an international call to his former flatmate one day, handed her the phone. Martin was prone to giving his telephone mid-conversation to whoever was with him at the time, whether the two parties at each end knew each other or not.

Victoria dined with Martin at the home of Francis James, the flamboyant former Anglican Press publisher who had shared a court bench with Martin during the *Oz* and *Tharunka* cases. (In a still mysterious episode, Francis had since then spent three years in a Chinese prison, allegedly for spying; he had been released only after intense lobbying by his friend Gough Whitlam, by then prime minister.)

When Martin arrived at Victoria's family house one day with a Polaroid camera and a little blank journal with the words *My Trip* on its cover, she was willing to share the journey that Martin wanted to document. But this was no road trip; Martin and Victoria didn't get beyond Bellevue Hill. Their trip was on LSD. The only journal entry that was made recorded how the trip got off to a slow start. As the effects eventually took hold, they were startled to see Martin's red setter Danny bounding up. Danny had never been to the house before, but must have followed his master's scent from Martin's Cranbrook Lane house twenty minutes' walk away. They captured their acid trip in a series of grainy and unfocused black and white images, including of Danny the dog.

As their relationship continued, Victoria became pregnant. She did not tell Martin initially. By the time she did, Victoria had decided to have an abortion. Martin tried to dissuade her, and Victoria believed he discussed her pregnancy with his mother. Victoria went ahead with the termination.

Although their romantic relationship ended after about three years, they remained friends until Martin died. But during their relationship, Victoria was by no means his only lover. Indeed Martin's complex romantic life prompted his friend the art patron John Reed to write in 1970: '[Martin] is a lovely person, very creative, gentle and generous; but I am afraid that does not prevent his personal life from being in a bit of a mess.'

Martin shipped his Artoons, including those he had exhibited with Sigi Krauss, to Australia. He had originally planned to show them at the Holdsworth Galleries in Sydney's Woollahra, where his friend and a former Cranbrook teacher Peter 'Charlie' Brown worked. But by the time Martin arrived, Brown and the gallery's owner had fallen out. So Martin approached the Clune Galleries, where he had held his first exhibition before he left for London, and they agreed.

The Clunes had decided to put up for sale the building that housed the gallery, as well as an adjacent property. It seemed likely the demolishers would soon move in. Martin's show was intended as a 'last mad dance on the old decks of the Clune Galleries before the wreckers sank them forever,' as *The Bulletin* later described it.

But when the properties quickly sold, the building's future and the fate of Martin's exhibition became uncertain. The new owner of the properties was a young pastoralist named Ian Reid. Martin and Charlie Brown arranged to meet him at the gallery; the pair asked if they could go ahead with the exhibition. Ian had no immediate plans for the property's redevelopment and so he agreed.

In a strange synchronicity, Ian had crossed paths with one of Martin's London associates. Ian travelled overseas in 1969, including to Brazil where he met actor James Fox, who was on holiday there after starring with Mick Jagger in *Performance*. In the wake of the film, which Fox found traumatic to make, he had a mental crisis and abandoned acting for years. He became an evangelical Christian before returning to the screen; in recent years he has appeared most notably in *Downton Abbey*. Ian and Fox travelled together, including on a raft down the Beni River where Fox told him about David Litvinoff, who educated Fox in the ways of East End gangsters for his screen role. Ian little suspected he would soon come to know Litva himself.

Much of the building at 59 Macleay Street had been rented rooms; although it was rundown, it had good bones with high ceilings and graceful proportions. The three-storey Queen Anne-style terrace designed in the late 1890s had distinctive gables, little balconies and Roman arches. Martin gathered around him a group of people to help ready the gallery space. Terry Clarke, Martin's former maths teacher, arrived with a group of Cranbrook boys, including his young cousin Andrew Sharp, to lend a hand. Another cousin, Kate Sharp, became Martin's assistant. She would wake him up each morning amid overflowing ashtrays and unwashed coffee cups in the gallery building, where he was staying. He wrote hundred-dollar cheques for her to buy paint and supplies of prawns, avocado and coffee. And she helped him paint some of the unfinished works.

Kate met Ian, whom she later married, one day when she and Martin were struggling to unpack crates of art and Ian offered to lend a hand. Kate worried that the space would not be ready in time for the May opening, but other problems also threatened the show: some of Martin's works that were being shipped from London had been held up by a dock strike. 'Lots of work—too much—will miss the sun because I have to work,' he wrote to Eija.

Martin funded the exhibition with money his grandfather had left him. He thought if he was going to invest in anything, he should have the confidence to invest in himself: 'then there's no excuses, there's no one to blame, it falls back on me if I make a success or failure of it,' he told an interviewer.

Martin had begun collaging works by Australian artists into European landscapes, including William Dobell's portrait of *Billy Boy*, which he combined with van Gogh's *Starry Night*. The work arrived back from the framer's just as Martin learned of Dobell's death. The Clunes had championed Dobell, who had painted writer Frank Clune's portrait for the 1949 Archibald Prize. Martin's past was also on display—a schoolboy photograph and the original *Gas Lash*, as well as a book of his mother's collages.

As he prepared the show, *The Sydney Morning Herald* paid a visit in May 1970, keen to see the impact of London on the enfant terrible who had left Sydney as a satirist. Martin's vivid London works—Artoons, paintings, posters and works on plastic—caught the newspaper by surprise. They were a radical departure from his previous incarnation as the acerbic black and white cartoonist of *Oz*. His work still offered social commentary but was 'less cruelly ironic than in the days when he bit the hand that fed him'. He had become preoccupied with van Gogh. 'The more I come to know him, the more I feel he was a saint,' Martin told the *Herald*.

Martin was dismayed to discover that some things had not changed during his absence in London. A new crop of editors at the student newspaper *Tharunka* was being threatened with obscenity, including for publishing the ribald ditty 'Eskimo Nell'. When the case came to court, one of the editors, Wendy Bacon, later a prominent investigative journalist and academic, arrived in a nun's habit emblazoned with 'I have been fucked by God's steel prick'. After being arrested, she spent eight days in Silverwater prison, and was fined and given a two-year good behaviour bond.

Even the artworks of Aubrey Beardsley—the subject of a major London exhibition when Martin arrived in Britain—were still suspect in New South Wales: a Newcastle man was charged with obscenity for possessing some of his prints. These were not the only signs that Australia's censorious attitude endured. Martin told the newspaper that when he arrived at Sydney airport, customs had asked him if he possessed any pornography and scoured for smut his reading matter—Patrick White's *Tree of Man* and a book of van Gogh's letters.

Martin was putting the finishing touches to an image of Mickey Mouse fifteen minutes before guests arrived for his opening. The gallery's exterior was a psychedelic swirl of green, red and blue. The interior was no less dramatic, including one room painted black with a silver ceiling, another one orange, red and blue, and a staircase with pink bannisters. Surreal touches had been added—a plastic fried egg hung from a window. The place resembled a 'pop art haunted house', said *The Bulletin*.

Martin presided over the visual circus like a 'gleeful puppeteer' handing out novelties from a magic shop, the magazine continued. He wore a floppy hat and from his buttonhole a toy woman's leg cheekily emerged out of the centre of a plastic red rose. Tiny Tim and Vera Lynn crooned above the din of patrons. Martin had created an aural as well as a visual collage. Also blasting through the speakers were sound bites of cricketer Donald Bradman's final innings and the moon landing. Martin arranged live music, too. Sydney singer Jeannie Lewis, whose voice encompassed jazz, folk and opera, performed from the top of a staircase.

More than a thousand people crammed the gallery for their first glimpse of the work Sharp had created at the epicentre of the Swinging Sixties. Society dames—*Vogue Australia* editor Sheila Scotter among them—and clean-cut Cranbrook schoolboys rubbed shoulders with artists and long-haired hippies. A black and white fox terrier in a red coat negotiated a forest of sandals and stilettoes, and a figure in a gorilla suit bumped up against Thelma Clune on the stairs. Waiters in dinner suits and black eye masks moved precariously through the crowd holding jugs of red wine aloft. Many in the well-dressed Bellevue Hill set were en route to Checkers to see Shirley Bassey. In the crush, an expensive kolinsky fur stole fell from the shoulders of one of Jo Sharp's friends and was accidentally trodden underfoot by young artist Bruce Goold.

Bruce had not intended any mischief when he arrived at the exhibition with his friend Jon Lewis, the tearaway son of Tom Lewis, a minister in the Askin government and later a New South Wales premier. But during the revelries, an athletic Bruce removed one of Martin's paintings hanging high above the stairwell. Bruce and Jon climbed out of a bathroom window, along a rooftop and out to the street where they loaded the work into Jon's mother's Citroën and drove off.

But the thrill of taking the painting soon paled. They felt guilty and decided to return it. However, they needed to do so furtively. In the dark, they nervously unloaded the painting, entered the gallery's backyard and left it near the rear door. The pair subsequently fessed up to Martin—who until then had been oblivious to the art heist, although mystified how his painting had ended up by the back door.

The social columnists gushed. The exhibition was an 'event to be seen at, a swinging party', said one; 'the wildest most way out scene of the week,' said another. But author Patrick White was unimpressed. It was a 'sleazy exhibition … which even a lot of the social squares have been getting groovy about, but it gave me the horrors. I felt we'd all be better dead, and that the Chinese should take over immediately,' he wrote to a friend in London.

The *Herald*'s critic had a bob each way. The work showed great energy, but was largely parasitic: 'Martin Sharp seems to be still mainly a borrower and commentator, adding only an enormous verve and gusto to the redeployment of familiar ideas and images. But the verve is real, and the impact of the exhibition as a whole—objects and context—is quite uncommonly powerful.'

For all the exhibition's colour and exuberance, *The Bulletin*'s critic Elwyn Lynn detected something darker: '[Sharp] examines his past not through nostalgia or a golden haze but with an anxious eye'. And Lynn noted how van Gogh's bandaged head appeared throughout the show as a symbol of loneliness.

Martin was buoyed by his hastily arranged exhibition and especially by the help he had received from friends, cousins and other artists. He wanted to take this further. He later recalled: 'The enthusiasm was terrific ... And with that enthusiasm I thought you could do [more], because I'd pretty much thrown that show in and created the spaces and things. It was very effective, but you could conceive it more thoroughly.'

Martin was seated in the window of Mrs Beeton's Tent, a small chic Potts Point café where he lunched most days, when he spotted Bruce Goold passing by. Martin sent a waiter to invite Bruce to join him. They dined on smoked salmon and spoke about the exhibition. Martin said he wanted to make the exhibition ongoing and invited Bruce to take part. Martin also met a young Sydney artist, George Gittoes, who had recently returned from New York. They quickly discovered their mutual love of van Gogh, whose letters George had also read.

Martin had been re-reading his book of van Gogh's letters, which he had brought with him from London. In particular he seized on a late episode in van Gogh's life. In 1888, the troubled artist arrived in the southern French town of Arles, where he rented a small run-down house in a seedy neighbourhood. The four-roomed house, full of sunlight beneath a deep blue sky, had a green door and shutters and the outside was painted yellow.

There van Gogh dreamed of establishing an artistic family, drawing like-minded companions to a place of refuge and renewal. Van Gogh created many now-celebrated works there, including *The Night Café* and several versions of his sunflower paintings. But Paul Gauguin was the only painter to join van Gogh in his utopian dream at the Yellow House, as it became known. Although the pair were initially inseparable—their days filled with painting, drinking, visiting brothels and more painting—it was not just the cramped house that made the dream unworkable. Van Gogh and Gauguin were men of strong but vastly different temperaments, and they soon quarrelled. In addition, van Gogh was mentally unravelling. Within three months the dream was over. Van Gogh severed part of his left ear and soon after entered an asylum.

Martin never visited Arles, and the Yellow House was destroyed in World War II. But he was captivated by van Gogh's idealism of a creative community in the sunny south—little matter that the short-lived experiment ended so disastrously. An idea began to take shape as he prepared to leave Australia.

CHAPTER 11

THE YELLOW HOUSE

Martin arrived in Zambia with his new love Ingrid Boulting in August 1970. The South African-born model was an ethereal, pre-Raphaelite beauty. As the poster-girl for Biba, she was one of the era's most recognisable faces. Martin had met her in London, where she had visited the Pheasantry and dined with Martin at the neo-Byzantine Criterion in Piccadilly—Martin had a taste for expensive restaurants. When *Vogue* magazine sent Boulting on a fashion shoot to Zambia in August 1970, Martin joined her.

This was a top assignment. The shoot was to be conducted by leading photographer David Bailey. He had photographed sixties celebrities—from the Stones and Nureyev to the Kray twins—squired a string of beautiful women, and inspired Michelangelo Antonioni's film *Blow-Up*. Also on assignment was model Penelope Tree. Since being photographed at Truman Capote's Black and White Ball in New York City in 1966, Penelope had become one of the fashion world's most in-demand models.

It was unusual for a model's boyfriend to tag along on a shoot, especially on such a high-end assignment. There were deadlines to meet and logistics to manage as they flew around the country for three weeks, in and out of remote airstrips.

Martin was hardly an unobtrusive presence. Penelope recalls: 'Martin was extremely eccentric. We had all these planes to take us to here and there, and appointments we had to make, and he was always incredibly late. He looked like he was just getting out of bed the whole time.'

They travelled to Lake Tanganyika, Lusaka, Kafue National Park and Victoria Falls to produce an eighteen-page spread for the glossy magazine's December issue. Ingrid and Penelope posed in jumpsuits beside zebras, leopards and elephants. They danced around fires with local shamans, who were adorned with feathers and had painted faces. They encountered hippos, antelope and impala.

Meanwhile, Martin became preoccupied with hyenas. And he discovered a new musical instrument—the kalimba, a hand-held African piano. 'He became obsessed with the least attractive animal in the entire animal kingdom,' Penelope says. 'He thought he could communicate with these hyenas . . . he would play to the hyenas on the African piano for hours and hours.'

Martin's eccentric behaviour tested the patience of photographer David Bailey, at that time Penelope's boyfriend: 'David got very fed up with Martin being late for everything. He was just frustrating—the hyenas, the African piano, waiting for him endlessly in hotel lobbies. He was really in his own imagination. We were there for work, we weren't there for cruising around.'

Zambia was an interlude between Martin's London years and his relocation to Australia. By the time he returned to London after Zambia, he was weary of the city that had once enchanted him. The optimism of the mid-sixties had wilted like flowers left over from the Summer of Love. Bohemia was moving out of King's Road and commercialism was moving in.

This was highlighted by the fact that Martin, previously impervious to the noise from the Pheasantry's basement nightclub, now struggled to sleep. 'I remember one night being woken up by a burglar alarm, some boutique with awful clothes going off in the middle of the night. It went on and on forever … they stole everyone's sleep trying to protect their awful clothes … Carnaby Street was moving into King's Road.'

Politically, too, 1970 was a turning point. Harold Wilson's Labour government—on whose watch The Beatles were awarded MBEs—was tossed out by mid-1970. The Conservatives were back in power, Edward Heath was prime minister and his new cabinet included Margaret Thatcher, who quickly busied herself axing supplies of free school milk.

The sixties party was over. The Beatles broke up amid acrimony; the hedonism, excess and drug-taking were exacting a price. By September, Jimi Hendrix—whose electrifying energy Martin had encapsulated in paint—was dead. The musician, twenty-seven, choked on his own vomit while affected by barbiturates. A few weeks later, singer Janis Joplin died of a heroin overdose. Their deaths came on the heels of the drug-related deaths of Beatles manager Brian Epstein, who had encouraged Robert Whitaker to travel to London, and Rolling Stones guitarist Brian Jones.

It was not only rock stars who succumbed. John Weiley recalls the toll drug use took on friends: 'It was as if World War I was still on, and now and again you would hear about a friend who had been lost in the trenches.'

John was among early friends who worried about the effect on Martin of his use of LSD and marijuana. John observed Martin become increasingly withdrawn in London, a far cry from the witty, assured man he had known in Sydney: 'I felt we lost him. Those of us who had claimed to be close friends felt a bit that we had lost him during those London times. He was heavily into acid particularly and that just cuts you off completely … basically it was just drugs that intervened.'

Martin's relationship with Eija Vehka-aho eventually broke down and she moved to Paris by 1971. There she worked with designer Karl Lagerfeld, who designed a collection around her, photographer Helmut Newton and fashion illustrator Antonio Lopez, who filled his French *Vogue* sketchbooks with images of her. Although she loved Martin deeply, she had tired of his infidelity and his emotional ambivalence. Martin's words and actions never matched the images of hearts, suns and rainbows that filled his letters to her. 'He couldn't give his love and commit himself. At the same time, in all the letters he draws the symbols of love, but he could never say "I love you"', says Eija.

Martin told her he felt incapable of love and attributed this to his upbringing. '[He said] his father had held him in his arms once or twice when he was a baby and never after that—that was a big sorrow for him—and that his mother was socialising a lot and a nanny was taking care of him. But also that his mother loved him too much, that was a problem too ... The core of his life was because he was not loved in the right way when he was a child, so he didn't learn to love either, and he never could commit himself.'

Martin had also grown apart from London *Oz* magazine, which had become more overtly political. And he was incensed at the treatment of an image he had sent from Sydney for the April 1970 issue of the magazine. It depicted two figures, Mickey Mouse and the lone artist from van Gogh's *Road to Tarascon*. It was in black and white, but editor Jim Anderson was working on a highly coloured Acid *Oz* issue. Jim added orange stripes to Martin's work and made another embellishment. In the space between Mickey Mouse and van Gogh, he wrote: 'Acid is good for you.'

Jim recalls: 'Martin was furious, but he never said anything to me. He did say things to just about everybody else about how upset he was that his artwork had been treated like this.' Jim's relationship with Martin, which was not close, never recovered. After that, whenever they met, Martin greeted Jim with a formal handshake.

Martin had made no contribution to the May issue of *Oz,* which was guest-edited by a group of teenage schoolchildren. Fifteen-year-old schoolboy Vivien Berger had created for it a sexually explicit cartoon strip of Rupert Bear, a much-loved children's character. The infamous School Kids *Oz* would see Richard Neville, Jim Anderson and Felix Dennis at the centre of Britain's biggest obscenity case.

The more Martin read and re-read van Gogh's letters, the more the idea of realising the Yellow House in the south in the sun grew. Martin wanted to do so not in the south of France—or Formentera—but in the southern hemisphere. In London, he talked about the idea with his filmmaker friend from Sydney, Albie Thoms, who was encouraging. 'I would never have had the opportunity to do it in London. I wouldn't have had the support,' Martin said.

Estranged from Eija, distanced from *Oz* and unable to get another exhibition in London, Martin decided it was time to leave. His Pheasantry companions—Eric and Philippe—had already left the building. Martin's decision to move back to Australia—so far from the centre of the art world—struck some as unusual and sudden. Some wondered why he wanted to leave London at all, having made such an impact with *Oz,* his posters and album covers. If he wanted to move, why not relocate to New York and capitalise on the attention his award-winning *Wheels of Fire* album cover had garnered?

Yet Martin was never driven by strategic career moves or a desire to play the art world game. Martin had taken what he needed from London. His Chelsea years had been his university, from which he graduated with flying psychedelic colours. Martin's images were pervasive during the late sixties, but they were not to be found in art galleries. His posters, especially of Dylan, Jagger, Hendrix, Donovan and *Plant a Flower Child*, captured the imaginations of a generation of young people. Martin's posters adorned their bedroom walls, his album covers were in their vinyl collections, his cover for Timothy Leary's hippie manifesto *The Politics of Ecstasy* was on their bookshelves along with copies of *Oz*.

His travels had prompted artworks, song lyrics and soul searching. In London, he had worked in film, discovered the writings of van Gogh and encountered his eccentric muse, Tiny Tim. Martin had arrived in London as a cartoonist, but left as an artist. He packed up his belongings and flew to Sydney in November 1970.

Martin sat at his large circular wooden table in the bay window with its view over Sydney's Macleay Street. The table was covered with papers, books, magazines, cartoons, scissors, pens, coffee cups, overflowing ashtrays and half-empty packets of Camel cigarettes. He had been working on a book to accompany his next exhibition. *Catalog* would become a collaged book: part manifesto, part scrapbook, part autobiography. For imaginative detail it would rival The Magic Theatre *Oz*. He filled its thirty-six pages with images from his childhood, from *Oz* days and the Pheasantry, and lines from his various influences, from *The Little Prince* and Paracelsus to Teilhard de Chardin and Leonard Cohen.

But it was van Gogh's art and words that featured most prominently. The cover image of van Gogh included the artist's words to his brother Theo: 'The more I think it over, the more I feel there is nothing more truly artistic than to love people.' The quote read like a mission statement for what would become the Yellow House in Sydney.

Martin wandered downstairs to where a space known as the Cloud Room was taking shape. The walls were being painted pale blue and covered in fluffy white clouds. The door, window frames and skirtings were painted silver and a small stage was being installed. It would be the focus of his next exhibition.

His work had gathered pace after he had spent part of the summer since he returned to Sydney up at Palm Beach, where he shared a house with friends, including Bruce Goold, Jon Lewis, and brothers Dick and Greg Weight. Artist Brett Whiteley and his wife, Wendy, had rented the house next door. Whiteley was by then the golden-haired boy of Australian art. Martin had known Whiteley in London, but it wasn't until they returned to Sydney that they spent much time together. The two artists had different temperaments—Whiteley as energetic and talkative as Martin was languid and reserved—but they shared a love of van Gogh.

At Palm Beach, Martin worked on a series of pen and ink drawings, *Footprints on the Road to the Yellow House*. The Yellow House in Macleay Street was still a work in progress. It was yet to be named—or painted—yellow. Indeed, the outside had been painted silver, as had much of the inside. Silver was the colour of Andy Warhol's original Factory, his influential New York studio which drew the hip and creative—artists, musicians, filmmakers and drag queens.

Martin had bought gallons of household silver frosted paint, the type used to paint pipes underneath sinks. He had a way of wordlessly encouraging visitors to assist. His unwritten code was that if you wanted to be part of this artistic experiment, you had to contribute. Bruce Goold recalls: 'He would put the paintbrush on the windowsill and give people this sort of look, as if to say, "You can take over now."'

Martin wanted to create a special environment. He borrowed some furnishings and antiques from his grandmother's home. When Sydney's Trocadero dance hall closed, Martin and Bruce attended the auction of the contents. Martin had his eye on a series of bas-relief Art Deco sculptures of figures from around the world—of Native American, Cossacks and Balinese dancers. 'They were about six feet high, massively heavy, they were beautifully sculpted and painted … and Martin wanted them. I think he got them all for a thousand dollars—but it cost another three thousand dollars to have them cut them down off the walls,' says Bruce.

Martin shipped a large mirror ball from England and installed mirrored doors at the front of 59 Macleay Street. The doors evoked Jean Cocteau's film *Orphée*, in which characters pass through a mirror to an underworld, a portal to a different reality.

Martin spared no expense or effort on the house. He was cavalier about money. He left his Mini Moke parked on the street, untroubled by the dozens of parking fines it attracted. When he reached into his pocket for a cigarette, money fell out like confetti, recalls John 'George' Harrison, a former Cranbrook student who helped out ahead of the exhibition. Harrison gathered up the notes, put them aside and returned them to Martin at the end of the day.

Juillet's restaurant next door, run by Frenchman Patric Juillet and his Australian wife, Chrissie Brett, fed many of the artists. A few paid cash, others ran up lengthy tabs or bartered for their meal or drinks. Juillet's attracted journalists, writers, poets—including Allen Ginsberg—and the odd underworld figure, among them Kings Cross nightclub owner Abe 'Mr Sin' Saffron, who ran much of the city's vice trade, including brothels and gambling activities. Martin would come to learn a great deal about Saffron.

Martin planned to exhibit in his new show his Artoons and other works from his Sydney exhibition a year earlier. But with a twist: the works for *The Incredible Shrinking Exhibition* were reduced to a fraction of their original size. Greg Weight had photographed the previous show, and these formed the basis for the new exhibition. Some were reduced to fifteen centimetres by ten and, as in London, surrounded by mirror mounts in silver frames. Others were just five centimetres square and surrounded by gold mounts and frames. Mirrors were a vital element in the show, which would be entered through the house's mirrored front door.

The exhibition would be in honour of Tiny Tim, Martin told the press ahead of the opening, and 59 Macleay Street had been named the Yellow House after van Gogh's failed venture. Martin was optimistic: 'It didn't work, but it might now.' He was photographed with a group of friends preparing the show. He sat at the bottom of a ladder. A few rungs above him on the ladder was a muscle-bound bare-chested figure, his arms crossed, wearing only a pair of shorts. He was older than the fey, long-haired hippies who stood surrounding Martin. At a casual glance, the older man looked like a builder. It was David Litvinoff.

Litvinoff had arrived in Sydney from Bali. He hinted he was on the run, possibly from the Kray twins. Litva had spent the previous two years in a cottage in the village of Llanddewi Brefi in rural Wales. Exactly why he left London was unclear. He appeared to have had a falling out with his criminal associates, possibly related to his work on *Performance,* which drew on his underworld activities. Martin had visited him in Wales and found him extremely depressed. Martin told him of his plan to start the Yellow House in Sydney and invited him to come for a change of scene.

Litva moved into an upstairs room with walls painted black near Martin's quarters. He was ostensibly the Yellow House's cleaner, or 'garbologist' as he styled himself, but his role was far more complex. He was part court jester, part presiding spirit of Mercury—god of trickery, thieves and guide to the underworld—part Scheherazade, the spellbinding storyteller of the *One Thousand and One Nights*, and part provocateur. He was also a source of dope, which he brazenly smoked on the street. Bruce Goold recounts: 'He had a little joint-rolling machine. He would make the most perfect-looking joints, because he smoked Camel plain [cigarettes], and he would put them into the packet with the Camel plain. And he would think nothing of wandering around [in public] smoking a joint, even though there were cops walking around.'

But Litva had an instinct for self-preservation, as Jon Lewis discovered when the pair drove in Lewis's Renault near Sydney's Central railway station one day: 'The car was full of marijuana smoke and we got pulled over by the police. As we waited for the policeman to walk up to the car, we had all the windows wound down and Litva just got out and said, "Bugger this. I'm not staying here," and he just took off... The policeman suspected nothing and so we were let off. But Litva was looking out for number one.'

Litva became friendly with Brett Whiteley, whose manic energy and fast talk could match his own. Wendy Whiteley was less impressed—she found him a dangerous character. *The Sydney Morning Herald* soon picked up the rumour that Litvinoff, who it described as a London raconteur and sound-recording collector, was the basis for 'Jumpin' Jack Flash'. Although the song has the driving energy redolent of Litva, he was not its inspiration. The spark, according to Keith Richards, was his one-time gardener Jack Davey and the insistent stomping of his heavy rubber boots.

Litva arrived in Sydney with a tea chest containing about two hundred reel-to-reel tapes. How he had acquired them was uncertain. He claimed to have rescued some from the garbage at Abbey Road studios, others from the Library of Congress in the United States. Some were of music, including blues musician Ma Rainey and bootleg Dylan tapes. Others were of the Pheasantry's resident madman John Ivor Golding and of a young man Litva had helped to regain his ability to speak.

Litva played the tapes to Kate and Ian Reid at their property near Cooma in rural New South Wales. He arrived for a weekend, but stayed for more than two months. His stay was prolonged when, helping out on the property, he had an accident on a tractor and injured his hand. As he recuperated, he and Kate catalogued the tapes. He presented his hosts with a red and white striped jacket he said had been worn by Dick Van Dyke in the movie *Mary Poppins*. His tales were always entertaining, even if they were unverifiable or untrue. He gave Kate a shoulder bag he said he had acquired in a desert from a Bedouin sheik. She was carrying the bag one day when she met Martin; he recognised the bag as one Anou had given him as a present, and he wanted it back.

Litva was a showman. On the eve of *The Incredible Shrinking Exhibition,* he stood before a television camera wearing a Fantômas mask. The comic book antihero—who struck terror in the hearts of the bourgeoisie—was much admired by Martin and other Yellow House artists. With Martin's images behind him, Litva taunted the interviewer like a cat with a mouse. Asked how might the public react to the show, Litva bit into an apple and spat out: 'I think it will be one of massive indifference. And I believe the public will stay away in their thousands.' The show would be a 'great leap backwards', he declared.

The lights dimmed in the Cloud Room as people jammed in. The crowd overflowed out the door, down the corridor and up the staircase of the Yellow House. A seventeen-year-old in her mother's white silk 1930s slip took to the little stage. Her lips and nails were red, her eyelids sparkled with silver eye shadow, her hair curled into a prewar bob. On her feet were a pair of ruby sequined tap shoes.

She had rehearsed Alice Faye's 'Wake Up and Live'. But as the lights came up, instead of the familiar 1930s big-band trumpets of the song's introduction, a different tune blasted through the record player. Little Nell knew the show must go on. And so she improvised. She tapped and shimmied across the stage and into the hearts of those watching, including Martin's.

The Incredible Shrinking Exhibition was launched on April Fools' Day, the day on which Sydney *Oz* had been launched eight years earlier. Martin was dazzled by his girlfriend's panache. 'She just went on and ad-libbed another song and completely stole the show. It was a brilliant performance. That's when I saw what a great artist she was,' said Martin.

Laura Campbell had been dubbed Little Nell, a figure from Dickens' *The Old Curiosity Shop*, by her journalist father, Ross Campbell. A Rhodes scholar who studied at Oxford at the time of C.S. Lewis and J.R.R. Tolkien, Campbell was a columnist for *The Daily Telegraph* and *The Bulletin* who wrote about his family life at the home he called Oxalis Cottage. In his tales, he gave his four children nicknames. Little Nell would go on to dance her way to stage and screen stardom as Columbia in *The Rocky Horror Show*.

'Little Nell stole the thunder,' reported social columnist and man-about-town Leslie Walford after the opening. Walford arrived overdressed in a black dinner suit and velvet bow tie as he was en route to the more formal Peter Pan Ball at the city's upmarket Wentworth Hotel. He was among about thousand people who turned up for Martin's opening—double the number of invites that had been sent out.

As with his previous shows, Martin's invitation had displayed trademark wit. Written in ever-tapering typeface was the exhibition's name: *The Incredible Shrinking Exhibition*. The invitation had been the size of a business card. In black beret, a blue smock splattered with red paint, patchwork velvet trousers and a black bow tie, Martin was now joined by his mother, father, cousins and grandmother, other artists, hippies in love beads and Litva.

'Where do all these miraculous people live, who sport old top hats, flowing capes, bits of lace, Tempe-tip trappings worn like royal robes?' Walford gushed. 'The art world has seemed dull for long, and all the young—and the old, for that matter—are looking for a new excitement. Nobody has given them a moment like Martin Sharp. More madness please!'

Martin's shrunk-down mirror-mounted works hung in the Cloud Room. Viewers simultaneously saw the artworks and themselves reflected back. Some drew comparisons with Lewis Carroll's *Through the Looking-Glass*: down a hallway, Martin's smiling-mouth image reminded Albie Thoms of the book's vanishing Cheshire Cat, which slowly fades leaving only his grin. Certainly the Yellow House was about to get curiouser and curiouser.

Martin's cousin Andrew Sharp was perplexed by the exhibition and spoke to Charlie Brown about it. Andrew recalls: 'I said, "I don't really get it. Martin's just taken pictures of all of his pictures and just shrunk them down." And Charlie said, "It's the most wonderful comment on the acquisitive society."'

The Sydney Morning Herald's critic Donald Brook was not impressed. He ignored the images but admired the frames: 'The best bit is environmental ... There is moody music and a sense of bohemianism.' But *The Sunday Telegraph*'s Daniel Thomas saw friendship reflected in Martin's mirrored world. The figures in the artworks—van Gogh, Mickey Mouse, Ginger Meggs and Picasso—were like old friends to Martin: 'The opening party must have been intended as the ultimate work of art: the real live friends—old, young, new, familiar and all very pretty—were gathered to meet the other friends that were in the pictures.' Thomas found Martin's looking-glass world enchanting. The exhibition also launched Martin's book *Catalog*. Disjointed as it was, its argument was consistent, observed critic Joanna Mendelssohn, who later noted, '[There is] a belief in the importance of the life of an artist, the need to pursue noble ideals for the sake of art.'

Idealism inspired the imaginative mirror world Martin created within the Yellow House. But the reality outside the dream-like walls was a bleak contrast. On the day the exhibition launched, the Australian government released for the first time a list of more than a hundred books it had banned in the previous two months alone: works it considered blasphemous, indecent or obscene, works that unduly emphasised sex, horror, violence and crime or encouraged depravity. Among them was Andy Warhol's *Blue Movie,* the British edition of the girlie magazine *Penthouse* and a range of pulp fiction. And as the crowds spilled out of the Yellow House, in the White House US President Richard Nixon picked up his pen and ordered that William Calley, the only US officer convicted over the Mỹ Lai massacre of unarmed Vietnamese civilians, be transferred from jail to house arrest.

With the launch of *The Incredible Shrinking Exhibition*, Martin's filmmaker friend Albie Thoms, just back from London, had an idea for a program to accompany the show. The program needed a name. Since childhood Martin and Albie had admired the Australian comic hero Ginger Meggs, a cheeky redheaded boy who spent his days dodging school and bucking authority, an embodiment of the larrikin spirit. And so the Ginger Meggs School of Arts was born. Its creation was a mischievous swipe at the stultifying formality of the teaching at the National Art School.

The school's 'curriculum' was events rather than classes, including screenings of old movies and new works by young filmmakers. In an upstairs room, artist George Gittoes created a puppet theatre, covering the walls and floor in richly coloured swirling arabesques. He made puppets—of angels, birds, dragons and of Medusa, Medea, Oedipus. He wrote and presented puppet plays based on ancient Greek and Persian mythology and on the wives of great artists. His shows were 'the most haunting delight so far at the Ginger Meggs school', the *Herald* said.

George was one of the few Yellow House artists to have attended a public, rather than private, school; as a precocious schoolboy in working-class Rockdale, he had been drawn to Islamic art and culture. He drew on its imagery as he created his puppet room. His ceramicist mother,

Joyce Gittoes, helped create pairs of surreal ceramic feet that evoked Magritte for the Yellow House.

The Yellow House was open round the clock and hosted a range of 'happenings', including film screenings, music performances and cabarets from Wednesdays to Sundays. An eclectic range of old movies—from Leni Riefenstahl's *Olympia* to Walt Disney's *Dumbo*—were screened. More significantly, so were the works of local filmmakers, some of whom would go on to international careers. Peter Weir, Phillip Noyce and Jim Sharman were among the directors whose early films were shown at the Yellow House.

There were soirees in the Cloud Room, where tables were installed and alcohol illegally served in coffee cups. An evening was devoted to tightrope walkers, in which actor Arthur Dignam read from Genet's 'The Funambulist', a poem dedicated to his highwire lover. There were performances inspired by Dada, Surrealism, Expressionism, and a 'séance' invoking the spirit of Anton Artaud and his Theatre of Cruelty. Singers Jeannie Lewis and Marion Henderson performed music and artist Peter Kingston performed magic, with Brett and Wendy Whiteley's six-year-old daughter Arkie as a magician's assistant.

Wendy Whiteley recalls how Arkie, later an actress, set her sights on a performing career after first taking to the stage in the Yellow House: 'She decided she'd get up and do a little tap dance and sing a song ... She was this beautiful little blonde child. She said [afterwards] that's what she wanted to do, she wanted to be an actor/performer. She didn't deviate from that. She got a huge round of applause. Her little face lit up.'

Even Litva did a one-off performance, telling tales and playing his bootleg recordings in an evening billed as 'The Incredible David Litvinoff'. At times the tables were turned, and the passers-by became the performance. Jon Lewis observed a group of schoolkids arrive and set up rows of chairs in the Yellow House's entrance, as if in a theatre.

The chairs faced out onto the street; people sat on them and watched bemused pedestrians wander past.

By then Jon had moved into an alcove in the Yellow House; he bought a parachute to curtain it off and called it home. When Martin handed him a paint-splattered camera one day, Jon began to shoot—and began his photographic career.

A range of performers and artists were drawn to the Yellow House. George Gittoes' Ukrainian girlfriend, artist Marie Briebauer, joined him from the United States and moved in. So did Peter Royles, a musician, drifter and one-time jockey. Peter was busking in the Domain when he ran into Litva, who invited him back to the Yellow House. Peter erected a tent in an attic, which he reached by clambering up a rope. He removed roof tiles to create a window, but this simply let in the rain.

Photographer Juno Gemes, an experimental performer who had worked in London with Yoko Ono, was inspired by the Yellow House's atmosphere, as was Fairlie Kingston, Peter Kingston's teenage sister, who offered to cook. Fairlie recalls: 'It was a disaster. I made this big lentil dish because I thought that's what people eat these days. Peter Royles said, "There's better food in prison."'

The Yellow House attracted some high-profile visitors. Comedian Marty Feldman dropped in, as did Pink Floyd. The band watched films and invited several Yellow House residents to their concert at Randwick Racecourse. Ingrid Boulting, with whom Martin had travelled to Zambia, stayed at the Yellow House for a while.

British designer Zandra Rhodes, on her first trip to Australia, visited the Yellow House, where she met Martin. It was the beginning of a long friendship. Martin stayed with Rhodes on a visit to London a few years later, when he painted a mural in her Notting Hill Gate home: 'He did it as a gift. It had Mickey Mouse and those wonderful swirls and it went up the staircase,' Zandra says. And he created a collaged portrait of her that still hangs on her bedroom wall.

Martin took his mirrored pictures to Canberra for the Aquarius Festival of University Arts, an alternative lifestyle festival. There he hung his works from trees on the Australian National University campus. Some compared the festival to Woodstock, the 1969 counter-culture festival in upstate New York, billed as three days of peace and music. Although, as *The Sydney Morning Herald* noted coyly, unlike Woodstock, men and women would have separate sleeping quarters in Canberra's tent city.

Martin organised a small exhibition of cartoons by Livingston Hopkins, or Hop, to help fund activities soon after he returned to Sydney. Martin had bought the cartoons on his twenty-first birthday from a Sydney shop that sold art supplies. Barry Humphries opened the exhibition, but as a fundraiser it was a fizzer. The works sold didn't cover the cost of the framing. Money was becoming an issue, as most of the artists existed hand-to-mouth. So, too, was organisation. The Yellow House had an abundance of artists but lacked anyone with management, administration or financial skills. 'Whoever was available at the time would be the front-door bitch,' says Greg Weight. Entry fees were invariably spent on food.

CHAPTER 12

GINGER MEGGS SCHOOL OF ARTS

The building took on the golden hue of van Gogh's *Sunflowers*. But the paint the Yellow House artists used to give the building its distinct colour had more prosaic origins. It was the type the Department of Main Roads used to mark traffic lines on public streets.

In the aftermath of Martin's *Incredible Shrinking Exhibition*, work got underway that would see the Yellow House become far more than an exhibition space, performance venue or artists' collective, although it would be all of these too. It would become a work of art itself, as derelict rooms were transformed by elbow grease and flights of imaginative fancy. The Yellow House expanded into the adjoining building, part of which had been damaged by squatters who had lit fires in some rooms. A hole was knocked into a wall between the two buildings, and its surrounds were painted to evoke pop artist Roy Lichtenstein's explosive work *Whaam!*. It was dubbed the Whaam Wall.

Martin presided over the Yellow House like Andy Warhol over the Factory. Photographer Greg Weight recalls regular meetings to talk about the transformation of the various rooms into distinct environments. 'Martin was the primary art director of that whole thing. It was with his consent that certain rooms went ahead or had a certain look about them ... but he pretty much left you to it once he believed in the people who were early founding members.' Weight began work on a room where he planned to display the black and white photographs he had taken of sand dunes at the Sydney beachside suburb of Cronulla. He realised the need to attend the meetings when he skipped one and found his all-white room had been reassigned. He was given one upstairs with black walls: 'It was a shock, but in the end I thought, okay, I'll go with it.'

In a ground-floor room, floorboards were sanded and the walls painted white; this was what would become Brett Whiteley's Bonsai Room. Whiteley invited artist friends to sketch or paint his Moreton Bay bonsai tree, mounted on a white cylindrical plinth in the centre that was strategically placed to conceal a persistent scorch mark. Bruce Goold created what he dubbed a 'Belgian bourgeois interior' using a red theatre curtain and a two-seater couch covered in a polar bear skin, the latter borrowed from Martin's grandmother. The bear retained its head over time, but someone removed its claws and possibly turned them into a necklace.

Other rooms drew on the images of Martin's art heroes, including Magritte. The words 'This is not a pipe'—from Magritte's *The Treachery of Images*—were painted on the wall and clouds on the floor and ceiling of the Magritte Room. Martin had brought back to Australia from Paris some Magritte etchings. Jo Sharp painted clouds on their mounts and Martin offered them for sale for $300 each. On a wall where the etchings were hung, Martin wrote lines of poetry. Goold recalls Litvinoff scoffed: 'What are you doing? It's not a kindergarten, you know.'

A white table and a chair covered in feathers were the centrepieces of the Infinity Room, a light installation illuminating 'Spookyland', as Arkie Whiteley dubbed the otherwise darkened room. A rollcall of artists—among them Peter Wright, Peter Powditch, Ellis D. Fogg, Richard Weight, Julia Sale and Vivienne Pengilley—helped create the rooms or contributed artworks. Altogether about twenty rooms were transformed into magical, disorienting spaces. There were cheeky nods to high art—not least in Whiteley's portrait of Rembrandt, with a three-dimensional nose—and there were comic book heroes, including

Fantômas. In a white-walled room, Martin showed his series *Footprints on the Road to the Yellow House.*

Few of the Yellow House artists had any money, other than Martin. Some funded their art work through other means. George Gittoes drove taxis and Bruce Goold sold clothes and ephemera in Paddy's Market. Although several of the key artists lived elsewhere, they spent long hours creating at the Yellow House.

The work was as constant as the smell of marijuana. Albie Thoms recalled receiving a thirtieth birthday present of a tennis-ball-sized lump of hash that went into a communal curry. With the Yellow House attracting young visitors and a wild reputation, some parents became alarmed. Eighteen-year-old Andrew Sharp was with a group of friends in Martin's upstairs room late one night when there was a knock on the door. Andrew's mother was on the doorstep with a coat over her nightdress, urging her son to come home.

Greg Weight documented the magical rooms including the Stone Room, which was among the most dramatic. In it, everyday objects appeared to be made of rock, including the walls, a door and a table. Weight photographed Martin in the Stone Room and suggested he hold something other than a cigarette. Martin returned with a novel he was reading at the time, Dickens' *The Old Curiosity Shop.* Dignified and stylish, despite a crochet beanie, Martin was photographed before a painted homage to Hokusai's *Great Wave off Kanagawa,* an image that had been a source of friction between Martin and Brett Whiteley. Jon Lewis had watched as Martin painted it one way one day and Brett repainted it his way the next. Jon recalls: 'When Martin saw it, he just painted over it and brought it back to Hokusai again. I think this went on for at least three or four days, or five days.' Then Jon saw Martin one day pick up more than a brush: 'He was on a ladder and Brett came in … Martin hurled a hammer across the room. He hurled it towards Brett and it crashed into the other side … I remember Brett downstairs [afterwards] pacing furiously back and forth, saying, "He's really lost it this time. He's gone completely over the edge."'

Martin insisted he threw to miss. Nonetheless, Jon was unnerved by his friend's behaviour. Perhaps it was an indication of the mounting pressure ahead of an exhibition planned for September 1971. Tempers began to fray. David Litvinoff, too, turned his acerbic tongue on Martin. Andrew Sharp was horrified as Litva stomped up and down a staircase shouting abuse at Martin. Andrew recounts: 'He said Martin was a complete poseur, he was a snob and he had bought his way into success in London. And I remember Martin just stood there and took it. He didn't defend himself. David went on this tirade against him, listing all his faults and weaknesses … Martin was embarrassed and speechless and hurt.' Litva moved to Lavender Bay shortly before the unveiling of the Yellow House's landmark *Spring Exhibition*.

About three weeks before the opening, tragedy struck one of the Yellow House residents. George Gittoes arrived at the house one August morning to visit his girlfriend, Marie Briebauer. He recalls: 'Everyone was standing there like statues. They all seemed too frightened to say something.' Eventually Martin broke the news: 'Martin came up to me and hugged me and said, "I am terribly sorry, she's gone."' Marie had died of an overdose.

As work towards the *Spring Exhibition* continued throughout the Sydney winter, half a world away in London, Martin's friends were in the dock at the Old Bailey. Richard Neville, Jim Anderson and Felix Dennis were on trial over the School Kids issue of *Oz*. They had been charged with obscenity, sending indecent material through the post and conspiracy to corrupt the morals of young children. The latter archaic charge was the most serious, and potentially carried a life sentence. Yet the issue was one in which the three editors had little direct involvement since it had been guest-edited by a group of teenagers.

Clytie Jessop held a fundraising exhibition at her gallery to help their legal battle. David Hockney gave a drawing of the three *Oz* editors naked, Germaine Greer offered up a bikini crocheted with pubic hair and John Lennon, who had once been an art student, contributed drawings. Lennon and Yoko Ono also recorded a song in support, 'God Save Oz'. Martin gave a van Gogh image he'd made on red perspex, which Jessop bought and still has. Philippe Mora premiered his *Trouble in Molopolis* at an *Oz* benefit at Chelsea's Paris Pullman Cinema. Critic George Melly introduced the film and sang a couple of songs. Clapton, who funded the film, had a front-row seat, as did the film's madman star, John Ivor Golding. The latter passed out in a drunken stupor and had to be removed.

Martin wrote to Richard Neville ahead of the case, urging him to use the forum of the court case to make a courageous public stand. 'If you call the right witnesses, you can place the whole education system on trial . . . It can be a first in all the world, a unique opportunity—don't miss it. Truth is the most revolutionary force of all.'

The trial had many similarities with the Sydney *Oz* case nearly a decade earlier. When the trial began in June, the three had a crack London legal team, led by John Mortimer QC—later best known for creating the *Rumpole of the Bailey* series—and Australian Geoffrey Robertson, later a prominent human rights barrister. They called high-profile defence witnesses, including DJ John Peel, comedian Marty Feldman, critic George Melly and conservative psychologist Hans Eysenck.

The trial had elements of farce, not least when Melly, asked to explain to the court the meaning of cunnilingus, drew on an expression from his naval days to describe it as 'yodelling in the canyon'.

Justice Michael Argyle scolded: 'This is not a theatre but a court of law'—echoing magistrate Gerald Locke's 'This is a court of law not a circus' in the Sydney *Oz* case.

At the end of the six-week trial—then the longest obscenity case in British legal history—the three were convicted in August of the two lesser charges, but not guilty of corrupting the morals of England's children. They were carted off to Wandsworth Prison, where their long hair was shorn. Martin telegrammed his support. There was a public outcry when Richard was sentenced to fifteen months' jail and Jim to a year. Felix received nine months, because Justice Argyle considered him 'much less intelligent'.

Felix had the last laugh and went on to become a millionaire publisher. The convictions were overturned on appeal; *Oz* continued to publish for a couple more years and the case remains one of the greatest debacles in British legal history.

A spectacle of a different sort—one to 'dazzle the eye, caress the ear and stimulate the mind'—kicked off at the Yellow House with the opening of the *Spring Exhibition* on 1 September 1971. It was Herman Hesse's Magic Theatre brought to life, according to Albie Thoms—although the price of admission was not one's mind but a dollar, and entrance was not restricted to madmen. People came to wander the rooms, to listen to live music, to watch cabarets and puppet shows, or to sit in the garden, where some of the former Trocadero dance palace statues had been installed. The producer of *Hair*, Harry M. Miller, recommended his cast take a look.

With the *Spring Exhibition*, Martin believed he had finally fulfilled van Gogh's unrealised dream of a house in the sun, where artists would work, create and live together. He considered Sydney's Yellow House was 'one of the greatest pieces of conceptual art ever achieved'.

But the critics were divided. Some dismissed the Yellow House as a fun palace and slammed its co-operative ideal as naïve and woolly. *Nation* condemned it as amateurish, cloyingly sentimental and ill thought out. *The Sunday Australian*'s Terry Smith decried its vague romanticism, nostalgia and lack of originality. And he pointed the finger at Martin: 'Why always borrowed forms?' *The Sydney Morning Herald*'s Noel Hutchison was disoriented by its blend of 'the serious and unserious, the sophisticated and the slapstick, the vulgar and the nice … I suffered an increasing anxiety that I was doomed never to escape from the place.'

The Bulletin's Elwyn Lynn appreciated the unsettling ambiguous environment of the 'psychedelic phantasmagoria', and found the Stone Room particularly inspiring. *The Sunday Telegraph*'s Daniel Thomas summed up the show as 'marvellous'. The Yellow House was more festivity than art exhibition, according to *The Australian*'s Laurie Thomas. But he admired its mad optimism. He returned to the subject of the Yellow House a few weeks later, noting Martin's fascination with strange juxtapositions and putting familiar objects in unusual contexts. Martin was 'concerned with unsticking the mind, with making us see things anew'. He declared the Yellow House a 'unique experiment. There is nothing like it anywhere.'

By then the Yellow House had closed its doors, temporarily at least, and was in crisis. Tensions that had simmered—over money, artistic direction, administration and personalities—erupted. Greg Weight recalls: 'It really took a toll on everybody. When you've got that many artists in one space, it's like a hornet's nest. In a way, we all co-operated with each other, but artists are pretty intense, and I think by the time this [*Spring Exhibition*] had happened … it had run its course. And it didn't have a structure that would guarantee its survival.'

George Gittoes felt the Yellow House was drawing hippies, oddballs and hangers-on, rather than artists. He recalled one night a visitor fell from a table, hit his head on one of Joyce Gittoes's ceramic lamps and smashed it in retaliation as onlookers cheered. George had had enough. So, too, had Martin. 'It's over,' Martin told George.

Over breakfast together in a café a few days later, Martin read a newspaper account of the latest casualty figures in the Vietnam War. 'We should be doing the Yellow House in Hanoi—that's where we are needed,' Martin told George. But by then both were exhausted. George advised Martin to get away.

Martin's involvement with the Yellow House ended by late October. He left for London. Jo Sharp arranged for his artworks, antiques and other belongings to be removed to Wirian.

Other artists, including Albie Thoms, left around the same time. David Litvinoff, having worn out his Sydney welcome, returned to England, selling his tapes to Ian Reid in exchange for an airline ticket home. Litva died of an overdose of sleeping pills in 1975 at Davington Priory in Kent, then the home of Christopher Gibbs, the Chelsea antique dealer caught up in the Redlands bust. The Yellow House eventually reopened and became more of a music and performance venue until it closed its doors in early 1973. But the *Spring Exhibition* had been its high point. The building's fortunes have fluctuated in the years since. After a period as a boarding house, 59 Macleay Street comprises a restaurant and apartments today. The exterior is painted yellow, an acknowledgement of its artistic past.

At its best, the Yellow House had a larrikin heart and an expansive soul. It continues to exert a pull on artists and others who encountered it. For Greg Weight, the Yellow House was 'the icing on the cake of the sixties. It had all of that pop alternative culture, revolution, social revolution, embodied in one building ... It was intended to actually change people.'

Some were. Jon Lewis found his vocation at the Yellow House. 'I stumbled into the realm of the Yellow House and was completely and utterly changed,' he says. He has pursued photography ever since Martin handed him his first paint-splattered camera. Jon, who calls himself the only graduate of the Ginger Meggs School of Art, has also been an environmental campaigner.

George Gittoes has taken the spirit of the Yellow House to one of the most strife-torn places on the planet, Afghanistan. After spending much of his professional life in war zones, as a filmmaker and artist, he set up the Yellow House Jalalabad in 2011. It has been a sanctuary for a group of young local artists with whom he works on film, circus skills and music; a small school has also been established there. George painted the walls of a room within the house with the vivid swirling images that evoked his original puppet theatre.

Film producer Sandy Lieberson, who visited the Yellow House from London, saw it as a flame of creativity and artistic refuge in an otherwise conservative Australian society: 'Here was a place where like-minded people could meet, and exchange ideas, and have fun, and do alternative things, so it was a beacon of a new kind of culture. It felt very powerful and prominent in Sydney.'

More than four decades later, Martin believed the utopian dream to realise van Gogh's vision in Sydney's Yellow House had worked. 'You have to put things out there. Some things were stolen, there were risks. It came off in a strange way.'

Martin arrived in London at the end of 1971 eager to see his new girlfriend Nell Campbell. Soon after she opened *The Incredible Shrinking Exhibition*, she had left for Europe with her family. They exchanged letters; Martin covered his in drawings and occasionally enclosed presents, including a feather boa.

Martin was her first boyfriend. She was seventeen and just out of high school when she fell for the sophisticated man eleven years older than herself. 'He looked marvellous, he dressed wonderfully, he and I both loved 1920s and thirties music ... Boys of my own age didn't interest me. And he had this really interesting life, so that's what captivated me.'

She loved his style, his dark blue velvet suit, bowler hat and two-tone shoes. But the man she had fallen for in Sydney was very different from the one who arrived in London in the northern autumn. The Yellow House had taken a toll on Martin financially and mentally. Martin said: 'I was totally exhausted. I went to see Nell in London ... But I didn't have any money. It had been too much for me, the Yellow House. George [Gittoes] told me, "You've got to get away." He was right in a way. But I should have just gone somewhere quiet in Sydney and had a holiday. Instead I went to London. I love London of course, but I only had about two hundred dollars with me so we couldn't go anywhere.'

Martin arrived just as the *Oz* legal appeal was about to get underway. He and Nell stayed for about a month with Sandy Lieberson and his family in Mayfair. There he met some of Sandy's art and film world friends, including Jeremy Thomas, who later produced Bertolucci's *The Last Emperor* and *Stealing Beauty* and would visit Martin on his annual trips to Australia.

Martin asked Sandy if he could paint a mural in the three-storey Mount Street apartment. But he didn't stop at one wall and it eventually covered all three floors. Sandy recalls: 'It was all very van Gogh being driven out of Paradise. All of a sudden the whole flat became decorated.'

Despite the eye-popping presence of Martin's artwork in Sandy's home, the film producer found Martin himself elusive. 'I don't think at the end of that time I knew him any better than before he came to stay. Even when he was there, he was a slightly shadowy figure. He could sort of make himself disappear. Although he was a powerful presence, nonetheless you didn't always see him. He was never in the way, because he always managed just to insert himself in a very quiet and somewhat obscure way into our family and our life.'

Martin and Nell stayed briefly at the home of Ed Victor, who was to become a prominent literary agent. Ed had gone to Los Angeles on a short visit and a mutual friend had given Martin and Nell the keys. They assumed the friend had told Ed, but he was in the dark.

After his long-haul flight, Ed was relieved to be home—he had missed his neat and tidy Primrose Hill flat. He put his key in the door. Ed recounts: 'It looked as though a tornado had blown through it. Everything was upside down. Clothes everywhere, plates everywhere, dishes full of old food.' As he surveyed the debris, he noticed his space heater. Melted over it was his favourite Carole King record: 'It looked like a Salvador Dali painting.'

Martin stayed with various friends in London but had no regular base or studio. Nell joined her older sister Sally in renting a flat in West Kensington. Their Comeragh Road flat had previously been shared by model Christine Keeler and showgirl Mandy Rice-Davies, who played starring roles in one of the 1960s great political scandals. Keeler's affair with government minister John Profumo rocked the Tory government and helped sweep it from power in 1964. The famous photograph by Australian Lewis Morley of Keeler seated astride a chair became an iconic image of the 1960s.

Martin attempted to get a second exhibition in London with Sigi Krauss. He wrote to Sigi saying he had fifty works ready. They were similar to those he had previously shown at Sigi's Neal Street gallery—*Sharp Martin and His Silver Scissors*—but were of higher quality, he wrote. They were framed in gold and included thirty large images. He wanted to create a particular atmosphere with the show. 'The idea is to create an ambience rather like a "Bond St Art Gallery", so the viewer has the feeling of walking into one of those elegant rooms filled with expensive pictures only to find the paintings aren't what they seem. To take it to the furthest degree one could have an actor playing a dealer.' But the show did not go ahead. Sigi did not receive the letter.

Martin wanted the show to coincide with the 1972 release of a little book about his artworks. Titled simply *Art Book*, it consisted of thirty-eight of his collaged images of well-known artworks—art about art. He surrounded Botticelli's *Birth of Venus* with the menacing naked prostitutes of Picasso's *Les Demoiselles d'Avignon*, Andy Warhol's portrait of Marilyn Monroe bloomed amid van Gogh's *Sunflowers*, the nude girl in Edvard Munch's *Puberty* perched on the edge of van Gogh's billiard table in *The Night Café*. He dedicated the book to his old art teacher, Justin O'Brien. Published by the innovative visual art publishers Mathews Miller Dunbar, its founders included Anthony Mathews, an early promoter of the collaborative duo and Turner Prize winners, Gilbert & George.

In a review of *Art Book* for *The Guardian*, critic George Melly admired Martin's skill in combining unlikely images which were more than mere avant-garde in-jokes based on famous works of art: 'Modern icons tend through constant reproduction to lose their magic. Sharp's grafts, looking simultaneously so familiar and extraordinary, help to recharge the originals.'

Towards the end of 1972, Stanley Cohen invited Martin to stay at his Left Bank home. Cohen was a close friend and lawyer to sculptor Alexander Calder, and he worked with many prominent figures in the worlds of art and film, including Helmut Newton, David Puttnam and Sandy Lieberson, who had introduced him to Martin in London.

Stanley went away for Christmas, leaving Martin in the house he rented at 1 Villa Seurat. It was an address with a distinguished art world pedigree. Owned by Surrealist Kurt Seligmann, its previous tenants had included artist and poet Dorothea Tanning, art dealer Julien Levy and sculptor Isamu Noguchi. But when Stanley Cohen returned, he was aghast at what confronted him: 'Every square metre of floor and walls, closets and toilets were covered in Disney characters,' says Stanley. 'Luckily the ceiling was too high for him to reach.'

When he wasn't transforming Villa Seurat into Villa Disneyworld, Martin browsed art shops in search of Japanese prints. He was particularly keen on images by Hokusai. He loved Hokusai's *Great Wave off Kanagawa* and had drawn inspiration from it in several works, including at the Yellow House.

As he combed through Japanese prints in a shop on the Rue du Bac, one image caught his eye. The print depicted a female abalone, or ama, diver. These sea women made their livings diving deep to the ocean floor to return with treasures. Their seemingly superhuman ability—they could descend more than ten metres and hold their breath for up to two minutes—had made them a popular subject of Japan's woodblock prints from the Edo period. At times the ama divers had been depicted erotically—often entangled with octopuses—including by Hokusai in *The Dream of the Fisherman's Wife*. The image Martin found in the Paris shop was unlike anything he had seen by Hokusai and yet he was convinced the print was by the Japanese master.

In this particular image, the woman held an abalone shell aloft. With her body half-in and half-out of the water, she occupied the liminal place where the ocean and sky met, as though mediating two worlds. Her half-naked body, clad in a loincloth, was submerged; but her head, shoulders and upstretched arm were above the water. She held in her mouth a chisel with which she has prised the abalone shell from a rock. Her long black hair moved fluidly behind her.

Her swirling hair captivated Martin. It evoked for him van Gogh's *The Starry Night* with its whorl of the Milky Way. Martin even wondered if van Gogh, who had a deep interest in Japanese art, had seen the print and whether it had planted a seed in the Dutch artist's mind.

The price of the print was a thousand francs. But Martin had only ten francs, which he gave as a deposit. He then scraped together the balance and returned to collect his print. But the shop was closed. He persisted every day for three weeks; he eventually found the shop open and left with the print. He took it to the owner of a specialist Japanese print shop by the Seine to try to have it verified. She, too, believed the work was by Hokusai. Martin was overjoyed. Yet the print was a mystery. He could find no record of it.

Nell got a series of jobs, including on a stall at Kensington Markets. There she talked with a young neighbouring stallholder, Freddie Mercury. The flamboyant singer had yet to achieve fame as Queen's frontman. She worked as a phone counsellor at Release, the agency that gave legal support to people on drugs charges. It had been founded by Caroline Coon, who had been associated with *Oz*. And Nell began modelling for Martin's friend Zandra Rhodes, who recalls: 'Nell came dancing into my studio, and I mean tap dancing ... waving a hat she was wearing.'

Nell graced the pages of *Vogue* magazine. So, too, did Martin, appearing in a shoot with Nell for Zandra's knitwear. For Nell, London was exciting. But for Martin—with no house, studio, exhibition or money—London had lost its charms. Nell recalls: 'He was a fish out of water ... he was conflicted because he felt he had more chance of things going better for him in Sydney.' He returned to Australia.

He maintained a long-distance romance with Nell for several years and made a number of visits to London to see her. During that time she became part of the hottest show in town, *The Rocky Horror Show*. Nell was Columbia alongside Tim Curry as Frank-N-Furter and Richard O'Brien as Riff Raff. The show was directed by Jim Sharman, who had worked with Martin years earlier with *On Stage Oz*. The musical premiered at the tiny Upstairs at the Royal Court Theatre in Chelsea in June 1973. The high-camp spoof of B-grade sci-fi and horror movies became an international hit and eventually a movie, in which several original members, including Nell, appeared.

She was riding high on the musical's early success when Martin travelled to London and came to see her perform. By then the show was playing to packed houses in a former cinema in Chelsea. The cast was in good spirits backstage in their communal dressing room when Martin arrived to see her after the performance. She asked him whether he liked it. He did not. 'He picked up one of my lipsticks and wrote on the dressing table "nasty"', says Nell.

When Nell had a modelling assignment for Zandra in New York, Martin went along. During the visit, Martin took Nell to meet Tiny Tim. Martin was horrified when she fell asleep in front of his idol. Around 1974 Nell flew to Australia to see her parents; she also saw Martin, but by then both realised their romance was over. Nell later moved to New York where she established her hugely successful eponymous Manhattan nightclub.

CHAPTER 13

THE EMBASSY OF ENCHANTMENT

Beneath the Sydney Harbour Bridge, the face of Luna Park grins over the water to the majestic Sydney Opera House. At night, Luna Park's lights seem to wink cheekily across, like a child pulling a face behind the back of a dignified relative. Martin would play a crucial part in both places, one a paean to pop art, the other a temple of high art. But it would be the funfair that would dominate the rest of his life.

Martin arrived back in Australia on his thirty-first birthday in January 1973 and soon began working on Luna Park. He was rarely eager to have his work in art galleries, but at Luna Park he had a chance to paint a massive clown face and grin—a feature in so much of his work—on the canvas of Sydney Harbour. It was his biggest artwork.

Since it opened in 1935 on waterfront land once used for workshops for the Sydney Harbour Bridge, Luna Park had amused generations of Sydneysiders. Children had screamed in delight at Coney Island's crazy mirrors, stomachs had churned on the Big Dipper and courting couples had stolen kisses in the River Caves. Its entrance had always been a huge face with a gaping mouth, supported on either side by two towers inspired by New York's Chrysler Building. The initial face, with an unsmiling mouth, appeared rather sinister. But as the face was remodelled over the years, the mouth was transformed into a huge grin.

Martin had been commissioned to rejuvenate the look of Luna Park, including its welcoming face, by businessman Leon Fink,

Margaret Fink's then husband. Fink had leased the site in 1969 with business partner Nathan Spatt, a manufacturer and property developer. They initially planned to redevelop the site into a high-rise world trade centre, but when the Askin government refused permission, the funfair continued.

Hope and optimism were in the air. In December 1972 more than two decades of conservative government had been swept away. The Labor government's reforming new prime minister, Gough Whitlam, had ended conscription, introduced free tertiary education, and put arts and culture centre stage. The Opera House was finally due to open, albeit without Jørn Utzon, theatre companies were springing up and a generation of playwrights were finding their voice. Suddenly it was a good time to be an artist.

Martin embodied much of the creative energy of Australia in the 1970s, just as he had in sixties London. He was prolific and his impact diverse, working in theatre, film, with musicians and especially on Luna Park. He always worked collaboratively, and at Luna Park he worked with a group of friends, including Garry Shead, Peter Kingston, Richard Liney and Tim Lewis.

Much of the funfair's colourful look had been the work of Arthur Barton, a sign-writer, portrait artist and cartoonist who was hired as one of the park's first artists and stayed until his retirement in 1970. Dubbed the Rembrandt of Luna Park, Barton painted murals inside Coney Island, and carried out a much-loved remodelling of the giant entrance face. Until 1972 the funfair closed each winter, when rides could be overhauled, painted and new attractions added. Until 1969 the site had been run by showmen, notably Ted Hopkins, and had operated mostly without incident.

Although Martin rarely visited the funfair as a child, he came to love its colourful artwork, especially that by Barton. For Martin, Barton made Luna Park unique. The funfair was run down when Martin arrived, yet he had big dreams. He believed it could become the best place on earth. It was filled with figures from his childhood and the popular imagination that never got into art galleries. Yet he considered Luna Park more dense with images, sculptures and paintings than any gallery. 'The spirit of the place obsesses one,' he told a reporter as he worked on the site.

He blasted out the music of Al Bowlly and Tiny Tim as he worked. As he transformed the giant entrance face, he created eyes that critic Elwyn Lynn found 'enticingly and mesmerically beautiful'.

Martin wrote about the spell Luna Park wove over him in an eloquent article for *Quadrant* magazine. In it he described the funfair as a work of art, 'a city state of illusion' and an 'embassy of enchantment': 'One has to look through the eyes of a child to comprehend Luna Park,' he wrote. Here he could touch the spirits of Ginger Meggs, Mickey Mouse, Boofhead and others: 'Luna Park is their home. Great as they are, the twinkle in their eye has excluded them from those more formal clubs of the celebrated: the Art Galleries and the Museums and the Libraries. One can't help but feel this neglect is a serious flaw, a blind spot in society's assessment of some of its finest cultural blooms.'

Martin saw Luna Park and the Sydney Opera House as related to each other. When he finished painting the face he wrote *Ha! Ha!* in big letters at the base of Luna Park's twin towers. It was his way of mocking those who opened the Opera House without its architect Jørn Utzon.

Sunset was his favourite time, when the funfair was at its most bewitching. It was closed on weekdays, and so it was silent and deserted as the fading light cast an unearthly glow. He wrote: 'Then the Spirits of the Carnival came shimmering from the walls and hidden corners … guardians of strange and esoteric secrets, a tattered faded band of clowns and ghouls, denizens of the Labyrinth of a child's heaven and hell.' He had walked warily through the run-down Ghost Train, 'looking for old horrors that had fallen on hard times'. He expressed unease about Luna Park, with her 'glittering necklace of lights showing gaps that bare [sic] ominous tidings of unstrung pearls'. He questioned his infatuation with the imagery of childhood: 'I find myself dangerously fascinated by the world's discarded toys . . . windows to another world. The child who once played with this or that toy may now be a boring old man, and yet that toy can be a key to a childhood he had completely forgotten, and that he could never otherwise regain.'

Martin's preoccupation with childhood, especially his own, worried his mentor and former teacher. Justin O'Brien warned Martin about dwelling on this. O'Brien invoked St Paul's words in Corinthians: 'When I was a child, I talked like a child, I thought like a child, I reasoned like a child. When I became a man, I put the ways of childhood behind me.'

O'Brien wrote: 'You refer so often to your childhood Mart, that perhaps you should think a little more of the second part of St Paul's quotation? I wonder if it is so wise to think so often of your school days. It's now that is important. Yesterday is over, it's tomorrow that's so important. Leave your yesterdays and posterity (if they will still remember us) and you'll always be young if only you'll think of the future.'

The stacks from the BHP steelworks belched smoke by day and orange flame by night, like a parody of the promised land. The acrid stench filled noses and grit filled eyes. In the backyards of Newcastle, the industrial city that had helped Martin's Ritchie forefathers grow rich, Hills hoists were regularly wiped clean before washing was hung over their lines.

Newcastle Workers Club was a galaxy away from the Albert Hall and a television audience to rival the moon landing. Tiny Tim's star had well and truly fallen by the time he took to the club's stage in January 1974. His marriage to Miss Vicki was over, his manager had departed and the man who could once command fifty thousand dollars for a week's residency at Caesar's Palace in Las Vegas was broke. Then

Martin painted *The Toff* as a schoolboy at Cranbrook, where he was mentored by Justin O'Brien. (© the Estate of Martin Sharp)

Port Hacking, Fishing Day, 1963, was painted at art school. The river where Martin spent childhood holidays exerted an imaginative pull. (© the Estate of Martin Sharp)

Martin's cheeky Mona Lisa cover for Sydney *Oz*, 1964.
(© the Estate of Martin Sharp)

Ahead of his time. Martin created the psychedelic *Seventeen minutes to four*, 1965, before he discovered LSD. (© the Estate of Martin Sharp)

Martin's comic-book hero Ginger Meggs featured in advertising he created for Binkie's Burgers in Sydney *Oz* magazine. (© the Estate of Martin Sharp)

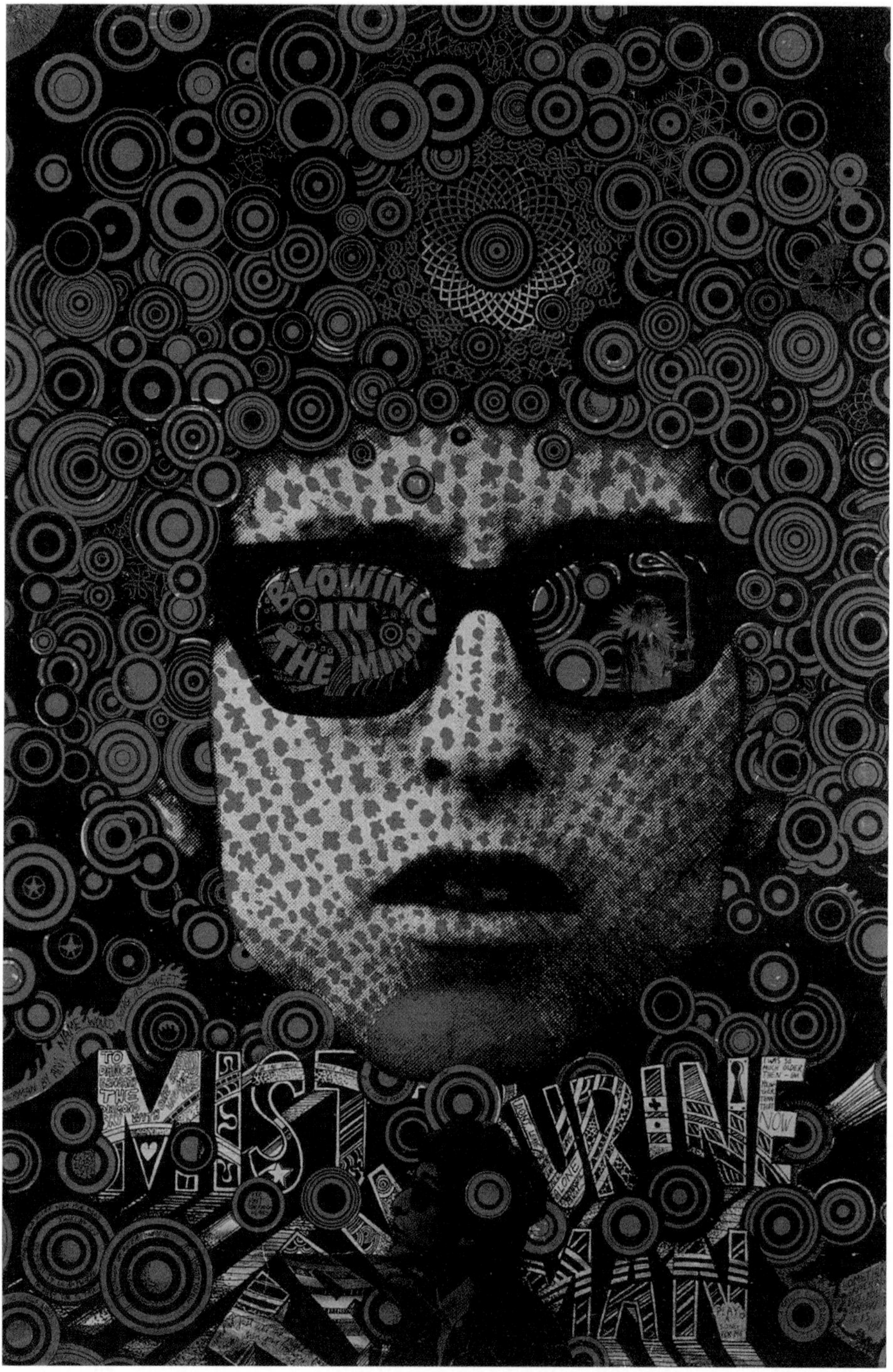

'Blowin' in the mind'. Martin's Bob Dylan poster *Mr Tambourine Man*, 1967, is an icon of sixties psychedelia. (© the Estate of Martin Sharp)

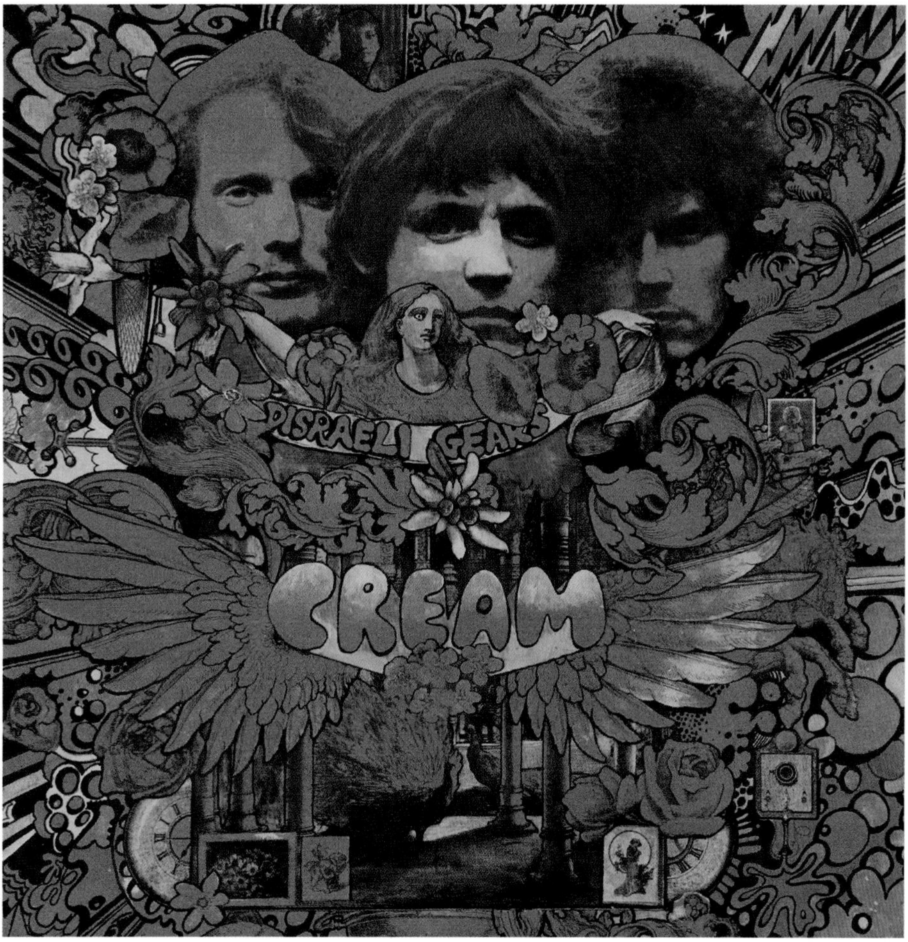

Martin created Cream's *Disraeli Gears* album cover, 1967, while sharing his London flat with Eric Clapton. The album included *Tales of Brave Ulysses*, for which Martin wrote the lyrics. (© the Estate of Martin Sharp)

Plant a Flower Child embodied the hippy spirit of 1967s Summer of Love.
(© the Estate of Martin Sharp)

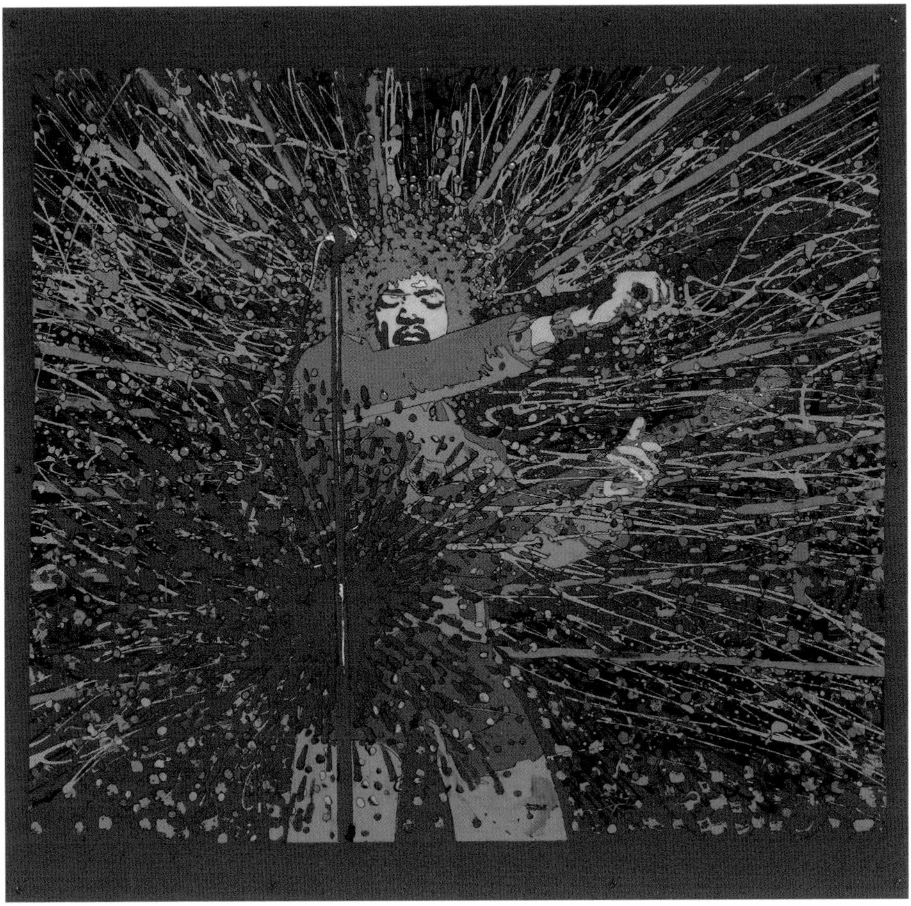

Martin captured Jimi Hendrix's electrifying energy. Unaware the guitarist was left handed, Martin later reversed his 1968 image to correct the mistake.
(© the Estate of Martin Sharp)

The Magic Theatre cover for the all-graphic London *Oz* 16 in November 1968 was later hailed as 'the greatest achievement of the underground press'.
(© the Estate of Martin Sharp)

The kabuki-like *Young Mo*, 1978, was created for the ground-breaking Nimrod Theatre Company.
(© the Estate of Martin Sharp)

Eternity Haymarket! 1977. Martin was captivated by the eccentric Arthur Stace, who chalked the word 'Eternity' on Sydney pavements.
(© the Estate of Martin Sharp)

Martin based *Abalone*, 1990–2006, on a Japanese print he found in Paris. He saw it as an oriental equivalent to Botticelli's *Birth of Venus.* (© the Estate of Martin Sharp)

The comic-book hero ventures to the Floating World with *Ginger Meggs in Japan,* 1996. (© the Estate of Martin Sharp)

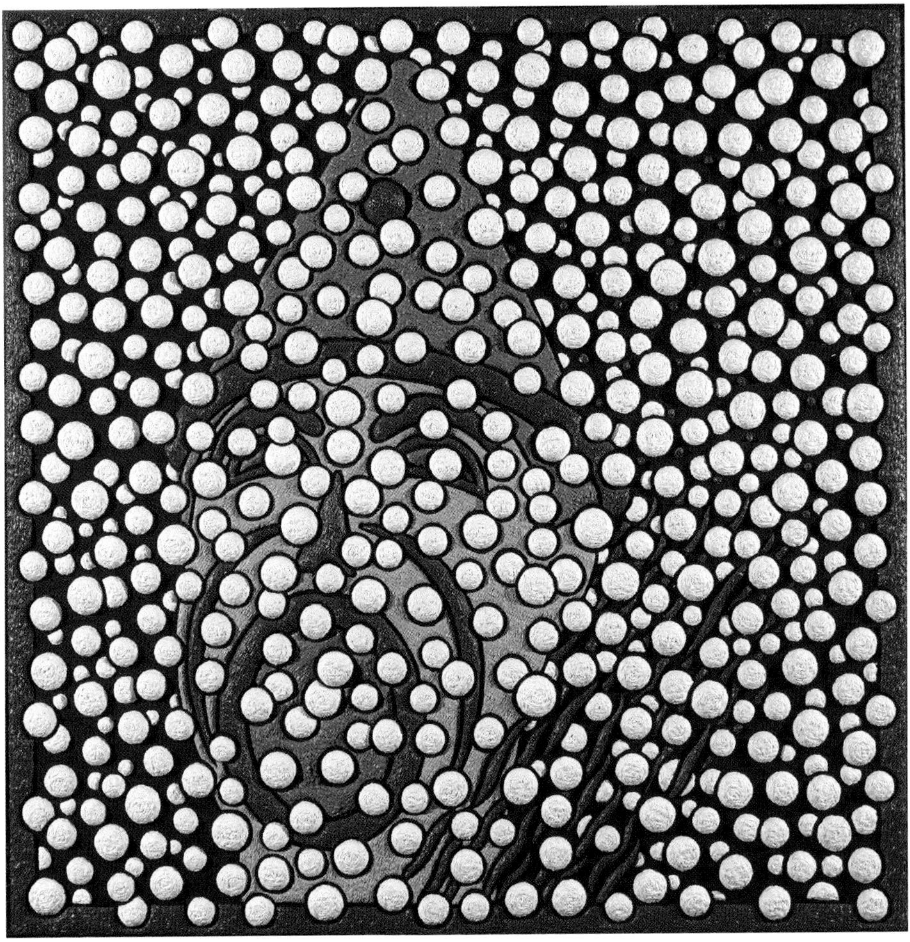

Snow Job,1980–95, reflected Martin's conviction that the cause of the Luna Park fire had been covered up. (© the Estate of Martin Sharp)

Andy Warhol's Marilyn Monroe blooms amid van Gogh's sunflowers in Martin's *Still Life*, 1999. (© the Estate of Martin Sharp)

Pentecost, 2001, combined Matisse's dove and van Gogh's chair.
(© the Estate of Martin Sharp)

Babylon the great is fallen, is fallen (Revelations 18 v.2), 2000–06, depicted Luna Park's entrance towers sinking beneath Hokusai's *Great Wave off Kanagawa.*

(© the Estate of Martin Sharp)

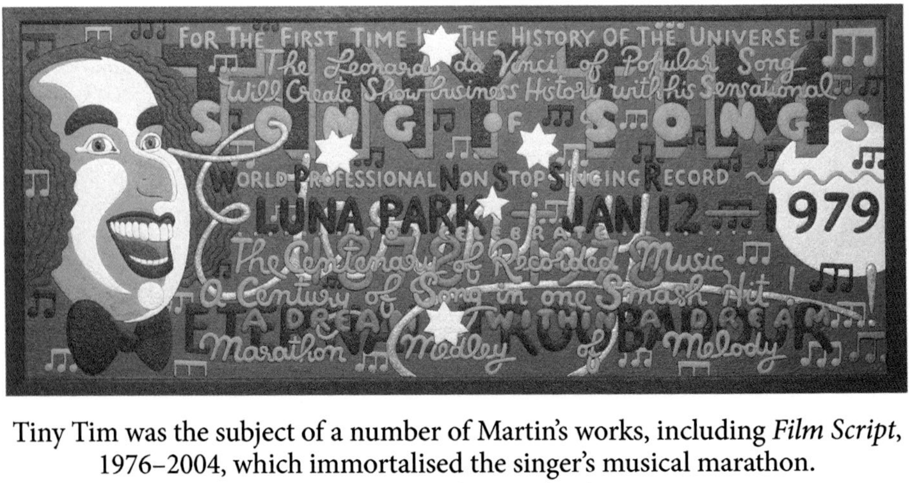

Tiny Tim was the subject of a number of Martin's works, including *Film Script*, 1976–2004, which immortalised the singer's musical marathon.

(© the Estate of Martin Sharp)

Courage My Friend, c. 1988–99, was based on a van Gogh print that once hung in his father's surgery. (© the Estate of Martin Sharp)

Boofhead meets Rodin's *The Thinker* in *Art Galaxy*, 2000. (© the Estate of Martin Sharp)

Martin's portrait of actor David Gulpilil, *The Thousand Dollar Bill,* c. 2012, hung in the Archibald Prize. (© the Estate of Martin Sharp)

he could afford to indulge a whim and order the luxury hotel's entire room-service menu, including dessert, before waving away the trolleys of silver-domed morsels without touching a mouthful. Now he was on clubland's rubber-chicken circuit.

Amid an audience of bemused shiftworkers downing dark beer and women with tight perms and polyester frocks, Martin had come to see his idol. In the six years since he first saw him in London, Martin's enthusiasm for Tiny Tim was undimmed. He knew people had come to the club to laugh at his idol. He knew his friend Eric Clapton—who had urged him to see Tiny Tim in the first place—found the tremolo in his voice frightening. But none of that mattered to Martin. To him, Tiny Tim was an artist without precedent, an eternal troubadour, an encyclopaedia of popular song, a Tin Pan Alley Orpheus. Martin was keen to work with Tiny Tim and he began to formulate ideas.

Martin had long been fascinated by Joan Lindsay's novel *Picnic at Hanging Rock*, which tells of the disappearance of a party of schoolgirls and their teacher during a picnic at Victoria's Hanging Rock on Valentine's Day 1900. What happened to the girls is never explained. When Martin learned Peter Weir was to direct a movie of the novel, he wanted to speak to the young Sydney filmmaker about the book. Until then, Peter had been aware of Martin only from a distance, through *Oz* and the Yellow House.

They arranged to meet and Martin handed Peter a sketchbook with a grey cover. Inside, Martin had pasted a leaf from each page of *Picnic at Hanging Rock*. And he had annotated every page with his thoughts, drawings and images about the enigmatic tale. Peter was astonished at how Martin had broken down the book, and they talked about the novel.

'What he said to me that influenced me deeply was that "There's much more to this than meets the eye. This is a sort of mystery of mysteries". And the fact that [the story] had no solution, it was really a way of making a film about the mystery of life and the insolubility of things,' says Peter.

Martin's sketchbook included references to Botticelli's *Birth of Venus*, a richly symbolic work in which the Goddess of Love, with flowing golden hair, stands naked on a seashell. Lindsay had made one fleeting reference to the beautiful schoolgirl Miranda as a Botticelli angel, rather than as Venus, but Peter recalls: 'He saw the book as encoded in some way. Whether intentionally by Joan Lindsay or by chance didn't interest him. The theory didn't make much sense to me, but I was impressed by Mart's intensity and the work he'd done breaking down the book. I left that meeting knowing that if I couldn't accept Martin's interpretation, then I'd better find my own.'

Peter, who ultimately became a renowned international director for films such as *The Year of Living Dangerously*, *The Truman Show* and *Master and Commander*, asked Martin to work on the film. He is credited as artistic adviser to the director. The shooting of what would become one of Australia's most influential movies, and the first to gather international critical and box-office acclaim, began in February 1975 and Martin joined the cast and crew in South Australia's Clare Valley. There a Georgian mansion, Martindale Hall, was used as the location of the girls' boarding school, Appleyard College, a crucible of repressive Edwardian discipline and burgeoning sexuality. Martin was on set for the six-week shoot and involved in 'dressing' the set, choosing objects and props to include.

'He particularly was interested in what the girls had in the way of personal property in their rooms, and also the headmistress. So he would find a beautiful seashell for one of the girls, certain little stones or rocks or bits of glass. So particularly, in the title sequence when you see the girls in their rooms getting ready for the day, for the picnic, they will see these things and they're often Martin's ... He was always looking for powerful objects,' says Peter.

Martin had a novel way of drawing Peter's attention to some of these—an approach that might have tested the patience of many a director. As a shot was being lined up, a shadowy blur occasionally appeared in front of the camera. Peter recalls: 'I'd look around the lens, and there'd be Martin, holding up a snail shell or an interesting vase. I'd say, "Martin, it won't work. It's out of focus."' Unorthodox as Martin's approach was, it did at times prompt Peter to take another look at what his artistic adviser had waved before the camera.

The film's cast included Karen Robson, who Martin had suggested for the role of Irma—the girl found on Hanging Rock a week later with no memory of what had happened. Martin had given Karen, his girlfriend at the time, a copy of the book and told her she reminded him of the character Irma. 'She wasn't a natural performer. She had no experience, but she had the sensibility and the quality. And he was right, so I put her in the film,' says Peter.

Karen recalls visiting Martindale Hall one night with Martin, Peter and actress Helen Morse. As they wandered around the house, Karen came across an old piano stool. She lifted the lid and inside, set to music, was a copy of Edgar Allan Poe's poem 'A Dream Within a Dream'. 'I showed it to Martin. He thought that line was very Miranda,' says Karen. Poe's words, slightly reworked, are the opening lines of the film.

Martin met Joan Lindsay, a writer with a deep interest in visual arts. She had trained as a painter and met her artist husband, Daryl Lindsay, when both were art students. As an art student himself, Martin had visited Daryl's brother, artist Norman Lindsay. Joan Lindsay loaned Martin a Victorian-era book of pasted cut-outs—full of little cherubs, hearts, flowers and other romantic imagery—once popular for making Valentine's Day cards.

'Martin was fascinated by it,' says Peter. 'He took it away, and it became a project for him. He wanted to surprise Joan. He rearranged the pages … and remounted them along the lines of his interest. It was a work of art.'

Martin added images that reflected his own concerns, including of Botticelli's *Birth of Venus* and some biblical quotations. He returned the book to Joan Lindsay, assuming she would be pleased with what he'd done. She was furious. She felt Martin had ruined her treasured book. Martin had photographed the reworked book before he returned it. He reduced each photographed page to the size of a postage stamp—as he had done with the images in *The Incredible Shrinking Exhibition* at the Yellow House. And he turned these pages into a little folded concertina book. He gave a copy to Peter, who still keeps it in a tiny box.

A few months after filming the disappearance of the fictional schoolgirls, the disappearance of a Sydney woman made headlines and raised questions about the cost of confronting powerful forces. Like Martin, Juanita Nielsen was a blueblood, heiress to the Mark Foys retail fortune. With her beehive hair, she cut a glamorous figure around Kings Cross. She was involved in the alternative press and published *Now* magazine from her terrace in Victoria Street, round the corner from the Yellow House.

As property developers cast covetous eyes over Kings Cross, the Rocks and other old parts of the city, Juanita used *Now*'s pages to campaign against them. She backed the Builders Labourers' Federation, which had imposed green bans to halt the bulldozers. In particular, she wanted to stop the demolition of the gracious terraces along Victoria Street, which a developer, Frank Theeman, wanted to replace with high-rise.

Juanita was a major obstacle to Theeman's multimillion-dollar plans when she entered Kings Cross's Carousel Club on the morning of 4 July 1975 for a business meeting. The club was owned by powerful crime boss Abe Saffron and run by his associate 'Big Jim' Anderson. Both men had connections with Theeman. Juanita was never seen again. It is widely believed she was murdered; her body has never been found.

Throughout this year, Prime Minister Gough Whitlam was under siege. His government, which had ushered in an era of optimism and hope, was disintegrating. And on 11 November 1975, the governor-general, Sir John Kerr—the man who had once defended the *Oz* editors—sacked the elected government. By then Martin had retreated to Wirian, the home of his ailing grandmother, Vega Ritchie, where he lived initially not in the main house but above the garage. Vega Ritchie's death on 19 August 1976 left Martin a wealthy man. She had divided her $400,000 estate, which included Wirian, equally between her daughter, Jo, and Martin. It meant Martin had the freedom to work at his own pace—which then was extremely fast. He had the luxury of only working on what captured his imagination and pursuing only what genuinely interested him. For good or ill, he could pursue his interests to the point of obsession.

Cressida Campbell rollerskated into the kitchen of her family's home on Sydney's North Shore. The house was known as Oxalis Cottage to readers of her journalist father's newspaper columns, in which she was dubbed Baby Pip. There she encountered a tall man with sapphire eyes and two-tone shoes who reminded her of the sad clown Pierrot. Her older sister Nell had brought her boyfriend home. Cressida was ten and Martin was probably the first artist she had met. Cressida announced she wanted to be an artist when she grew up. Martin took her at her word and encouraged her. He listened to children, and they in turn were drawn to him. 'He got on brilliantly with children and got on brilliantly with dogs. He was absolutely fantastic with both,' says Cressida.

Martin would occasionally appear in his Mini Moke with his red setter Bloke and drive Cressida to his mother's house. There Cressida experimented with Martin's paints. She loved the witty, chain-smoking Jo and her elegant Cranbrook Lane house. Jo had a gift for creating dramatic, colourful interiors. Cressida was enchanted by Jo's collection of blue glass, silver balls, images of hands and her sitting room with its warm yellow ceiling, the colour of dusty saffron. 'She had a magical eye,' says Cressida. 'I remember saying to her how much I loved the colour of the ceiling. And she said, "Daaarling, it's all nicotine."'

When Cressida and Martin stood before a large blank canvas he had prepared one day, he suggested she draw on it. The teenager was hesitant to make a mark on the canvas, which was at least as tall as her. But she picked up a pencil. 'I sketched in a face, very loosely. And then he worked over on that, and it turned into *Miss Australia*,' Cressida recalls. The painting is of a young woman with a vivid blue body and red hair, lips, nipples and a necklace of hearts. With a mane of wavy hair, the young woman resembles Cressida. Yet the 1975 painting, attributed to both artists and now in the Art Gallery of New South Wales, also has an uncanny likeness to Martin's favourite nanny, the Miss Australia contestant Roma Leonard.

Cressida is today a leading artist known for her unique single-edition woodblock prints and painted woodblocks of interiors, still lives, landscapes and gardens. As a young artist, Cressida was impressed by Martin's ability to draw from memory and cut a shape from paper without drawing a line. And she likens his fluid, graphic ability to Toulouse-Lautrec. 'Martin was a brilliant artist, an incredibly clever drawer and painter. I think his best work is works on paper ... When he got into that incredibly thick, layered and layered paint, it just didn't interest me much.'

After Martin's off-on long-distance relationship with Nell Campbell ended, Cressida became romantically involved with Martin. It was a 'very, very intense relationship' that spanned several years, but was at its most consuming when she was between nineteen and twenty-two years, she says. Her youth and her involvement with a man nearly two decades older raised eyebrows in some circles. But her parents were muted in their response. 'There wasn't a lot of judgement from Dad, and Mum didn't say much, but I don't think she was thrilled,' she says. '[Nell] always made it clear to me that she was never jealous of the fact that I had the relationship with Martin.'

Although Cressida and Martin were both obsessively driven artists, they worked in vastly different ways. Cressida worked by day, Martin by night. She worked alone, Martin with others. 'I always wanted an intimate set-up. I couldn't stand having people coming and going and that was one of the reasons we didn't work out because he always liked having all sorts of droppers-in and all that stuff and I hated it.'

Cressida found Martin's attitude to families unrealistic. 'He had a sort of fantasy of what families were … I suppose because he didn't have any brothers and sisters and hadn't been brought up in a family situation—much as he craved it.' When she was nineteen, Martin suggested marriage—but withdrew his proposal a few days later. Cressida was mortified at the time. '[He] could never commit because he would feel trapped … There was a cruel side to him. And he may not have meant to be cruel, but … when you got too close, then he got a bit claustrophobic and pushed you away. And when you'd get to the point where you'd be feeling strong enough not to need him, then he would find you interesting again … He had that strange sort of going hot and cold on people, and that's a difficult thing to deal with.'

His ambivalence was part of what eventually drove them apart. Although there was, she says, great love on both sides, Cressida realised she could not be what Martin needed, nor he what she needed. She did not wish to become immersed in Martin's world: 'I ended it, but it was a case of many turbulent fights and, like a lot of relationships, the other person makes it impossible, and then you end it.' She acknowledges that there is much about the relationship she is unwilling to discuss.

Nonetheless, she and Martin maintained a friendship to the end of his life, mostly by telephone, and they would talk for hours as they worked. Cressida recalls: 'A lot of people found Martin difficult on the phone because they always said there were these long silences. But for some reason, that never worried me at all … Whenever we saw each other physically, in later years, we never got on in the same way that we got on on the phone. It was almost like we needed that. He'd make funny comments and I'd feel self-conscious [in person]. But we got on brilliantly on the phone.'

CHAPTER 14

WIRIAN

After Martin inherited Wirian, he rarely left it. He had little desire to see more of the world. He rattled off a long list of places he never intended to visit: Tokyo, Vancouver, not even the former gold rush hamlet and Australian artists' mecca of Hill End. Like the hero of his favourite childhood book, *The Little Prince*, Martin had ventured far from home and returned to his tiny planet. Martin's 'planet' was a mansion in Sydney's Bellevue Hill. Wirian became not just the centre of his universe but his entire universe. Martin was often described, in later years especially, as reclusive. Paradoxically, Martin was a recluse whose Mickey Mouse telephone rarely stopped ringing. The world came to Martin.

In one sense, little had changed in the house from when Martin's grandparents lived there, not even the thirties-era green and cream Kooka gas stove, which remained in the kitchen. In another sense, Martin transformed the house where he would live for the rest of his life into a reflection of his wayward, chaotic, creative spirit. He became the centre of a galaxy around which a range of artists, friends and oddballs orbited.

The heart of the house was his studio, which he set up in the former dining room. Outside its French doors, the harbour sparkled beyond the sloping garden. Inside, even on the sunniest of days, the north-facing studio was dark, and in winter it was frigid. The gloomy atmosphere was underscored by dark brown brocade wallpaper, another legacy from his grandparents' era. Natural light, so essential to most artists' studios, was not a priority for Martin. He said he didn't require it since he didn't mix paints, but used them straight from the tube.

The dining table overflowed with ashtrays, coffee cups, paints, pens, notebooks, books and the odd oyster shell—Martin loved oysters—before the latter was flung from the kitchen window to where a midden built up. Across the dining table, whatever image he was working on would be propped on an easel in front of the fireplace. The room had no sofa or easy chairs, but a battered assortment of mismatched unyielding wooden chairs. It was not a room for resting in.

The once-elegant drawing room, which ran the width of Wirian's western end, became his 'Dream Museum', which he filled with the toys and fairground art he collected in large and expensive quantities. He bought Mickey Mouse figures by the dozen, as well as statues of Ginger Meggs and comic-book heroes. He bought vintage children's games, and once spent three thousand dollars on an early-model train set and an Edwardian throwing game called Ring My Nose. Some of his collection went on display at the Art Gallery of New South Wales' *Fairground Arts and Novelties* show in 1978, together with memorabilia from Luna Park. In the run-up to that show he was excruciating to deal with, debating for hours with gallery curator Jackie Menzies on the merits of which of his many Mickey Mouse statues to include.

While Wirian's Dream Museum filled with toys, the rest of the house filled with people. Wirian was a human collage in which disparate denizens rubbed shoulders. Martin's friends from London dropped in on their Australian visits, among them Eric Clapton, Marianne Faithfull, Jeremy Thomas and Zandra Rhodes. Other friends moved in. Richard Neville and his journalist wife Julie Clarke, artist Garry Shead and photographers Jon Lewis and William Yang were among the first of hundreds of people who lived under Martin's roof. William captured Wirian's early atmosphere in his book *Sydney Diary*, with photographs of parties, visitors and residents. William photographed Bob Geldof playing ping-pong with Richard Neville, entertainer Peter Allen reclining on a chaise lounge and knockabout Peter Royles sporting a black eye. The house cast a spell, William recalls: 'When you lived at Wirian, you were in this kind of fantasy world, a kind of dream world, and I think Martin encouraged that ... There was a pull there, but you kind of had to escape from it.'

In later years Martin installed two statues at the top of the central staircase. A figure of Christ, in flowing robes and long hair, looked out to Victoria Road. The benevolent figure offered blessings to all who approached. But looking inwards was a more ambiguous figure—a bust of the wily god Mercury, the trickster and guide to the underworld. The two figures on the stairs were the presiding spirits at Wirian, and within Martin, where generosity and kindness met chaos and contradiction. The balance constantly shifted.

Free-spirited as he was, Martin retained some patrician trappings. He was a bohemian with a butler. For when he inherited Wirian, he also 'inherited' his grandmother's factotum. Known only as Albert, he lived upstairs in the servants' quarters. He was energetic, wiry, opinionated, intimidating to some of the lodgers and proprietorial about the house. When Albert burned some papers belonging to Martin's grandparents, Martin was unforgiving. The long-serving Albert was sent packing.

Martin rarely tackled people head-on, he had more subtle ways of showing his disapproval. He would simply wander off when he was bored or considered someone had outstayed their welcome. Cousin Russell Sharp, an early resident, recalled a few ups and downs with Martin that focused on the placement of a tricycle Russell had given him as a present. 'When I was out of favour, it would go out the front [of the house]; when I was in favour it would be in the foyer,' says Russell.

Julie Clarke noticed Martin was particular about how rooms were allocated to lodgers: 'He divided people up socially as to those who would be in the servants' quarters or in the main house.' She and Richard Neville lived at Wirian until the birth of their first child, Lucy, one of Martin's many godchildren, when they needed a less chaotic environment.

The house was full of people day and night. No one was quite sure who was living in the house at any time. Wirian's most colourful resident was Harold 'the Kangaroo' Thornton, an artist known as much for his eye-popping clothes, including his hand-painted shoes, spectacles and hat, as for his naïve, brightly coloured artworks, most notably one that adorned the front of the Bulldog coffee shop in Amsterdam. Thornton's 'spirit of childhood' appealed to Martin.

A menagerie of animals was part of the household. Martin had a dynasty of dogs over the years, among them a bull terrier called Tiger and a corgi named Jane. Later came short-haired Smudge, long-legged Pompom, and Imelda, a terrier with a fondness for devouring shoes. He could take his affection for dogs to extremes, once eating from a can of dog food, insisting that if he was feeding the mush to his pets, he needed to know what it tasted like. Rocky the lamb grazed in the garden and a pair of roosters pecked their way around the studio—'they were very aggressive,' Jeremy Thomas recalls. Possums invaded the ceiling and termites chomped through the woodwork. Martin built nesting boxes for the possums rather than evict them, and when told of the termites his initial response was 'everyone's got to eat'.

Not everyone who stayed was an artist. Some who arrived on Wirian's doorstep struggled with mental illness or addictions, had experienced domestic violence or had criminal pasts. Martin, as his mother once put it, liked to collect strays. But the unspoken rule was that they had to contribute, whether helping Martin with his projects or around the house. Lin Utzon, who stayed at Wirian on her regular visits to Australia, observed the passing parade over many years. 'Wirian became a haven for people who could not manage life,' says Lin. Martin's openness to people from all walks of life was seen by some friends as epitomising his generosity and charity. Others were wary of hangers on.

Martin, who had grown up without siblings, needed people around. With the parade of people, visitors, residents and activity, Wirian recreated what was familiar from his youth. Cressida Campbell observes: 'One of the reasons he could handle all those people living in Wirian was because in a way it was like boarding school. And even though there were times when he used to loathe having people around him and he'd get sick to death of it, he also relaxed. He could paint in front of lots of people. If you think of boarding school, a lot of the people there you're not actually that intimate with.'

Although Wirian was always full of people, relatively few were artists. 'They were either helping Martin frame or … they'd do things like gardening. But it wasn't necessarily a whole lot of artists,' says Cressida. Martin had a wide network of friends throughout his life, but Cressida believes there were few he truly confided in.

Actor Andrew Sharp, who lived at Wirian in the 1970s, recalls a rare candid conversation with Martin. As the two cousins stood together in the garden during a party, Martin described how, when his parents were getting divorced, he had taken a boat out on the Port Hacking River. 'It was night-time, and he went out in the dingy by himself and he looked up at the stars. And he suddenly became gripped with this terrible existential loneliness,' says Andrew. 'And it shocked him. I think that's why his door was always open to everybody. He was always looking for a family.'

Martin never forgot the word he had seen chalked on the pavement near his childhood home: *Eternity*. He incorporated the word into his art, always in yellow and in copperplate script. He drew on it for one of the most striking images he created during his early days at Wirian, *Eternity Haymarket!* Created at a time when a battle was underway over Sydney's old market area, the work paid exuberant homage to

Arthur 'Mr Eternity' Stace and Martin's other cultural heroes. Martin placed the word Eternity over van Gogh's starry night sky, above a crowd of pop culture figures—among them Popeye, Mickey Mouse and Boofhead.

Martin loved rescuing figures and images from the past, and seeing how images migrated. The single copperplate word chalked by the lone eccentric Arthur Stace would become synonymous with Martin, finding its way into his paintings, prints and tapestry. *Eternity Haymarket!* was among a number of powerful artworks he created soon after he inherited Wirian. The late seventies were a fertile period for Martin as the city became his canvas and inspiration.

As he worked on Luna Park, he was also drawn to the theatre. A generation of young Australian playwrights, directors and actors were emerging in the early 1970s, keen to tell Australian stories. In Sydney this was spearheaded by the energetic, brash Nimrod Theatre Company based in Kings Cross. The innovative company, formed by John Bell, Richard Wherrett and Ken Horler, produced new Australian drama and took an irreverent approach to the classics. Martin captured the company's spirit in a poster for Nimrod's production of playwright Steve J. Spears' *Young Mo,* about the life of Australian vaudevillian star Roy Rene. The kabuki-like image, with its sinister grin, became the face of the Nimrod Theatre, which had by then moved to a former tomato sauce factory in Belvoir Street, Surry Hills.

Martin designed a series of posters for the company as well as some of the sets, including for the Weimar-style cabaret *Kold Komfort Kaffe*. He hung cottonwool snowballs from the ceiling of the little Downstairs Theatre, the more experimental of the two Nimrod venues. And he painted a galaxy of popular figures around the deep blue walls, including Barry Humphries as Edna Everage. The design was integral to the success of the show, which starred singer Robyn Archer and actor John Gaden, who had by then abandoned the law for the theatre. 'People loved being in that room,' says John. Martin worked quickly, creating the space—with the help of friends—in just a week as the performers rehearsed around them. And he created a poster, with snowballs falling on the two actors, a tangible record of the landmark 1978 show.

He also worked with the imaginative but short-lived Paris Theatre Company. Jim Sharman—having directed *Hair*, *The Rocky Horror Show* and *Jesus Christ Superstar* around the globe—and director-designer Rex Cramphorn set up the company in an old cinema near Hyde Park. Patrick White, who had received the 1973 Nobel prize for literature, chipped in $10,000. It had bold ambitions and an ensemble of fine actors but was a financial disaster. It folded after just two productions: the musical *Pandora's Cross* by Dorothy Hewett and *Visions* by Louis Nowra. Martin created arresting posters for both.

None of Wirian's early residents were more mysterious than Yensoon Tsai. In white face makeup and long Chinese gowns, she glided through Wirian like a character from the Peking opera. No one ever saw her without her full-face makeup. Some said she was a Chinese princess from Taiwan, others said she was from the North Shore. Some thought she was in her late teens, others in her forties. When Shanghai-born Alex Popov addressed her in Mandarin, he was surprised she did not respond—although she rarely spoke. Wendy Whiteley reduced Yensoon to tears once, annoyed at being shadowed about the house by her. But Martin was captivated by his Asian lover as she silently attended to his needs, and later his mother's.

The pair went to visit Alex at his northern beaches home one weekend, where it was Martin's attire, rather than Yensoon's, that most captured Popov's attention. Martin was walking around the house when he spotted a nearby gathering of 'muscle' cars—Martin loved unusual cars. The hotted-up vehicles had their bonnets up, displaying their gleaming chrome engines. Dressed only in white underpants, Martin walked across to chat with the owners, oblivious to the incongruous sight he made amid the highly polished vehicles.

An image of a Japanese woman continued to obsess Martin. He was determined to have the print of the female abalone diver he had found in Paris in 1972 confirmed as the work of Hokusai. He consulted experts in London, including at the Victoria and Albert Museum. He sent photographs of the print to Japan and close-up shots of its signature. Quite why he needed to do so puzzled even himself. Part vanity—to prove himself right—he acknowledged.

But his tenacity led to the loss of the print. He entrusted it to a friend who was travelling to Japan, where Martin wanted it shown to experts. But it went astray, left in a women's washroom at Tokyo airport. Martin was distraught. After its loss, in April 1978, he wrote a seventeen-page letter about the print to Jackie Menzies, then curator of Asian Art at the Art Gallery of New South Wales. 'I do believe I have been one of the few people to understand that print,' he wrote.

He saw it as an oriental equivalent to Botticelli's masterpiece *Birth of Venus,* a work he loved. While Botticelli's goddess stands on a cockle shell—a bivalve shell Martin described as symbolising requited love—in the abalone shell he saw its counterpoint. He had read in Japanese mythology that the univalve abalone shell symbolised unrequited love.

But that was not all he saw in the Japanese image. He also saw an expression of the complex, painful relationship of the artist to his art and to his muse. He thought the rock on which the diver stood resembled an old sea creature and symbolised the artist. The female diver was the muse, who had extracted from the old sea creature his art and unrequited love, in the form of the abalone. The diver 'like an angel, or a muse, comes from the higher realm of air, the artist dwells in the lower water world, more pressured, more turgid, darker,' he wrote to Jackie Menzies.

Martin was ecstatic whenever Tiny Tim was about to arrive. The singer Martin dubbed the Eternal Troubadour became a regular visitor to Wirian during his Australian tours, which Martin helped organise. William Yang recalls: 'Martin would get so excited when Tiny was about to come. Like a child. And then when Tiny would come, Martin would be in a state of excitement, and could hardly wipe this huge grin off his face. He was so totally enraptured by his presence.'

Enthroned in a large chair within Wirian's Dream Museum, Tiny Tim would hold court. He told stories of his life and gave opinions punctuated by musical interludes when he pulled his ukulele from a paper bag. He had no more devoted courtier than Martin, who was often at his feet with a tape-recorder capturing the singer's every utterance. To Tiny Tim, Martin was always 'Mr Sharp'. The singer never called people by their first names, always honorifics. Martin called his muse Tiny.

Martin accommodated the singer's whims. Musician Mic Conway recalls Martin never smoked marijuana in front of Tiny, who disapproved of drugs, but stepped outside to roll a joint. Martin knew Tiny liked to win at games and offered John Weiley advice when playing ping-pong with the singer at Wirian. 'I had to pretend to lose. He could not abide losing. He was like a very big bullying bad-tempered child,' says John.

Martin began sinking vast amounts of his inheritance into Tiny Tim. Martin flew Tiny to Australia—the singer demanded, and got, a first-class ticket. Martin booked venues, paid his expenses and hotel bills, for even in Sydney, Tiny never stayed at Wirian. Within a year of Martin's grandmother's death, he sold part of the land surrounding Wirian to Cranbrook School for $150,000. It didn't matter to Martin that Tiny was down on his luck; with his high-profile marriage over, the singer was so broke at one point that he returned to live with his mother. Martin had big plans for Tiny.

When Tiny Tim toured Australia in 1978, Martin took him to meet Peter Weir, who was then living in Adelaide. Peter was struck by Tiny Tim's charm and innocence. Peter recalls: 'At first, you thought that might be manufactured. And then you began to sense that actually it was true. And I think it might have remained at the heart of Martin's love for him. He was the eternal—not the eternal troubadour, but the eternal child.'

Martin wanted Peter to make a film about Tiny Tim. Peter explained that fiction, not documentaries, was what he was drawn to. Martin was unfazed. So Peter came to Sydney to get to know Tiny Tim and try to understand Martin's fascination with him. Peter wanted to know what kind of film Martin had in mind. It couldn't simply be a recording of Tiny's performances.

They met Tiny Tim in his room at the Cosmopolitan Motor Inn in Double Bay late one night after a performance. Peter wanted to see whether Tiny Tim could act and had devised a couple of improvisations. In one, Tiny played a schoolboy about to be expelled for poor marks. It produced much laughter, not least from Peter and Martin, but little in the way of acting ability.

Then Tiny was asked to leave the room and re-enter. When he did, Peter and Martin assumed the roles of doctors and told their 'patient', Tiny Tim, that he had advanced throat cancer and would soon be unable to sing. Peter recalls: 'He said, "Really? What do you mean? Not at all?" And suddenly he was acting. He fell straight into it and was totally involved.'

Peter returned to Adelaide to think through the idea. Despite many long conversations with Martin, Peter was unable to fathom Martin's fascination with the singer. 'I finally picked the phone up to Martin, and I felt terrible, and said, "I think I've got to pull out. I think the film isn't about Tiny, it's about you and Tiny. I think you should make it. You have a feeling about it that I don't have."'

Martin and Peter remained friends. And although the filmmaker never understood Martin's obsession with the singer, Peter observed their evolving relationship: 'I did at least glimpse enough of Tiny to see him go through a phase where he was flattered then even irritated by Martin's constant attention. I heard him a couple of times say, "Mr Sharp, if you don't mind, I can't possibly make myself available for that."' And he saw a deep accord between the pair. 'I said to Tiny, "It must be a very special thing to have somebody so devoted to you and believing so much in you." And he agreed.'

Classical musician Nathan Waks got a phone call one evening from Martin. Could Nathan come to Wirian and bring his cello? Martin was with Tiny Tim. Nathan, who had been friends with Martin since the Yellow House, knew little of Tiny beyond 'Tiptoe Through the Tulips', but he went over to the house and it was the beginning of an unlikely collaboration between the two musicians.

Nathan was impressed by Tiny Tim's encyclopaedic knowledge of songs, their history and context. And his uncanny ability to remember lyrics. Nathan recalls: 'He had a quasi *Rain Man*-type ability. I know of no one [else] who can do that.' Although Tiny was known for his high falsetto voice, his natural voice was a rich bass-baritone, and Nathan encouraged him to use that.

Martin, wanting to record Tiny, booked Sydney's best studio to do so, EMI's Studio 301 in Castlereagh Street. Nathan was musical director when Tiny entered the recording studio on 11 January 1979. They had already done a couple of days of recording, but this day they were about to embark on a particularly demanding session. It was to be recorded direct to disc rather than on magnetic tape, a format that appealed to audiophiles, whose finely tuned ears appreciated the lack of hiss and hum heard on magnetic tape.

But it was a nerve-racking way to record, since the session had to be captured without a break. Errors could not be spliced out, so it required great musical dexterity. Nathan spent part of the session under the piano whispering directions to Tiny Tim before crawling from beneath it to resume playing his cello. There was little time to draw breath after the session. For the next day, Martin had choreographed an even more challenging event.

Tiny Tim stepped onto a stage at Luna Park's Floating Palais and blew kisses to the crowd. In a red shirt, white bow tie, red hair and tail coat printed with comic strips that Martin created for him, the singer looked tailor-made for the venue. Tiny Tim was about to embark on a singing marathon, the 'world non-stop professional singing record'. He planned to sing for two hours without a break, not even to acknowledge applause.

Martin had organised this event and it combined his twin obsessions: the funfair he adored, which bore the giant face he had painted, and the singer he idolised. Martin planned to film the concert; it would be the backbone of the film he wanted to make about Tiny. By then he had decided to make the movie himself.

The audience was filled with Martin's friends by the time Tiny Tim arrived by speedboat at Luna Park on the evening of 12 January 1979. Some wore costumes. Russell Sharp dressed as a clown. Bruce Goold, in Panama hat and a linen suit covered in little tin religious folk charms, evoked a colonial missionary. Singer Jeannie Lewis donned a mask and a Pierrot outfit and opened the marathon show. The compere introduced the 'eternal troubadour, the human lyrebird, the superman of popular song', before Tiny Tim ambled onto the stage, holding a brown paper shopping bag containing his ukulele. He began with 'My Name is Mr Phonograph', a nod to Thomas Edison's invention. For the event was also to mark the centenary of recorded music.

As musical director, Nathan did not perform, but kept the show on track. That was no mean feat because of Tiny's seat-of-the-pants way of performing without a set list. Musicians never knew what song would come next, only the musical key Tiny wanted it played in. Nathan recalls: 'He'd call out during the song he was doing, "Maestro key of G" or "Maestro key of C", then we all had to shift ... We had a number of songs we knew he would do, we would know they were coming, but not necessarily when or in which order.' Or what other songs he might include.

Tiny embarked on a journey through a hundred years of popular song, segueing without pause from one song to another as the audience danced in front of him and the band scrambled to keep up. His repertoire included songs from the music hall, vaudeville, gospel and even disco: 'Don't Sit Under the Apple Tree', 'Shine on Harvest Moon', 'Pennies from Heaven', 'He's Got the Whole World in His Hand'. He ended with the Bee Gees' disco number 'Stayin' Alive'. He exceeded his goal and sang for two hours and seventeen minutes. It was one of the happiest nights of Martin's life.

CHAPTER 15

THE KING IN YELLOW

Jason Holman was on his first evening outing with friends unaccompanied by an adult. Twelve-year-old Jason was the youngest in a group of Waverley College school friends whose parents, after much debate, had agreed that they were old enough and responsible enough to go by themselves to Luna Park. But their parents had imposed one condition: the boys must attend mass on their way.

After attending the service at Rose Bay's Mary Magdalene church on this wintry Saturday evening of 9 June 1979, the excited boys caught a bus to Circular Quay and the ferry across to Luna Park. They entered the funfair by passing under the giant smiling face Martin had created and spent the evening sharing thrilling rides and laughter.

When it was getting near closing time, they found that their tickets only entitled them to just one last ride. They walked to the dodgem cars, but it had closed for the night. So they looked around for a ride still operating, because they did not want to squander the chance for one last adventure. The Ghost Train was still running at 10.15pm.

Nearby was Jenny Godson. She and her truck driver husband John had brought their two sons, six-year-old Damien and four-year-old Craig, to Sydney for a treat from their home in Warren in central western New South Wales. They'd visited Taronga Park Zoo during the day and had dinner in the city. At Circular Quay the boys were photographed with a man, possibly a busker, wearing a horned-beast mask and a tiger-skin loincloth, and then they caught a ferry to Luna Park.

By the end of the night the Godsons, too, had just one ride each left. Although it was midwinter, Jenny Godson decided she wanted an ice-cream. Her boys, keen to get on the Ghost Train before it closed, raced ahead. She thought they would wait for her. But when she got there, her husband and sons had entered the Ghost Train's twisting corridors without her.

Jason's friends had scurried ahead of him to climb into the Ghost Train's carriages. Two got in together and disappeared through the entrance doors into the spooky darkness. Then his two other friends did the same. Just seven seconds separated each carriage; Jason sat alone in the last carriage. He later recalled: 'As my carriage went [forward], the doors opened and a man came out saying, "Get out, it's on fire." I could smell the smoke, just as I went through the door.'

The fire spread quickly and engulfed the mostly timber building. Jason did not know the fate of his schoolmates when a policeman later drove him home. Nor did the rest of Sydney. Jason's mother was angry when she opened the door and saw her son accompanied by a policeman and assumed he had got into mischief. 'What have you done?' she asked.

Jason went with his parents to the home of Jonathan Billings, his best friend, who lived a couple of doors away. Jonathan was among the boys who had entered the Ghost Train ahead of him. Jason climbed into his missing school friend's bed while the anxious families turned on the radio and television.

In the early hours of the morning, Jason heard howling in the house. Jonathan's father had just learned that his thirteen-year-old son had perished in the flames. The fire claimed seven lives: the four Waverley schoolboys—Jonathan Billings, Richard Carroll, Michael Johnson and Seamus Rahilly—and John Godson and his two sons, Damien and Craig.

Martin had held fears about the park's safety even before the fire. He had been alarmed by an accident two months earlier when thirteen people, mostly children, had been injured after two cars collided on the Big Dipper. He had even written a letter to New South Wales Premier Neville Wran in the wake of that accident. Martin warned Wran—who had defended Martin years earlier over his *Gas Lash* cartoon—that the public was at risk at the funfair. The repair and restoration needed were too big a job for the park's management. The government needed to step in, develop a long-term plan to put Luna Park on safe ground, he wrote.

But Martin didn't send the letter. Advised by a friend that the language was too strong and needed rewriting, Martin had put it in his bottom drawer. Now Martin drove to Luna Park as soon as he heard about the fire, unaware that anyone had died. He belatedly delivered his letter to Wran the morning after the fire. Less than six months earlier, Luna Park had been the setting for one of the greatest nights of Martin's life, but now the childhood fantasy world in which Martin had invested his hopes, dreams and his art was in ashes.

Police immediately ruled out arson believing the cause was an electrical fault. Artist Garry Shead was working at Luna Park the day before the fire and had walked into the Ghost Train. 'There was so much litter there, no one had cleaned up the papers. It was easy to see how a fire could happen,' says Garry.

Martin's initial response to the media recognised the Ghost Train was rundown, but there was no indication of the elaborate conspiracy he would soon develop and which would overshadow the rest of his life. He said simply: 'It's eerie that that is where the fire should have started. It was a real labyrinth of wood, plywood and cloth. Nothing had been done to it for years.'

At the time of the fire, the park was leased week-to-week to Leon Fink and Nathan Spatt, whose earlier six-year lease had run out. They wanted a new long-term lease to justify the cost of improvements they wanted to make. Fink claimed he had lobbied Wran in a bid to secure a longer lease but the premier refused. The coroner's report, released three months later, concluded that the fire had been 'reasonably foreseeable' and that an electrical fault was unlikely to have caused the fire. A cigarette or match 'carelessly or recklessly discarded' by someone in the train was the most probable cause; the fire had started near an imitation fire.

The coroner reprimanded management for a 'serious breach of duty of care'. There had been a reluctance to spend money on fire safety measures. That could be explained, but not excused, by the company's insecure week-to-week tenure. The coroner dismissed as 'false and mischievous' a claim made to police shortly after the fire that it had been deliberately lit. Nonetheless, rumours persisted that the fire was no accident—that it had been started by an underworld figure who coveted this prime piece of Sydney waterfront real estate.

The burden of responsibility for the fire weighed heavily on Martin. He felt guilty that he had put an enticing smiling face on a place that proved deadly. And he soon saw the fire at Luna Park as suspicious and sinister. Within a couple of months of the coroner's report, Martin drafted an unpublished article in which he likened the deadly fire to a medieval morality play in which 'a vengeful God demanded a sacrifice of innocence from a complacent city … It was an event so shocking that Sydney has so far been unable to bring itself to face the significance of the ghost train fire. Yet it cannot be sidestepped. The silence surrounding the tragedy has its roots in a deep civic embarrassment. Sydney had neglected Luna Park until the inevitable happened.'

Luna Park was inextricably connected with childhood and innocence. But Martin's pursuit of the symbolic meaning of the fire led him into a dark psychic labyrinth from which some believe he never returned. He became deeply religious and, to many who had known him in his early life, perplexingly so.

His early cartoons had taken aim at Christianity and even poked fun at God. But he now began studying the Bible and saw in Luna Park an epic battle between good and evil. He began attending services at Catholic and Anglican churches, and developed a fire and brimstone element in his form of Christianity. His approach to spirituality was unorthodox and drew on disparate elements; it was as much a collage as his artworks. He delved into the writings of psychiatrist Carl Jung and studied Jung's theory of synchronicity—that it is possible to see meaningful connections behind apparent coincidences. 'Synchronicity, I think that's how God talks,' he said.

He saw meaning in the fact that the Waverley schoolboys had come from mass; he saw as demonic the horned figure the Godson boys had been photographed with just before they left for Luna Park, and then there was the name Godson itself. With Sydney in the midst of a train strike at the time of the fire, he saw meaning in the fact that the Ghost Train was the only train running. He likened the Luna Park fire to the biblical temple to Moloch, in which ancient tribes were said to sacrifice boys to the flames. The fire had occurred in the International Year of the Child. He began studying occult imagery. He saw numerological significance in the seven deaths—associating them with the seven biblical plagues and the Seven Seals of the apocalyptic Book of Revelations, which he began analysing in depth.

Fearing what might happen in his absence, he became reluctant to leave the house. He acquired fire extinguishers for Wirian, which he insisted should be checked regularly. When he claimed he was being followed and his house was being watched, some feared he was becoming paranoid. Others believed he had reason to be on his guard because he insisted the fire was no accident.

Martin began work on one of his most powerful artworks within a year of the fire. *Snow Job* depicted a laughing clown's face almost obliterated by falling snow. He had used snowballs in *Kold Komfort Kaffe*, but the ominous *Snow Job* expressed Martin's unwavering belief that the cause of the Luna Park fire was suspicious and had been covered up. He consistently responded to the tragedy in his art. He painted in the form of a cross portraits of the seven who died and called it *Golgotha*, a reference to the hill known as the 'place of the skull', where Christ was said to have been crucified.

In 1991 Martin created the poster *Lest We Forget* for an exhibition at the Hyde Park Barracks of his own and other Luna Park memorabilia. The poster had the face of Luna Park with a sinister smile, above which the letter 'f' in 'funfair' has broken away, so it read 'unfair'. With an economy of lettering, he transformed the meaning—just as he had when he changed a single letter of Dylan's 'Blowin' in the Wind' to 'Blowin' in the Mind' when he created his celebrated poster *Mr Tambourine Man*.

Martin became friends with Jason Holman, the schoolboy who survived the fire, and with Jenny Godson (later Poidevin), who had lost her husband and two sons. Martin and Jason visited the graves of his school friends who perished. Until his death, on the anniversary of the fire each year Martin telephoned Jenny.

With Luna Park closed immediately after the fire, Martin took up the fight to save the funfair. With Peter Kingston he formed Friends of Luna Park to lobby for its preservation. Martin, Peter and others prepared a report for the state government on the park's history and significance. Michael Barker was a young photographer who had helped document the park; when Michael was killed in a hit-and-run accident while riding his motorcycle around the time when the report was being completed, Martin dedicated the report to him.

Parts of Luna Park were sold in mid-1981, by which time a consortium called Harbourside Amusements was poised to take up a thirty-year lease. Martin and Peter Kingston attended the auction of memorabilia, posters, Arthur Barton's signs, costumes and rides, including a carousel and horses and a Burmese buddha. Auction-goers booed when the carousel was sold to an American collector, who planned to ship it off to the United States. The auction raised half a million dollars. Martin spent nine thousand dollars buying memorabilia and rides, including Coney Island's Turkey Trot, Barrels of Fun and the Joy Wheel, all of which remained on site. Peter bought the River Caves for twenty dollars, but he was unable to remove them; they were then bulldozed together with much of the park—but not Coney Island—to make way for new rides when the park reopened in 1982. But the park closed again in 1988 and the smiling face and towers were removed. Plans were drawn up by a new lessee for an adult entertainment centre with high-rise buildings.

Allegations of criminal involvement in the fire persisted. They were aired at a New South Wales Police Internal Security Unit inquiry in 1985, during which a witness claimed the fire was started by a group of bikies working for an underworld figure who was trying to gain control of the park. Questions were raised in state parliament that year about the involvement of notorious crime boss Abe Saffron in the ownership of the park. Saffron was by then a much-feared—if rarely prosecuted—figure. The nightclub owner and property developer controlled the vice trade, and bribed and corrupted senior police and politicians to protect his empire.

The Corporate Affairs Commission attempted to untangle the web of ownership of Luna Park. It learned that Harbourside Amusements, the consortium who leased the funfair in the wake of the fire, included two of Saffron's cousins as directors and a nephew as company secretary. Nonetheless it could find no evidence that Saffron was the beneficial owner of the funfair.

Martin compiled a thick file of press clippings and other material on Saffron. (He kept extensive files on many areas of interest—so many that Richard Neville satirically likened him to 'a little Stasi officer' with his assiduous document-keeping.) Among the headlines in hundreds of articles that dated back to the 1950s were: 'Saffron named as crime boss', 'Saffron: I'm not Mr Sin', 'Saffron denies vice or gambling links', 'Abe Saffron accused of link with drug buying'.

Martin included in his file a page from a Sydney phonebook with the telephone number of a company linked to Saffron, Arcadia Amusements, which provided vending machines to Luna Park. With Martin's interest in the Book of Revelations, it would not have escaped his notice that the phone number ended in 666, the number of the Beast. Martin titled his file 'Criminal Connections: Saffron, The King in Yellow'. It was a reference to the colour of his name, but also an allusion to a theme in a book of supernatural short stories by nineteenth-century American writer Robert W. Chambers. *The King in Yellow*, referred to throughout the stories, is a fictional play that induces despair or madness in anyone who reads it.

Martin's film about Tiny Tim became inextricably bound up with the Ghost Train fire. Called *Street of Dreams*, it has elements of nightmare. Part-documentary, part-visual collage, the film's uniting thread is Tiny Tim's singing marathon at Luna Park, but it is also intertwined with the fire and Martin's response to it. In the film Martin alleges there was a cover-up and that police had told him this at the time but were powerless to act. At its heart it is also a self-portrait of Martin. It is full of striking and disturbing images, chaotic juxtapositions and meanderings that—like his speech and letters—trail off without conclusion.

Martin worked on the film obsessively throughout the 1980s, and it cost him a fortune. It almost cost him his house. He put Wirian up for auction through real estate agents L.J. Hooker in 1983, then changed his mind. He mortgaged the house instead. Indeed, he used the house as a piggy bank—he mortgaged Wirian more than a dozen times between 1978 and 1984.

The near-auction of Wirian came on the heels of one of Martin's most quixotic Tiny Tim ventures. In September 1982 he hired the Sydney Opera House's opera theatre for a performance by the singer. He designed a poster for the concert depicting the Opera House shells morphing into Tiny Tim's face. And he placed an advertisement in *The Sydney Morning Herald*. It read: 'Martin Sharp presents against all reasonable advice, once only, the one and only Tiny Tim, Eternal Troubadour.' But Martin never did accept reasonable advice.

The audience applauded loudly as the singer performed his repertoire, including 'Street of Dreams', 'Sweet Rosie O'Grady' and 'Heartbreak Hotel'. But the concert was hardly a sell-out. The 1500-seat theatre was only half full. It was not just the enormous amounts of money Martin sank into Tiny Tim, who made at least eight trips to Australia between 1971 and 1993, but the vast amounts of time. Some friends questioned what he was doing, including Nathan Waks. '[I'd say,] "You're a great artist, Martin, and I hate to see you subjugating your own art to anyone else." He said, "I'm not, I'm learning from Tiny." … He was like a child at Tiny's feet sometimes,' says Nathan.

Martin remained immovable. He did not see his involvement with Tiny Tim as being at the expense of his work—it was integral to it.

Martin remained in contact with his father and stepmother, and attended their annual family Christmas gatherings at Mosman. But as the new year began in 1984, Henry Sharp became ill. He died on 23 January 1984, two days after Martin's forty-second birthday. Henry left his estate of $880,000 to his widow, Dorothy. Martin's mother's health also deteriorated around this time. Jo Sharp had lived in an apartment in Darling Point for nearly a decade after selling her large Cranbrook Lane residence, Martin's childhood home. As she became increasingly frail, she moved to Wirian in 1984, where Alex Popov designed quarters for her upstairs.

Jo developed diabetes and scoliosis, and her already tiny bird-like figure became stooped as her spine curved. Yet Jo, who Brett Whiteley dubbed the little sparrow, retained her wit. Peter Kingston sat with an ailing Jo and Martin around an open fireplace one winter night at Wirian. Jo was aware of Martin's growing religious beliefs, but did not share them or appreciate his efforts to 'convert' her. Peter recalls: 'She pointed to Martin, and said, "He's religious but, as far as I am concerned, there's only possums up there."'

Jo died at St Luke's Hospital, where Martin had been born, just after midnight on 24 November 1986. Her death notice read: 'The sparrow has flown. God bless her loving soul.' She asked for 'Hello, Young Lovers' to be sung at her funeral service on 2 December at St Mark's in Darling Point, the church in which she married. Martin's childhood friend John Gregory-Roberts gave the eulogy. Martin held a wake at Wirian for his great champion, the woman who had encouraged his art and was his first art teacher.

Jo's estate was valued at $1.7 million. She left bequests of a thousand dollars each to several of Martin's friends, including Marilyn Karet and musician Alastair Jones, who both worked on the Tiny Tim film, Yensoon Tsai and to Martin's early girlfriend Anou Kiisler. Martin inherited the remainder and became the sole owner of Wirian. 'I miss her so, but feel she is with me,' he wrote to Eija, his former London girlfriend, soon after Jo's death.

As he went through Jo's treasures in the wake of her death, he discovered a series of letters. Most were more than forty years old, written during World War II. They were love letters between his parents. The letters transformed Martin's understanding of his parents' marriage. Until then, he had known their relationship only for the unhappiness it had brought. Martin learned that Jo and Henry Sharp had once truly loved each other.

He wrote a long letter to Eija about his startling discovery: 'My childhood was spent in the midst of their dissapointment [sic] and being the manifestation of their love that had been vanquished I never experienced their love. I was the result of it, but I never knew it even existed until I read those letters, with gratitude. I knew something was missing but I didn't know what it was. To many my life appears very priviliged [sic] but the greatest privilige [sic] is to have parents who love each other. And if they can't love each other and separate after years of coldness one hopes they could talk to each other, be friends. But such was the great failure of their marriage that they only spoke once ... And it was brief and polite, and they both told me afterwards how the other had aged.'

Martin recalled with regret that he had let slip a moment that might have brought some peace to all. Shortly before his death, Henry Sharp telephoned Martin. Jo was living at Wirian at the time. 'He rang up drunk and lonely. I was in the room with my mother and some friends. There was a moment I could have put her on the phone to him and it might have brought a blessing to us all. I was so apprehensive that one or the other would refuse. I failed to make the connection that may have brought some redemption. I regret my lack of courage.'

He felt he had disappointed his mother and had been unable to fully reciprocate her love. 'I surely know my mother loved me a great deal more than I could love her and [feel] a sense of failure about my relationship with her, almost a reaction about being loved too much. I know my parents tried their best with each other, and certainly with me, though my father was never close, perhaps because he only held me briefly when I was a baby.'

The woman he had confided in during the sixties, Eija Vehka-aho, had re-entered his life shortly before Jo Sharp's death. In the intervening years Eija had moved to Stockholm; her days as a high fashion model were over and she had studied alternative healing. Martin had unexpectedly received a letter from her in the mid-1980s, when she was curious to learn what had happened to him.

He had replied in an upbeat letter, updating her on their mutual London friends and his life. Eric Clapton—who had overcome battles with heroin and alcohol—had recently visited him on tour. 'It was wonderful to see him, very well and slim and clear. I think we got on better than ever, friendship grows.' Philippe Mora was living in America and making horror films; Richard Neville was about to make a television series, *Extra Dimensions*, which looked at sustainability and human potential.

Martin had told Eija that he kept a photograph of her framed in pink wood on his wall. He spent a lot of time 'tidying up'—it was a favourite expression. He was still disorganised. He was to be godfather to a friend's child the next day and, although he had found a pair of matching socks to wear, he had no buttons on his coat. He was also suffering from kidney stones—he had repeated bouts of this excruciating condition over the years. But mostly he was busy being an artist, and his Tiny Tim film was the most important part of that. 'It's my Sistine Chapel ceiling,' he wrote.

But after his mother's death, Martin's letters to Eija took on darker hues. He gave an unsettling description of the role the house played in his life and art. He hardly ever left it, he explained. 'This house is a studio which is the front line in a strange warfare. I suppose you could describe it as Art against Black Magic.' Part of the battle was against heroin. Although Martin continued to smoke marijuana throughout his life, he regarded heroin as evil. 'Things are very tense in Australia,' he wrote. 'The serpent is pumping heroin into the veins of our youth. World War 3 is being waged on the streets of every city and country town. Hostages are held on the point of a needle.' By then he was aware of the price heroin exacted on some of those around him. His artist friend Brett Whiteley was battling addiction—and would fatally overdose in 1992—and a former Wirian resident, Sallie-Anne Huckstepp, was dead.

Sallie-Anne was a prostitute, heroin addict and police corruption whistleblower, although Martin knew little about her when she arrived at Wirian. Richard Neville, who had encountered Sallie-Anne through his work in the media, had asked Martin if he could shelter her. With her gap-tooth smile and forthright manner, she was charismatic and intelligent, with an aura of danger.

She mingled with Wirian's artists and she began to write. Martin thought she could become a successful writer. She certainly had stories to tell, and they were every bit as compelling as David Litvinoff's. Sallie-Anne's boyfriend, Warren Lanfranchi, a drug dealer and armed robber, had been shot dead in an inner-city laneway by a Sydney detective, Roger Rogerson, in June 1981. Rogerson was at that time one of the police force's most decorated officers. But Sallie-Anne claimed Rogerson had murdered her boyfriend in retaliation for Lanfranchi having ripped off another drug dealer the detective was protecting. Rogerson claimed self-defence. She believed Rogerson had a corrupt relationship with notorious criminal Neddy Smith, who had brought Lanfranchi to the laneway. She believed the New South Wales Drug Squad and Armed Hold Up Squad were corrupt and had made that allegation to the New South Wales Police Internal Affairs Branch. She was frequently in the media spotlight. She claimed on national television to have been paying off police for more than a decade. 'But when the police become judge, jury and executioner, then somebody has to speak out.'

Since disgraced, Rogerson has been described as 'possibly the most corrupt police officer Australia has known'. He was dismissed from the police force in 1986, jailed for perjury and, in 2016, convicted of the murder of a twenty-year-old university student and alleged drug dealer, Jamie Gao, and jailed for life.

Sallie-Anne's life was cut violently short at the age of thirty-one. She was strangled in 1986 and her body was found floating in a lake in Centennial Park. Neddy Smith later confessed to her murder, but was acquitted. He subsequently claimed that she was killed because she was making trouble for Rogerson. Her murder remains unsolved.

Martin admired Sallie-Anne's outspokenness and large personality. After her death, he described her as: 'A mythic figure. Very brave, she showed exemplary courage. Ultimately one of the great women.'

If Sallie-Anne's murder—like the disappearance of Juanita Neilson—raised questions about the price paid by whistleblowers and activists, Martin was not about to be silenced in his crusade over the Luna Park fire. He organised an exhibition at the Hogarth Galleries in June 1987 in memory of those who had perished in the fire. Ahead of the opening, he stood alongside widow Jenny Poidevin while she called for the reopening of an inquiry into the blaze. And he reiterated claims that the fire had been started by bikies working for an underworld figure trying to gain control of the park. He told *The Sydney Morning Herald*: 'There is a strong smell of injustice around this case. It only requires a brave police force and judiciary to delve deeper into this awful web of evil.'

CHAPTER 16

'WHILE OFTEN EXTREME AND ECCENTRIC ...'

The tall ships rounded the heads and sailed past Wirian en route to Sydney Harbour. More than two million people crowded the foreshore on Australia Day 1988 to watch a re-enactment of the First Fleet of British convict ships arriving. It was the beginning of a year-long celebration to mark Australia's bicentenary of white settlement.

But for Australia's Indigenous community, the bicentenary was no cause for celebration and Australia Day was viewed as Invasion Day. For them, the two hundred years that followed the British arrival had been marked by massacres, displacement from country, the forced removal of children from families, high rates of incarceration and low life expectancy. For Australia's Aboriginal people, the bicentenary was a year of mourning and resistance.

As the ships arrived and flags were waved, in Sydney's Hyde Park 40,000 people gathered in protest, the largest demonstration since Vietnam. That evening Indigenous Australians gathered at La Perouse, a south-eastern Sydney suburb across Botany Bay from where Captain Cook stepped ashore. Martin and Jenny Kee joined them. Fires were lit and ceremonies performed, to the sound of the didgeridoo and the scent of smouldering eucalyptus. At daybreak, the Aboriginal flag was raised. Martin later told his friend, art curator Ace Bourke, it was one of the most significant nights of his life.

Martin's concern for the plight of the first Australians grew slowly. Although he had created a poster advocating for Indigenous land rights in the 1980s, it was only in his later years that this concern would be consistently reflected in his art. Among his first Indigenous friends was actor David Gulpilil. Martin had been impressed with the young actor, a Yolngu man from north-east Arnhem Land, since he first saw him in Nicolas Roeg's film *Walkabout* and met him when he appeared in Philippe Mora's film *Mad Dog Morgan*. David visited Wirian, where Martin filmed him for his Tiny Tim film; when Tiny recorded the Bee Gees disco song 'Stayin' Alive', David played didgeridoo and clapsticks.

Martin travelled to Britain a few months later where Tiny was to stage another singing marathon and where Martin's film *Street of Dreams* was to premiere at the Brighton Arts Festival in May 1988. Martin designed a vivid poster for the festival, with stars and fireworks illuminating the night sky above Brighton Pier. Some friends from Australia accompanied Martin, including Nathan Waks, who invited eminent British musicologist Sir Christopher Hogwood to the marathon. 'Christopher immediately understood the musicological significance,' says Nathan.

Tiny Tim broke his Luna Park record, singing continuously for three hours and eleven minutes and soldiering on through a power failure during 'Life is Just a Bowl of Cherries' that briefly silenced his accompanying band. Despite Nathan's reservations about the amount of time and money Martin invested in Tiny Tim, his view of the performer's musical ability remains unchanged: 'I believed him to be a serious musician who wasn't taken seriously.'

As Martin prepared to screen the film, which he edited and re-edited until the last minute, he told Eija how the film had dominated his life for a decade. He acknowledged people wondered why it was taking him so long to finish it—and he wondered the same. The difficulties were connected to the Luna Park fire: 'It was very carefully planned to look like an accident. It spun a web of delusion over the city like an evil spell. I have been working to break that spell,' he wrote. He described *Street of Dreams* as a religious film and hoped it would be a healing film. 'I'm certainly going to feel better when it's finished,' he quipped.

As a portrait of Tiny Tim, *Street of Dreams* is far from hagiography. In it, the man *Newsweek* once described as 'The Last Innocent' seems anything but. The film is an unsettling portrayal of a controversial, complex and contradictory figure. Tiny's extremely conservative views on contraception and sexuality are intercut with scenes of him at Wirian watching a stripper. Its most bizarre scene was shot in New York, where Martin had sent a film crew. It shows an apparently drunk Tiny Tim, beer in hand, on a bed in a cheap hotel removing the bra from a woman otherwise clad only in black panties. As the unsettling scene unfolds, the perplexed cameraman can be heard asking: 'Tiny Tim, why did you bring me here tonight to film?' Quizzed about the scene later, Martin commented: 'We all have strange sexual fantasies.'

By the time the film screened in Brighton, Martin's preoccupation with Tiny had become far more than childlike hero worship or admiration for the singer's musical ability. Tiny Tim struck a chord with Martin that was as complex and unsettling as the singer himself. Martin's muse was a strange brew of contradictory spiritual and sexual tensions. Tiny espoused fundamentalist Christian beliefs and rejected women's liberation and birth control, saying the latter was like 'stuffing a Brillo pad up the faucet to stop the water flowing'. He advocated purity and abstinence, coyly spelt out the word s-e-x, and yet acknowledged, 'I'm the biggest sinner in the world.'

Tiny Tim led Martin into his unorthodox form of Christianity. In time, Martin came to share some of Tiny's puritanical beliefs and turned to him for advice. 'Being a lost soul I was somehow drawn to Tiny just by loving his singing and his courage, and his love of romance … Tiny was the first Christian I could listen to because the formal church was beyond me.'

Tiny Tim divided Martin's friends. An astonished Victoria Cobden recalls Tiny giving her advice before she got married: 'He lectured us for four hours while he sipped cocktails. He said, "Remember s-e-x is only for blessed events within wedlock."'

Some were concerned that Martin was manipulated by Tiny Tim. George Gittoes enjoyed the singer's music, but was wary of his motives. George was backstage with Tiny on one occasion when the singer badgered him for some business contacts. He struck George as a go-getting showbiz professional. But as soon as Martin appeared, Tiny pulled a Bible from a bag and began quoting scriptures: 'I was amazed by the brazenness of the switch from the hustler to a born-again, evangelistic hell-and-brimstone preacher. It was clear Tiny knew how to maintain Martin's fantasies about Tiny Tim as a Prophet of Song. Obviously Tiny knew he was on a good wicket … [Tiny] knew how to manipulate Martin's peculiar obsessions. Martin made Tiny into a Christ-like figure and would quote him and his songs as if they were from a Biblical verse.' Tiny shared Martin's Christian fundamentalism and a fondness for young women. 'This was perfect for Martin as it endorsed his own moral contradictions.'

Throughout his life, Martin was surrounded by beautiful young women. At Wirian, he had a string of young female assistants who helped him in the studio. Some were the daughters of artist friends, or aspiring artists themselves, whose art he encouraged. In turn they watched him work.

But as he got older and the age gap widened between himself and the women in his orbit, some longstanding friends and observers wondered about the nature of his relationships with women. By then he had embarked on a number of relationships with women younger than himself, including Victoria Cobden, and Nell and Cressida Campbell.

His relationship with Yensoon Tsai ended after Martin became convinced she was older than he initially believed her to be.

Why did he not form long relationships with women? Why was he drawn to young women? No one was sure. Martin's fascination with young women was well known among his circle and a source of unease to some. Friends observed Martin infatuated by some of the young women around him. Critic Robert Hughes described what he called Martin's 'relentless, rather wistful pursuit' of young women as a testament to his childishness.

Julie Clarke believes Martin was drawn to the perfection of young women. 'He loved the beauty of youth. It wasn't about shagging … So many painters, all they want to do is root their models. Martin was not like that,' she says. He was interested in the aesthetics of women. 'He just liked the way their white shoulder was reflected in a mirror, the lines of a nude body and the beauty of a face, but not wanting to be close to a person … The younger the woman the more perfect the lines of the face and the body.'

Martin was voyeuristic, says Jenny Kee. He was fascinated by beauty, especially youthful beauty. He was an observer. 'I don't think he liked women getting older. He loved the glow of youth, he loved the romance … His intrigue was always about not who the person was, but their beauty. And that was wonderful, but it was also a bit eerie because he couldn't show his emotions.' Nor could he sustain a long-term intimate relationship: '[Martin] damaged women because he couldn't commit,' says Kee.

Wendy Whiteley felt Martin's impact on women was corrosive: 'I don't think he was good to any of the women in his life. He confused them and fucked them up.' She sensed an unresolved conflict in Martin: 'There was an element of Martin's darkness that was deep. He was afraid of it … I always thought he had a dark pit in there somewhere that he struggled against all the time.'

Martin arrived at Sydney's Sacred Heart hospice with an early version of his painting *Pentecost.* A friend of his, writer Edda Walker, was dying of cancer and she had asked friends to bring into her room something of themselves, something beautiful. With its biblical allusion to the descent of the Holy Spirit, Martin's painting drew on Magritte's dove from *The Great Family* and Henri Matisse's *Large Red Interior*. Edda's daughter Kathryn stuck little red hearts on the hospice room's walls, and then added one to the eye of the dove that dominated Martin's painting.

After his friend died, Martin remained in contact with her two daughters and became particularly close to the youngest, Emma Walker. She was an aspiring artist in her late teens when she came to help Martin at Wirian. She carried out a range of chores, from sorting boxes of photographs to vacuuming the stairs. He mentored her art. She was impressed with Martin's openness to people from all walks of life. Emma says: 'He accepted everyone through that door: strangers, vagabonds, psychotics.'

In time, Emma became Martin's muse, and by 1989 he was captivated by her. Emma recounts: 'He liked having a muse. He needed that, beyond Jesus Christ. He needed a female, preferably a young one.'

Martin wrote long passionate letters to Emma, full of biblical quotations, meandering observations and declarations of love. Theirs was not a physical relationship. It was primarily a romance of letters. Emma recounts: 'There was definitely love there. It was romantic without needing to be sexual, as far as I was concerned. And I don't think it really mattered to him either. His prime motivation was something else. Because he was an artist, and your muse becomes all encompassing. It burns brightly and when that inspiration flickers out, you are on to the next one.'

His letters reveal a deep conflict between his Christian ideals and his behaviour. He acknowledged his actions had fallen short of standards he aspired to. He felt remorse over his previous relationship with Yensoon Tsai and expressed this in Old Testament language: 'I lay with her in fornication and caused her and myself to sin though I knew God's Law.' Martin had even turned to Tiny Tim for advice on sexual morality: 'Tiny was most explicit in his recent instructions to me, "God HATES fornication" and yet twice since recieving [sic] that most definite advice I fell from Grace.'

Although Martin and Emma kissed only once—under the stars on Cranbrook's oval—Martin wanted to marry her, and to remain chaste until he did. 'I pray God gives me the strength to be married to you before we are together. I feel in His eyes we are married in our spirits. If we are to be married in the flesh, let it be in a manner which is pleasing to God.' His words are a far cry from the free-love advocate of the 1960s.

Good and evil were recurrent themes in his letters to Emma and in their many long conversations. Emma did not share his religious beliefs, nor did he try to convert her; she sensed that for Martin good and evil were tangible forces. She recalls: 'He was like a detective trying to work things out, and it felt like he had a mission to do that. The reason for that mission was complicated, but I think on the whole it was about good and evil, getting to the bottom of those forces and finding ways to work with goodness.'

He also wrote to Emma about his art, giving a frank assessment of his abilities and aware that the diverse art forms in which he had worked had impacted on his ability to be taken seriously. 'I'm not a real painter, though sometimes I have done some good paintings. It's been an extraordinary and unexpected life in art. I never dreamt I would work in so many areas—from funfairs to fine art—it could be viewed as being a dilletante (if that's the right spelling?) I don't consider myself too bright, but I have been granted insights, inspirations.'

Having worked in film and theatre, he had ventured into another field: nude photography. 'I really only want to photograph beautiful nudes like a book my mother had which aroused my boyhood interest. It was called *Light and Shadow* and I used to look at it often. I have tried to paint nudes—not too well—and I have written a bit about the subject . . . questioning my motives. I don't know if it's a yearning for a woman or a yearning to paint an eternally fascinating subject.'

The insights he had gathered, not least from his pursuit of the symbolism of Luna Park, weighed heavily. 'Sometimes I feel that I am pushing my health too far. Too many cigarettes, too much coffee and not enough sleep and food and exercise. Sometimes I feel I am under house arrest with my burden of the knowledge I have been granted of the dark side of town . . . Mine is not the life of an ordinary man—much as I have tried to make it so at times, wished I could be more normal—this is not a comfortable life, but it is a wonderful one.'

Martin gave Emma his painting *Pentecost*, but later asked for it back. He wanted to rework it. Martin often asked for works back, claiming they were unfinished. But once returned to Wirian, the works were extracted from Martin's tenacious grip with great difficulty. To Emma's surprise, he returned the work about six years later. By then he had made many changes. But the one that resonated with her most was one of the smallest. Over the eye of the dove, he had painted a little red heart.

Martin never wavered from his conviction that the Luna Park fire was deliberate and that Abe Saffron was behind it. Martin believed bikies had lit the fire at Saffron's bidding as a means of having the park closed, evicting the incumbent tenants and gaining control of the lease. By 1989 the circumstances of the Luna Park fire were being investigated by the National Crime Authority (NCA). Martin provided material to the authority during its two-year inquiry. It gave consideration to his theory that Abe Saffron—by then linked to seven other Sydney fires—had coveted the Luna Park site for more than twenty years. It considered allegations of bikie involvement and learned that they were regular visitors to Luna Park.

The NCA's report, tabled in New South Wales parliament in mid-1989, was scathing about the original police investigation, which it described as 'grossly inadequate'. It concluded that, because of this, the coronial inquest had been rendered 'ineffective'. Legitimate avenues of inquiry had not been thoroughly pursued; these included claims by two witnesses to have seen bikies near the Ghost Train just before the fire. As a result, possible leads had faded. But there was no evidence that the inadequate police investigation was due to dishonesty or corruption.

Martin annotated a copy of the ninety-page report. In it he found himself described as well-motivated but obsessed: 'as a result his judgment has become clouded, if not warped ... it is unlikely that Mr Sharp will ever be satisfied that the fire was caused by other than deliberate criminal behaviour on someone's part.'

The NCA failed to discover the cause of the fire and could not say whether or not it was deliberately lit. But the report noted that because of the failure of the initial police investigation to provide a credible explanation, the fire had remained the subject of rumour and innuendo. The NCA concluded that Martin's theories, 'while often extreme and eccentric, arose from public dissatisfaction with the original findings, which in this case was not without cause'.

The young Thai woman brought light and laughter into Wirian. The house always looked beautiful on the days when the new housekeeper had visited. And the scent of lemongrass and lime filled the kitchen as she prepared fragrant Thai food for the house.

Martin hired Paiwan Phongsitthisak in February 1991 and she worked at Wirian five days a week, cooking, washing and gardening. She had a sense of fun and cheekiness, although she missed the young son she had left behind in northern Thailand. Paiwan wanted a better life for the little boy, who lived with her brother; she regularly sent money back to support him and dreamed of bringing him to Australia.

Wirian's residents adored Paiwan, and she became close to Gria Shead, Garry's daughter, who was living at the house while she studied at art school. Gria enjoyed Paiwan's company and her food. Paiwan would often have dishes ready when Gria came downstairs mid-morning. They would sit together eating and chatting, and planned a trip to Canberra together.

Paiwan shared her Centennial Park flat with her Australian boyfriend of two years, David Smedley. She had met him when she worked in a Kings Cross strip club, where she was known as Pepsi. The well-spoken man appeared kind and gentle. She tried hard to make the relationship work, even paying all the bills. But the relationship was troubled. David, an unemployed financial adviser and bankrupt, would become violent, especially after drinking.

Late one night, a distressed Paiwan phoned Martin and told him David had beaten her. Martin drove over to Centennial Park at about 2am and found her in tears in the street. He brought her back to Wirian. She stayed the night in a spare bedroom but returned to her flat next day. Martin was working late one night in October when there was a knock at his studio door at the rear of the house. It was Paiwan. David had bashed her again. She was frightened and desperate to get away from him.

Martin agreed she could stay at Wirian and she moved into a spare room beneath his studio. He wanted her to stay in a room within the main house, which he considered safer. But she insisted on staying in the downstairs room, which had a separate entrance. David began telephoning Wirian and was each time told she was not there, triggering verbal abuse and threats to Martin or whoever answered the phone.

Martin and Gria helped Paiwan take out a restraining order against Smedley. Despite this, he continued telephoning, although he seemed polite when he did. Martin was unhappy about obfuscating on the phone, and eventually told David that Paiwan was living at Wirian and that she was well. 'I was uncomfortable about lying,' he said. '... I thought she would be safe.' Paiwan was distressed when she learned Martin had disclosed her whereabouts. David arrived at Wirian one morning and sat in the garden talking with Paiwan. It was the first time Martin had set eyes on her 42-year-old boyfriend.

Paiwan, twenty-nine, had been living at Wirian for a few weeks when she arranged a night out with a girlfriend. She asked Gria if she would babysit her girlfriend's child while the two women went out. Gria could mind her in Paiwan's downstairs room. But at the last minute, the arrangements were changed. Paiwan asked Gria to look after the little girl at the friend's house at Maroubra, several kilometres away. Gria had no car, but she reluctantly agreed and stayed overnight.

Back at Wirian, Martin was working on his poster *Fragments of a (F)unfair* ahead of his exhibition of Luna Park memorabilia in the early hours of 9 November 1991. A friend, William de la Vega, had called around and they sat talking late into the night and playing loud music. It was about 3am when Martin's dozing dogs suddenly became excited.

'I heard the dogs barking, but I thought they were barking at possums,' said Martin. He let the animals out and continued working. Then he heard a noise and went into the kitchen to investigate. He found nothing but, as he walked back, he smelt smoke and saw a haze in the room above Paiwan's room. Her room was alight, but he did not know whether she had returned home from her night out.

Martin and William grabbed some fire extinguishers that the artist had kept at Wirian since the Luna Park fire. Martin said: 'We broke into the room and she was there. I could hear a little noise from her.' Paiwan was lying facedown on the floor, her nightdress largely burned off. A birdcage was at her feet and the bird was dead inside. David lay next to her; he was conscious. Martin said: 'His hair had been burned off, his skin had gone blue ... I said, "You monster."'

Martin called an ambulance, but Paiwan could not be saved. She died in the room. Despite his injuries, David stumbled around to the front of the house, where Martin saw him leaning on a lamppost. He was wearing only underpants and his burnt skin was peeling off. He was taken to hospital, where he made an allegation that Gria had also been present in Paiwan's room. This may have been intended as a final act of villainy. David, who died of his injuries less than twelve hours later, knew that Gria had helped Paiwan take out the restraining order.

Unable to locate Gria, police contacted her father, who drove to Wirian from his home more than an hour away. Gria knew nothing of the night's horrific events until she returned from her previous night's babysitting and found the usually unlocked gates of Wirian locked. She arrived at the same time as her father.

Martin attended the inquest, at which he heard that David Smedley had arrived at Wirian that night with two four-litre drums of petrol. He had left his shoes in the car so as not to make a noise on the gravel driveway. Inside Paiwan's room, he had hit her twice over the head with the metal stand of the birdcage, knocking her unconscious. Then he doused her and himself with the fluid and struck a match.

The coroner offered condolences to Martin, who had lost the friend he had tried to help: '[Paiwan was] someone you knew, a friend you tried to help, unfortunately it didn't come out the right way.' In the aftermath, Martin arranged for various religious rituals to be performed. Her funeral was held at Wirian, presided over by an Anglican priest who also performed a cleansing ceremony in her downstairs room. Martin, Gria and William de la Vega went to the Buddhist temple in western Sydney that Paiwan used to attend, where monks performed a ritual in her honour.

Martin knew that the Wirian fire could easily have consumed the house, his life's work and the lives of all within it. His erratic nocturnal hours may have prevented the tragedy from taking an even higher toll. 'If I hadn't stayed up so late talking, the whole place would have gone up,' he said.

Despite witnessing the horrendous scene, the deadly fire at Wirian did not haunt Martin the way the Luna Park fire did. He did not see it as laden with symbolism, as he had with the Ghost Train fire, but as a violent domestic tragedy. He said: 'It wasn't that the guy … wanted to destroy me or the house. He wanted to destroy the relationship, or he wasn't going to live without her.'

The inquest into Paiwan's death coincided with Tiny Tim's penultimate visit to Australia. The singer opened an exhibition of Martin's works on paper at the Australian Galleries in Paddington. It was a crowded, exuberant opening night, at which the singer performed some songs in his high falsetto voice, surrounded by Martin's vividly coloured works, many of which featured Tiny Tim.

Gallery director Stuart Purves saw parallels between the singer and Martin's art, between Tiny's vibrato voice and Martin's vibrating colours, Tiny Tim's singing marathons and the length of time Martin took to complete—or not—an artwork. Stuart observes: 'Martin transferred that style into a visual artist … None of this might be deliberate, it might be subconscious.'

The show included original artwork for record covers, posters, ink drawings and silkscreens—most of it from the seventies and eighties, some even earlier. Only a few of the works were new, and many were not for sale, as was often the case with Martin's occasional shows at commercial galleries. Throughout the month-long show, Martin went into the gallery almost daily to rehang works or add new ones.

Tiny's visit coincided with the singer's sixtieth birthday. Martin arranged a celebration concert at Sydney's Paddington RSL. Tape recorder in hand, Martin stood grinning amid the crowd as the eternal troubadour, in brightly coloured tails, performed his medley of old songs. At the end of the concert, Martin emerged with a birthday cake for his muse. As the singer blew out the candles and the crowd sang 'For He's a Jolly Good Fellow', Martin continued clapping long after everyone else had stopped.

Martin sat up all of one night in September 1994 writing about Luna Park. Although more than fifteen years had passed since the Ghost Train fire and the media's attention had long moved on, Martin's focus had not faltered. By then the planned high-rise for Luna Park had been spiked. A trust—the Luna Park Reserve Trust—had been established to preserve the site, which was poised to reopen as a funfair. Martin and Peter Kingston had spent three months restoring the park's iconic Coney Island, which contained the rides Martin had bought years earlier.

Martin gathered his thoughts in a 24-page handwritten letter to New South Wales arts minister Peter Collins. The letter, lengthy even by Martin's standards, traversed his symbolic understanding of the fire, which he described as 'an act of terrorism designed to destroy the Justice system'. Its perpetrators were worshippers of Moloch, Mammon and the Devil, he insisted.

Martin's main purpose in his letter was to argue for the creation of a permanent memorial on what he called the 'sacred site' of the Ghost Train. He had agitated for this for years but, with the funfair poised to reopen, the need was becoming more pressing. Martin wrote: 'I haven't lived as morally as I should and no doubt that has an effect on my credibility, however I do believe . . . it would be wrong to place an amusement on the site of the Ghost Train.' Peter Collins backed Martin's call for a memorial on the site, writing to the minister responsible for Luna Park, George Souris: 'It is, as Martin Sharp has put it, a sacred site in terms of European Australia and should be treated as such in the Luna Park redevelopment.' He added that Martin's name was synonymous with Luna Park, and noted that many questions about the fire remained unanswered.

Martin attended Luna Park's reopening in January 1995 with Jenny Poidevin, whose husband John Godson and two sons had been among those who perished in the fire. Jenny had remarried in the intervening years and had had a daughter, and she brought seven-year-old Emily with her. It was Jenny's first visit since the night her family perished. Her decision to return to the funfair had been made with difficulty. 'I had to come tonight, to overcome my fear of the place and the fear of my daughter going on a ride,' Jenny told an interviewer.

A memorial tree was eventually planted on the site and Martin donated an antique cast-iron garden bench inscribed with the names of the seven who died. Their faces were a constant presence at Wirian, where Martin's image *Golgotha*—containing the portraits of the boys and John Godson—hung in the shape of a crucifix on a wall. Martin was determined not to let Sydney forget the victims of the fire, and he even wrote an entry on John Godson for the *Australian Dictionary of Biography.*

Martin worked tirelessly for the preservation of Luna Park and for the victims of the Ghost Train fire. He did not work alone, but he marshalled the fight—just as years earlier he had galvanised the artists of the Yellow House. While few shared Martin's interpretation of the fire's symbolism, no one doubted his conviction and dedication. The fact that Luna Park remains today as a pop art counterpoint to the Sydney Opera House—and that those who perished are remembered—is in large part due to Martin's tenacious advocacy.

The deaths of two major figures in Martin's life bookended 1996. Artist Justin O'Brien died in Rome in January and Martin attended a memorial at Sydney's Christ Church St Laurence later that month for his 'art father', the teacher who had encouraged Martin's early paintings and hung them on the walls at Cranbrook School.

In America, Tiny's health was failing and he suffered heart problems. He ignored medical advice and appeared at a ukulele festival in Minneapolis on 30 November where he suffered a heart attack and collapsed on stage. He died shortly after in hospital, aged sixty-four. Martin called him 'the most amazing human being I've ever known and the greatest artist I will ever meet'. But Martin's adoration did not end with the singer's death and he planned to continue working on the material he had recorded, including more than a thousand cassettes of music and conversations—whether the world wanted it or not.

As Justin and Tiny departed, a young artist arrived in Martin's life. Luke Sciberras was an art student when he looked up Martin's phone number; he subsequently moved into Wirian and worked as an assistant. He observed at close quarters the senior artist's intensity and perfectionism, in the way Martin ensured that every detail was exactly the way he wanted it—from the type of paper used to the exact colour. Luke observes, 'He wouldn't put up with the wrong colour blue, he would never settle for second best on any level. It always had to be exactly what he saw in his mind's eye. Because every colour, every layer, every compositional element had a meaning.'

Among the works Luke helped Martin with was *Abalone.* Martin had begun the giant painting based on his lost 'Hokusai' print years earlier, but had set it aside. One night, while Martin was sleeping, Luke dragged the work, nearly three metres by two, into the studio. Luke recalled Martin had been in a 'bit of a funk' at the time and hoped the work would liven him up. But when Martin took to the work with coloured pencils, Luke feared he would ruin it.

Martin began endlessly crosshatching over the painting. Then he took a tea towel and began to polish the pencil marks. Martin and Luke polished and polished for days. The work slowly transformed.

Eventually the surface acquired a glowing patina like mother of pearl. Luke recalls: 'I have never seen anyone do that before. And so the work had this incredible luminosity.'

Paint on many of Martin's older canvases kept building up into thicker and thicker layers. The snowballs on *Snow Job*—Martin's work about the Luna Park fire—became almost a centimetre thick. Other works too were painted and repainted, including *Courage My Friend* (based on van Gogh's lost *Road to Tarascon*), *Film Script* (about Tiny Tim) and *Still Life* (his combination of van Gogh's sunflowers and Andy Warhol's image of Marilyn Monroe). The layers of paint made the works so heavy that they could barely be lifted.

As he painted and repainted, he vanished from the public eye. Martin worked largely outside the commercial gallery system, determined to retain control and mistrustful of the art establishment. At his infrequent exhibitions, the paintings often had 'not for sale' tags on them. When a show ended, they went back into a dark corner of Wirian. He rarely parted with his paintings and worked on some for decades. He even tried to buy back some of his paintings. He had only a handful of shows throughout his career and shifted from one gallery to another. Over the years he had exhibited in Sydney at the Hogarth, Coventry, Roslyn Oxley9 and Australian Galleries, but he never had a long-term representative.

Filmmaker Jeremy Thomas, who visited Martin on his annual trips to Australia, observed: 'He didn't paint to live, he lived to paint. I suppose that is why his output was smaller. He was a perfectionist, he didn't want to let go of things.' He was similarly reluctant to relinquish his Tiny Tim film. Thomas saw a ninety-minute version of the film and considered it perfectly viewable. 'But Martin did not want to let go of it and said, "I haven't finished it," but nothing was finished really.'

With his various inheritances, and without a family to support, Martin did not have the imperative to have exhibitions or meet deadlines. Wendy Whiteley observed: 'I always felt if Martin had to paint to work to actually pay the gas bills and keep things going, if he'd have had to keep a family, we would have seen a lot more from Martin Sharp.'

Australian Galleries director Stuart Purves observes that while Martin produced fine works, his reluctance to show his work came at a cost: 'He sabotaged his own career really by not exposing himself to gallery exhibitions and to the public and letting them judge his work. He held his art very close to his chest and never allowed them to make an opinion on it. He showed things that weren't for sale or works and paintings that took ages and ages. It shows a great vulnerability because he just didn't want to be exposed.'

The speed with which he worked in the sixties and seventies was the opposite of his pace in later life. His early success may have had an impact, says Fairlie Kingston: 'It is very hard for people that have an amazing success when they are young, and you have to keep pulling rabbits out of hats, and I think he lost his confidence a little bit. He could still do amazing work, but if he had a show it was always old work that was being brought out. And I think that whether he was conscious of it or not, I think it ate away at him.'

In his withdrawal to his decaying mansion he reminded Nell Campbell of a figure from Dickens' *Great Expectations:* 'He became like Miss Havisham in a tattered artist's smock.' Money slipped through Martin's fingers. Occasionally his stepmother, Dorothy, would help him out. He received more in royalty cheques for 'Tales of Brave Ulysses' than he earned from his visual art.

Martin, who as a young man had danced through life, became subject to sudden dark moods that permeated Wirian. 'The whole house felt it,' says Luke Sciberras. 'Martin's moods were all pervasive, and so there was a lot of tiptoeing around. He was so mercurial, you could never really tell what triggered a bad mood, because you could never really know what he had been up to in the last forty-eight hours, who had been to the house, or who had been on the phone. There was always someone coming and going, in and out of his life, that we never found out about.'

And as quickly as the mood arrived, it could lift. Visitors were never sure which Martin would greet them: cantankerous or charming. Penelope Tree, who had witnessed Martin's eccentricity on the *Vogue* fashion shoot to Zambia in 1970, reconnected with Martin after she moved to Sydney in the early 1980s. And she saw his extremes. When her infant daughter presented Martin with a Babar the Elephant book in which she had drawn, he put it in his studio cabinet with his most precious belongings. Years later he would bring it out to show Penelope when she visited. 'It was one of his favourite possessions. It was the sweetest thing,' says Penelope.

But she found Martin hard to have a direct conversation with and was wary of his sharp tongue. 'He'd say these things which could be quite devastatingly hurtful out of the corner of his mouth … he said them sotto voce. He said these things in a laughing way, so he was also sending you up … But at the same time—and that's what was confusing—he was very affectionate and had this very sweet side of him. It was very hard to reconcile those two opposites.'

CHAPTER 17

LOSS AND RECONCILIATION

Harmonie Downes, a free-spirited hippie, was keen to finish her secondary education. She had grown up in communes around Mullumbimby in northern New South Wales and was living in coastal Byron Bay in her mid-teens. Seeking a more conducive environment in which to study than the alternative communities with which she was familiar, she decided to head south. She was sixteen when she arrived in Sydney alone.

Harmonie enrolled in Randwick TAFE and found a share flat near Bondi Beach. She knew few people in Sydney. But through a friend of her mother's, who knew some of the people living at Wirian, she was invited to visit there. She had never seen a house like Wirian. The vast creative, chaotic mansion full of artists, music—Downes was a talented musician—dogs and paintings impressed her. 'I was absolutely blown out by the house. It was something I'd never dreamed of. I didn't know that that kind of place could exist. It absolutely had a major impact on me,' Harmonie says.

She found Martin open and generous. Although he was thirty-five years older than her, they became lovers. Harmonie gathered up her two bags and guitar, left her share flat and moved into Wirian. She had her own room, but often slept in Martin's bed. Although he was not her first lover, he was the first man she loved.

Harmonie was not concerned about their age difference. Martin spoke to Tiny Tim about her—he was still alive during the early part of his relationship with Harmonie. The singer had married his first wife, Miss Vicki, when she was seventeen years old.

But Harmonie began to feel uncomfortable in the house that had initially seemed so appealing. She felt out of her depth amid so many people, most of them much older than her, and there were so many demands for Martin's attention. Also, she was unsure where she stood in her relationship with Martin. She recalls: 'I fell in love with him, and I didn't know how to quite deal with it. It was a push-pull thing. He would say, "Harmonie, I belong to the world, I don't think I'm ever capable of having a normal relationship." That was a big part of his life, he felt like he was owned by so many other people.'

She moved in and out of Wirian several times as the relationship continued over about four years. Then in early 1997, twenty-year-old Downes was pregnant. Martin was shocked initially and told Luke Sciberras of his fears. Luke recalls: 'He said to me, "I don't know how this is going to work. This house is no place for a kid." He didn't know how to look after himself, let alone a child. He didn't have the strength ... It wasn't selfishness, it was just a practical fear. He felt that huge house could have been a dangerous jungle to a child.' Greg Weight worried about Martin's ability to cope with fatherhood. 'I don't think Martin was emotionally equipped properly to be a father. He was very nervous about it,' Greg says.

As Harmonie's pregnancy advanced, Martin's attitude to impending fatherhood shifted. A nursery was readied for the new arrival; Martin asked Sciberras to be godfather. Luke says: 'He was prepared and loving it.' Harmonie, too, saw a change in Martin. 'In winter, we'd sit down by his fire and talk about it and try and think of names.' She and Martin discussed marrying, and he visited her grandmother to ask permission. They became engaged and Martin gave her Jo's engagement ring. But the marriage didn't go ahead. 'It was never going to happen,' she says.

Harmonie was about eight months pregnant when, in need of peace and emotional support from her family, she left for her father's home in Burringbar in northern New South Wales. She initially planned a homebirth—she was young and healthy. Martin wrote her a letter that was less than reassuring: an artist such as himself could not be a husband and a father, and he felt it was important she understood that. He wrote: 'I am under a great deal of pressure, the resolution of this pressure can only help the kid. I can hardly leave the house, like a captain I have a responsibility to the good ship Wirian, and needs be a good captain [who] will go down with his ship ... I am on the edge of my life at the moment and I don't know if I will survive.'

As Harmonie prepared for the birth of her first child, Martin travelled to northern New South Wales to join her. They stayed with Martin's old friend John Weiley in Bangalow. But one morning late in her pregnancy, Harmonie felt something was wrong. She recounts: 'I just woke up and I said, "My belly is cold. I think I need to go to the hospital." All the temperature had dropped out of my body.' She and Martin rushed to Lismore Base Hospital, where Harmonie had an ultrasound. No heartbeat from the baby could be detected. The medical staff left her and Martin alone as they absorbed the reality. She recalls: 'We both bawled, burst into tears. He was like, "We're not strong enough." He felt like we'd failed the test. We'd failed as human beings to be able to have this child.'

Martin's friends arrived, including Richard Neville, Julie Clarke and George Gittoes, as well as Harmonie's mother and her friends. Harmonie gave birth to their stillborn son on 14 October 1997. They named him Marcello, a name that combined Harmonie's music and Martin's art. George painted Marcello's tiny coffin bright blue with the word *Eternity* in yellow copperplate script on the side. On the lid was a small red heart. Red roses were laid in the casket before Marcello was buried in Mullumbimby cemetery.

Martin returned to Sydney and wrote to Harmonie a few weeks later: 'We all had hopes in our different ways, and you had to handle the toughest part. And I wish I could help you to get stronger and give you what you lost … We were dangerous to each other and I should have known better but we were both surprised and overwhelmed by each other … I hope we can all grow and learn from what we've been through. Cello expects and deserves that.'

After the devastating loss, Martin and Harmonie continued their relationship intermittently for several years. They visited each other and phoned. Martin also wrote her hundreds of letters over more than a decade. They were affectionate letters running to many pages in which he frequently signed off as 'Crustie' or 'The Crust'—her nickname for him—and addressed her as 'Grumpo' or 'Ha'. He enclosed clippings, cartoons, cards and images. Eight years later, when she had a child with another partner, Martin offered to be godfather, which she declined. They remained in contact for the rest of his life. Harmonie recalls: 'He could be laconic, acid-tongued and cut you down with a look—and he did that with a lot of people—but then he could be wonderfully open and generous and available and spiritual and a mentor and could teach you a lot. And in a way he became more a mentor than a lover as we got older.'

Martin wrote about his loss to his friend Sandy Lieberson: 'It's rather like being father to a spirit child, perhaps that's as close to earth as I'll get … as to trying again, it's more than I could say. Sometimes I'm rather sure that I'm too much of an artist to be a human being.' Martin continued to grieve for his stillborn son. He attended a remembrance service for children who had died at Sydney's St Andrew's Cathedral three years later, where he laid a rose in Marcello's memory on the altar. After the service, he wrote to Harmonie about it: 'I wish it could have been otherwise. I really, really do.'

Whenever Lin Utzon visited Sydney, she and Martin would drive around the harbour. And when the Sydney Opera House came into view, he would exclaim: 'Look at that! Look at that!' Martin had always loved the Opera House. Over the years, he incorporated it into his art. He designed a poster to mark its tenth anniversary, and he featured it in his poster for Tiny Tim's 1982 Opera House concert and in a poster he created for the prestigious Adelaide Festival, where he wittily included a woman wearing a hat in the shape of its shells.

Martin was hardly alone in his admiration for Jørn Utzon's masterpiece. Australia had taken the building to its heart in the decades since the architect and his family had quietly left Sydney, aided by Jo Sharp. The Sydney Opera House had become one of the world's most identifiable buildings. Tourists and art lovers flocked to it. The building that had risen from the site of a rundown tangle of tram sheds had helped transform the harbour into a breathtaking waterfront.

The Opera House, which had been so bravely commissioned when there was little to put inside it, had been the site of unforgettable performances and had helped Australia overcome its cultural cringe. Professional theatre and contemporary dance companies—mere thought bubbles when its construction began—regularly graced its stages, together with the Australian Ballet, Opera Australia and the Sydney Symphony Orchestra. The great soprano Dame Joan Sutherland, La Stupenda, gave her final performance on its stage in 1990, the same year South African leader Nelson Mandela, then newly released from twenty-seven years in prison, spoke from its steps.

But the Opera House had cast a long shadow over the life of Jørn Utzon and his family. For years, whenever Lin stayed at Wirian on her Sydney visits she did not want to discuss it, or entertain the possibility of a happier ending. But Martin did. He told Lin that people loved the magnificent building and that it had changed Australia forever. And he told her: 'It's your history, too; you can't escape it.'

Many thought a rapprochement was long overdue with Jørn Utzon, whose name was not even mentioned when the Queen opened the Opera House in 1973. Keen to see some tangible recognition of the architect—perhaps a plaque with his portrait— New South Wales arts minister Peter Collins contacted Lin Utzon. Martin accompanied her in 1993 when she unveiled a bronze plaque that showed Jørn Utzon's spherical solution to his architectural puzzle.

Martin was thrilled and threw a party at Wirian to celebrate. The house was filled with flowers for the party, which was held on a sparkling autumn afternoon in March 1994; the guests included Opera House advocates and politicians—among them Peter Collins, Opposition Leader Bob Carr and architect Harry Seidler. And Lin Utzon.

———

Martin again accompanied Lin when she presented her father's scale model of the main hall to the Sydney Opera House Trust, its governing body, in 1995. But the building was now approaching its twenty-fifth anniversary and there was no clear plan as to how to move beyond symbolic gestures—such as the plaque and the scale model—or how to achieve a deeper re-engagement and reconciliation with Jørn Utzon. According to Joe Skrzynski, who was appointed chair of the Trust in 1996, there was a general assumption that to do so would mean closing down the Sydney Opera House, getting hold of Utzon's original plans for the interior, demolishing everything that wasn't according to his design, and rebuilding. Joe recalls: 'That was obviously politically a very difficult idea so that had slowed down a lot of peoples' thinking.'

Yet time was pressing. Beyond the landmark anniversary, it was apparent the building would soon need substantial internal work, and Utzon was no longer a young man. 'We could already see that in the next twenty-five years, major works would have to be done at the Opera House … you couldn't in all honesty be thinking about those major works while he was alive and ignore him,' says Joe.

Soon after his appointment, Joe held a private dinner in the Opera House boardroom with several of the key figures including architect

Alex Popov, Martin's friend and Lin Utzon's former husband. Alex made a comment during the dinner that helped overcome the stalemate. Alex said that going back to the original plans was a dead end. No architect would want to simply dust off their decades-old plans and effectively say, 'Here they are, go build it.' He would want to consider them afresh and look forward, not backwards.

The dinner was a breakthrough. The idea took shape of engaging Utzon to set down his big-picture thinking for the future of the Opera House. Joe recalls: 'So not saying use a brass knob on that door handle, but design principles rather than design details that should inform anybody working on it.' But a key question remained: how to approach Jørn Utzon after his inglorious exit from Australia so long ago?

Joe Skrzynski was in his office when he received a phone call from Martin. The pair had crossed paths from time to time since their student days, but the call came unexpectedly. Martin had some news that made Joe's ears prick up. Lin Utzon was in Sydney and staying at Wirian. Would Joe like to come over?

Joe walked down the gravel drive at Wirian on a January day in 1998. He sat at the wooden kitchen table with Lin and Martin. As they talked, Joe assured Lin that the Opera House Trust was sincere in wanting to have Jørn Utzon back. Joe recalls: 'Martin's involvement was crucial to create the link as a trusted friend to introduce me to Lin and for Lin to feel confident about the discussion.' Joe outlined the possible way forward.

It was a 'marvellous conversation', says Lin. She agreed to talk to her father on her return to Europe. And when she did, not only was he open to the idea, but she saw a change in his spirit: 'He was an old man, so he did not have a real ambition nor illusion that it would have been possible to go back and change the whole inside. He was very light hearted after that. And that was my motive for doing it.'

Joe and prominent Sydney architect Richard Johnson flew to Denmark to meet Utzon. In collaboration with his architect son Jan Utzon and Johnson, Jørn Utzon developed a set of design principles to guide the building's future. And he redesigned the Opera House's reception hall, to be renamed the Utzon Room, and designed a fourteen-metre wide and three-metre tall tapestry, inspired in part by the music of C.P.E. Bach, to hang within it.

Lin oversaw the tapestry's installation, and Martin was with her for its unveiling. Indeed he accompanied her to every milestone involving the architect and the Opera House until, by the time of its fortieth anniversary, Martin's failing health prevented this.

In the wake of the reconciliation, the world appeared to rediscover Jørn Utzon. He was awarded architecture's top honour, the Pritzker Prize, in 2003. Although he never saw his completed masterpiece, when Utzon died, aged ninety in 2008, his building was hailed by British architecture critic Deyan Sudjic as having 'transformed the world's view not just of Sydney, but of Australia'. Lin regards the meeting around Wirian's kitchen table as pivotal: 'That first meeting with me and Joe Skrzynski and Martin ... was when everything started cooking.'

In later years, blue and white plates created by Lin stood on a dresser in the kitchen where that conversation had taken place. Others were set into the white walls outside Wirian. They were Royal Copenhagen porcelain commissioned by the Danish government to mark the bicentenary of the birth of Hans Christian Andersen, a children's author Martin loved.

Martin and Lin occasionally sailed on Joe Skrzynski's boat in the aftermath of that meeting. Martin always brought along a bag of bread to feed the fish. He maintained his fascination with fish and other creatures. Lin recalls: 'You could ask him anything about fish or snails or insects or anything that lived in Australia.' Martin would constantly pull out books from his vast library to show her.

He could take his passion for animals—and literature—to extremes, as Lin found when she invited Martin to join her and her husband, Hugues de Montalembert, at Mackerel Beach on Pittwater, on Sydney's northern fringe, where the couple had rented a house at the hamlet accessible only by ferry. A writer and artist, Hugues had lost his sight in a violent attack in New York. Through her window at their holiday house, Lin observed Martin dragging a large, heavy suitcase across the sand from the ferry wharf in her direction; every so often he would stop for a smoke, and then resume heaving it along.

Lin went to help him and asked what was in his case to make it so heavy. He had packed no clothes for the two-week stay but had completely filled his luggage with books of poetry. Lin recounts: 'Because Hugues is blind, Martin was going to read to him. So there was all the poetry, and one tiny, well-used little toothbrush.'

Generous, if eccentric, Martin could test the patience of friends. He remained at the house with Hugues after Lin left. Provisions had to be conveyed to the isolated hamlet by ferry, and Lin had ensured that she had provided enough food for this time. But she hadn't counted on Martin's preoccupation with animals. Lin recalls: 'He proceeded to feed it all to the kookaburras. Hugues was absolutely furious.'

Martin was dedicated to his art, but Utzon sensed the price he paid. 'When you are so devoted to your art, and it is your soul, it doesn't make it easy to include someone in your life. There was a deep loneliness in his life,' she says. Yet he had an ability to inspire and mentor others. 'A lot of people came away from being in his house as artists one way or another, just by being in his world.'

As the millennium approached, Sydney prepared to celebrate. Thousands gathered around the harbour to share the revelries of the city's greatest party. They watched as lanterns in the shape of giant creatures floated up and down the harbour, ahead of the main event. On the stroke of midnight on New Year's Eve, the champagne corks popped and the sky above the hedonistic harbour city filled with the snap, crackle and pop of fireworks. They shot from the top of the Sydney Harbour Bridge, and cascaded down like a burning waterfall. As the fireworks ceased and the sky darkened, a single word lit up on the bridge itself. A word written in copperplate script: *Eternity.*

The word was beamed around the world, an intimation to the future. It was sent from the new millennium as the rest of the world—much of it in many time zones behind Sydney—remained in the old. Martin watched the celebrations from a boat on Sydney Harbour, thrilled and amazed that the image had been carried around the globe. He had nothing to do with the word being put on the Sydney Harbour Bridge, he said.

But he had a great deal to do with the image capturing the popular imagination. Martin had turned a piece of graffito into art, and made the image his own. He had combined the word Eternity with Tiny Tim and with Mickey Mouse, and with a map of Australia in a design he was working on for a tapestry to mark the centenary of Federation. And he had let the word stand alone—in yellow with a lapis blue background—on a five-metre canvas in the window of Sydney's funky design store Remo in 1990. Yet he never forgot Arthur Stace, whom he regarded as Australia's greatest writer: 'He writes an entire novel in that word,' Martin said. How far the word Eternity had entered Sydney's cultural imagination—courtesy of Martin's art—was underscored later in the year when the city hosted the Summer Olympics. At the opening ceremony, the word was again up in lights.

But in that ceremony it was the Indigenous dancers and the sight of Cathy Freeman lighting the Olympic torch that most impressed

Martin. And later Cathy winning gold. The 2000 Olympics threw a spotlight on Australia's treatment of its indigenous people.

In May, when an unprecedented quarter of a million people marched across Sydney Harbour Bridge in support of reconciliation between black and white Australians, Martin was among them. He believed that healing generations of injustice was the country's most pressing issue. He said: 'It is much more important to fix up the things with the indigenous people than the wars [the government] get involved with.'

He began several works in the first decade of the new millennium that reflected his concern for, and growing friendship with, Indigenous Australians. When he visited his friend David Gulpilil at his Sydney hotel one night, he was struck by the actor's ability to straddle two worlds—his ancient traditional culture and the contemporary sphere. Martin said: 'I realised how tough it was to come down [from Arnhem Land] into this world and how brave he was and also how brilliant.' As he left the hotel, he thought: 'I've got to do something. A portrait was the only thing I could think of.'

Luke Sciberras was at Wirian when Martin began the portrait. Luke recalls: 'He made up a big pot of beautiful blue ink, a cobalt blue.' Martin held in his hand a Chinese horsetail brush and in the other a Polaroid photograph Jon Lewis had taken of Gulpilil in Martin's studio, an image Martin thought captured the actor's wise humour. 'He marked out this drawing of David's face ... In about ten minutes he had this incredible portrait done. It's a brief, very economical drawing. That was one of the elements of the genius in Martin's work. The economy with which he could use a line to describe so much.' It was the starting point for a work that would evolve over about a decade into one of Martin's finest late works, *The Thousand Dollar Bill.*

The portrait's subject—who has since starred in *Rabbit-Proof Fence*, *Australia*, *Charlie's Country* and *Ten Canoes*—began to stay at Wirian when he was in Sydney. Around a camp fire in the back garden, David shared his stories with Martin. Other Indigenous friends also stayed or visited Wirian, where they held traditional smoking ceremonies. The house filled with the smell of eucalypts. Some he helped financially, quipping as he wrote out a cheque that he was 'just paying the rent'. For Martin believed white Australia was deeply indebted to its original inhabitants.

Martin also began a work based on a Phil May cartoon, *A Curiosity in Her Own Country.* The nineteenth-century cartoon, originally published in *The Bulletin*, depicted a group of well-dressed white figures staring down at an impoverished black mother and child. Martin's version, which he called *Australia,* resembled a nativity scene, with yellow halos around the mother and child.

For a church in Sydney's inner-city Redfern, a suburb with a large Indigenous congregation, he painted a series of wooden crucifixes in the colours of the Aboriginal flag—red, black and gold. And he painted a crucifix on the cover of his Bible in the same colours.

Martin was alert to the need for reconciliation, not only between white and black Australia. In April 2001, he attended a ceremony at Sydney's St Mary's Cathedral that brought together Japanese and Australian veterans of World War II and others affected by the conflict. Martin accompanied his friend Jan Ruff-O'Herne, a woman he considered as one of his heroes. Jan had grown up in the former Dutch East Indies and was living on the island of Java when Japan invaded during the war. She was twenty-one when she was taken prisoner and held as a 'comfort woman' or sex slave of the Japanese military. She had kept silent about her experience before penning a memoir, *Fifty Years of Silence*. She campaigned consistently on behalf of former comfort women and demanded Japan acknowledge and apologise for the wrongdoings of the past. Only then, she believed, was reconciliation and healing possible.

Martin admired his friend's courage in speaking up for the forgotten victims of war. 'We hear of Gallipoli, Dunkirk and the Battle of the

Coral Sea, and the heroic men who died and killed on those endless and distant lands. Few of us have heard of the women and girls, the nurses or the "comfort women"', he later wrote.

In the years after the death of his son, Marcello, Martin began to reflect on his own life and on the impact he had had on women. His behaviour was a source of remorse. He acknowledged the pain he had caused in letters to Eija Vehka-aho: 'I'm not so pleased at what I see of myself. Such a confused life with too many "sweeties".' He had moved from one woman to the next, including from Anou Kiisler to Eija and back to Anou, to Ingrid Boulting, to Victoria Cobden, to Nell and Cressida Campbell, to Yensoon Tsai and Harmonie Downes: 'I realise there was something disturbed about me.'

By then Anou was dead. Martin's early girlfriend, who had inspired 'Tales of Brave Ulysses', died suddenly in her fifties of an aneurysm. Martin had remained in contact with Anou, and he attended her Sydney funeral in 1999. There he met her daughter Clare, then an art student, and they became friends.

Martin returned to the theme of his reckless behaviour in a melancholy letter to Eija written in the early hours of a sleepless winter morning in June 2001. 'One lives one's early life so thoughtlessly so one can spend one's later years trying to cope with the results,' he wrote. 'I have certainly failed in "love". I have "loved" at times, intensely, but never brought love to fruition. I think because I grew up in a house with parents who had lost their love and a father who didn't know how to love his child under those circumstances. I didn't comprehend what love was between a man and a woman. (I would say I have loved, but I have difficulty with being loved.) … I am sorry for both myself and for you and others who I have been loved by and who I have tried to love—not realising the responsibility involved.'

Even as he pointed the finger at his upbringing and his parents' loveless marriage, he acknowledged his justifications seemed pathetic. And although he looked at times in horror at his conduct, he stopped short of resolving to change his ways. 'I have been responsible for so much discomfort in the lives of others and it appals [sic] me to realise it, and yet I still find women so attractive, and may cause more discomfort before I am in the grave.' He could not forgive himself, yet he struggled with the notion of forgiveness: 'to be forgiven one must confess and be contrite—it is hard to do both'.

Martin arrived at Eija's Stockholm apartment in August 2002. Although they had corresponded for nearly two decades, they had not seen each other since they were in their twenties. After a modelling career in Paris and New York, Eija had studied alternative health, including psychological health.

Although Martin always smoked, Eija was not prepared for just how much. She asked him to smoke outside. This quickly proved impractical—he smoked so heavily, he was constantly out in the street. She allowed him to smoke in the toilet, but that, too, became similarly impractical. So she allowed him to smoke in the kitchen.

But it wasn't just the reek of cigarette smoke that concerned her. She was aware that Martin had become deeply religious, but she was unnerved by the form this took. His talk was full of hellfire sermons about punishing those who didn't acknowledge Jesus. She could not find in him the open-minded young man she had known in sixties London or the thoughtful Martin of his recent letters. His extremism in religion, his cigarettes and even his diet—she later recalled he lived entirely on shrimps during the visit—did not make for a happy reunion. Although they spoke on the phone a few times after that meeting, his long correspondence ceased with the woman to whom he had written some of his most candid letters.

Martin visited Eija during what turned out to be his last trip to Europe. He had left Sydney mid-year for what his assistant Wendy Evans thought would be a three-week visit, but it turned into nearly six months. After about a week with Eija, he flew to Majorca to visit Lin Utzon and Hugues de Montalembert, who had a home on the Spanish island. He then travelled on to London, where friends welcomed him back. Sandy Lieberson threw a party for him. 'I do love London and all my friends there,' he later wrote to Lieberson. Martin's cousin Andrew Sharp recalled Martin was buoyed by seeing so many old friends. Some urged him to stay in London, but he insisted he could not leave Wirian.

Shortly before he left Britain, Martin attended a concert at the Royal Albert Hall, where he had first seen Tiny Tim perform and been so transfixed more than three decades earlier. This concert, which Eric Clapton co-directed and performed at, was a tribute to George Harrison. The former Beatle, Eric's long-time friend and occasional Pheasantry visitor, had died a year earlier.

CHAPTER 18

ETERNITY

In Sydney, eminent art curator Nick Waterlow had never forgotten seeing Martin's anti-Vietnam image of former US president Lyndon Johnson excreting bombs. The image had riveted English-born Nick when he visited Australia in the mid-sixties and picked up a copy of Sydney's *Oz* magazine. When Nick returned to England after a year, he encountered Martin's work repeatedly on posters, record albums and in London *Oz*. Martin's works seemed to be everywhere in Britain. Nick said: 'If there's one graphic artist who defined the era, it's still Martin Sharp.'

Nick had been struck, too, by the number of Australians—artists, writers, filmmakers and photographers—who were at the forefront of the social and cultural upheaval in Britain at that time, and by their irreverent and offbeat humour. 'So much of it was brought to a head through the Australians. They were able to cut through the class system and in a sense cock a snoot at the colonial [attitude],' Nick said.

With the fortieth anniversary of the founding of *Oz* magazine in 2003, Nick decided the time was ripe to revisit the work of the upstart expats in an exhibition. An erudite man with a dry wit, quiet manner and an astute eye, Nick was ideally placed to do so. He had a gift for putting Australian contemporary art in an international context, and he was one of the most influential figures on Australia's visual arts scene. He had directed three Sydney biennales before taking the reins of Sydney's Ivan Dougherty Gallery, part of the University of New South Wales' College of Fine Art.

Larrikins in London, which opened at the gallery in September 2003, was the first significant acknowledgment of the contribution of the expat Australians. The show included some of Martin's collages, posters and album covers, as well as works by Brett Whiteley, Colin Lanceley, photographs by Robert Whitaker, Lewis Morley and Juno Gemes, as well as David Hockney's lithograph of a naked Richard Neville, Jim Anderson and Felix Dennis. The group show also screened several films, including Bruce Beresford's *The Adventures of Barry McKenzie*, Philippe Mora's *Trouble in Molopolis*, as well as a film made for the exhibition to acknowledge the work of Australian women in London in the sixties, entitled *Womenzone*. The show was a landmark, sparking debate and reassessment of the impact of the sixties generation of expat Australians artists, activists and ratbags.

Martin wrote to Sandy Lieberson to tell him about the exhibition. *Molopolis* had 'a quaint innocence contrasted with the darker weavings of *Performance* ... both seem to get better as time flys [sic]'. And he had been impressed by the film *Womenzone*. 'Louise Ferrier, aghast at the male orientation of the proposed exhibition made a film with Jenny Kee's help of the "girls" and their memories of the 60s. ... It was a very good film. Surprisingly interesting and not as critical as we ("boys") might have expected.'

Faces flashed before Martin's eyes. Some were comic; others grotesque and malevolent. He saw a goblin peeking through a curtain, and also a pig's head. He had been warned he might hallucinate. But these were not flashbacks to his LSD-fuelled sixties. In August 2004 he had a triple bypass following a heart attack. Friends feared he would not survive the open-heart surgery. As he recovered, Martin's response was more sanguine, and he was typically curious about the experience: 'I kept my eyes wide open. I kept a notebook,' he said.

He documented his visions and wondered about their source. He had never seen such images before. Were they simply the by-product of the heavy medication after the surgery? He wrote: 'Is this an act of creation or an invasion? I suggest the latter as I've not seen these little folk before. They aren't sourced for a film or a book illustration. They appear freshly minted behind my eyelids. They want to be seen. They look intently … Are they only seen by [some] individuals or does everyone see them?'

He had by this time given up his four-pack-a-day cigarette habit. Or, as he described it, they had given him up: 'Benson and Hedges dropped me like a ton of bricks because I was looking too ill. They just turn off a switch at headquarters and I didn't want to smoke anymore.' Not that he was filled with the missionary zeal of the reformed smoker: 'I'm not against smoking, they're useful at certain times of our lives.' He remained cavalier about his health. He was given an exercise regime following his surgery, but he never followed it. He had rarely encountered the health system—so rarely he hadn't even obtained a Medicare card until Richard Neville helped him apply for one.

No one seemed more surprised to have survived the operation than Martin himself. Yet he made light of his brush with mortality when he quipped to an interviewer that the surgeons at St Vincent's Hospital had sentenced him to the responsibilities of his calling: 'I thought I was going to leave a big mess behind—that at last I didn't have to do all that work. But now, thanks to them, I have a lot more work to do,' he said. He made the comment as it was announced that he had received an award in the Queen's Birthday Honours in June 2005. He became a Member of the Order of Australia for his contributions to pop art and support for young artists.

The artist who had once poked fun at the monarchy was well aware of the irony of accepting such an honour. By then, Martin was no longer the scourge of the establishment. He admired the Queen's dedication. Although he considered an Australian republic inevitable, he would not be drawn on whether he supported this: 'It will happen naturally. It doesn't worry me one way or the other.' Martin's politics remained a mystery, even to his closest friends. Not even Richard Neville knew how Martin voted. Richard considered his friend in later life as 'an outsider with a Tory propensity'.

In the wake of his award, Martin received a congratulatory letter from one of his former teachers from Cranbrook, Miss Beatrice Peel. She had been his favourite childhood teacher until she sent him to the headmaster's office for a misdemeanour, where he had been strapped. Miss Peel suggested having lunch. Martin was reluctant. For decades he had nurtured the hurt of the beating and what he believed was her knowing role in it. He ignored her letter.

But when Miss Peel wrote a second letter, he agreed to meet. They were the sole diners in the plush old world surrounds of the Royal Automobile Club that day. Martin broached the subject of the long-ago incident. She was shocked when Martin told her he had been beaten as a result; she had assumed he would be verbally disciplined. She had never knowingly sent a boy to be beaten, she told him. After more than half a century, Martin felt released from the painful episode that had haunted him.

Martin's health had improved enough by mid-2006 for him to make his only trip to Central Australia. He flew to Alice Springs in July for the wedding of his friend, photographer Greg Weight, to artist Carol Ruff. Martin was to be best man. But he was as eccentric a wedding guest as he had been a house guest when he stayed with Lin Utzon at Pittwater. In Alice Springs, he arrived with a heavy bag containing little but old books. They had belonged to his father. Martin's trip coincided with his late father's birthday, and he wanted to acknowledge that by reading works from his father's library. He spent part of the wedding day seated in the sun poring over them.

Martin did remember to pack his navy pinstripe suit for the ceremony. He wore it for years at formal occasions, the trousers invariably held up with a piece of cord rather than a belt. But he forgot to pack a shirt and had to borrow one. Also at the wedding was the bride's mother, Jan Ruff-O'Herne, the former wartime 'comfort woman' with whom Martin had attended a reconciliation ceremony a few years earlier. Martin and Greg breakfasted together on the morning of the wedding, during which Martin attempted to talk his old friend out of getting married. Perhaps he was joking. In the end, he gave a generous speech.

In Alice Springs he visited the grave of the Indigenous watercolour painter Albert Namatjira, who Martin admired. Greg and Carol took him to the Lutheran Mission at Hermannsburg, where Namatjira was born and where he had inspired a school of painting. Martin spent time at the art centre at Hermannsburg and met some of the celebrated women potters there.

Nick Waterlow wanted to do a solo show of Martin's work. The focus would be on Martin's paintings rather than on his better-known early graphic work. Nick believed the paintings were under-recognised. As he worked on the exhibition, *The Everlasting World of Martin Sharp*, which opened at the Ivan Dougherty Gallery in November 2006, Nick reflected on Martin's art: 'What's so important about Martin is there are eternal truths—there are not many artists in this country who are really involved with those eternal truths—and his particular grasp of this part of the world. And he's been able to communicate that wherever he's been. He's a kind of visionary larrikin in a way ... there seems to be a deep love at the basis of his work, apart from a remarkable visual talent that enables him to somehow scan horizons that others don't seem to be aware of. He's part social commentator, part shaman ... Because it's often presented in a gentle way, people don't see it as hard-nosed, but it's very observant.'

Nick prepared a small catalogue, in which he reiterated words about Martin he had written years earlier: 'He is one of those very rare creatures, whose alchemy makes visible the invisible ... one of a handful of international guerrillas bringing light to these dark ages.'

Among the paintings in the show were *Ginger Meggs in Japan*, *Pentecost*, his David Gulpilil portrait and *Babylon the great is fallen, is fallen*. The latter depicted the twin towers of Luna Park being swept away by Hokusai's wave. He had started this work in 2000—and based it on a chapter in the book of Revelations—but when the painting went on show, it seemed unnervingly prescient. By then the twin towers of New York's World Trade Center had fallen and the 2004 Asian tsunami had claimed more than a quarter of a million lives.

Martin had become friends with Nick Waterlow and he agreed to contribute to another exhibition Nick co-curated around this time, about schizophrenia. *For Matthew and Others: Journeys with Schizophrenia* was held in part to draw attention to the condition. Martin had long been sympathetic and non-judgmental towards those suffering from mental illness. He had sheltered some, from John Ivor Golding at the Pheasantry to others at Wirian. And he knew of the mental torments of his hero van Gogh. At an event held in conjunction with the exhibition, Martin spoke about his own schizophrenic-like visions in the wake of his heart surgery.

Nick had personal reasons for wanting to present the show. His adult son, Antony, battled mental illness. As their friendship grew, Nick confided in Martin about his troubled son. Nick had sought help for Antony, who had declined to take anti-psychotic medication.

Antony's untreated mental illness would have terrible consequences. In 2009, Antony Waterlow arrived at the home of his sister, Chloe Heuston, in the eastern Sydney suburb of Randwick. Nick was visiting his daughter and her three small children when Antony arrived.

In a frenzied attack, Antony used a kitchen knife to stab to death his father and sister in front of the three children. Antony Waterlow was ultimately found not guilty of murdering Chloe and Nick on the grounds of mental illness.

Martin remained in contact with his stepmother, Dorothy Sharp, during her two-decade-long widowhood. He would take her out for lunch and speak to her on the phone, and at times she helped him out financially. As her health failed, she moved from Mosman into aged care at Lulworth House in Elizabeth Bay—once the maternity wing of St Luke's Hospital where Martin was born—where she died on 5 October 2006.

Dorothy Sharp had no children of her own, but she gave more than twenty members of her extended family—including godchildren, cousins and members of the Sharp family—gifts of between $20,000 and $30,000 plus $50,000 each to ten charitable and health institutions. She left Martin the annual income from her considerable estate, but not the capital. This would go, on Martin's death, to two institutions associated with her late husband and Martin's father: Cranbrook School and St Paul's College at Sydney University. Dorothy also left the two institutions bequests of $300,000 each. The bounty destined for Cranbrook and St Paul's was a source of unhappiness to Martin, who fought a legal battle over his stepmother's estate. His rancour continued to smoulder.

Martin's life had been dominated by the Luna Park fire for nearly thirty years when *The Sydney Morning Herald* dropped a bombshell in May 2007. The face of Sydney crime boss Abe Saffron stared out from the front page, superimposed on the smouldering ruin of the Luna Park

Ghost Train. Above this image were photos of the seven who perished in it.

Abe Saffron was behind the fire, according to his niece Anne Buckingham. She told investigative journalist Kate McClymont that Saffron had sought control of the funfair in the wake of the fire. 'I don't think people were meant to be killed,' Buckingham said. She said her uncle liked to 'collect things' and that Luna Park was one of them. The story appeared a year after Saffron died.

For Martin, the story confirmed what he had always believed—that the fire was no accident and that Saffron was behind it. 'It was an act of terrorism,' he told the *Herald*. 'If you can get away with burning children in public on a Saturday night in an amusement park, you can get away with just about anything.'

In the wake of the story Jenny Poidevin called for an inquiry to be reopened, but this has not happened. Martin remained in contact with Jenny and others affected by the fire. As an adult, Jason Holman—the schoolboy who survived the fire—lived at Wirian for a couple of years and came to regard Martin as a father figure.

Martin was tenacious in maintaining friendships over long periods. Once someone struck a chord with Martin, he rarely let go. He remained in contact with his childhood nanny Roma Leonard, whom he always invited to his exhibitions. After his mother died, he gave Roma the silver pendant Jo had loaned her when she entered the Miss Australia contest. When Roma died in 2008, Martin attended her funeral and her ashes were scattered at Wirian. Her granddaughter, Ella Sperling, was one of his last assistants.

He still held occasional parties at Wirian, including one for Sydney photographer Régis Lansac. Martin's friend Kylie Kwong, a leading chef, made the food, and guests included composer Elena Kats-Chernin, choreographer Meryl Tankard (Regis's partner) and several dancers. Two of the dancers agreed to give an impromptu performance in the garden and shed most of their clothes. As one of them twirled near Martin, he had an idea of his own. Meryl recalls: 'Martin painted her with house paint. It was winter and the paint was really cold. I kept seeing Martin reaching out from behind a tree with a paintbrush ... It was like a sixties happening.'

Martin continued to widen his network of Indigenous Australians. He became friends with Maggie Walsh, a Bwgcolman woman from Queensland's troubled Palm Island. Maggie was in her forties when she arrived in Sydney for the first time and was introduced to Martin. He offered her a room at Wirian, where she lived on and off for several years. There she began writing poetry for the first time. Maggie recalls: 'One day I said I feel like writing on the walls. Martin said, "Go ahead, it's your room."' She picked up coloured pens and covered the room with lines of her verse. She credits Martin with her transformation from karaoke singer to poet: 'I graduated from Wirian.' She loved its timeless atmosphere—there were no clocks visible—and Martin's acceptance of people from all walks of life. A homeless man would turn up periodically, Martin would make him a sandwich, give him a few dollars and he'd disappear for a few months. He would occasionally send a Wirian resident to Hyde Park with fifty dollars to give to a vagrant sleeping rough there.

Maggie was visiting friends in the Blue Mountains, about a two-hour drive west of Sydney, in 2009 when Martin phoned and asked her to return to Wirian. He was expecting a 'couple of backpackers' and needed some help. Maggie was seated in the garden with Martin and his assistant Wendy Evans when a chauffeur-driven vehicle arrived. Out stepped Princess Eugenie, plus a friend of hers and her aunt, Jane Ferguson. Maggie read some poems and showed the young princess her room covered in poetry. The princess, daughter of Britain's Prince Andrew and Sarah Ferguson, played the piano in Wirian's hallway. 'You never knew who would turn up,' says Maggie.

By then, Martin was working towards a solo show and his health was deteriorating. He endured several bouts of pneumonia that required hospitalisation, and suffered from kidney stones and abscesses on his legs. He may well have realised this show would be his last exhibition. It would be held not in an art gallery but in a social history museum. His curator friend Ace Bourke was overseeing the show for the Museum of Sydney. By then Ace had become an unlikely international star—thanks to the pet lion he and his flatmate John Rendall had owned in sixties Chelsea. The pair had long ago released Christian the lion into the wilds, but when footage emerged of their emotional reunion in Africa, the YouTube clip went viral, and Ace and John appeared on *The Oprah Winfrey Show*.

But handling an adult lion was easy compared to dealing with Martin. Ace, who worked with Louise Ferrier on the show, wanted to re-create Martin's Wirian studio for the exhibition. Martin had other ideas. He did not want to be curated or his studio re-created. Although contracts were signed, Ace worried that Martin would pull out. A catalogue was planned but Martin resisted, much as he had resisted approaches for books, films and even newspaper profiles over the years. In the end, the show was largely self-curated.

Within walls painted Martin's favourite cobalt blue, the show surveyed his life's work, from his childhood images and *Oz* cartoons to the paintings he had worked and reworked for decades. His Tiny Tim film screened on a loop at one end of the room. Maggie Walsh performed at the opening of *Martin Sharp: Sydney Artist*. It was a riotous, celebratory night, but behind the scenes the journey there had been fraught.

The Sydney Morning Herald's critic John McDonald noted the ambiguity of the exhibition's title, and of the artist himself. Martin was one of a few Australian artists with an international reputation, McDonald noted: 'Sharp has all the makings of gargantuan commercial success and not the slightest interest in pursuing it. He is an intensely private person devoted to public causes ... For all the frustrations he inflicts on his friends and admirers, there is nobody like him—nobody who has given up the entire world in order to be a Sydney artist.'

Martin turned seventy in 2012. He continued to sleep poorly, and as he lay awake at dawn a couple of weeks after his birthday he contemplated life's inscrutability. He wrote in his notebook: 'Here we are, in the midst of the creation, endless, mysterious, unknowable, magnificent, beautiful and terrible. How? Why? One can only be humble to the Creator and hope to be useful whilst one can. I have always found friendship one of the greatest vehicles of usefulness ... As I sit here at my table in my studio at Wirian surrounded by the pieces of my life, in this physical feebleness, at the beginning of my seventieth year I wonder about the mystery of life ... not for the first time, and probably not the last, but there will be a last time. It is not too far away. I am feeble in my body so I very much live in this room, a tube brings me oxygen. My friends bring me food. In these words I hold on to my life. I am not ready to leave, I have things I must do before I go, God willing!'

His portrait of David Gulpilil, *The Thousand Dollar Bill*, was selected for the Art Gallery of New South Wales' Archibald Prize in 2012. Although it did not win the coveted prize, it was placed in prime position at the entry to the exhibition and became the cover image for the catalogue. A portrait of Martin by Garry Shead was also hung; it depicted a white-bearded skeletal Martin, clear-eyed but wary, with Luna Park in the background and in front of him toy figures, including Tiny Tim and Mickey Mouse.

Garry was with Martin and artist Fairlie Kingston when, in November 2012, they boarded a ferry on the Port Hacking River. Martin wanted to see Telford again, his grandparents' holiday home where he had been happiest as a child. The trip had taken a great deal of planning. Martin by now had advanced emphysema and constantly required oxygen. His friends, needing to ensure he had enough oxygen for the journey from Sydney and back, loaded his tank onto the ferry.

Also on the ferry was one of his earliest friends, Ian Skinner, the caretaker's son from Telford. Martin had lost contact with Ian for decades. But around the time of the Museum of Sydney exhibition, he had made efforts to find his long-lost friend and was thrilled Ian could join him.

Martin wore his grandfather's pith helmet as the ferry sailed the clear green waters. He looked across at the rocks where as a child he had played with Ian and his sister Jan Skinner, and gone beachcombing for treasures with his mother. And he scoured the waters where he had once been enchanted by the sight of a blue groper.

Back at Wirian, Martin was cared for three days a week by Angelica Tremblay, a New Zealand gospel singer who had been a backing singer for Tiny Tim and known Martin for about twenty years. Angelica helped take Martin to his medical appointments, answered his calls when he became too sick to reach the phone himself, prepared food and brought his many visitors cups of tea and coffee.

Others, too, helped with his care, including Fairlie Kingston, who cooked him dinner twice a week for about eighteen months. Martin was a picky and erratic eater. When she cooked flathead one day, he said he couldn't eat such an ugly fish. When his health allowed, friends took him in his wheelchair around Centennial Park so he could feed the fish and ducks, along the Rose Bay foreshore or to Watsons Bay, where he threw chips in the air for seagulls. His cousin Roslyn Sharp spent Sundays with him and encouraged him to sit in the sun; for four years she oversaw his medical needs. Musician Mic Conway brought his ukulele and sang; classical pianist Gerard Willems played Beethoven on the honky-tonk piano in the hallway.

Martin became increasingly anxious if anything in the house was touched without his permission. Despite the apparent chaos of his studio, he was quick to notice if items had been moved. When he returned in a wheelchair from a medical appointment one day, he was furious to discover a small picture had been turned upside down in his absence. His suspicion of others increased. When his much-loved little white terrier, Imelda, died suddenly, he was convinced she had been deliberately poisoned and ordered an autopsy. She was buried in the garden beside Martin's dynasty of dogs. She was his last.

His most regular outing was to St Vincent's Hospital for fortnightly transfusions to treat a blood disorder, myelodysplastic syndrome, which compromised his immune system. He had bouts of pneumonia and a number of admissions to hospital. On one occasion he sketched the view beyond, in an image that drew together the threads of his artistic life. Through the window of the hospital that shared the name with his much-loved van Gogh—who Martin considered a saint—he could see a cross on the nearby hospice's chapel and beyond that to the National Art School, where he had studied as a young man. He sketched this view in blue ink and added the star of Bethlehem. It was part of what he called his Blue Series, a number of small ink drawings of places important to him, including Nielsen Park on Sydney Harbour and Telford. These were his final series of drawings.

Martin was pleased when his former school, Cranbrook, used his drawing from his hospital window for their annual Christmas card. The school had had a new headmaster, Nicholas Sampson, since July 2012 and he called in periodically. Martin enjoyed these visits; he loaned the school a number of his works and made two crosses, one for the school's chapel and one for the senior boys' study room. When Cranbrook acquired a work by Martin's former art teacher Justin O'Brien, Martin went to its unveiling.

The oxygen tube hissed. The clear plastic tube snaked its way from Martin's nose to a tank near the open door of his studio. Beneath two sash windows was a single four-poster bed. Martin could no longer get upstairs to his bedroom. Rake-thin and pale, Martin sat—as he often did—with his back to a glass cabinet in which he kept his most treasured objects: among them were the Babar the Elephant book Penelope Tree's daughter had given him; his parents' love letters; a stubbie of beer from a friend who had battled the drink and vowed this bottle was the last liquor he would ever touch. A newspaper clipping about artist Margaret Olley, who had recently died, was taped to the cabinet's glass door.

From the studio's picture rail, some of the dark childhood portraits Martin painted at Cranbrook glowered down. Also hanging on the walls were the faded print of van Gogh's *Road to Tarascon* from his father's surgery, Justin O'Brien's schoolboy portrait of Martin and a black and white photograph of O'Brien himself. The room overflowed with images from throughout his life, including of Tiny Tim and Luna Park. On an easel across the dining table was his famous image of Jimi Hendrix, which he was reworking. 'All my art history is in this room,' he said.

The dining table was cluttered with papers, notebooks, pens, coffee cups. And a pouch of tobacco. Martin had taken up smoking again. He rolled a cigarette and, with the oxygen tube in his nostrils, puffed away. Orange flames shot from his nostrils as if from a fire-breathing dragon.

Artist Margaret Olley, who had lived nearby, had been on his mind. He had visited her Paddington home-studio shortly after she died in 2011. He had been enchanted at how her house appeared from the outside to be a simple old terrace attached to a former hat factory, but inside was an endless realm of 'mysterious, fruitful interiors' and he thought her garden was as wonderful as Monet's at Giverny.

Like Martin, Margaret had been a lifelong heavy smoker. Towards the end of her life, she was given the choice of either oxygen or tobacco.

She opted for tobacco. Martin was convinced Margaret could have had both. And, as I sat beside him at the dining table to interview him for *The Sydney Morning Herald* in May 2012, he wanted to prove his point.

He removed the oxygen tube from his nose and flicked his cigarette lighter close to its hissing end. Flick. Flick. Flick. He had been reading about oxygen, he said. Flick. Flick. Flick. 'It's not combustible,' he insisted. Combustible or not, a flame shot from the end of the tube. The studio and all in it seemed poised to be consumed by energy more explosive than that from Hendrix's guitar. Martin threw down the tube and leapt to his feet. He quickly stamped out the flame that was advancing along the tube towards the oxygen tank a couple of metres away. Then he picked up the blackened tube and conceded his reckless experiment had failed. 'Cancel that argument,' he said. 'Life's a total experiment. You never know what's going to happen and you've got to be able to move fast.'

Having no heirs, Martin was preoccupied with the fate of Wirian. He wanted the house and all it contained to remain as a haven for creative spirits. 'It can be an awful vanity wanting to save everything. I don't believe that's the case. But I question myself many, many times.'

Some wondered whether Martin would bequeath the house to his former school and next-door neighbour, Cranbrook. Yet his relationship with the school was complex and ambivalent. He valued the education, especially his art education and mentorship by Justin O'Brien. Yet he nurtured the hurt of the bullying he had received at the hands of another student. And he was unhappy that his stepmother had bequeathed a large amount of money to the school, money he believed was his birthright.

He signed his will on 20 September 2012, appointing as executors his cousins Roslyn and Alexander Sharp and journalist Johnny Barker.

Martin had become friends with Johnny after his brother Michael, who had worked on Luna Park, had been killed in a hit-and-run accident. He appointed two literary executors, Marilyn Karet, who had worked with him on the Tiny Tim film, and artist Luke Sciberras.

But Martin had a sting in the tail of his will, and it was directed at Cranbrook. He wrote: 'I note the unfortunate and antagonistic relationship that has arisen over a number of years with my neighbour Cranbrook School and I direct my trustees not to deal with or favour that School in the administration of the trusts under this will.' He wanted the school to stop using his name for its Martin Sharp Art Prize. He had not consented to this, he wrote. He left no individual bequests. He wanted his entire estate, valued at more than eleven million dollars, held in a trust known as the Street of Dreams Martin Sharp Trust. Its purpose would be to preserve Wirian as a centre for art education, to foster awareness of Martin's work and the significance of Luna Park and Tiny Tim.

Martin's work *Graceland* was the centrepiece of a group show in August 2013 at Damien Minton's gallery. For the opening, Angelica pushed Martin in his wheelchair through the gallery, where he sat in his well-worn pinstripe suit, navy tam o'shanter and red plaid scarf. The patrons paid court. *Graceland* was a homage to Giorgio de Chirico's surrealist *The Song of Love*. Martin thought the head of Apollo that dominated de Chirico's painting—with tousled hair and the hint of a curled lip—resembled Elvis Presley. Martin began the work in 1973, but forty years on it remained unfinished. Martin wrote a sign taped to the wall beside his painting. It read: 'Still a work in progress.'

Martin had stopped listening to Tiny Tim by 2013 and, after a brief musical interlude when Scottish pop singer Susan Boyle captured his attention, he rediscovered Elvis Presley. But in his last weeks, he preferred silence. Old friends came to say farewell, among them Alex Popov with whom Martin shared an eccentric meal. Martin requested kippers. Unable by then to eat solids, Martin's kippers went through a blender. Nonetheless, he declared his kipper shake delicious.

Martin kept the Bible he had painted in Aboriginal colours by his bedside and asked visitors, including Cranbrook's headmaster, Nicholas Sampson, to read from it. Notwithstanding the barb he had in store for the school, Martin welcomed Nicholas's visits.

Martin retained his religious faith and his curiosity. As death approached, he wanted to know what might be ahead. He asked Luke Sciberras to scour biblical sources in a fruitless attempt to find an explanation of the Kingdom of Heaven. Luke recalls that he was like a man waiting at a bus stop, but unsure where the bus was going. 'There was always a sense that he was looking for absolution of some kind, or a blessing of some kind, because I think he felt a little lonely. He was scared of that loneliness. He wanted the comfort of spirituality,' says Luke.

No one had a more moving final meeting than Peter Weir. Martin and the filmmaker had remained good friends over the years since *Picnic at Hanging Rock*, although Peter found Martin's fractured conversation—peppered with staccato, unfinished sentences and long pauses—did not make for fluid dialogue. But when Peter visited Martin a couple of weeks before he died, those obstacles to communication had vanished. Peter recounts: 'We talked for an hour and a half in a way that we'd never talked before. Without anything between us. Without any barrier. And it was at death's door. It was one of the most wonderful conversations of my life.' They galloped freely across many subjects, including art, religion and creativity. 'We could have been anywhere. We could have been in the middle of the Gobi desert, or on horseback riding through New England, or on a ship or something. It was just two souls talking. Two men. And I forgot he was ill and he forgot I was well.'

In late November, Martin wrote a codicil to his will and added Angelica to his list of executors. By then she had been staying at Wirian for most of the month. He was bedridden in his studio where Angelica provided comfort and companionship, and agency nurses attended Martin's increasing medical needs. On the evening of Sunday 1 December 2013, the nurse on duty prepared a painkiller and Angelica readied to lift Martin's head so he could more readily swallow the tablet. 'I love you, Martin,' she told him, as she often did. As she reached her arm around his head, she felt his last breath, like a wind, on her shoulder. It was just after 11pm on the first day of Advent and a day after his muse, Tiny Tim, had died seventeen years earlier.

Obituaries appeared in the international press. Martin's psychedelic posters were cultural icons of the era, said London's *The Telegraph*. He had helped shape the imagery of late 1960s rock, said *The New York Times*. He turned seemingly trivial or ephemeral images into monuments, said *The Sydney Morning Herald*'s critic John McDonald.

Friends, too, paid tribute. 'Martin moved far beyond the world of pop art; he was a philosopher using paint,' wrote Richard Neville. George Gittoes described him as 'a stranger in a strange land' who left behind a 'trail of stardust'. Filmmaker Jeremy Thomas believed Martin's art is yet to be appreciated. 'He will have his day because his work is so unique. There is nobody else but Martin who chose to paint what he chose to paint.'

Martin's white coffin was covered in sunflowers. About eight hundred people sweltered inside Christ Church St Laurence in Sydney's downtown Haymarket. The church where Martin worshipped and wished to be farewelled was too small for the crush of mourners who leaned against walls and overflowed onto the street in the hot December sunshine.

The hard pews filled with artists, filmmakers, musicians. Reg Mombassa, Jimmy Barnes, Germaine Greer, Margaret Fink, Jenny Kee, Richard Neville and Julie Clarke, Wendy Whiteley. There were politicians and dignitaries, including the New South Wales governor Marie Bashir, Aboriginal friends and a Buddhist nun.

Andrew Sharp acknowledged his cousin belonged to many families: 'It would be remiss to think we owned him.' Philippe Mora recalled their youthful Pheasantry days in London, the drug bust and late-night duets of art and music as Eric Clapton played and Martin painted. Martin had the iron will and heroic stubbornness needed to be a real artist: 'He was the real deal.'

Eric sent a message: 'Thank you Martin for your friendship, inspiration and for just being you. An entire section of my youth is interwoven with your memory, a time of freedom, joy and fellowship that I will never forget. I will miss you, my friend, until we meet again somewhere down the road. Your old pal, Eric.'

Jon Lewis stepped up to speak with his camera around his neck and cheekily photographed those assembled. Goddaughter Lucy Neville, critic John McDonald, Cranbrook's headmaster Nicholas Sampson and Marie Bashir also paid tribute. Several of his Tiny Tim collaborators performed. Mic Conway and Jeannie Lewis sang 'Somewhere Over the Rainbow'. Cellist Nathan Waks accompanied Lewis for 'There is a Green Hill Far Away'—Martin's favourite, if mournful, childhood hymn. Angelica Tremblay sang 'Little Sparrow', a song she and Martin had composed.

Artists Greg Weight, Peter Kingston, Garry Shead and Luke Sciberras and Martin's young relatives Alex Lloyd and Nicholas Sharp carried his coffin down the nave to the waiting hearse. The crowd applauded as the vehicle departed down Sydney's George Street. Mourners picked up pieces of chalk and wrote a single word on the pavement outside the church. It was the word Australia had sent as a message to the world, the word that Martin had, through his art, made his own. *Eternity.*

Martin wanted his ashes scattered at the two places he loved most. Half were buried near to his dynasty of beloved dogs in the garden at Wirian, his grandparents' home and the house in which he had lived, created and died. The remainder were disbursed when friends and family gathered on the banks of the Port Hacking River a year after his death. Some were spread on the ground near Telford, where he had spent the happiest days of his childhood. The remainder were cast into the sparkling water. Martin had returned at last to the realm of his mysterious, majestic blue groper.

ACKNOWLEDGEMENTS

As a teenage fan of Bob Dylan, I was riveted when I saw Martin's image of *Mr Tambourine Man* reproduced in a magazine. I cut out and pasted it on the cover of my school book. I can still see the red psychedelic swirls against the book's green cover.

It was small, just a few centimetres across. When I later saw the image reproduced much larger in London's *Observer* colour magazine, I squirrelled away the supplement and packed it in my bag when my family emigrated from Liverpool to Australia in late 1968.

I had no idea who had created the image—or that I was sailing towards his birthplace. Indeed, it would be many years before I learned Martin Sharp's name and that he lived in my adopted town of Sydney.

By then, various well-worn T-shirts with his artworks on them—of Ginger Meggs and *Eternity*—had been my companions on travels around the globe. So I had been drawn to his art for decades before I walked down Wirian's path in 2003 to interview him at his home for *The Sydney Morning Herald.*

In the years after, we spent many hours sitting at his dining table—amid a parade of visitors, phone calls, dogs and an irascible rooster—drinking fiendishly strong coffee and talking. Those meandering conversations are the genesis of this book.

But a biography does not take shape without great generosity, surprising encounters, memorable conversations and a dash of good luck. Many people agreed to be interviewed for this book. I wish to thank especially Philippe Mora for his insight, enthusiasm and willingness to open so many, and for reading early sections. Eija Vehka-aho entrused me with a biographer's dream: a collection of Martin's letters written over more than thirty years.

Others, too, shared letters and insights—Sandy Lieberson, Harmonie Downes, Jackie Menzies, Peter Collins and Emma Walker, while John Weiley made available excerpts from his diary from the mid-1960s. Roslyn Sharp was a font of knowledge of Sharp family history, and Luke Sciberras on details of Martin's art and later life. I thank Martin's executors for their support and willingness to answer my many queries.

Thank you also to the following for making time for interviews, and in some cases several. Anthony Abrahams, Jim Anderson, Johnny Barker, Deborah Beck, John Bell, Birgitta Bjerke, Ace Bourke, Cressida Campbell, Nell Campbell, Ruby Challenger, Julie Clarke, Lynne Clarke, Terry Clarke, Victoria Cobden, Mic Conway, Lois Cook, Wendy Evans, Martin Fabinyi, Marianne Faithfull, Louise Ferrier, Margaret Fink, Roger Foley-Fogg, John Gaden, Juno Gemes, George Gittoes, Bruce Goold, Linda Gumbert, John Gregory-Roberts, Pamela Griffith, Anthony Haden-Guest, John 'George' Harrison, Michael Hobbs, Jason Holman, Clytie Jessop, Jenny Kee, Annie Kelly, Fairlie Kingston, Peter Kingston, Lisa and Sigi Krauss, Kay and the late Colin Lanceley, Justice David Levine, Jon Lewis, John McDonald, Craig McGregor, David McKay, Freya Mathews, Charlotte Martin, Tina Micklethwait (Date), Mike Molloy, Mirka Mora, Aunty Val Murphy, the late Richard Neville, Peter Powditch, Alex Popov, Stuart Purves, Kate Reid, Ian Reid, Zandra Rhodes, Karen Robson, Peter Royles, Carol Ruff, Nicholas Sampson, Jim Sharman, Andrew Sharp, Russell Sharp, Bob Seidemann, Gria Shead, Garry Shead, Ian Skinner, Joe Skrzynski, Ella Sperling, Karla Sperling, Timothy Street-Porter, Meryl Tankard, Jeremy Thomas, Penelope Tree, Angelica Tremblay, Robert Tilley, Lin Utzon, Ed Victor, Maggie Walsh, Richard Walsh, Nathan Waks, the late Nick Waterlow, Greg Weight, Peter Weir, the late Robert Whitaker, Wendy Whiteley, Mandy Wright and William Yang.

Others answered email queries and assisted in myriad ways. Thank you Rebecca Baillie, John Blandy, Stanley Cohen, Michael Esson, Felicity Fenner, Christine France, Peter Hannan, Marilyn Karet, Rupert Latimer, Michael Organ, Annabel Pegus, Keiron Pim, Sandy Sharp, Brook Turner, and past and present curatorial staff at the Art Gallery of NSW, especially Wayne Tunnicliffe, Natalie Wilson and Barry Pearce, and UNSW Galleries.

Many librarians and archivists helped me document aspects of Martin's life. I thank Steven Miller and Eric Riddler at the Art Gallery of NSW library, Simon Drake at the National Film and Sound Archive, staff of the State Library of NSW, the National Library of Australia, the NSW State Archives, the University of Sydney library, Karen Stitt at the Sydney Opera House, Dominique Novak d'Hennin at Cranbrook School archives, Helen McDonald at Sutherland Shire Library and Anne Doughty, Luna Park historian. Youthworks Outdoors kindly let me see through Telford and the caretaker's cottage at Port Hacking.

Joanna Mendelssohn and Anne Coombs read early sections and gave perceptive feedback. Anne also put a roof over my head as I researched and travelled, as did Susan Varga, Rae and Yuri Bolotin, Matthew Westwood and Andrew Harris. Other friends and former colleagues helped in precious ways, including Robin Aylott, Clare Morgan, Philippa Drynan, Darren Goodsir, Barbara Harper, David Marr and Kate McClymont. Brenda O'Neill and Dianne Quinn undertook many hours of patient transcription.

At Allen & Unwin, publisher Richard Walsh has been an energetic champion and offered wise counsel and encouragement. Editorial director Rebecca Kaiser has brought this book into reality with enthusiasm and sensitivity. Simone Ford has been an incisive editor. My agent Lyn Tranter has been supportive throughout.

Conrad Walters has lived with my obsession with Martin Sharp. Thank you for your love, patience, astute comments on several drafts and for doing more than your share of the dog walks for the past two years.

SELECT BIBLIOGRAPHY

Anderson, Patricia, *Robert Hughes: The Australian Years*, Pandora Press, Sydney, 2010.

Bell, John, *The Time of My Life*, Allen & Unwin, Sydney, 2002.

Burton, Pamela, *The Waterlow Killings*, Melbourne University Publishing, Victoria, 2012.

Clapton, Eric, *Eric Clapton, The Autobiography*, Century, London, 2007.

Clarkson, Wensley, *Bindon: Fighter, Gangster, Lover*, John Blake, London, 2007.

Cockington, James, *Banned: Tales from the Bizarre History of Australian Obscenity*, ABC Books, Sydney, 2005.

Coombs, Anne, *Sex and Anarchy: The Life and Death of the Sydney Push*, Viking, Victoria, 1996.

Dale, John, *Huckstepp, A Dangerous Life*, Xoum, NSW, 2014.

de Leeuw, Ronald (ed), *The Letters of Vincent Van Gogh*, Penguin, London, 1996.

de Saint-Exupéry, Antoine, *The Little Prince*, Thorndike Press, USA, 2005, (first published 1943).

Drew, Philip, *The Masterpiece: Jørn Utzon, A Secret Life*, Hardie Grant, Melbourne, 1999.

Du Noyer, Paul, *In the City: A Celebration of London Music*, Virgin Books, UK, 2010.

Dutton, Geoffrey, *The Innovators: The Sydney Alternatives in the Rise of Modern Art, Literature and Ideas*, Macmillan, Australia, 1986.

Faithfull, Marianne, *Faithfull*, Penguin, London 1994.

Fountain, Nigel, *Underground: The London Alternative Press, 1966–74*, Routledge & Kegan Paul, London, 1988.

Green, Jonathon, *All Dressed Up: The Sixties and the Counterculture*, Jonathan Cape, London, 1998.

— *Days in the Life: Voices from the English Underground 1961–1971*, William Heinemann, UK, 1990.

Gittoes, George, *Blood Mystic*, Pan Macmillan, Sydney, 2016.

Hathaway, Norman and Nadel, Dan, *Electrical Banana, Masters of Psychedelic Art*, Damiani, New York, 2012.

Grunenberg, Christoph and Harris, Jonathan (eds), *Summer of Love: Psychedelic Art, Social Crisis and Counterculture in the 1960s*, Liverpool University Press, UK, 2006.

Hall, James and Sandra, *Australian Censorship: The XYZ of Love*, Jack de Lissa, Sydney, 1970.

Hayward, Philip (ed), *From Pop, to Punk, to Postmodernism: Popular Music and Australian Culture from the 1960s to the 1990s*, Allen & Unwin, Sydney, 1992.

Hesse, Hermann, *Steppenwolf*, Penguin, 2009 (first published 1927).

Hickie, David, *The Prince and the Premier*, HarperCollins, Australia, 1985.

Keen, Graham, and La Rue, Michel (eds), *Underground Graphics*, Academy, London, 1970.

Lowey, Ian and Prince, Suzy, *The Graphic Art of the Underground: A Counter-cultural History*, Bloomsbury, London, 2014.

Moraes, Henrietta, *Henrietta*, Hamish Hamilton, London, 1994.

Hoskins, Donald, *Foundation Stones, The Contributions of the Loveridge, Ritchie, Hudson and Hoskins Families to Australian Industry*, Mittagong, NSW, 1997.

Hughes, Robert, *Things I Didn't Know*, Vintage, London, 2007.

Kee, Jenny, *A Big Life*, Penguin Australia, Victoria, 2006.

McCoy, Albert, *The Politics of Heroin, CIA Complicity in the Global Drug Trade*, Chicago Review Press, Chicago, 2003.

McGregor, Craig, *People Politics and Pop: Australians in the Sixties*, Ure Smith, Sydney, 1968.

McGregor, Craig et al, *In the Making: Australian Art and Artists*, Thomas Nelson, Australia, 1969.

Marr, David, *Patrick White: A Life*, Random House, Sydney, 1991.

— *The Letters of Patrick White*, University of Chicago Press, Chicago, 1994.

Marshall, Sam, *Luna Park: Just for Fun*, Luna Park Reserve Trust, Sydney, 1995.

Melly, George, *Revolt into Style: The Pop Arts in Britain*, Penguin, London, 1972.

Mendelssohn, Joanna, *The Yellow House, 1970–72*, Art Gallery of NSW, Sydney, 1990.

Miles, Barry, *London Calling: A Countercultural History of London Since 1945*, Atlantic, London, 2010.

Mora, Mirka, *Wicked But Virtuous*, Viking, Victoria, 2000.

Naifeh, Steven and Smith, Gregory White, *Van Gogh: The Life*, Profile Books, London, 2011.

Neville, Richard, *Hippie Hippie Shake*, William Heinemann, Port Melbourne, 1995.

O'Neill, Helen, *A Singular Vision: Harry Seidler*, HarperCollins Australia, 2013.

Owen, Ted and Dickson, Denise, *High Art: A History of the Psychedelic Poster*, Sanctuary Publishing, London, 1999.

Pearce, Barry et al, *Brett Whiteley: Art & Life*, Thames and Hudson, Australia, 1995.

Pearce, Barry and Wilson, Natalie, *Justin O'Brien: the Sacred Music of Colour*, Art Gallery of NSW, Sydney, 2010.

Pim, Keiron, *Jumpin' Jack Flash: David Litvinoff and the Rock'n'Roll Underworld*, Jonathan Cape, London, 2016.

Richards, Keith, *Life*, Little, Brown & Co, New York, 2010.

Sharman, Jim, *Blood & Tinsel, A Memoir*, Miegunyah Press, Victoria, 2008.

Sharp, Martin, *Martin Sharp Cartoons*, Scripts, Sydney, 1966.

— *Catalog No. 3*, Reid Books, Sydney, 1971.

— *Art Book*, Mathews Miller Dunbar, London, 1972.

Tarling, Lowell, *Tiny Tim: Tiptoe Through a Lifetime*, Generation Books, Katoomba, NSW, 2013.

Thoms, Albie, *My Generation*, Media21 Publishing, Sydney, 2013.

Timmers, Margaret (ed), *The Power of the Poster*, V&A Publications, London, 1998.

Trinca, Helen, *Madeleine: A Life of Madeleine St John*, Text, Melbourne, 2012.

Tunnicliffe, Wayne and Jaspers, Anneke (eds), *Pop to Popism*, Art Gallery of NSW, 2014.

Walding, Murray and Vukovic, Nick, *Plastered: Poster Art of Australian Popular Music*, Miegunyah Press, Victoria, 2005.

Wallace, Christine, *Germaine Greer: Untamed Shrew*, Pan Macmillan, Sydney, 1997.

Waterlow, Nick (ed), *Larrikins in London*, Ivan Dougherty Gallery, Sydney, 2003.

Waterlow, Nick and Pegus, Annabel (eds), *The Everlasting World of Martin Sharp*, Ivan Dougherty Gallery, Sydney, 2006.

Wilson, Ashleigh, *Brett Whiteley: Art, Life and Other Things*, Text, Melbourne, 2016.

Yang, William, *Sydney Diary, 1974–1984*, James Fraser, Sydney, 1984.

NOTES

ABBREVIATIONS

MS Martin Sharp
JS Jo Sharp
HS Henry Sharp
EVA Eija Vehka-aho
JM Joyce Morgan
SMH *The Sydney Morning Herald*

CHAPTER 1

BEGINNINGS

'lecturer-general': *The Cumberland Argus and Fruitgrowers Advocate*, 22 August 1891, p. 9.

'sluggish action of the bowels': *The Cumberland Argus and Fruitgrowers Advocate*, 22 August 1891, p. 9.

He was a 'man of ceaseless mental activities', and 'more the captious and destructive critic': *The Cumberland Argus and Fruitgrowers Advocate*, 22 August 1891, p. 9.

Employed more than 800 men: 'Ritchie Bros rolling stock works, Auburn', *SMH*, 18 October 1919, p. 14.

The government should stick to owning the tracks: 'The Locomotives', *The Cumberland Argus and Fruitgrowers Advocate*, 3 May 1905, p. 3.

He took an unwavering line: 'Wages board', *SMH*, 19 August 1913, p. 5.

James Ritchie was hailed as a pioneer: 'James D. Ritchie', obituary, *SMH*, 10 December 1925, p. 15.

Born in Stockholm: 'William Kopsen', obituary, *SMH*, 18 August 1930, p. 6.

lifelong interest in England's folklore: 'W.H. Sharp, political veteran's death', *SMH*, 8 October 1929, p. 12.

He raised his family in an atmosphere that was spartan: 'Dr W.A. Ramsay Sharp, an appreciation', *SMH,* 16 November 1937, p. 8.

William Sharp chaired: 'Trades movements: East Sydney Labour League', *SMH,* 11 April 1891, p. 7.

William Sharp was elected: 'William Henry Sharp', obituary, *SMH*, 8 October 1929, p. 12.

He graduated from Sydney University in 1902: 'Dr W.A. Ramsay Sharp', obituary, *SMH*, 11 November 1937, p. 7, and 'Dr W.A. Ramsay Sharp, an appreciation', *SMH*, 16 November 1937, p. 8.

The wedding at St John's: 'At Hymen's altar', *Southern Star*, Bega, 15 June 1907, p. 2.

His will provided for the establishment: 'Late Dr Ramsay Sharp', *SMH*, 28 March 1938, p. 9.

'hotbed of Labor sympathisers': 'Liberal Reform Association', *The Southern Record and Advertiser*, 30 July 1910, p. 3.

'degenerate' element: 'Flats at Vaucluse', *SMH*, 8 November 1929, p. 14.

The centre of attention was: 'Happy birthday party', *SMH*, 16 July 1936, p. 17.

The young woman was presented: 'Back from abroad', *The Age*, 10 February 1940, p. 21.

He sailed the Atlantic: 'Henry Sharp', obituary, *Australasian Journal of Dermatology*, vol. 25, issue 2, 1984, pp. 94–5.

He arrived just a few days before: 'Engagement announced', *SMH*, 3 August 1940, p. 10.

Jo's parents held an afternoon tea party: 'Engagement celebrated', *SMH*, 19 August 1940, p. 4.

A marquee was erected: 'Reception in marquee', *SMH*, 9 December 1940, p. 4.
'then I could be with you': JS, letter to HS, 12 December 1941.
'I get the feeling that you don't love me': JS, letter to HS, 4 December 1941.
'to the wife of Flight-Lieutenant Henry Sharp': *The Sydney Morning Herald*, 23 January 1942, p. 10.
The keen singer joined his fellow servicemen: Australian War Memorial (ref no: SUK10510).
'He said the worst thing': MS to JM, 31 August 2007.
'Mum's broom': JS, letter to HS, 17 November 1943.
'quite one of the naughtiest': JS, letter to HS, circa 1945.
Jo, too, was worn out: JS, letter to HS, circa 1945.
'the child has just been': JS, letter to HS, circa 1946.
Jo loved horseracing: JS, letter to HS, 25 November 1938.
'I am still being told': JS, letter to HS, November 1943.
She promised to be a good wife: JS, letter to HS, November 1943.
'The more we are parted': JS, letter to HS, 17 November 1943.
'you love me a little bit—don't you?': JS, letter to HS, 17 November 1943.
Exhausted after a week: JS, letter to HS, 27 November 1943.
'I heard quite a few people': JS, letter to HS, 1 December 1943.
'he got through God bless': JS, letter to HS, 7 December 1943.

CHAPTER 2
THE LITTLE PRINCE

'It was quite jolly for a while': MS to JM, 31 August 2007.
Jo purchased the print: MS to JM, 15 May 2012.
he insisted it was an animal: JS, letter to HS, 26 May 1944.
A Campbell's soup can: MS to JM, 10 August 2006.
But to fit it in the frame: *The Everlasting World of Martin Sharp*, Nick Waterlow and Annabel Pegus (eds), Ivan Dougherty Gallery, Sydney, 2006, p. 4.

The illustrations for: MS to JM, 3 March 2012.

He first saw a statue: *Martin Sharp*, Survey series, 14, Open Channel, 1981, film for National Gallery of Victoria.

But Martin was disappointed: MS to JM, 1 November 2012.

Walt Disney's *Fantasia:* MS to JM, 3 February 2012.

Martin was surrounded by books: MS to JM, 3 February 2012.

Martin's father was a great reader: 'Henry Sharp', obituary, *Australasian Journal of Dermatology*, vol. 25, issue 2, 1984, pp. 94–5.

'Jo's family were a lot looser': Roslyn Sharp to JM, 25 July 2014.

'[Jo] was winsome': Anthony Abrahams to JM, 15 December 2014.

'I did think you could fly': MS to JM, 13 May 2013.

'I was a very untidy boy': MS to JM, 13 May 2013.

'It was my pride and joy': MS to JM, 1 November 2012.

'No one said': MS to JM, 1 November 2012.

Martin believed his father: MS to JM, 1 November 2012.

'I think it was because': MS to JM, 10 August 2006.

'I could feel it': MS to JM, 9 November 2012.

'Breakaways were': John Gaden to JM, 13 August 2015.

'He really put in': Anthony Abrahams to JM, 15 December 2015.

'He said, "Open your fly"': MS to JM, 1 November 2012.

'That was my first political act': MS to JM, 13 May 2013.

'He was given': MS to JM, 1 November 2012.

'I did want': MS to JM, 13 May 2013.

'There was a roar': MS to JM, 31 August 2007.

'art father': MS frequently referred to Justin O'Brien this way, including in a letter to curator Barry Pearce, 25 January 1996.

'almost monosyllabic': John Elder, 'The razor's edge', *M Magazine,* November 1990, p. 16.

O'Brien joined Cranbrook in 1946: David Thomas and Mark McAndrew, *Born in the Hour of Victory: Cranbrook School 1918–1993*, Playright Publishing, Sydney, 1998, p. 76.

'He provided lovely colours': MS to JM, 31 August 2007.

O'Brien had given his student: MS to JM, 10 August 2006.

A 1957 still life: *The Everlasting World of Martin Sharp*, p. 7.

'He was a confident boy': Terry Clarke to JM, 4 February 2015.

'[Bell's class] was next to the physics lab': MS to JM, 24 August 2007.

'If you got one there': MS to JM, 13 May 2013. The Archibald Prize is awarded annually by the Art Gallery of New South Wales for portraiture.

'It was considered quite cheeky': MS to JM, 24 August 2007.

'I don't know if he liked it': MS to JM, 13 May 2013.

'I realised [for the first time]': MS to JM, 24 August 2007.

'An indefensibly bad exam': MS, Cranbrook School report, 1957.

'He has the ability but': Cranbrook School report, 1957.

'Martin has been very busy again': Cranbrook School report, 1957.

'He is coming on': Cranbrook School report, 1957.

'My father had been given': MS to JM, 9 November 2012.

'I've had enough': MS to JM, 9 November 2012.

Jo and Henry did not officially separate: *Sharp v. Sharp*, divorce petition, 14 May 1965.

'My mother wasn't the first one': MS to JM, 9 November 2012.

She had an abortion: MS to JM, 9 November 2012.

'And she did give Keith up': MS to JM, 9 November 2012.

'It was Justin's suggestion': MS to JM, 9 November 2012.

CHAPTER 3

ART VERSUS ALFS

'There was no art world': Colin Lanceley to JM, August 2003.

'Great swarming teeming Sydney': D.H. Lawrence, *Kangaroo*, Penguin, Victoria, 1983 (first published 1923), p. 33.

labelled as 'Alfs': Anne Coombs, *Sex and Anarchy: The life and death of the Sydney Push*, Viking, Victoria, 1996, p. 84.

'I wear's me hair long': *Honi Soit*, 17 April 1962, p. 8.

Martin produced a cartoon: *Honi Soit,* 20 July 1961, p. 2.

'College was like going back': MS to JM, 5 May 2012.

'I stopped going': MS to JM, 31 August, 2007.

'I took one look': MS to Deborah Beck, City of Sydney Oral History Program, <www.sydneyoralhistories.com.au/martin-sharp>, 25 July 2013.

He later destroyed much of this work: MS to Deborah Beck, City of Sydney Oral History Program.

His first was for the annual Artists' Ball: Deborah Beck to JM, 20 August 2015.

For Martin the balls were the high points: 'Art for Mart's sake', *SMH*, 8 December 1965, p. 6, and Hazel de Berg, National Library of Australia, Oral History Section, (TRC 1/519), 9 June 1970.

He dressed as a sea monster: Deborah Beck, City of Sydney Oral History Program.

Louise Ferrier had little recollection: Louise Ferrier to JM, 8 December 2014.

he lost his ability to paint: Deborah Beck, City of Sydney Oral History Program.

'I always remember Martin looking at that': Garry Shead to JM, 12 November 2014.

'He just was a total romantic': Jenny Kee to JM, 18 February 2015.

her 'way-out wardrobe': *The Australian Women's Weekly*, 1 July 1964, pp. 8–9.

Anou later caught: *The Australian Women's Weekly*, 28 April 1965, p. 63.

'I was driving with Martin': John Weiley to JM, 16 November 2014.

After the occupants had exited: Anthony Abrahams to JM, 15 December 2014.

'He kept touching the gutter': Alex Popov to JM, 27 April 2014.

he surreptitiously served alcohol: Tony Stephens, 'On the menu: Love, passion, style and one regret', *SMH*, 23 August 2003, p. 10.

'We wanted to celebrate': John Weiley to JM, 16 November 2014.

He had already been involved: Richard Neville, *Hippie Hippie Shake*, William Heinemann, Port Melbourne, 1995, p. 17.

The school's harsh discipline: Richard Neville, 'My school of hard Knox', *Crikey*, <www.crikey.com.au/2009/02/25/richard-neville-my-school-of-hard-knox>, 25 February 2009.

'I was getting terrible marks': Richard Walsh to JM, 26 November 2014.

En route to Pithiviers: Mirka Mora, *Wicked but Virtuous*, Viking, Victoria, 2000, p. 14.

He handed over many gold coins: Zelda Cawthorne, 'Treasure trove from Mirka', *Australian Jewish News*, <www.jewishnews.net.au/treasure-trove-from-mirka/35684>, 18 June 2014.

'I remember his first visit': Mirka Mora to JM, 7 July 2014.

'We got on like a house on fire': Robert Whitaker to JM, August 2003.

Martin later used a portrait: Robert Whitaker's grotesque portrait of Mirka Mora was the cover of *Oz*, no. 12, August 1964.

'I put peacock feathers around him': Robert Whitaker to JM, August 2003.

'And off I went': Robert Whitaker to JM, August 2003.

CHAPTER 4
THE TRIALS OF MARTIN SHARP

'It didn't occur to anyone': Richard Walsh to JM, 26 November 2014.

'Australia's greatest menace': Garry C. Wotherspoon, 'Delaney, Colin John (1897–1969)', *Australian Dictionary of Biography*, National Centre of Biography, Australian National University, <adb.anu.edu.au/biography/delaney-colin-john-9945/text17617>, published first in hardcopy 1993.

The correspondent advocated filling: *Oz*, no. 3, June 1963.

James had been a religious correspondent: see 'Francis James', obituary, *The Independent*, 28 August 1992, <www.independent.co.uk/news/people/obituary-francis-james-1542938.html> and Tony Stephens, 'James, Alfred Francis Phillip (1918–1992)', *Australian*

Dictionary of Biography, National Centre of Biography, Australian National University, <adb.anu.edu.au/biography/james-alfred-francis-phillip-16270/text28209>, published online 2016.

'we are unlikely to sail so close': *Oz*, no. 5, December 1963.

'We were intimidated by the incredible animal-like crowd': John Weiley, diary entry circa summer 1962–63.

'The beer garden was full of beery half-pissed blokes': John Weiley, email to JM, 4 August 2015.

'They have described': 'Police act on student magazine', *SMH*, 21 February 1964, p 1.

'The university is extremely concerned': 'Police act on student magazine', p. 1.

Martin hit back: Martin Sharp, 'Satirist defends *The Gas Lash*', *SMH*, 24 February 1964, p. 2.

'angriest young man': 'Angry wizard of Oz', *Sunday Mirror*, 19 April 1964, p. 23.

'Francis was a bit of a loose cannon': John Gaden to JM, 13 August 2015.

'There is a lady sitting': Gerald Locke, Central Court of Petty Sessions, 8 September 1964.

Magistrate Gibson found: 'Article by student obscene, S.M. finds', *SMH*, 13 August 1964, p. 8.

CHAPTER 5
'FILTHY AND DISGUSTING'

He had also designed: Martin's advertisement appeared on the back of *Oz*, no. 12, 1964.

Heads turned the night: see Jenny Kee, *A Big Life*, Penguin Australia, Victoria, 2006. p. 43, and Richard Neville, *Hippie Hippie Shake,* William Heinemann, Port Melbourne, 1995, p. 51.

'They drank so little': Jock Veitch, 'Now even Romanos goes au go-go', *The Sun-Herald*, 24 October 1965, p. 107.

'We didn't have a toothbrush': Richard Walsh to JM, 26 November 2014.

'They were standing there': John Gaden to JM, 13 August 2015.

'Congratulations to all': telegram, 25 September 1964, in Barrett Reid and Nancy Underhill (eds), *Letters of John Reed: Defining Australian cultural life, 1920–1981*, Viking, Victoria, 2001, p. 615.

A young law student: Geoffrey Robertson, 'To ban or not to ban?' *SMH,* The Guide section, 14 October 1991, p. 6.

'one of the most liberal': 'An enlightened judgement', *The Canberra Times*, 7 November 1964, p. 2.

'It smells as though the air's been locked up': Craig McGregor, *People, Politics and Pot*, Ure Smith, Sydney, 1968, p. 90.

'genuine, spontaneous bright thought': 'Satire in *Oz* praised', *SMH*, 16 December 1964, p. 6.

'It is a lurking fear of civic sculptors': 'Satire in *Oz* praised', p. 6.

'It does us no harm when our pretentiousness': 'If magazine is obscene, so is satire', *The Daily Telegraph*, 17 December 1964, p. 15.

For if *Oz* was allowed: 'Appeal by *Oz* men ends', *SMH*, 18 December 1964, p. 5.

He intended to quash: 'Judge intends to quash obscenity convictions', *SMH*, 27 February 1965, p. 4.

'After all, who could resist': Richard Neville and Richard Walsh, 'Satire in the dock', *The Australian,* 27 February 1965, p. 8.

'Perhaps it would be a good idea': Justin O'Brien, letter to MS, 22 April 1965.

'Fancy Levine white-washing us': 'Sharp's comment on the Oz judgment', *SMH*, 10 February 1966, p. 6.

'We are living in times:' 'Magazine found not obscene', *SMH*, 10 February 1966, p. 6.

The *Oz* decision was hailed: 'This Australia: A round-up of 1964', *The Bulletin*, 26 December 1964, p. 8, and 'Satire', *The Bulletin*, 6 March 1965, p.13.

'That was really a turning point': Edward St John to Veronica Keraitis, National Library of Australia, Oral History Project, 29–30 September 1980 (TRC830).

Gerald Locke sentenced another artist: 'Three months' hard labour for artist', *SMH*, 15 December 1966, p. 1.

The tragic tale began: 'School Sex!', *Daily Mirror*, 12 March 1964, p. 1.

But *Oz* did: see *Oz*, no. 8, April 1964, p. 4.

Geoffrey Robertson alluded to the case: <www.geoffreyrobertson.com/9questionsforRupert.html>.

'We were treading on toes': MS to Helen Topliss, National Library of Australia, Oral History and Folklore (TRC3150), 17 November 1994.

'The *Oz* Guide to the Sydney Underworld': *Oz*, no. 23, October 1965, pp. 10–12.

But it was not until the day of: David Hickie, 'Askin friend to organised crime', *The National Times*, 13–19 September 1981, p. 1.

'For Vietnam. Season's Greetings': *SMH*, 23 December 1965, p. 4.

Martin lampooned it: *Oz*, no. 29, July 1966, p. 7.

CHAPTER 6

THE WHITE-ANT OF BELLEVUE HILL

'I took my clothes off': Linda Gumbert to JM, 2 June 2014.

'[Martin's] ash kept constantly dropping': John Weiley to JM, 16 November 2014.

'Terry White was in charge': MS to JM, 5 May 2012.

Martin thought the work: Hazel de Berg, National Library of Australia, Oral History Section, (TRC 1/519), 9 June 1970.

'lying between humour and mild horror': 'Exhibition commentary', *Art and Australia*, March 1966, p. 301.

'But it was before I knew anything': MS to JM, 5 May 2012.

'Marijuana was something': John Weiley to JM, 16 November 2014.

'If one had to choose': 'Art for Mart's sake', *SMH*, 8 December 1965, p. 6.

'It can be rough': Wallace Thornton, 'Martin Sharp exhibition at Clune Galleries', *SMH*, 8 December 1965, p. 21.

Martin noted years later: Deborah Beck, City of Sydney Oral History Program, <www.sydneyoralhistories.com.au/martin-sharp>, 25 July 2013.

Henry filed for divorce: *Sharp v. Sharp*, divorce petition, 14 May 1965.

He submitted a note: Dr Alan McGuinness, letter, 1 December 1965.

Jo received the Cranbrook Lane house: deed of settlement, 16 December 1965.

'I was in awe of them': Lin Utzon to JM, 15 January 2015.

'Her own age group were pretty shitty': MS to Helen Topliss, National Library of Australia, Oral History and Folklore (TRC3150), 17 November 1994.

'She was the kind of person': Alex Popov to JM, 27 April 2014.

'She had the slacks': Jim Sharman to JM, 25 September 2015.

'Martin and Anou are going': John Weiley diary, circa May 1965.

'danced and danced': Craig McGregor to JM, 15 November 2014.

'It was an amazing song': MS to JM, 5 May 2012.

'Walking up Mart's driveway': John Weiley diary, 1 January 1966.

'You wouldn't catch me': in Martin Sharp, *Martin Sharp Cartoons*, Scripts, Sydney, 1966.

'It has made me feel glad': Patrick White, letter to Desmond Digby, 15 March, 1963, in David Marr, *Patrick White: A life*, Random House, Sydney, 1991, p. 412.

At an election-night dinner: Philip Drew, *The Masterpiece: Jørn Utzon, a secret life,* Hardie Grant, Melbourne, 1999, p. 311.

Hughes called a press conference: 'Utzon quits Opera House', *SMH*, 1 March 1966, p. 1.

'Brilliant move forcing': *Oz*, no. 26, March 1966, p. 4.

'On the practical level': Jim Sharman to JM, 25 September 2015.

'Although the material is never obscene': '*Oz* takes to the stage', *SMH*, 11 March 1965, p. 8.

They were the last passengers: 'Utzon off in secret', *SMH*, 29 April 1966, p. 1.

'Martin's mother organised': Lin Utzon to JM, 15 January 2015.

'That was such a blow to our hopes': John Weiley to JM, 16 November 2014.

'the enormousness of it': MS to JM, 19 April 2013.

'Suddenly to be plunged': MS to JM, 19 April 2013.

The *Herald* promoted: 'New comic today', *SMH*, 14 May 1966, p. 1.

In his first *Herald* article: Richard Neville, 'The youth of Singapore', *SMH*, 14 May 1966, p. 13.

Martin watched a wedding ceremony: MS to JM, 19 April 2013.

At the Thai border: Richard Neville, 'Hiking through Thailand', *SMH*, 27 August 1966, p. 19.

'It was a great place': MS to JM, 19 April 2013.

It provided inspiration: *SMH*, 27 August 1966, p. 19

'You'd buy grass': MS to JM, 19 April 2013.

Donald Duck impersonations: *Martin Sharp*, Survey series, 14, Open Channel, 1981, film for National Gallery of Victoria.

He marvelled at: The James Gleeson Oral History Collection, National Gallery of Australia, 7 November 1979.

He thought Angkor the most beautiful place: The James Gleeson Oral History Collection.

They wandered the streets: Richard Neville, 'French bread, opium and music in the rococo Strand', *SMH*, 19 November 1966, p. 13.

'It was a harmless': Neville, 'French bread', p. 13.

'mood of uncomfortable gloom': Neville, 'French bread', p. 13.

He drew Richard: Neville, 'French bread', p. 13.

'I was too sick to do that': MS to JM, 19 April 2014.

CHAPTER 7

SWINGING LONDON

Time magazine had just declared: 'Great Britain: You can walk across it on the grass', *Time*, 15 April 1966, p. 26.

'That wasn't quite the excitement': MS to JM, 19 April 2014.

'something between *Private Eye*': Richard Neville, *Hippie Hippie Shake,* William Heinemann, Port Melbourne, 1995, p. 70.

'one of the classics': Robert Hughes, *Things I Didn't Know,* Vintage, London, 2007, p. 287.

'[Whitaker] turned the big main room': MS to JM, 19 April 2015.

'It was right off the King's Road': Robert Whitaker to JM, August 2003.

lampooning swinging London's: see Sydney *Oz*, no. 31, November 1966 p. 21.

The US Central Intelligence Agency: see Maia Szalavitz, 'The legacy of the CIA's secret LSD experiments', *Time,* 23 March 2012, <www.healthland.time.com/2012/03/23/the-legacy-of-the-cias-secret-lsd-experiments-on-america>.

'a profound experience': Walter Isaacson, *Steve Jobs*, Simon and Schuster, New York, 2011, p. 41.

'I admired Syd Barrett': MS to JM, 5 May 2012.

Martin took his first acid trip: Norman Hathaway and Dan Nadel, *Electrical Banana: Masters of psychedelic art,* Damiani, New York, 2012, pp. 179–93.

'Another dimension of reality was revealed': Hathaway and Nadel, *Electrical Banana*, pp. 179–93.

'I didn't draw under its influence': Hathaway and Nadel, *Electrical Banana*, pp. 179–93.

It was Bing Crosby: MS to JM, 10 August 2006.

Litvinoff modified: Keiron Pim, *Jumpin' Jack Flash: David Litvinoff and the rock'n'roll underworld*, Jonathan Cape, London, 2016. p. 30.

'on the borders of art': Keith Richards, *Life,* Little, Brown & Co, New York, 2010, p. 202.

'It became apparent': MS to JM, 19 April 2015.

A better place: MS to JM, 19 April 2015.

The Bob Dylan poster: The James Gleeson Oral History Collection, National Gallery of Australia, 7 November 1979.

'I wanted to do a tribute': MS to JM, August 2003.

The circles were influenced by: The James Gleeson Oral History Collection.

'Martin was really messy': EVA to JM, 2 February 2015.

'I saw like an aura around him': EVA to JM, 2 February 2015.

'I didn't know anyone there': MS to JM, August 2003.

'A couple of weeks later': MS to JM, August 2003.

he acknowledged he had felt homesick: MS, interviewed in *Classic Albums: Cream: Disraeli Gears,* documentary, Isis Productions, UK, 2006.

Martin told his friend: Peter Hannan, email to JM, 8 August, 2015.

He had written the lyrics: MS to JM, August 2003.

To Martin's ultimate good fortune: Tina Micklethwait (Date) to JM, 8 September 2015.

'The twins walked into': Robert Whitaker to JM, August 2003.

Martin spiked Richard's tea: Neville, *Hippie Hippie Shake*, p. 87.

They beat up Kramer: Pim, *Jumpin' Jack Flash*, p. 157 and Richards, *Life*, p. 210.

CHAPTER 8

THE PHEASANTRY

'[Martin and Clapton] really clicked': Charlotte Martin to JM, 27 January 2015.

'Martin and I were amazed': Philippe Mora to JM, 6 June 2015.

'It was Eric being a friend': MS to JM, August 2003.

Beneath their portraits: MS to JM, 15 May 2012.

'Fluorescent paints': to JM, 15 May 2013.

'I went off with Eric Clapton': Robert Whitaker to JM, August 2003.

'Jimmy started playing that slow': Alex Popov to JM, 27 April 2014.
an acetate of: Eric Clapton, *The Autobiography*, Century, London, 2007, p. 105.
'Through David Litvinoff': Charlotte Martin to JM, 27 January 2015.
'We were working really hard': Philippe Mora to JM, 24 May 2014.
'I certainly remember him': Charlotte Martin to JM, 27 January 2015.
'Martin was very introverted': EVA to JM, 2 February 2015.
'You couldn't sleep': Freya Mathews to JM, 8 July 2014.
'I remember him on the phone': Freya Mathews to JM, 8 July 2014.
'It was the greatest show in the world': Birgitta Bjerke to JM, 2 June 2014.
Melbourne-born Lambert: Jane Mulvagh, 'Obituary: Vernon Lambert', *The Independent*, <www.independent.co.uk/news/people/obituary-vernon-lambert-1549427.html>, 5 September 1992.
Accompanied by Piaggi: Lucy Cavendish, 'The not so mad hatter', *The Telegraph*, <fashion.telegraph.co.uk/news-features/TMG3348824/The-not-so-mad-hatter.html>, 15 January 2006.
'While Eric was very modest': MS to JM, 5 May 2012.
'Jimi Hendrix could only': MS to JM, 5 May 2012.
'I was working with Mylar plastic': MS to JM, 5 May 2012.
'otherwise the colour would have run': MS to JM, 5 May 2012.
'I splashed that [paint] like': MS to JM, 3 February 2012.
'I know about music emotionally': MS to JM, 3 February 2012.
'I didn't know whether he was': MS to JM, 5 May 2012.
'The groups ruled': MS to JM, 5 May 2012.
'It was the turning': MS to JM, 5 May 2012.
'A hallucination of an English childhood': James Button, 'Sergeant Pepper's wild trip', *The Age*, Insight section, 2 June 2007, p. 3.
'If such a deliberately': George Melly, 'Poster power', *The Observer*, 3 December 1967, p. 13.
'Sharp's posters seem divided': Melly, 'Poster power'.
'king of the kinky-poster makers': 'Sharp Dylan', *SMH*, 14 December 1967, p. 6.

'Serving spirits ended up': Clytie Jessop, email to JM, 28 June 2014.
'Their friendly verbal fencing': Clytie Jessop, email to JM, 18 June 2014.
'He was so carried away by that': Clytie Jessop to JM, 29 June 2014.
'He was very taken with all the letters': Clytie Jessop to JM, 29 June 2014.

CHAPTER 9

'I NEED TO BE POSSESSED BY SOMETHING BIGGER THAN ME'

'Fancy meeting them here!': MS, letter to EVA, circa October 1967.
'There are so many stars': MS, letter to EVA, 28 October 1967.
'He was a fantastic ladies' man': *The Sharp Edge*: *The art of Martin Sharp*, documentary, Southern Pictures, 2013.
'He wasn't hiding it': EVA to JM, 2 February 2015.
'Eija left [Martin] about four in the morning': Louise Ferrier to JM, 8 December 2014.
'I feel so clumsy': MS, letter to EVA, 17 May 1968.
even hoped their relationship: MS, letter to EVA, 17 May 1968.
'The distractions here': MS, letter to EVA, 20 May 1968.
'I need to be possessed': MS, letter to EVA, 29 May 1968.
'London and all its confusion': MS, letter to EVA, 19 June 1968.
'Getting very sick of Anou': MS, letter to EVA, 9 July 1968.
'I feel free in the sea': MS, letter to EVA, 9 July 1968.
'I must rid myself': MS, letter to EVA, 9 July 1968.
'So Alf': MS, letter to EVA, 16 July 1968.
'The boy must become a man': MS, letter to EVA, 16 July 1968.
'can this man boy be trusted': MS, letter to EVA, 18 July 1968.
'We all went': Marianne Faithfull to JM, 22 May 2015.
'one singer who is all singers': Martin Sharp, 'The real Tiny Tim', *Quadrant*, January 1977, p. 13.
'It was drawn from all sorts': MS to JM, 15 May 2015.

'Sharp has assembled': Robert Hughes, letter to London *Oz*, no. 17, December 1968, p. 12.

'arguably the greatest achievement': Jonathon Green, *All Dressed Up: the Sixties and the Counterculture*, Jonathan Cape, London, 1998, p. 356.

He was dubbed 'Big John': Wensley Clarkson, *Bindon: Fighter, gangster, lover*, John Blake, London, 2007, kindle edition.

'a seething cauldron': Marianne Faithfull, *Faithfull*, Penguin, London, 1994, p. 159.

'a twister and a manipulator': Keith Richards, *Life*, Little, Brown & Co, New York, 2010, p. 253.

'David was very instrumental': Sandy Lieberson to JM, 28 May 2014.

'He created quite a bit of the artwork': Sandy Lieberson to JM, 28 May 2014.

'Ask him for my Boyhood paintings': MS, letter to EVA, circa December 1968.

'the culture of Swinging London': Philip French, 'Donald Cammell's wild side', *The Observer*, <theguardian.com/film/News_Story/Critic_Review/Observer_review/0,,338776,00.html>, 2 July 2000.

'It was Martin saying': Bob Seidemann to JM, 2 June 2014.

Clapton's manager, Australian Robert Stigwood: Philippe Mora to JM, 30 March 2016.

British government inquiry: Report of the United Kingdom Home Office Advisory Committee on Drug Dependence (the Wootton Report), 1969.

'The first day of the shoot': Philippe Mora to JM, August 2003.

'[Golding] hung around the Pheasantry': John Weiley to JM, 16 November 2014.

Ironically, after *Molopolis's* release: In Philippe Mora, 'Culture shock', *Art Monthly Australia*, issue 156, December 2002, p. 8.

CHAPTER 10
BACK AND FORTH

'so spectacular and over-decorated': MS, letter to EVA, December 1968.

'It was so much more': MS, letter to EVA, December 1968.

'pagan centre of Christendom': MS, letter to EVA, December 1968.

'I spent the whole time with homosexuals': MS, letter to EVA, December 1968.

'It was so beautiful': MS, letter to EVA, December 1968.

'Getting through to father': MS, letter to EVA, 31 December 1968.

'Had a few good discussions': MS, letter to EVA, 18 February 1969.

'A nice lot of heads': MS, letter to EVA, 31 December 1968.

'When I saw Martin's work': Sigi Krauss to JM, 6 July 2015.

A three-headed figure: The James Gleeson Oral History Collection, National Gallery of Australia, 7 November 1979.

'Martin was reinforced': Richard Neville to JM, August 2006.

'[Martin] is a lovely person': John Reed, letter to Mary Christina Sewell, 9 October 1970, in Barrett Reid and Nancy Underhill (eds), *Letters of John Reed: Defining Australian cultural life, 1920–1981*, Viking, Victoria, 2001, p. 755.

Brown and the gallery's owner: MS to JM, 13 May 2012.

'last mad dance': Marion Macdonald, 'A house of seduction', *The Bulletin*, 4 December 1971, p. 36.

'Lots of work—too much': MS, letter to EVA, 7 April 1970.

'then there's no excuses': MS to Hazel de Berg, National Library of Australia, Oral History Section, (TRC 1/519), 9 June 1970.

'less cruelly ironic': Margaret Jones, 'Whatever happened to Martin Sharp?', *SMH*, 16 May 1970, p. 17.

A Newcastle man: 'Beardsley drawings—charges dismissed', *SMH*, 9 July 1970, p. 4.

'pop art haunted house': 'One more week', *The Bulletin*, 30 May 1970, p. 20.

'gleeful puppeteer': 'One more week', p. 20.

'event to be seen at': Jane Perlez, 'Society and art in Sharp focus', *The Australian*, 23 May 1970, p. 16.

'the wildest most way out scene': Di Arthur, 'So many pictures, so many people', *Sunday Mirror*, 24 May 1970, p. 59.

It was a 'sleazy exhibition': Patrick White, letter to Margery Williams, 21 June 1970 in David Marr, *The Letters of Patrick White*, University of Chicago Press, Chicago, 1994, p. 365.

'Martin Sharp seems to be still': Donald Brook, 'Originals and multiples,' *SMH*, 21 May 1970 p. 14.

'[Sharp] examines his past not through nostalgia': Elwyn Lynn, 'Various anxieties', *The Bulletin*, 13 June 1970, p. 49.

'The enthusiasm was terrific': MS to JM, 19 April 2013.

CHAPTER 11

THE YELLOW HOUSE

'Martin was extremely eccentric': Penelope Tree to JM, 19 January 2015.

'I remember one night': MS to JM, 15 May 2013.

'It was as if World War I': John Weiley to JM, 16 November 2014.

'He couldn't give his love': EVA to JM, 2 February 2015.

'Martin was furious': Jim Anderson to JM, 14 September 2015.

'I would never have had the opportunity': MS to JM, 19 April 2013.

'The more I think it over': Vincent van Gogh, letter to Theo van Gogh, circa 17 September 1888, in Martin Sharp, *Catalog No 3*, Reid Books, Sydney, 1971.

'He would put the paintbrush': Bruce Goold to JM, 22 May 2014.

'It didn't work, but it might now': 'Watch out for the Incredible Shrink', *The Australian*, 1 April 1971, p. 30.

Martin had visited him in Wales: Keiron Pim, email to JM, 11 December 2015.

'He had a little joint-rolling machine': Bruce Goold to JM, 22 May 2014.

'The car was full of marijuana smoke': Jon Lewis to JM, 4 December 2013.

The Sydney Morning Herald soon picked up the rumour: Michael Symons, 'Puppets under the stars', *SMH*, 5 June 1971, p. 15.

The spark: Keith Richards, *Life*, Little, Brown & Co, New York, 2010, p. 240.

'I think it will be one': David Litvinoff, Channel 10, circa March 1971.

'She just went on': MS to JM, 13 May 2013.

'Little Nell stole the thunder': Leslie Walford, 'Our town', *The Sun-Herald*, 4 April 1971, p. 141.

'Where do all these miraculous people live': Walford, 'Our town', p. 141.

Martin's smiling-mouth image: Albie Thoms, *My Generation*, Media21 Publishing, Sydney, 2012, p. 380.

'I said, "I don't really get it"': Andrew Sharp to JM, 7 December 2015.

'The best bit is environmental': Donald Brook, 'Around the galleries', *SMH*, 8 April 1971, p. 8.

'The opening party': Daniel Thomas, 'An artist speaks', *Sunday Telegraph*, 18 April 1971, p. 72.

'[There is] a belief in the importance of the life': Joanna Mendelssohn, *The Yellow House, 1970–72*, catalogue essay, Art Gallery of New South Wales, Sydney, 1990, p. 10.

the Australian government released: 'Customs bans 106 books in 2 months', *The Australian*, 2 April 1971, p. 2.

'the most haunting delight so far': Michael Symons, 'Puppets under the stars', *SMH*, 5 June 1971, p 15.

'She decided she'd get up': Wendy Whiteley to JM, 4 November 2015.

'It was a disaster': Fairlie Kingston to JM, 30 June 2014.

'He did it as a gift': Zandra Rhodes to JM, 7 January 2016.

Although, as *The Sydney Morning Herald*: Robert Milliken, 'A swinging week in old Canberra town', *SMH*, 14 May 1971, p. 7.

Martin had bought the cartoons: MS to JM, 13 May 2013.

'Whoever was available': Greg Weight to JM, 3 July 2014.

CHAPTER 12

GINGER MEGGS SCHOOL OF ARTS

'Martin was the primary art director': Greg Weight to JM, 3 July 2014.

'What are you doing?': Bruce Goold to JM, 22 May 2014.

Albie Thoms recalled: Albie Thoms, *My Generation*, Media21 Publishing, Sydney, 2012, p. 390.

'When Martin saw it': Jon Lewis to JM, 4 December 2013.

'He said Martin was a complete poseur': Andrew Sharp to JM, 7 December 2015.

'Everyone was standing there': George Gittoes to JM, 4 August, 2014.

'If you call the right witnesses': MS letter to Richard Neville, in Neville, *Hippie Hippie Shake*, William Heinemann, Port Melbourne, 1995, p. 247.

'yodelling in the canyon': George Melly to Justice Michael Argyle, in Neville, *Hippie Hippie Shake*, p. 296.

'dazzle the eye, caress the ear': Yellow House newsletter, circa August 1971.

It was Herman Hesse's Magic Theatre: Albie Thoms, *My Generation*, p. 395.

'one of the greatest pieces': MS interviewed on *This Day Tonight*, ABC TV, September 1971.

Nation condemned it as amateurish: 'No greener in Sydney', *Nation*, 2 October 1971, p. 18.

'Why always borrowed forms?' Terry Smith, 'Bin for blurred rubbish', *The Sunday Australian*, 19 September 1971, p. 19.

'the serious and unserious': Noel Hutchison, 'Buried in sand of prejudice', *SMH*, 9 September 1971, p. 26.

'psychedelic phantasmagoria': Elwyn Lynn, 'Pleasant nightmares', *The Bulletin*, 18 September 1971, p. 44.

'marvellous': Daniel Thomas, 'Delights in an intelligent way', *The Sunday Telegraph*, 5 September 1971, p. 72.

The Yellow House was more festivity: Laurie Thomas, 'The art of spoofing the precious object', *The Australian*, 7 September 1971, p. 8.

'concerned with unsticking the mind': Laurie Thomas, 'The magic of an artistic Luna Park', *The Australian*, 5 October 1971, p. 8.

'It really took a toll': Greg Weight to JM, 3 July 2014.

'It's over': George Gittoes, *Blood Mystic*, Pan Macmillan, Sydney 2016, p. 90.

'icing on the cake': Greg Weight to JM, 3 July 2014.

'I stumbled into': Jon Lewis to JM, 4 December 2013.

'Here was a place': Sandy Lieberson to JM, 28 May 2014.

'You have to put things out there': MS to JM, 13 May 2013.

'He looked marvellous': Nell Campbell to JM, 5 December 2014.

'I was totally exhausted': MS to JM, 13 May 2013.

'It was all very van Gogh': Sandy Lieberson to JM, 28 May 2014.

'It looked as though': Ed Victor to JM, 7 January 2016.

'The idea is to create': MS, letter to Sigi Krauss, circa 1972.

Sigi did not receive the letter: Sigi Krauss, email to JM, 13 January 2016.

'Modern icons tend': George Melly, 'Double exposures', *The Guardian*, 28 December 1972, p. 12.

'Every square metre of floor': Stanley Cohen, email to JM, 10 March 2016.

Martin even wondered: MS, letter to Jackie Menzies, 18 April 1978.

'Nell came dancing into my studio': Zandra Rhodes to JM, 7 January 2016.

'He was a fish out of water': Nell Campbell to JM, 5 December 2014.

CHAPTER 13

THE EMBASSY OF ENCHANTMENT

'The spirit of the place': Lenore Nicklin, 'Boofhead wins the first round against Luna Bear', *SMH*, 3 April 1976, p. 13.

'enticingly and mesmerically beautiful': Elwyn Lynn, 'Those silver scissors', *Quadrant*, February 1977, p. 45.

Martin wrote about the spell: Martin Sharp, 'Notes from the river caves', *Quadrant*, February 1977, p. 34.

'You refer so often to your childhood': Justin O'Brien, letter to Martin Sharp, circa early 1970s.

order the luxury hotel's: Chris Campion, 'Hello stranger', *The Observer*, Music Monthly section, <www.theguardian.com/arts/features/story/0,,1871633,00.html>, 17 September 2006.

found the tremolo: Martin Sharp, 'My friend Tiny Tim', *The Daily Telegraph*, 3 December 1996, p. 15.

'What he said to me': Peter Weir to JM, 7 August 2014.

'I showed it to Martin': Karen Robson to JM, 12 October 2015.

'Martin was fascinated by it': Peter Weir to JM, 7 August 2014.

'He got on brilliantly with children': Cressida Campbell to JM, 26 May 2014.

CHAPTER 14

WIRIAN

spent three thousand dollars: Susanna Short, 'Child's dream world broken', *SMH*, 18 November 1980, p. 10.

'When you lived at Wirian': William Yang to JM, 1 July 2014.

'When I was out of favour': Russell Sharp to JM, 24 January 2015.

'He divided people up socially'; Julie Clarke to JM, 15 November 2014.

Thornton's 'spirit of childhood': *Australian Story,* ABC TV, broadcast 22 March 1997.

'they were very aggressive': Jeremy Thomas to JM, 29 December 2014.

'everyone's got to eat': Luke Sciberras to JM, 14 September 2014.

'Wirian became a haven': Lin Utzon to JM, 15 January 2015.

'One of the reasons': Cressida Campbell to JM, 26 May 2014.

'It was night-time': Andrew Sharp to JM, 29 November 2015.

'People loved being in that room': John Gaden to JM, 13 August 2015.

'I do believe I have': MS, letter to Jackie Menzies, 18 April 1978.

'Martin would get so excited': William Yang to JM, 1 July 2014.
'I had to pretend to lose': John Weiley to JM, 16 November 2014.
he sold part of the land: Memorandum of Transfer, Q307286, 14 July 1977, Registrar General of New South Wales.
'At first, you thought': Peter Weir to JM, 7 August 2014.
'He had a quasi': Nathan Waks to JM, 25 February 2016.
'He'd call out during': Nathan Waks to JM, 25 February 2016.

CHAPTER 15

THE KING IN YELLOW

'As my carriage went [forward]': Jason Holman to JM, 28 April 2015.
But Martin didn't send the letter: The James Gleeson Oral History Collection, National Gallery of Australia, 7 November 1979.
Police immediately ruled out arson: Paul McCloy, 'Ghost Train toll rises to 7', *SMH*, 11 June 1979, p. 1.
'There was so much litter': Garry Shead to JM, 12 November 2014.
'It's eerie that': Errol Simper, 'No more laughing crowds at the froth and bubble world', *The Canberra Times*, 24 June 1979, p. 2.
Fink claimed he had lobbied Wran: Kate McClymont, 'Niece links Saffron to Luna Park deaths', *SMH,* 26 May 2007, p. 1.
The coroner's report: 'Ghost Train fire was foreseeable, says coroner', *SMH*, 4 September 1979, p. 4.
'a vengeful God': unpublished article, quoted in The James Gleeson Oral History Collection, National Gallery of Australia, 7 November 1979.
'Synchronicity, I think that's how God talks': MS to JM, 10 August 2007.
Harbourside Amusements was poised: Susan Orr, 'New bids on old Luna Park dreams', *SMH*, 20 May 1981, p. 9, and Susan Orr, 'Fairground wheels ready to roll', *SMH*, 15 March 1982, p. 10.
The auction raised: '$0.5m sale at Luna Park': *SMH*, 2 June 1981, p. 10.
started by a group of bikies: Graham Gambie, 'Luna Park inquiry reopened', *The Sun-Herald*, 13 October 1985, p. 2.

included two of Saffron's cousins: Andrew Keenan, 'Luna Park's merry-go-round of ownership', *SMH*, 19 November 1985, p. 13.

no evidence that Saffron: Ross Coulthart, 'Saffron's close ties with Luna Park', *SMH*, 28 October 1987, p. 1.

'a little Stasi officer': Richard Neville to JM, August 2006.

He put Wirian up for auction: 'Artist to sell family mansion', *SMH*, 23 March 1983, p. 12.

He mortgaged the house instead: MS to JM, 10 August 2007.

he mortgaged Wirian: Certificate of Title, 13526-077 & 078, Registrar General of New South Wales.

he placed an advertisement: *SMH*, 28 August 1982, p. 74.

The 1500-seat theatre: Master Statistics Sheet for September 1982, Sydney Opera House archives.

'You're a great artist, Martin': Nathan Waks to JM, 25 February 2016.

'She pointed to Martin': Peter Kingston to JM, 22 July 2014.

'The sparrow has flown': *SMH*, 29 November 1986, p. 152.

'I miss her so': MS, letter to EVA, 8 April 1987.

'My childhood was spent': MS, letter to EVA, circa June 2001.

'He rang up drunk': MS, letter to EVA, circa June 2001.

'I surely know my mother loved me': MS, letter to EVA, circa June 2001.

'It was wonderful to see him': MS, letter to EVA, 24 September 1986.

'It's my Sistine Chapel': MS, letter to EVA, 24 September 1986.

'This house is a studio': MS, letter to EVA, 8 April 1987.

'The serpent is pumping heroin': MS, letter to EVA, 21 July 1987.

'But when the police become judge': Sallie-Anne Huckstepp, interviewed on *60 Minutes,* Channel 9, broadcast 5 July 1981.

'possibly the most corrupt police officer': Kate McClymont, 'Roger Rogerson's murder of Jamie Gao caps notorious career in and out of the law', *SMH,* <www.smh.com.au/nsw/roger-rogersons-murder-of-jamie-gao-caps-notorious-career-in-and-out-of-the-law-20160607-gpdx1f.html>, 15 June 2016.

‘A mythic figure’: MS quoted in John Dale, *Huckstepp: A dangerous life*, Xoum, NSW, 2014, p. 178.

‘There is a strong smell of injustice’: Simon Kent, ‘Widow seeks new Luna Park inquiry’, *SMH*, 12 June 1987, p. 2.

CHAPTER 16
‘WHILE OFTEN EXTREME AND ECCENTRIC …’

‘Christopher immediately understood’: Nathan Waks to JM, 25 February 2016.

soldiering on through a power failure: James Cockington, ‘Today’s people’, *SMH*, 8 January 1990, p. 24.

‘I believed him to be’: Nathan Waks to JM, 25 February 2016.

‘It was very carefully planned’: MS, letter to EVA, 2 November 1987.

‘I’m certainly going to feel better’: MS, letter to EVA, 2 November 1987.

The Last Innocent: *Newsweek*, 20 May 1968, p. 113.

‘We all have strange sexual fantasies’: Michael Visontay, ‘Tiptoe in Tiny Tim’s dreams’, *The Eastern Herald*, 7 June 1990, p. 17.

‘stuffing a Brillo pad’: Martin Portus, ‘Tiny Tim’s big comeback’, *SMH*, Good Weekend section, 21 May 1988, p. 10.

‘I’m the biggest sinner’: Joyce Morgan, ‘Tiny on love, sex and sin’, *The Newcastle Herald*, 5 September 1983, p. 3.

‘Being a lost soul’: MS, letter to Emma Walker, circa 1989.

‘He lectured us for four hours’: Victoria Cobden to JM, 14 December 2015.

‘I was amazed by’, George Gittoes, email to JM, 24 January 2016.

‘relentless, rather wistful pursuit’, Robert Hughes, *Things I Didn’t Know*, Vintage, London, 2007, p. 289.

‘He loved the beauty’: Julie Clarke to JM, 15 November 2014.

‘I don’t think he liked’: Jenny Kee to JM, 18 February 2015.

‘I don’t think he was good’: Wendy Whiteley to JM, 4 November 2015.

‘He accepted everyone’: Emma Walker to JM, 17 November 2014.

‘I lay with her in fornication’: MS, letter to Emma Walker, circa 1989.

‘I pray God gives me’: MS, letter to Emma Walker, circa 1989.

'I'm not a real painter,' MS, letter to Emma Walker, circa 1989.
'I really only want to photograph': MS, letter to Emma Walker, circa 1989.
'Sometimes I feel that': MS, letter to Emma Walker, circa 1989.
The NCA's report: 'Arson investigations in the Sydney Eastern Suburbs and North Sydney areas in the period 1979–1982', interim report, National Crime Authority, April 1989.
'I was uncomfortable about lying,' MS, witness statement to Rose Bay police, 9 November 1991.
'I heard the dogs barking': MS to JM, 10 August 2006.
The coroner offered condolences: Derrick Hand, Deputy State Coroner, Coroner's report, 24 April 1992.
'If I hadn't stayed up': MS to JM, 10 August 2006.
'It wasn't that the guy': MS to JM, 10 August 2006.
'Martin transferred that style': Stuart Purves to JM, 5 May 2016.
'an act of terrorism': MS, letter to Peter Collins, 2 September 1994.
'It is, as Martin Sharp has put it': Peter Collins, letter to George Souris, Minister for Land and Water Conservation, 25 October 1994.
'I had to come tonight': Clarissa Bye, 'Happy Luna landing', *The Sun-Herald*, 22 January 1995, p. 14.
'the most amazing human being': Martin Sharp, 'Bound for heaven—my amazing friend', *SMH*, 3 December 1996, p. 5.
'He wouldn't put up': Luke Sciberras to JM, 14 September 2014.
'I have never seen anyone': Luke Sciberras to JM, 14 September 2014.
'He didn't paint to live': Jeremy Thomas to JM, 30 December 2014.
'I always felt': Wendy Whiteley to JM, 4 November 2015.
'He sabotaged his own career': Stuart Purves to JM, 5 May 2016.
'It is very hard': Fairlie Kingston to JM, 30 June 2014.
'He became like Miss Havisham': Nell Campbell to JM, 11 May 2016.
'The whole house felt it': Luke Sciberras to JM, 14 September 2014.
'It was one of his favourite possessions': Penelope Tree to JM, 19 January 2015.
'He'd say these things': Penelope Tree to JM, 19 January 201.

CHAPTER 17

LOSS AND RECONCILIATION

'I was absolutely blown out': Harmonie Downes to JM, 1 November 2015.

'I fell in love with him': Harmonie Downes to JM, 1 November 2015.

'He said to me': Luke Sciberras to JM, 14 September 2014.

'I don't think Martin was': Greg Weight to JM, 3 July 2014.

'He was prepared': Luke Sciberras to JM, 14 September 2014.

'In winter, we'd sit down': Harmonie Downes to JM, 1 November 2015.

'I am under a great deal of pressure': MS, letter to Harmonie Downes, circa mid-1997.

'I just woke up': Harmonie Downes to JM, 1 November 2015.

'We all had hopes in our different ways': MS, letter to Harmonie Downes, December 1997.

'He could be laconic': Harmonie Downes to JM, 1 November 2015.

'It's rather like being father': MS, letter to Sandy Lieberson, 22 June 1998.

'I wish it could have been otherwise': MS, letter to Harmonie Downes, circa May 2000.

'It's your history, too': Lin Utzon to JM, 15 January 2015.

'That was obviously': Joe Skrzynski to JM, 2 February 2015.

'Martin's involvement was critical': Joe Skrzynski to JM, 2 February 2015.

'He was an old man': Lin Utzon to JM, 15 January 2015.

'transformed the world's view': Deyan Sudjic, 'Jørn Utzon', obituary, *The Guardian*, <theguardian.com/artanddesign/2008/dec/01/architecture-denmark-j-oslash-rn-utzon>, 1 December 2008.

'That first meeting': Lin Utzon to JM, 15 January 2015.

'You could ask him anything': Lin Utzon to JM, 15 January 2015.

'Because Hugues is blind': Lin Utzon to JM, 15 January 2015.

Martin watched the celebrations: Christine France, 'Martin Sharp: A democratic surrealism,' *Art and Australia*, vol. 47, no. 1, 2009, pp. 90–9.

Australia's greatest writer: France, 'Martin Sharp', pp. 90–9.

'He writes an entire novel': Sharon Verghis, 'One-word sermon we can't forget', *SMH*, 19 January 2005, p. 16.

But in that ceremony: MS, letter to Sandy Lieberson, circa 2000.

'It is much more important': MS to JM, 11 September 2006.

'I realised how tough it was': MS to JM, 11 September 2006.

'He made up a big pot': Luke Sciberras to JM, 14 September 2014.

reconciliation and healing possible: AM program, ABC Radio, 25 April 2001.

'We hear of Gallipoli, Dunkirk': MS, foreword to Jan Ruff-O'Herne, *Peace, Love and Joy: Liturgical church banners*, Falling Frangipani, Sydney, 2013. Martin wrote his foreword while in hospital in August 2013. It is probably his last published writing.

'I'm not so pleased at what': MS, letter to EVA, circa December 1994.

'I realise there was something disturbed,' MS, letter to EVA, circa December 1996.

There he met her daughter: Peter Hannan, email to JM, 22 July 2015.

'One lives one's early life': MS, letter to EVA 23 June 2001.

'I do love London': MS, letter to Sandy Lieberson, 29 December 2003.

CHAPTER 18
ETERNITY

'If there's one graphic artist': Nick Waterlow to JM, August 2003.

'So much of it was brought to a head': Nick Waterlow to JM, August 2003.

'a quaint innocence': MS, letter to Sandy Lieberson, 29 December 2003.

'I kept my eyes wide open': Joyce Morgan, 'He's part social commentator, part shaman', *SMH*, Spectrum section, 30 September 2006, p. 8.

'Is this an act of creation': MS notebook, 7 August 2004.

'Benson and Hedges dropped me': MS to JM, 10 August 2006.

'I thought I was going to leave': Matthew Thompson, 'Pop-art master accepts postie's advice', *SMH*, 13 June 2005, p. 11.

'It will happen naturally': MS to JM, 11 September 2006.

'an outsider with a Tory propensity': Richard Neville to JM, August 2006.

'What's so important about Martin': Nick Waterlow to JM, August 2006.

'He is one of those very rare creatures': Nick Waterlow, catalogue essay, *The Everlasting World of Martin Sharp*, Nick Waterlow and Annabel Pegus (eds), Ivan Dougherty Gallery, Sydney, 2006, p. 2.

As their friendship grew: Rick Feneley, Josephine Tovey and Georgina Robinson, 'Waterlow killings: family feared for "unstable" son', *SMH*, <www.smh.com.au/national/waterlow-killings-family-feared-for-unstable-son-20091110-i7uq.html>, 12 November 2009.

'I don't think people': Kate McClymont, 'They weren't meant to die', *SMH*, 26 May 2007, p. 1.

'It was an act of terrorism': Kate McClymont, 'The haunting questions that linger', *SMH*, 26 May 2007, p. 13.

'Martin painted her': Meryl Tankard to JM, 24 November 2015.

'One day I said': Maggie Walsh to JM, 5 April 2015.

'Sharp has all the makings': John McDonald, 'Sydney's master of familiarities', *SMH*, Spectrum section, 6 February 2010, p. 14.

'Here we are, in the midst': MS notebook, 5 February 2012.

'All my art history': Joyce Morgan, 'Life's a total experiment', *SMH*, Spectrum section, 2 June 2012, p. 4.

'mysterious, fruitful interiors': MS notebook, circa 2012.

'It can be an awful vanity': MS to JM, 12 May 2015.

'There was always a sense': Luke Sciberras to JM, 14 September 2014.

'We talked for an hour': Peter Weir to JM, 7 August 2014.

'Martin moved far beyond': Richard Neville, 'Singular artist's mind-blowing voyage in paint', *SMH*, 3 December 2013, p. 6.

'a stranger in a strange land': George Gittoes, The World Today, ABC Radio, 2 December 2013.

'He will have his day': Jeremy Thomas to JM, 30 December 2014.

LIST OF ARTWORKS

Artwork copyright of the Estate of Martin Sharp

The Toff, c1958
Poster paint on paper on board, 80 x 60 cm
Collection: estate of Martin Sharp
Photo: Greg Weight

Port Hacking, Fishing Day, 1963
Oil on masonite, 60 x 90cm
Collection: The National Art School, Sydney
Photo: Paul Morgan

Mona Lisa magazine cover
Sydney *Oz* 11, July 1964
Collection: University of Wollongong Library

Seventeen Minutes to Four, 1965
Oil, lacquer on paper mounted on board, 135 x 185cm
Collection: estate of Martin Sharp

Binkie's Burgers magazine advertisement
Sydney *Oz* 26, March 1963
Collection: University of Wollongong Library

Mr Tambourine Man, 1967
Screenprint, 75.4 x 49.8cm

Collection: Art Gallery of NSW
Photo: estate of Martin Sharp

Disraeli Gears, 1967
Album cover and screenprint
Photo: estate of Martin Sharp

Jimi Hendrix, c 1971
Enamel paint on synthetic polymer film between two sheets of perspex, 101 x 115cm
Collection: National Gallery of Australia
Photo: estate of Martin Sharp

Plant a Flower Child
Poster, London *Oz* 5, July 1967
Collection: University of Wollongong Library

Magic Theatre magazine cover
London *Oz* 16, November 1968
Collection: the author

Eternity Haymarket! 1977
Screenprint, 66 x 89cm
Collection: National Gallery of Australia
Photo: estate of Martin Sharp

Abalone, 1990–2006
Colour pencil, ink synthetic polymer paint on canvas, 293 x 180cm
Collection: estate of Martin Sharp
Photo: Greg Weight

Young Mo, Nimrod, 1978
Screenprint, 89.5 x 45.7cm
Collection: Art Gallery of NSW
Photo: estate of Martin Sharp

Snow Job, 1980–1995
Synthetic polymer on canvas, 122 x 122cm
Private collection
Photo: Greg Weight

Pentecost, c2001
Acrylic on Perspex (prototype for print 2006), 80 x 60cm
Private collection
Photo: Sam McAdam

Babylon the great is fallen, is fallen (Revelations 18 v.2), 2000-6
Wax crayon, acrylic on canvas, 184 x 280cm
Collection: estate of Martin Sharp
Photo: Greg Weight

Courage My Friend, c1988–99
Synthetic polymer on board, 172 x 150cm
Private collection
Photo: Greg Weight

The Thousand Dollar Bill, c2012
Acrylic on canvas, 190 x 120cm
Collection: estate of Martin Sharp

Still Life, 1999
Synthetic polymer on canvas, 149 x 117cm
Private collection
Photo: Greg Weight

Ginger Meggs in Japan, 1996
Oil stick on canvas 183 x 118cm
Private collection
Photo: Sam McAdam

Film Script, 1976–2004
Acrylic on paper mounted on board, 136 x 319cm
Collection: estate of Martin Sharp
Photo: Greg Weight

Art Galaxy, 2000
Acrylic on canvas, 162 x 162cm
Private collection
Photo: Greg Weight

Artwork copyright of the Estate of Robert Walker (b.1922, d.2007), licensed by Viscopy, Sydney

Martin Sharp and another man [possibly John Crittle] outside Dandie Fashions, Chelsea, London, 1967
From a colour transparency
Robert Walker Archive, Art Gallery of New South Wales Archive
Gift of the Robert Walker family 2008
AGNSW ARC262.14.1

Martin Sharp holding a lithograph related to 'Wot', Sydney, 1969
From a black and white negative
Robert Walker Archive, Art Gallery of New South Wales Archive
Gift of the Robert Walker family 2008
AGNSW ARC262.14.6

Martin Sharp, Sydney, 1969
From a black and white negative
Robert Walker Archive, Art Gallery of New South Wales Archive
Gift of the Robert Walker family 2008
AGNSW ARC262.14.11

INDEX

9 Collins Street 49–50
25 Cranbrook Lane 14, 19, 20, 22, 81–2, 84, 85, 86, 87, 146, 200, 225

A Curiosity in Her Own Country 260
Abalone 245–6
abalone diver print 188–9, 210–11
Abbey Road studios 168
Abbotsleigh School 65
Aboriginal people, concern for 230–1, 258–60, 272
abortion 34, 53, 77, 152
Abrahams, Anthony 24, 27
abstract works show 41–2
Adams, Eddie 113
Albert Hall 133–4, 194
Aldrin, Buzz 149
'Alfs' 39, 87, 92, 132
Allen, Peter 205
Aloszko, Michelle 108
Aloszko, Nicole 108
Amédée Joubert 99, 111
Anderson, 'Big Jim' 199
Anderson, Jim 110, 149, 162–3, 179–81, 265
Anderson, John 39, 40
Angkor 94
Anglican Press 55, 56, 60, 151
Angry penguins 71
animals, fascination with 21, 22, 25, 160, 206, 256–7
Annandale Imitation Realists 43
'Anyone for Tennis' 148
appearance 44
Aquarius Festival of University Arts 175
Arcadia Amusements 223
Archdale, Betty 65, 73, 75
Archer, Robyn 208
Archibald Prize 154, 274
architecture studies 40–1
Are You Experienced 121
The Argonauts Club 23
Argyle, Justice Michael 181
Armstrong, Neil 149
Art and Australia 83
Art Book 187
Art for Mart's Sake 82
Art Gallery of New South Wales 43, 68, 200, 204, 210, 274
  Fairground Arts and Novelties show 204
art school 3, 34–5, 40
Artaud, Anton
  Theatre of Cruelty 173
The Artist on the Road to Tarascon 20, 136, 162, 246, 277
Artists' Ball 42
Artoons 147, 152, 154, 166
The Arty Wild Oat 43–4, 52
Askin, Robert 79, 89, 90, 192
Australia cartoon 260
Australia Day 1988 230
Australia Hotel Sydney 12, 20–1

The Australian 75, 83, 182
Australian Ballet 253
Australian Broadcasting Commission 50, 66, 129
Australian Galleries 242, 246, 247
Australian Jewish News 51
Australian Journalists Association 71
  fancy dress ball 71–2
Australian National University 175
Australian Satirical Paper 52
The Australian Women's Weekly 44
Australia's bicentenary 230

Babar the Elephant book 248, 277
Babylon the great is fallen, is fallen 269
Bacon, Francis 111, 124, 136
Bacon, Wendy 154
Bailey, David 159–60
Baker, Ginger 107, 113–15, 140, 148
Balearic Islands 106–7, 127, 130
'Ballad of a Thin Man' 87
Bamford, Digby 78
Bangkok *see* Thailand
Bardot, Brigitte 44, 117
Barker, Johnny 278
Barker, Michael 221, 279
Barnes, Jimmy 282
Barrett, Syd 101, 102
Barton, Arthur 192, 222
Bass, Tom 59, 66, 74
Baxter, Professor John 58
Beardsley, Aubrey 104, 155
The Beatles 51, 59, 65, 87, 96, 97, 98, 100, 106, 122–5, 134, 138, 161, 263
  'butcher' cover 98
Bell, Colin Aubrey 31–2
Bell, John 39, 208
Bennie, Reverend Peter 64
Beresford, Bruce 39, 265
Berger, Vivien 163
Biba boutique 108, 115, 159
Big O Posters 105, 110, 122, 136
Billings, Jonathan 217
Billy Boy 154
Bindon, John 110, 137
Binkie's Burgers 55, 68, 93, 94
birth 15
Bjerke, Birgitta 119
Black & White Ball 42
black and white illustrations 94
Blake, Pete 123
Blake prize 22
Blue Series 276
bodgies and widgies 38–9, 40
Bogle, Dr Gilbert 55
Boo-Zoom 149
Boofhead 21, 90, 193, 208
books
  censorship 37, 171–2
  influence of 22
Botticelli's *Birth of Venus* 187, 196, 198, 210
Boulting, Ingrid 159–60, 174, 261
Bourke, Ace 120, 230, 273
Bowlly, Al 133, 193
Boyd, Arthur 82, 141
Boyd, David 125
Boyd, Hermia 126
Bradman, Donald 155
Breton, Michele 137
Brett, Chrissie 166
Briebauer, Marie 174, 179
Brighton Arts Festival 231
Britannia 89
Brook, Donald 171
Brown, Mike 77
Brown, Pete 125
Brown, Peter (Charlie) 152, 171
Browne, Frank 56
Bruce, Jack 113, 114, 115
Buckingham, Anne 271
Budinger, Victoria (Miss Vicki) 149–50, 194, 250
Builders Labourers' Federation 198
Bulldog coffee shop Amsterdam 206
The Bulletin 21, 43, 76, 152, 155, 157, 170, 182, 260
bullying 27–8, 48, 278
Burg, Alistair 137
Burma 95

Bush, Reverend Roger 62–3, 73
Bussell, Darcey 100
Button, James 123

Caesar's Palace Las Vegas 194
Café Balzac 50
Cahill, Joe 88, 89
Calley, William 172
Cammell, David 139
Cammell, Donald 137, 138, 139
Campbell, Cressida (Baby Pip) 199–202, 207, 233, 261
Campbell, Laura (Little Nell) 169–70, 184–6, 189–90, 199–201, 233, 247, 261
Campbell, Ross 170
Campbell, Sally 186
The Canberra Times 72
The Caretaker 141
Carnaby Street 119, 161
Carr, Bob 254
Carroll, Lewis 123
  Through the Looking-Glass 171
Carroll, Richard 217
cars 45–6, 114, 209–10
Carson, Johnny 149–150
cartoons 21, 40, 42–4, 54–8, 64–5, 77, 79, 80, 89, 90, 92, 93–5, 99, 113, 128, 175
Catalog 164, 171
censorship 76–7, 154–5
Chambers, Robert W
  The King in Yellow 223
Chandler, Margaret 55
Chelsea Antiques Market 119–20
childhood 1–34 17–19, 20, 21–2, 23–4
Children's Hour 23
Christ Church St Laurence 281
christening 16
Christian the lion 273
Christmas Carol, A 8, 21, 133
Clapton, Eric 106, 107, 112–19, 129, 133–4, 140–1, 148, 151, 163, 180, 195, 204, 227, 263, 282
Clarke, Julie 204, 205–6, 234, 251, 282
Clarke, Terry 30, 32, 153
Clune, Frank 154
Clune, Terry 82, 152, 154
Clune, Thelma 82, 152, 154, 156
Clune Galleries 82, 152–8
Cobden, Victoria 150–2, 233, 261
Coburn, John 41
Cohen, Leonard 164
  Suzanne 108
Cohen, Stanley 187–8
Cold War 37
Coleman, Ernest 61
collages 21, 81–2, 108, 117–18, 124, 147–8
Collins, Peter 243–4, 254
Coming 149
Communist Party 37
Concord Hospital, RAAF section 19, 29
Conway, Mic 211, 275, 282
Conyngham, Russell 60
Coon, Caroline 189
Courage My Friend 246
Coventry Gallery 246
Cramphorn, Rex 209
Cranbrook School 12, 16, 25, 26, 27, 139, 152, 153, 212, 245, 270, 276, 278, 279
  Martin Sharp Art Prize 279
Cream 100, 106, 113–14, 115, 118, 123, 125, 140, 148
Crittle, John 100
Crosby, Bing 102, 133
Crothall, Ross 43
Crowley, Aleister (The Beast) 138
Curry, Tim 189

Dada 173
Dadaists 147
Daily Mirror 56, 78
The Daily Telegraph 170
Darling Do You Love Me? 137
Date, Tina 71, 108
Davey, Jack 168
de Chardin, Teilhard 164
de Chirico, Giorgio 147, 279
de Groot, Francis 60
de la Vega, William 240, 241
de Montalembert, Hugues 257, 263

de Saint-Exupéry, Antoine 128
death 281–3
Delaney, Colin 55
Democratic Labour Party 37
Dennis, Felix 149, 163, 179–81, 265
Dharawal people 1
Dickens, Charles 8, 21, 133, 170, 178
Dignam, Arthur 39, 173
Ding a Ding Day 45, 48
Disraeli Gears 112, 113–14
Dobell, William 73, 154
dogs 14, 22, 23, 151, 199, 200, 206, 276, 283
  see also animals, fascination with
Donald Duck 94, 127
Donovan 141, 164
Downes, Harmonie 249–52, 261
Dr Seuss 17
Draffin, Peter 130
  Pop 94
Dürer, Albrecht 114
Dylan, Bob 83, 87, 94, 105, 121, 123, 134, 168
  Basement Tapes 116
  poster 102–3, 104–5, 124, 125, 139, 164

East Sydney Technical College 35, 41, 59, 84, 85
Edison, Thomas 215
Edward VIII abdication 13
Ellis, Bob 39
Ellis, Sergeant 61, 62, 66
Elvis Presley 94, 123, 279
EMI's Studio 301 213
English, Michael 124
Enright, Nick 30
Ensemble Theatre 41
Epstein, Brian 51, 97, 161
'Ern Malley' hoax 71
Ernst, Max 136
'Eskimo Nell' 154
Eternity 24, 43, 45, 207–8, 251, 258, 282
Eternity Haymarket! 207–8
Evans, Wendy 263, 272
The Everlasting World of Martin Sharp 268–70
Eviston, Gina 53
Expressionism 173
Extra Dimensions 227
Eysenck, Hans 180

Faithfull, Marianne 109, 120, 124, 134, 138, 151, 204
Fantasia 21–2
Fantômas 169, 177–8
fatherhood 250–2
Feldman, Marty 174, 180
The Female Eunuch 111, 137
Ferguson, Jane 272
Ferrier, Louise 42, 97, 98, 129, 134, 149, 265, 273
Fifty Years of Silence 260
Film Script 246
Fink, Leon 191–2, 218–19
Fink, Margaret 46, 68, 192, 282
First, No Pinky 45
first art exhibition 22
first drawings 21
first solo gallery show 81–4
fish, fascination with 1, 107, 127, 131, 256–7, 275, 283
Fogg, Ellis D 177
Fonteyn, Margot 46, 111
football World Cup 96
Footprints on the Road to the Yellow House 165, 178
For Matthew and Others: Journeys with Schizophrenia 269
Fox, James 137, 138, 153
Fragments of a (F)unfair 240
Fraser, Robert 109
Freedom Riders 74–5
Freeman, Cathy 258–9
Freud, Lucian 103, 138
The Fugs 123

Gaden, John 27, 30, 39, 60–1, 62, 63, 66, 70, 208
The Gas Lash 68, 72, 84, 154
The Gas Lash 57, 58, 59, 60–1, 66, 68, 72, 77, 218

Gauguin, Paul 104, 158
Geldof, Bob 204–5
Gemes, Juno 174, 265
Genet's 'The Funambulist' 173
German Expressionists 147
'Get folked' 64, 69
Gibbs, Christopher 109, 183
Gibson, Magistrate 67
Gilbert & George 187
Ginger Baker's Air Force 148
Ginger Meggs 171, 172, 193, 204
Ginger Meggs in Japan 269
Ginger Meggs School of Arts 172, 184
Ginsberg, Allen 110, 166
Gittoes, George 157, 172–3, 174, 178, 179, 182–5, 233, 251, 281
Gittoes, Joyce 173, 183
God Bless Tiny Tim 133
'God Save Oz' 180
'God Save the Queen' 36, 65, 75
Godson, Craig 216–17, 220, 244
Godson, Damien 216–17, 220, 244
Godson, Jenny 216–17, 220, 221, 229, 244, 271
Godson, John 216–17, 220, 244
Golding, John Ivor 141–2, 168, 180, 269
Golgotha 221, 244
Goodbye album 148
Goodchild, Jon 149
Goold, Bruce 68, 156, 157, 165–6, 167–8, 177, 178, 214
Goossens, Sir Eugene 37–8, 88, 89
Gore, Jane Ormsby 100
Gough, Archbishop Dr Hugh 40, 146
Graceland 279
Green, Jonathon 136
Greer, Germaine 39, 46, 99, 111, 137, 141, 180, 282
Gregory-Roberts, Doctor 23
Gregory-Roberts, John 23, 225
Greycliffe 10
Griffin, David 25
  The Happiness Box 25
groper *see* fish, fascination with
Grose, Peter 48, 52, 53, 56
The Guardian 187
Gulpilil, David 231, 259–60, 269, 274
Gumbert, Linda 81

Haden-Guest, Anthony 111, 117
Hair 150, 181, 209
Haller, Harry 134–5
Hamilton, Richard 109
  Just What is it That Makes Today's Homes So Different, So Appealing? 97
Hamlet 75, 88
Hannan, Clare 251
Hannan, Peter 107
Hanrahan, Barbara 125
Hans Christian Andersen 21, 256
Hapshash and the Coloured Coat 124, 125
Harbourside Amusements 222, 223
Harlech, Lord 100, 142
Harris, Max 71
Harrison, George 115, 123, 141, 142, 263
Harrison, John (George) 166
Hayward Gallery exhibition 126, 136
health 237, 265–6, 273, 274, 275, 276, 277, 278
Heartfield, John 136
Heath, Edward 161
Heide 50
Helena Rubinstein travelling art scholarship 68–9
Henderson, Brian 47
Henderson, Marion 173
Hendrix, Jimi 120–2, 161, 164
Hendrix poster 121–2, 277
heroin 161, 227–8
Heseltine, Dr Harry 63
Hesse, Herman 130, 134, 181
Hester, Joy 50
Heuston, Chloe 269–70
Hewett, Dorothy 209
Highway 61 Revisited 87
Hippie Hippie Shake 108
Hôch, Hannah 147
Hockney, David 180, 265
Hogarth Galleries 229, 246

Hogwood, Sir Christopher 231
Hokusai, 188–9, 210, 245, 269
  Great Wave of Kanagawa 178, 188
  The Dream of the Fisherman's Wife 188
Holdsworth Galleries 152
Hollingshead, Michael 101
Hollingworth, Keith 33–4
Holman, Jason 216–17, 221, 271
Holt, Harold 80, 99, 112
Homer's *Odyssey* 107
homosexuality 54–5, 144
Honi Soit 39, 40, 48, 84
Hopkins, John 102, 125
Hopkins, Livingston (Hop) 21, 175
Hopkins, Ted 192
Horler, Ken 208
Horton Hatches the Egg 17
Huckstepp, Sallie-Anne 228–9
Hudson Bros 6
Hughes, Davis 89–90
Hughes, Robert 39, 43, 46, 97, 98, 99, 126, 136, 234
Humphries, Barry 46, 97, 175, 208
  Edna Everage 208
Hutchison, Noel 182
Huxley, Aldous 101

'I am the Walrus' 141
The I Ching 130
Images of Modern Evil 83
The Incredible Shrinking Exhibition 166, 169–72, 176, 184, 198
inheritance 145, 154, 199, 205, 225, 270
The Innocents 126
International Times (IT) 99, 102, 125
Ivan Dougherty Gallery 264, 268

Jagger, Mick 68, 109, 134–5, 137–9, 151, 153, 164
jail sentence 69–70
James, Clive 39
James, Francis 55–6, 60–1, 62, 65–7, 69, 72–5, 151
Jessop, Clytie 125–6, 140, 180
Jesus Christ Superstar 209
Johnson, Lyndon 79, 80, 99, 264
Johnson, Michael 217
Johnson, Paul 99
Johnson, Richard 256
Jones, Alastair 225
Jones, Brian 115, 161
Joplin, Janis 140, 161
Joubert Studios 99–100, 104, 119, 124
Juillet, Patric 166
Juillet's restaurant 166
'Jumpin' Jack Flash' 103, 104, 168
Jung, Carl 123, 130, 220

Karet, Marilyn 225, 279
Kats-Chernin, Elena 271
Kee, Jenny 44, 68, 97, 106, 120, 134, 141, 230, 234, 265, 282
Keeler, Christine 186
Kennedy, Senator Robert F 131
Kenny, Mary 98
Kerr QC, Sir John 73, 74, 199
Kerr, Vadim Steven 46–7
Kiisler, Anou 44–5, 46, 48, 50–1, 57, 85, 86, 87, 107, 129–30, 131, 132, 144, 169, 225, 261
King, Carole 186
Kings Cross 150, 198
  Carousel Club 198–9
King's Road 100, 112, 119, 140, 160
Kingsclere, Potts Point 8
Kingston, Fairlie 174, 247, 274, 275
Kingston, Peter 28, 173, 174, 192, 221–2, 225, 243, 282
Kinsella, V J 40
Kippax, Harry 46, 73
Klippel, Robert 59
Knox Grammar 47
Kold Komfort Kaffe 208, 221
Kopsen, William 7
Kramer, Nicky 109, 110, 137
Krauss, Sigi 147–8, 152, 186–7
Kray, Reginald 103, 159, 167
Kray, Ronald 103, 138, 159, 167
Krummel, John 91
Kunemann, Leondra 86
Kwong, Kylie 271

Labor Party 8, 37, 88
Labour Electoral League of New South Wales 10
Lagerfeld, Karl 162
Laine, Denny 148
Laing, R D 116
Lambert, Vern 119–20
Lanceley, Colin 38, 43, 59, 68–9, 72, 98, 126, 265
Lanceley, Kay 98
Lanfranchi, Warren 228
Lang, Jack 60
Lansac, Régis 271–2
Larrikins in London 265
The Last Judgment 143
Laugh-In 133
Lawrence, D H 38
  Lady Chatterley's Lover 33, 37
Lear, Amanda 115
Leary, Dr Timothy 101, 124, 164
Ledeboer, Peter 105, 109–10
Legalise Pot rally 109
Lennon, John 122, 123, 135, 141, 180
Leonard, Roma (Nursie) 17, 18, 200, 271
Leonardo da Vinci 104
Lest We Forget 221
Letcher, Dean 146
Levine, Judge Aaron 73, 74, 75, 76, 77
Lewis, Jeannie 155, 173, 214, 282
Lewis, Jon 156, 165, 168, 173, 174, 178–9, 184, 204, 259, 282
Lewis, Tim 192
Liberal and Reform Association 11
Liberal-Country Party 37, 89
Lichtenstein, Roy
  Whaam! 176
Lieberson, Sandy 138–9, 184, 185–6, 187, 252, 263, 265
Light and Shadow 236
Lindsay, Daryl 197
Lindsay, Joan 195–8
Lindsay, Norman 43, 86, 197
Lindsay, Rose 86
Liney, Richard 192
Little, Stephen 66
Little Nell *see* Campbell, Laura
The Little Prince 22, 25, 128, 164, 203
'Little Sparrow' 282
Litvinoff, David (Litva) 103–4, 110, 115–16, 137, 138, 141, 153, 167–9, 173, 174, 177, 179, 183, 228
Living Theatre 116
Lloyd, Alex 282
Locke, Magistrate Gerald 63, 66, 68, 69, 73, 77, 94, 181
Lolita 76
London 8, 92, 95, 96–110, 160–1, 163–4, 184–9, 263
London Evening Standard 98
London's Lewisham Hospital 13
loneliness 157, 207, 257, 280
Lopez, Antonio 162
LSD 101–2, 108, 114, 132, 133–4, 151, 161, 265
Lulworth 15
Luna Park 191–4, 204, 208, 214–15, 221–3, 240, 243–4, 269, 274, 277, 279
  ghost train fire 216–221, 223, 229, 231–2, 237–8, 270–1
Lynn, Elwyn 65, 157, 182, 193

McAuley, James 71, 74, 75
MacCallum, Mungo 39, 73
McCartney, Linda (nee Eastman) 121
McClymont, Kate 271
McDonald, Frank 82
McDonald, John 273–4, 281, 282
McGregor, Craig 72, 87
  People Politics and Pop 94
McPherson, Lennie 78–9
Mad Dog Morgan 231
The Madonna of the Napalm 99
Magritte 135, 147, 177
  The Great Family 235
  The Treachery of Images 177
Maharishi Mahesh Yogi 124
Man in a Headscarf 103
Manfred Mann 96, 98, 115
Mao Zedong 46, 95

marijuana 83, 94–5, 109, 140, 161, 167–8, 178, 211, 227
Marlborough Gallery 147
Martin, Charlotte 106, 112, 116, 118
Martin, Reginald 61
Martin Sharp: Sydney Artist 273–4
Martindale Hall 196, 197
Mary Poppins 24, 124, 128
Mary Poppins 169
Mary White School of Art 59
Mathews, Freya 112, 118–19, 139–41, 142
Mathews Miller Dunbar 187
Matisse, Henri
  Large Red Interior 235
Maugham, Somerset 95
The Mavis Bramston Show 71
May, Phil 21, 260
Meanjin 63
Melly, George 124, 125, 180, 187
Member of the Order of Australia 266–7
Mendelssohn, Joanna 171
mental illness, sympathy towards 269
Menzies, Jackie 204, 210, 211
Menzies, Prime Minister Robert 37, 39, 53, 79–80
Mercury, Freddie 189
Michelangelo's *Pieta* 143
Mickey Mouse 21, 127, 149, 155, 162, 171, 174, 193, 203, 204, 208, 258, 274
The Mikado 39
Miller, Harry M 181
Minton, Damien 279
Mirka Café 50
Miss Australia (painting) 200
The Missing Links 71
Molière's *Le Bourgeois Gentilhomme* 30
Molloy, Mike 81, 83, 87, 114
Mombassa, Reg 282
Mona Lisa 82
Monet, Claude 147, 277
Monroe, Marilyn 123, 187, 246
Montefiore, John 30
Monty Python 83
mood swings 247–8
The Moody Blues 148, 149
moon landing 149, 155
Mora, Georges 49–51
Mora, Mirka 49–51, 132
Mora, Philippe 112–13, 116–18, 121, 125, 135, 139–42, 147, 163, 180, 227, 231, 265, 282
Moraes, Henrietta 124
Morley, Lewis 186, 265
Morse, Helen 197
Mortimer QC, John 180
'Mr Tambourine Man' 87, 105
Mr Tambourine Man poster 102–3, 105, 110, 221
Mrs Beeton's Tent 157
Munch, Edvard 147
  Puberty 187
Murdoch, Rupert 56, 78
Muriel's Wedding 14
Murphy, Ron 68
Murray, Les 39, 46
Museum of Sydney exhibition 273, 275
Muybridge, Eadweard 135, 148
Mỹ Lai massacre 113, 172

Namatjira, Albert 268
nannies 2, 4, 16, 17, 23, 162
Nation 182
National Art School 172, 276
National Crime Authority 237–8
national maritime strike 9
National Times 79
Nature Key to Beauty 59
Neilson, Juanita 229
Neville, Jill 98
Neville, Lucy (godchild) 205–6, 282
Neville, Richard 47–8, 52–3, 56–7, 62, 69, 71, 73, 75, 79, 85, 87, 90, 92–5, 97–9, 108, 110, 125–6, 129, 131, 134, 140–1, 149–50, 163, 179–81, 204–5, 223, 227–8, 251, 265–7, 281–2
New South Wales Police 222, 228
New Statesman 99
New York 8, 190
New York Art Directors' Prize 148
The New York Times 281

New York World Trade Center 269
Newcastle 2, 5, 36, 194
Newcastle Workers Club 194–5
Newport Arms 57, 59
Newsweek 232
Newton, Helmut 162, 187
Nielsen, Juanita 198–9
The Night Café 158, 187
Night Flight 128
Nimrod Theatre Company 208–9
Nixon, President Richard 172
Nolan, Sidney 50, 82
  Leda and the Swan 43
Norman Normal 83
Norton, Rosaleen 38
Notanda Gallery 20
Now magazine 198
Nowra, Louis 209
Noyce, Phillip 173
nude photgraphy 236–7

Oakes, Laurie 39
O'Brien, Justin 28–30, 31, 32, 46, 75, 144, 187, 194, 244–5, 276–8
  Virgin Enthroned 22
O'Brien, Richard 189
The Observer 111, 124, 125, 128
O'Dowd, Bernard
  'Australia' 31, 47
Old Bailey 179
The Old Curiosity Shop 170, 178
Olley, Margaret 277–8
Olsen, John 59, 61, 64, 66, 73, 82
Ono, Yoko 135, 174, 180
open-heart surgery 265–6
opium 95
Orphée 166
Ostin, Mo 133
Oxalis Cottage 170, 199
Oz magazine 50, 52–7, 59–60, 68, 77–8, 81–4, 90–3, 99, 100, 124–5, 139, 142, 146, 154, 164, 169, 189, 195, 264, 273
  appeal 70–1, 72–6
  Australian obscenity case 61–7, 68, 69–70, 85, 151, 180
  English obscenity case 179–81, 185
  final issue 146
  London version 98–9, 100, 108, 110, 113, 119, 149–50, 162–3, 264
  On Stage Oz 90–1, 150, 189
  School Kids *Oz* 163, 179–81
  The Magic Theatre issue 135–6, 148, 164
  'The Oz Guide to the Sydney Underworld' 78

P & O fountain 59–60
Packer, Clyde 56
Packer, Kerry 56
Packer, Sir Frank 56
Packer family 25
Pallenberg, Anita 120, 137, 138
Pandora's Cross 209
Paolozzi, Eduardo 116
Paracelsus 164
Paradise Now 116
parents' separation 26, 33–4, 84–5, 207
Paris Pullman Cinema 180
Paris Theatre Company 209
Passmore, John 41
Paterson, Banjo 71
Peel, John 125, 180
Peel, Miss Beatrice 25, 267
Pengilley, Vivienne 177
Pentecost 235, 237, 269
Performance 137–9, 141, 153, 167, 265
Perkins, Charlie 74–5
Peter Pan Ball 170
Peter Pan Kindergarten, Point Piper 24
Petticoat Lane 120
The Pheasantry 111–26, 129, 132, 134–5, 138–42, 147–49, 159–61, 163–4, 263, 282
Phnom Penh 95
Phongsitthisak, Paiwan 238–42
Piaggi, Anna 119–20
Picasso 171
  Les Demoiselles d'Avignon 187
Picasso Café 117, 119, 139
Picnic at Hanging Rock 195–8, 280

Pilcher, Detective Sergeant Norman (Nobby) 140–1
Pink Floyd 101, 102, 123, 174
Pinter, Harold 141
Plant a Flower Child poster 108, 164
Plate, Carl 20
Poe, Edgar Allan
'A Dream Within a Dream' 197
Poidevin, Emily 244
Poidevin, Jenny *see* Godson, Jenny
politics 266–7
The Politics of Ecstasy 164
The Politics of Experience 116
Pollock, Jackson 122
pop art 97, 116, 123, 191, 244, 266, 281
Popeye 208
Popov, Alex 46, 48, 52, 53, 60, 72, 85, 86, 115, 209, 225, 255, 280
'pornography' scandal 89
Port Hacking River 2, 283
Portobello Road 120
The Portrait of the Artist as a Young Man 54
posters, creation of 42, 97, 102–5, 108–10, 117–18, 121–2, 124–5, 136, 163–4, 208–9, 221, 224, 230–1, 240, 253
Powditch, Peter 46, 177
Princess Eugenie 272
Private Eye 54, 55, 97, 99
The Procurer 103
The Prodigious Snob 30
Profumo, John 186
'Purple Haze' 121
Purves, Stuart 242, 247
The Putting Together of the Heads 109–10
Puttnam, David 187

Qantas 91
Quadrant 193
Quant, Mary 100
Queen Elizabeth 36, 53, 89, 111, 266
Queen Victoria Building 43

RAAF, 453 Spitfire squadron 16
Radio Caroline 96
Rahilly, Seamus 217
Rainey, Michael 100
Ramsden, Michael 125
Ready Steady Go! 96
Red Menace 37
Reed, John 50, 70–1, 152
Reed, Sunday 50
Rees, Lloyd 41
Rees-Mogg, William 109
Reid, Ian 152–3, 168, 183
Reid, Kate (nee Sharp) (cousin) 153, 168–9
relationships 44–5, 86, 105–8, 127–33, 152, 162, 200–2, 233–4, 235–7, 261–2
religious beliefs 219–20, 225, 232–3, 235–6, 262, 280
Rembrandt 177
Rendall, John 120, 273
Revolver album 98
Rhodes, Zandra 174, 189, 190, 204
Rice-Davies, Mandy 186
Richards, Keith 68, 103–4, 109, 110, 137, 138, 168
Ritchie Bros 3, 6–7
Ritchie, James (maternal great-grandfather) 6–7
Ritchie, John (maternal great-great-great-grandfather) 5
Ritchie, John (maternal great-great-uncle) 5
Ritchie, John (maternal great-uncle) 6
Ritchie, Robert Adam (maternal great great-grandfather) 5–6
Ritchie, Stuart Douglas (maternal grandfather) 2, 4, 7, 8, 21, 34, 117, 145
Ritchie, Vega (nee Kopsen) (maternal grandmother) 7, 21, 34, 145, 199, 212
Robertson, Geoffrey 71, 78, 180
Robertson, Michael 60
Robeson, Paul 38
Robson, Karen 197
The Rocky Horror Show 91, 170, 189–90, 209
Roeg, Nicolas 114, 137, 231
Rogerson, Roger 228–9

Rolling Stones 96, 100, 103, 109, 120, 123, 134, 137, 138, 141, 159, 161
Rome 143–4
Ropert, Denise 57
Rose, Murray 24, 89
Roslyn Oxley9 gallery 246
Rowe Street 20–1
Roxon, Lillian 151
Royal Albert Hall 133–4, 263
Royal family dress-up 71–2
Royal George pub 39
Royal National Park 2
Royles, Peter 174, 205
Rudy Vallée 20
Ruff, Carol 267–8
Ruff-O'Herne, Jan 260–1, 268
Rupert Bear 163

Saffron, Abe (Mr Sin) 166, 199, 222–3, 237, 270–1
Sale, Julia 177
Salmon, William 41
Salvador Dali 115, 186
Sampson, Nicholas 276, 280, 282
schooldays 25, 26–32, 34, 267
  art class 28–30, 31–2
Schwitters, Kurt 147
Sciberras, Luke 245–6, 247–8, 250, 259, 279, 280, 282
Scotter, Sheila 155
Seidemann, Bob 139–40
Seidler, Harry 90, 91, 254
Seligmann, Kurt 187
'Semolina Pilchard' 141
Seventeen Minutes to Four 83
Sgt Pepper's Lonely Hearts Club Band 123
Shahn, Ben 42
Sharman, Jim 86, 90–1, 150, 173, 189, 209
Sharp, Alan (uncle) 11, 13–14
Sharp, Alexander 278
Sharp, Alfred Ramsay 9
Sharp, Andrew (cousin) 153, 171, 178, 179, 207, 263, 282
Sharp, Dorothy (nee Muller) (stepmother) 145–6, 224, 247, 270, 278
Sharp, Eliza Alice (nee Ramsay) (paternal great-grandmother) 8–9
Sharp, Elizabeth (auntie) 11, 14
Sharp, Elizabeth (Bessie) (nee Ritchie) (paternal grandmother) 11, 13, 14, 18, 146
Sharp, Frank (uncle) 11, 13–14
Sharp, Henry (father) 2–4, 11–16, 18–20, 22, 33–4, 40, 70, 145–6, 170, 224, 226
  birth 11
  childhood 12
  courtship 13
  death 224
  engagement 14
  love letters 226, 277
  love of animals 22
  love of literature 22
  love of popular music 22
  marriage 14, 26
  marriage breakup 33–4, 84, 226
  medical studies 12
  remarriage 145–6
  siblings 4
  WWII service 14–15, 16, 19, 20
Sharp, Joan Sheila (Jo) (nee Ritchie) (mother) 7–8, 12–22, 24, 33–4, 85–6, 91, 132, 144–5, 152, 156, 170, 177, 183, 199–200, 206, 209, 224–6, 250, 253, 271
  abortion 34
  affair 33–4
  birth 7
  courtship 13
  death 225
  first art teacher 21
  inheritance 199
  love letters 226, 277
  love of animals 22
  love of art 22
  love of popular music 22
  marriage 14–15, 18, 19, 26
  marriage breakup 33–4, 84, 226
  motherhood 16, 17–19, 21
  relationship with mother-in-law 18
  socialite 8, 12–13, 20–1

Sharp, Katharine (auntie) 11, 14
Sharp, Marcello 251–2, 261
Sharp, Nicholas 282
Sharp, Roslyn (cousin) 22, 275, 278
Sharp, Russell (cousin) 205, 214
Sharp, Walter Alexander Ramsay (paternal grandfather) 9–13
Sharp, William Henry (paternal great-grandfather) 8–10
Sharp Martin and his Silver Scissors 147–8, 186
Shead, Garry 43, 45, 53, 87, 192, 204, 218, 239, 274, 282
Shead, Gria 239, 240, 241
Shearston, Garry 71
Shrimpton, Jean 44
Simpson, Mrs Wallis 13
Singapore 92–3
Sistine Chapel 143
Skinner, Alfred 2, 3
Skinner, Ian 2, 275
Skinner, Ida 2
Skinner, Jan 2, 275
Skrzynski, Joe 254–6
Smart, Jeffrey 23
  'Art Gallery of the Air' 23
Smartiples 148–9
Smartoonist 147
Smedley, David 239–42
Smith, Jimmy 115
Smith, Neddy 228, 229
Smith, Terry 182
smoker 2, 44, 48, 82, 127, 151, 167–8, 237, 262, 266, 277–8
Snow Job 221, 246
The Somewhat Incredible Turning on of Mervyn Limp, Bank Clerk 99
The Song of Love 279
Souris, George 243
Spatt, Nathan 192, 218
Speakeasy Club 106, 108
Spears, Steve J 208
Sperling, Ella 271
'The Spirit of Popular Song' 150
Spring Exhibition 179, 181–3
St John QC, Edward 73, 74, 77
St Luke's Hospital, Elizabeth Bay 15, 225
St Mark's Church, Darling Point 14, 225
St Paul, Corinthians 194
St Peter's, Rome 143
St Vincent's Hospital 266, 276
Stace, Arthur (Mr Eternity) 45, 208, 258
Standing 149
Starry Night 154, 188
'Stayin' Alive' 215, 231
Steppenwolf 130, 134–5
Stewart, Harold 71
Stigwood, Robert 140
Still Life 246
'Strange Brew' 106, 114
'Street of Dreams' (song) 224, 231–2
Street of Dreams, (film) 223
Street of Dreams Martin Sharp Trust 279
Sudjic, Deyan 256
The Sun 70, 108
The Sunday Australian 182
The Sunday Telegraph 171, 182
Sunflowers 176, 187
Surrealism 173
Sweeney Todd 30
Swinging London 109
Sydney Harbour Bridge 60, 88, 191, 258
The Sydney Morning Herald 15, 26, 46, 55, 58, 73, 76, 79, 82–4, 91–3, 95, 125, 154, 156–7, 168, 171–2, 175, 182, 224, 229, 270–1, 273, 278, 281
Sydney Olympics 258–9
Sydney Opera House 38, 87–90, 191–3, 224, 252–6
Sydney Push 39
Sydney Symphony Orchestra 37, 73, 88, 253
Sydney University 36, 39, 44, 45
  Dramatic Society 12
  St Paul's College 12, 40–1, 64, 270
  Students' Representative Council 48
  William Henry and Eliza Alice Sharp Prize 11

Tahiti 10
'Tales of Brave Ulysses' 106, 107, 114, 127, 129, 148, 247, 261
Tankard, Meryl 272
Tanner, Les 73
Taronga Zoo 36, 216
Teale, Leonard 71
The Telegraph (London) 281
Telford 1–4, 6, 7, 145, 274, 276, 283
'ten-pound Poms' 36, 50
Thai Song Greet 93
Thailand 93–5
Tharunka 47, 57–8, 60, 62, 64, 66, 72, 73, 77, 84, 115, 151, 154
That Was the Week That Was 71
Thatcher, Margaret 161
Theeman, Frank 198–9
This Is Tomorrow exhibition 97
Thomas, Daniel 171, 182
Thomas, Jeremy 114, 185, 204, 206, 246, 281
Thomas, Laurie 182
Thoms, Albie 163, 171, 172, 178, 181, 183
Thomson, Ross 91
Thornton, Harold (the Kangaroo) 206
Thornton, Wallace 84
The Thousand Dollar Bill 259, 274
Time magazine 96
The Times 109, 123
Tiny Tim 133–5, 144–5, 149–50, 155, 164, 167, 190, 193–5, 211–15, 224, 231–3, 236, 242–3, 245–6, 249–50, 258, 263, 274–5, 277, 279, 281, 282
  film 212–13, 223, 225, 227, 231–2, 246, 273, 279
'Tiptoe through the Tulips' 133, 134, 213
Tolarno 50
The Tonight Show 149–50
Top of the Pops 96
Topliss, Helen 85
Toth, Laszlo 143
Toulouse-Lautrec, Henri de 43
Trades and Labour Council 9, 10
Tree, Penelope 159–60, 248, 277
Tremblay, Angelica 275, 279, 281, 282
Trocadero 42
Trouble in Molopolis 141–2, 180, 265
The Truman Show 196
Tsai, Yensoon 209, 225, 234, 236, 261
Tucker, Albert 50, 83
Two Innocents Abroad 92
Tynan, Kenneth 123

UFO Club 101–102, 125
Ulysses 107, 131
United Australia Party 11
United States Library of Congress 168
University of New South Wales 47, 264
Utzon, Jan 256
Utzon, Jørn 38, 85, 88–92, 192, 193, 253–6
Utzon, Lin 85, 86–7, 88, 91, 115, 206, 252–7, 263, 267

Vadim's 46, 73, 75
Vallée, Rudy 133
Van Dyke, Dick 169
van Gogh, Theo 164
van Gogh, Vincent 30, 104, 126, 131, 135–6, 146, 147, 154–5, 157–8, 163–5, 167, 171, 176, 180–1, 184–5, 187–8, 208, 246, 269, 276
Vehka-aho, Eija 102–5, 112, 117–19, 127–33, 135, 139, 143–5, 149, 153, 162, 163, 225, 227, 231, 261–3
Venus Room 150
Vestey, Lord 74
Victor, Ed 186
Victoria and Albert Museum 104, 210
Vietnam War 79, 112–13, 150, 183
Village Voice 54
Vincent 136
Visions 209
Vogue 159, 189, 248
  French 162
Vogue Australia 155
Voormann, Klaus 98

Waks, Nathan 213–14, 215, 224, 231, 282
Walford, Leslie 170
Walker, Edda 235

Walker, Emma 235–7
Walker, Kathryn 235
Walsh, Maggie 272, 273
Walsh, Richard 39, 48–9, 52–3, 56, 57, 60, 62, 69–70, 71–3, 75, 90, 146
Wandsworth Prison 181
Warhol, Andy 165, 176
Blue Movie 172
Campbell's Soup Cans 21, 97
Factory 165, 176
Marilyn Monroe portrait 187, 246
Warner Bros 138
Waterlow, Antony 269–70
Waterlow, Nick 264–5, 268–70
Waverley College 216, 217, 220
Waymouth, Nigel 100, 124
Weight, Greg 81, 165, 166, 175, 176–8, 182–3, 250, 267–8, 282
Weight, Richard 165, 177
Weiley, John 45, 47, 57, 81–3, 86, 87, 91, 97, 117, 134, 142, 161, 211, 251
Weir, Peter 173, 195–8, 212–13, 280
West, Morris 73
Wheels of Fire 148, 163
Wherrett, Richard 208
Whidborne, Timothy 111
Whitaker, Robert 50–1, 95, 97–8, 99–100, 102, 104, 106, 108, 110, 114, 119, 124, 137, 161, 265
White, Patrick 15, 86, 89, 90, 155, 156, 209
White, Terry 82
White Album 115
'white-ant from Bellevue Hill' 84
White Australia policy 36
White Goddess of Moral Indignation 59
Whiteley, Arkie 173, 177
Whiteley, Brett 165, 168, 173, 177, 178–9, 225, 228, 265
Whiteley, Wendy 165, 168, 173, 209, 234, 247, 282
Whitlam, Gough 150, 151, 192, 199
will 278–9, 281
Willems, Gerard 275
Wilson, Harold 96, 112–13, 161
Windsor Castle (hotel) 54, 82
Wirian 8, 14, 17, 26, 145, 183, 199, 203–7, 209, 211–12, 220, 223–4, 225, 233, 238–42, 249–50, 259–60, 271, 272, 273, 278, 283
Albert (the factotum) 205
Womenzone 265
Woodstock 175
Wootton of Abinger, Baroness 140
The Word Flashed Round the Arms 62–4, 66, 69, 75, 77, 90
World Psychedelic Centre 101
World War II 14, 55, 96, 113, 158, 226, 260–1
The Worship of Bacchus 60
Wot! 149
Wran, Neville 61, 72, 73, 218–19
Wright, Peter 177

Yang, William 204–5, 211
Yasmar 9
The Year of Living Dangerously 196
Yellow House 104, 157–8, 163, 164–7, 169–72, 172–9, 181–3, 183–4, 185, 195, 198, 213
Yellow House Jalalabad 184
Yesterday and Today 98
Young Mo 208
Young Romance comic 97
youth culture, emergence of 38–9

Zambia 159–60